# JONES VERY

*The Effective Years, 1833–1840*

Jones Very, taken during the "Effective Years"
*Courtesy the Essex Institute, Salem, Mass.*

# JONES VERY

## *The Effective Years*

### 1833–1840

*

EDWIN GITTLEMAN

1967

COLUMBIA UNIVERSITY PRESS

NEW YORK & LONDON

Edwin Gittleman is Assistant Professor of English
at Dartmouth College

This study, prepared under the Graduate Faculties
of Columbia University, was selected by a committee of those Faculties to receive one of the Clarke
F. Ansley awards given annually by Columbia
University Press.

B 68012294

*In Memory of Ralph L. Rusk*
*1888–1962*

*Preface*

MANY OF THE pleasures and fewest of the frustrations experienced during the preparation of this work were due to the unfailing courtesy, cooperation, and thoughtfulness shown me by the staffs of the various institutions I visited between 1958 and 1961. I am especially indebted to the officials and personnel of the Essex Institute, Houghton Library and the Harvard University Archives, the Andover-Harvard Theological Library, Wellesley College Library, the Rare Book Room of the Boston Public Library, the Massachusetts Historical Society, the Unitarian Historical Society, the Boston Athenaeum, the American Antiquarian Society, the Berg Collection in the New York Public Library, and the Special Collections of Columbia University.

I am particularly grateful to Mrs. Julia Barrows of the Essex Institute. She made it possible for me to meet Truman Nelson, and to benefit from his delightful conversation during a summer afternoon spent wandering through Salem while he patiently explained how the "matrix of place" affected Jones Very.

I am appreciative too of the generosity of Mr. Parkman D.

Howe of Needham, Mass., who allowed me to examine Jones Very's copy of Emerson's *Nature,* and thoughtfully provided photostats of all pages in which I had special interest. Mr. Howe thereby implemented his conviction that the private collector has an obligation to encourage research and scholarship.

Special thanks are due to the staff of the Emerson House in Concord. They indulged my sentimental fancy, allowing me to wander through that lovely memorial for several hours, undisturbed by the talk of guides and the chattering of sightseers.

Thanks are due also to Pat Harrison of the Fruitlands Museum at Harvard, Mass., for his hospitality and general encouragement, and to Marie L. Ahearn of Belmont, Mass., for her specific views about Very's sermons.

Kenneth Walter Cameron encouraged me without realizing it. His interest in Jones Very (reflected often in the pages of the *Emerson Society Quarterly*), and his amazing energy and commitment to the ideals of transcendence everywhere, continue to sting my conscience.

I am indeed fortunate in having been exposed to the contagious enthusiasms of Lewis Leary. During seven long years I was often rescued from lethargy and discouragement by recalling that he had granted me the rare privilege of working out the form and content of this study by myself. In addition to strategic expressions of confidence, which I have tried hard not to betray, I am indebted to him for his periodic reminders that I should complete this project and get on to other work. As he well knew, these were essential correctives to my apparent willingness to spend a lifetime with Jones Very's effective years—at the expense of my own.

I am thankful too that Quentin Anderson criticized my original manuscript with stunning thoroughness and brilliance. He illuminated its every weakness, and made me aware—as if for the first time—of what I had done. I only regret that I have been unable to incorporate all his suggestions, or to correct every one of the deficiencies which he detected. I have learned much from him nevertheless.

I also am grateful for the comments and advice of Charles W. Everett, Horace L. Friess, Joseph L. Blau, and Sacvan Bercovitch.

I am indebted to the Ralph Waldo Emerson Memorial Association for permission to consult and to quote from Emerson manuscripts in the Houghton Library at Harvard University, and from the "Typescript Journals" in Butler Library at Columbia University.

I am greatly indebted to the trustees and directors of important research centers who kindly gave me permission to consult and quote from manuscript material in their custody: the Essex Institute, for Samuel Johnson, Jr. letters to Dr. Samuel Johnson, for Elizabeth Palmer Peabody letters to Ralph Waldo Emerson and Lidian Emerson, for an Emerson letter to Jones Very, for Jones Very's manuscript of "Epic Poetry," and for C. F. W. Archer's "Clippings from the Salem *Evening News,* 1922–1924"; the Wellesley College Library, for "Letters of Jones Very to Ralph Waldo Emerson, 1838–1846," and "Notebooks of William P. Andrews on Jones Very"; the Harvard College Library, for Bronson Alcott's "Manuscript Journals," for Sarah Freeman Clarke letters in the James Freeman Clarke Manuscript Collection, for Margaret Fuller's "Extracts from Journals, 1833–1839," for "Tappan Papers: Ossoli-Tappan," for one George B. Loring letter in the "James Russell Lowell Manuscript Collection," for "Manuscript Poems" by Jones Very, and for two Jones Very letters in the Autograph Collection—all in Houghton Library; the Harvard University Archives, for Jones Very's undergraduate essays and orations, and "Three Commonplace Books," for *College Papers, Faculty Records,* and *Overseers Reports,* for "Library Charging Lists," and "Institute of 1770" papers; the Massachusetts Historical Society, for three letters by Jones Very, for one Richard Henry Dana, Sr. letter in "Dana Papers," and for "Samuel Gray Ward's Account of a Visit from Jones Very in

1839"; the Boston Public Library, for Sarah Freeman Clarke's "Impressions and Recollections of Miss Peabody" in the Mellen Chamberlain Autograph Collection, and for one Jones Very letter in the Manuscript Collection; the American Antiquarian Society, for George Moore's "Diary"; the Andover-Harvard Theological Library, for "Records of the Theological School"; the Brown University Library, for Jones Very manuscripts in the Harris Collection of American Poetry; the Berg Collection of the New York Public Library, for letters by Elizabeth Palmer Peabody, Mary Peabody, and Sophia Peabody; and the Yale University Library, for "Spiritual Navigation" by Jones Very.

I am also grateful for the permission to quote from and refer to published sources, which has been granted by the following: Charles Scribner's Sons, for Ralph L. Rusk's *Life of Ralph Waldo Emerson* (1949); the Essex Institute, for articles appearing in *Essex Institute Historical Collections;* Kenneth W. Cameron, for articles appearing in the *Emerson Society Quarterly;* Houghton Mifflin Co. and the Ralph Waldo Emerson Memorial Association, for *The Journals of Ralph Waldo Emerson* (1909–1914), edited by Edward Waldo Emerson and Waldo Emerson Forbes; Little, Brown and Company, for *The Journals of Amos Bronson Alcott* (1938), edited by Odell Shepard; Duke University Press, for William Irving Bartlett's *Jones Very: Emerson's "Brave Saint"* (1942); Columbia University Press and the Ralph Waldo Emerson Memorial Association, for *The Letters of Ralph Waldo Emerson* (1939), edited by Ralph L. Rusk. (I regret that the edition of Jones Very's poetry prepared by Nathan Lyons was published too late for me to benefit from it.)

Many, many thanks are due Peg and Jack Fife for giving me "Mabel's Place" in which to work during the summer of 1962, and for introducing me to Vermont's magnificent Northeast Kingdom.

Obligations of a special and private sort must be acknowledged to my wife and eleven-year-old son. Rosalyn Leinwand Gittleman bore her sorrows patiently for an eternity, and then performed brilliantly a series of essential if irksome clerical assignments. Neal Jay Gittleman bore his sufferings less patiently, perhaps, but contributed significantly by discovering the first name of the gentleman who was president of Amherst College in 1836.

But my greatest indebtedness is to a man who died in 1962. Ralph L. Rusk—an unforgettable teacher and scholar, humanist and gentleman—first saw the possibilities of my attempting to wrestle with the shadow of Jones Very. He was always helpful, not only opening his personal files to me, but helping by his conduct of life. By this most of all. The extent to which Jones Very still remains a shadow is due entirely to the narrowness of my unaided vision.

E. G.

*Norwich, Vermont*
*February, 1967*

"Be spontaneous, be truthful, be free and thus be individuals. Nature made us individuals as she did the flowers and pebbles; but we are afraid to be peculiar and so our society resembles a bag of marbles—or a string of mould candles—"

—from the untitled prose prayer by Jones Very which follows his "Spiritual Navigation," in Yale University Library.

# Introduction

DURING THE years 1838 and 1839 a young man from Salem
gained a considerable reputation among that heterogeneous
company of adventurers of the mind and heart who, for convenience, are called Transcendentalists. What Jones Very did to
impress those idealistic intellectuals, those liberal ministers and
egocentric writers, those radical reformers and confident talkers,
those daring visionaries and hopeful prophets—all of whom were
practical New Englanders intent upon cultivating their own
sensitivities as individuals—deserves to be remembered. Jones
Very was as controversial a figure to them as he was to more
cautious men and women who were scarcely sympathetic to
Transcendentalism. He was a curious young man, full of intrigu-
ing contradictions which puzzled his contemporaries and
which even now cannot be completely comprehended or resolved.

He was an irritating mixture of brilliance and absurdity,
profundity and simplicity, piety and blasphemy, equanimity and
anxiety, excitement and dullness, innocence and guilt, humility
and messianic delusion. He was a lonely, isolated man even

among his friends, capable of despising those men and women he admired most. He was a thought-bedeviled man even when he was not thinking. He was a self-confident man tormented by doubts about himself. He was a man who loved himself because he could hate himself. He was a man trapped by his love of God and his love for an infidel mother. He was a man who at an early age lost his father through death, only to find him many years later by the fantastic expedient of being himself reborn. He was a man who discovered Byron at a crucial point in his life, learned from him, and thereby learned to condemn him. He was a man who labored hard to lead an impulsive, instinctive, effortless life. And he was a man who had little regard for consistency.

His personality was disclosed through his work as a student and teacher, as a scholar and literary critic, as a lecturer, moralist, and conversationalist, and above all as a poet and essayist. He wrote delicate sonnets about flowers, fields, rivers, and sky; and he wrote wild, tormented sonnets about the decay of external nature and of human nature, and about the end of the world. His essays are both brilliant and outrageous, disciplined as well as irresponsible. While he theorized about artistic creativity and the function of the imagination, and speculated about the relationship between genius and saintliness, he was at the same time analyzing and evaluating himself and his own private predicament. He was a thoroughgoing if imprecise critic of contemporary society, but the reforms he advocated were individual and personal rather than institutional and public, and while criticizing others he was simultaneously accusing himself.

What is most exasperating—and engaging—about Jones Very is that all this was crammed into the first twenty-seven years of his life, although he died in his sixty-seventh year. Had he died in 1840 instead of 1880 the basis for present interest in him would not be affected in the least. All his constructive energies and significant activities were concentrated in a relatively short span of years. It is the purpose of this book to examine Very's *effective* life, to indicate what made it possible, and to show why it ended so quickly.

To understand his achievements it is necessary to examine the mode of his development as a distinctive being (to the extent that is now still possible), and to trace the growth of that personality which in 1838 and 1839 made such a startling impact on Ralph Waldo Emerson, Elizabeth and Sophia Peabody, Nathaniel Hawthorne, Bronson Alcott, and Margaret Fuller. The sources of Very's ideas, emotions, and attitudes—in terms of family, temperamental, literary, theological, and philosophical influences—must be taken into account, along with the consequences of such influences. Otherwise his effective life will have little if any present meaning. And his growth as a poet and essayist needs to be considered in order to recognize the value of his poems and essays, and to distinguish the striking qualities which make a surprising number of them memorable contributions to nineteenth-century American literature.

What Jones Very did which was significant, how he did it, why he did it, and how and why others reacted to him, have never been adequately understood by those who have subsequently become interested in Jones Very or the Transcendental Movement.[1] In part this failure has been due to the elusive qualities of the man, in part to the nature of the undertaking, and in part to the amount and kind of evidence available. Since important sources of information have recently been discovered, sources heretofore unknown to modern scholars and critics (or else not used by them), the last difficulty has to some extent been surmounted, and provides justification for the present attempt to place Very's life into meaningful focus.

Part One of this study, entitled "Preparations," deals with the origins and growth of Very's distinctive style of life, especially with his emergent personality and intelligence while he was a student at Harvard College. To some extent this section of the work is speculative and the evidence presumptive. It depicts the development of ideas and attitudes which may reasonably be assumed to provide the special basis for his later accomplishments as a writer and as a man. Unfortunately, much of what one should like to know about Jones Very, especially about his relationships with his mother and father, is still unknown, and may possibly be undiscoverable and unknowable. Nevertheless, with the aid of his Commonplace Books, the general outline (if not the specific detail) of his inner life becomes clear. This is possible because the keeping of such notebooks was a significant means by which he attempted to overcome the isolation and anxiety which characterized these years. A number of his entries therefore disclose not merely what he was actually thinking at particular moments, but the texture and basic patterns of his mind as well. Even when Very himself was silent, the recurrence of themes and the internal logic which connect his quotations provide a consistency of outlook which reveals what he must have considered important, particularly since these entries seem to be integrally bound to his later life.

The poems he wrote during these years are similarly instructive. Even if many of them are unsuccessful as poetry, these early poems nevertheless enable his growth as a poet to be charted. Here too patterns of development are to be found. In terms of theme and technique they directly relate to his subsequent, more distinctive and substantial achievements, and thereby they acquire value. Together with relevant evidence from the Commonplace Books, they show that Very was a conscientious poet, one who was trying to learn his craft, was trying to locate himself in a vital poetic tradition, and was gradually discovering that it was necessary for him to use his poems to release the ideas and feelings which were growing within him.

The second and third sections of the present study, "Performances" and "Visions and Revisions," need no special introduction or justification. In them is depicted a man whose ambitions and anxieties combined to make him a writer of considerable merit and a personality of considerable brilliance, who managed for a brief time between 1837 and 1840 to give additional interest to an already interesting period in American literary and cultural history. What follows therefore is neither a clinical study of a paranoiac, nor a reverential study of a mystic. It is instead a genetic study of a man who, even if a marginal figure in American literature, still did not lead an ineffectual *literary* life, and therefore does not deserve to have his accomplishments either forgotten or misunderstood.

# Contents

[ xix ]

## Contents

# PART ONE: PREPARATIONS

"It is the little petty affairs of life that waste our time and prevent us from accomplishing anything truly great. The mind given up to trifles or involved in little . . . disputes is incapable of taking large and just views of things, of seeing everything in its due proportions, and consequently, of doing anything worth doing. Says Shakespeare, 'Rightly to be great Is not to stir without great argument' or occasion, and in this consists the true rule for all action."

—*from Jones Very's*
*Commonplace Book "III," p. 65.*

# *The Matrix of Maturity*

## 1813-1833

SOMETIME BEFORE 1640 the widow Very of Salisbury left
England for the New World. She was accompanied by two
grown sons and a daughter. Religious reasons presumably
prompted her departure, coinciding as it did with the mass
migrations precipitated by William Laud's vigorous enforcement
of High Church worship after he became Archbishop of Canterbury in 1633. Upon her arrival in America, Bridget Very enrolled
in the first Non-conforming church organized there, the church
from which Roger Williams was expelled as minister in 1635.
When she subsequently remarried, her second husband was
Edward Giles, a member of that Puritan congregation since 1636.

The widow settled with Samuel, Thomas, and Mary Very near
Danvers, about five miles west of Salem. In a wooded area
broken by scrub pasture on the north side of Cedar Pond, they
cleared a large tract of land. For more than a hundred years
thereafter, descendants of the Very brothers were Essex County
farmers. By the middle of the eighteenth century, however, Verys
had moved into Salem, drawn there by the remarkable prosperity

being brought to that semi-rural town by maritime commerce. At a time when shrewdness and sweat were overcoming the obstacles posed by barren hinterlands and a mediocre harbor, they became sailors and shipmasters, sailmakers and mechanics, ship-provisioners and customs officials. Other members of the family fought against the Narragansett Indians and died in the War of Independence. One was taken prisoner by the British during the War of 1812 while serving aboard the privateer *Montgomery*. He was interned at Halifax, Nova Scotia, where he suffered "harsh and cruel treatment" until the end of the war in 1815. This was Captain Jones Very (1790–1824), son of Captain Isaac Very.[1]

During the first year of the war the younger Captain Very set up an irregular household with an unseasonably emancipated woman, his strong-willed first cousin, Lydia Very (1794–1867), daughter of his uncle Samuel.[2] Apparently she was a capable, resourceful, clever young woman. Although she may have been somewhat of an intellectual, may have had bookish habits, and like her lover she wrote poetry,[3] hers was not essentially a delicate personality. She was unusually aggressive; and it was this aggressiveness, a willful, headstrong quality, rather than any refinement of taste and interest, which was the most conspicuous element in Lydia Very's character.

An outspoken woman, particularly in behalf of certain radical notions which touched upon her personal life, she expressed her opinions with "great energy." Neighbors were offended equally by the matter and the manner of her discourse. They considered her a "tiger of a woman." At times, according to the local gossips, she was "almost a maniac." But more than the "simple vehemence" of her "passion" distinguished her from the gentle folk of Salem. She was considered a "coarse materialist." By this the gossips meant that she was a proud, self-proclaimed atheist. She had "doubts of another world and of the existence of God." For "Atheism's sake," they said, she had been "long at war with the world." Her "coarse materialism" subsequently led her to be recognized as a "disciple" of Fanny Wright. By then it had been known in Salem for many years that Lydia Very had strange ideas about marriage. She considered it a relationship which was based upon a moral rather than a legal obligation, one which was consecrated by love rather than by civil law and provided its own sanctification. Such were the advanced ideas upon which her own non-contractual marriage to Captain Very had been based.[4]

On August 28, 1813 the first child of this latter-day Hester Prynne was born. He was named Jones Very, after his father.

Until he was nine years old, the outward life of young Jones was no more eventful than that of any other child of a Salem seafaring family. Inwardly, however, he must have been troubled by his mother's outbursts of strong feeling and by intense family relationships. At a suitable early age he was enrolled in Salem's West School. Here he received his share of scholastic honors and less than his share of canings, for he was an alert, studious child. He was also shy and solitary. Taking "little part in the boyish sports of his fellows," he preferred instead to explore by himself the banks of nearby North River and the rocky neighborhood fields. By contrast with his own, the lives of those close to him seemed far more momentous. His "sweet smile" and bright, dark eyes did not prevent him from being a sad-faced child.[5]

From 1817 to 1821 his father commanded the brigantine *Concord* for America's wealthiest shipowner, William Gray, whose ships sailed the world from their home port of Boston. (Gray had the foresight in 1807 to move most of his fleet from Salem—an omen of the town's impending maritime decline.) In 1818 Captain Very was publicly commended for his "humanity and benevolence" while transporting 117 German emigrants from Amsterdam to Philadelphia. From 1821 to 1824 he commanded Gray's small but swift three-masted bark *Aurelia* in voyages to European ports.[6] Until 1823 his son saw little of him. However, young Jones must have thought often about his tall, handsome, sandy-haired father, a father so generous to strangers.[7] His father, he also knew, found time in spite of long absences at sea to be active in the Essex Lodge of Freemasons, having become a member immediately after his release from the Halifax prison at the end of the War of 1812.[8]

His mother, separated from Captain Very for long periods and cut off from polite society by her radical ideas, her defective "marriage," and subterranean moods, needed her growing family. Other sons were born in 1815, 1818, and 1820; and daughters in 1821 and 1825. When two of her children brought her more than ordinary maternal pain, her "doubts of another world and of the existence of God" seemed confirmed. She had, it was said, a "severe experience of life." [9] Franklin was blind at birth and died in 1822 when four years old. Horace, her youngest son, lived only a month. But Jones, his brother Washington, and his sisters Frances Eliza and Lydia Louisa Ann were able to endure the flow of unstable blood which pounded within their young bodies. Their total dependence upon their mother brought her a measure of comfort. They spent their childhood years close to her, living uneasily in the homes of their grandfathers and their families.

The brother captains Isaac (1745–1831) and Samuel Very (1755–1824) had given up the sea, one for the life of a minor official at the Derby Wharf customs station, the other for that of a merchant and shopkeeper. They lived in adjacent houses at Buffum's Corner (the busy intersection of Boston and Essex streets) and at May Street.[10] The youngest Captain Very was away from Salem too much of the time to provide a separate home of his own for his wife and children. His father and father-in-law he believed could best protect his family during his long absences at sea.

When he returned from Spanish ports in the autumn of 1822 and understood the nature of his nine-year-old son's "diffidence," [11] it seemed best for the boy to accompany him on the next voyage of the *Aurelia*. From his own experience Captain

Very knew the sea could provide the manly education lacking in a woman-dominated family. Lydia Very's possessiveness toward her surviving children doubtless caused a domestic crisis, but when the ship unfurled sail in Boston Harbor in January 1823 the boy was aboard.

Shipboard routine "seemed strange and new" to him. He realized his home "had fled" when he looked back and saw "the ocean's deep green brow," and cried without shame. His mother and all he loved "seemed dead." He "crept beside the grey-locked man" to be comforted. Soon he grew to love his father's authoritative voice.[12]

Bound for the North Sea ports and for Kronstadt (the old port city of St. Petersburg), the *Aurelia* called at Helsingor to pay the Oresund tolls before passing into the Baltic. While waiting for the ship to be cleared, the young cabin boy visited Helsingor's gloomy Kronborg Castle, made famous by Shakespeare.[13] There, amid ghosts from a medieval past, he may have first dreamed of a son's self-destructive loyalty to his beloved father.

After the voyage was resumed and cargoes exchanged at Kronstadt, the *Aurelia* returned to Boston in August 1823. In the judgment of Captain Very, the seven-month separation from Salem had benefited young Jones, and he thought seriously about a career as a sailor for his son. In October 1823 the boy was once again aboard the *Aurelia,* bound this time for New Orleans. As before, the ocean seemed "so lonely, so vast"—and so full of "wonders." Off Key West a pirate ship gave chase. The swift three-masted vessel eluded her. After sailing two or three days in the Gulf of Mexico, the *Aurelia* entered Cat Island Channel and was soon unloading at New Orleans.

When negotiations for a cargo of cotton proved more time-consuming than Captain Very had anticipated, he arranged for his son to attend a local school for the winter of 1823–1824. Now the boy had the opportunity to learn something of the Mississippi River and its flatboats, of slaves and Indians. "At every turn" he

[7]

saw "something new" as he explored the city in much the same aimless way he had Salem.[14]

By spring the *Aurelia* was again readied for sea. She sailed east-northeast to the English and French channel ports of Cowes and Le Havre with her cargo of Mississippi-delta cotton. After unloading she visited Portugal's Bay of Setúbal and returned to Boston harbor with "St. Ubes" salt in her hold. At the end of August 1824, after ten months, the family was finally reunited in the house of the recently dead Samuel Very. This was to be the last voyage for Captain Very and the last for his son, now eleven years old, tall, and no longer sallow-complexioned.

Captain Very had not long to live. In "failing health from a disease of the lungs" contracted during his imprisonment in Halifax, he was bedridden upon his return from Portugal. During the voyage the boy must have been terrified to see his father's strength rapidly fail while his own wiry body was growing stronger. In September the haggard and completely enervated Captain was relieved of his command of the *Aurelia*.[15]

As he had done in happier circumstances, he occupied himself during his illness—whenever he was strong enough—by writing verses which he included in mischievous notes directed to his wife and children in other rooms of the large house.[16] In October he drew his will. His "beloved wife Lydia Very" was to receive the income from fifteen hundred dollars, and each of his four children a bequest of one thousand dollars. Captain Isaac Very was named executor.[17] Ten weeks later he reconsidered, rewrote his will, and instead of his father, designated John Pickering administrator of the estate and Benjamin Cheever guardian of his children.[18] The next day, three days before Christmas 1824, he died. Lydia Very bought suits of mourning for Jones and his nine-year-old brother Washington with a twenty-dollar bill she found in her late husband's pocketbook.[19] He was buried with "Masonic honors" in the old Danvers burying ground.[20]

The day after the funeral Isaac Very stormed into the May

Street house. In the presence of his grandchildren, he demanded from Lydia Very twelve hundred and fifty dollars, a quadrant, a sextant, and a spyglass. These, he said, had been mentioned in a memorandum sent him by his son the day before he died. Lydia angrily refused. She denied having the money and told him that since she was Captain Very's widow and "these were his children," they had "best rights" to his effects. He cruelly reminded her that she lacked legal proof she had been his son's wife. To this she could not reply directly. Instead she blamed her mother-in-law, Rachel Jones (Isaac Very's third wife), for having roused ill will in the family.[21]

Bitterness had been long standing and had prompted the changes in the will. Certainly bad feelings did not soon subside. A year later John Pickering, the administrator of the estate, accused Lydia Very of having "concealed, embesseled [*sic*] or conveyed away" the money. A court action followed in July 1826. Although she was at a disadvantage once testimony was received that she could produce no certificate of marriage, she was cleared of the criminal charges. The following year she moved from the Samuel Very house and purchased her own on River Street, an investment which must have infuriated Isaac and Rachel Very while giving further comfort to the neighborhood gossips. By 1833 she and her four children had moved again, into a larger but still modest frame house at 154 Federal Street. It was situated on a gently terraced slope which reached the banks of the North River, several hundred feet beyond. Here the family of the late Captain Jones Very was to live until the death in 1901 of the last survivor, Lydia Louisa Ann, the younger daughter.[22]

During thirty-five years she spent in the Federal Street home Lydia Very confirmed the suspicions of relatives and neighbors that she was a willful eccentric, a shameless person whom it was best to avoid. At times when less individualistic housekeepers were busied with kitchen and laundry and other domestic duties, she could be seen in her garden tending the flowers, preparing the soil, trimming the shrubs, or setting in one of eighteen varieties of fruit and shade trees.[23] (In Salem the devil had always worked in unaccountable ways.) When winter deprived her of a garden, the sitting room was transformed into a makeshift hothouse, with geraniums and other plants blooming on window sills and odd tables, in wall-hangings and ornamental stands. She was a resourceful women, but she gave herself up completely to her fancies—and these went beyond gardening.

What in another woman might seem a whimsical crotchet was in Lydia Very a fearful passion to be taken quite seriously, as when, before incredulous neighbors, she would periodically gather up (with excessive fuss) the stray cats, forsaken kittens, and injured birds of the vicinity. She would care for them in her home long after the need had passed. There was something frightening in the intensity of even her kindliest feelings. Yet, in her own aggressive way, she was a loving woman, one who did not neglect her children for the sake of plants and pets. On the contrary, she was a devoted mother. Her devotion, however, verged on frenzy: she pampered them during illnesses; she gloried in their youthful triumphs; she overpowered them with intimacy and affection; and she constantly reminded them of their self-sufficiency as a family. Above all, she dominated them, relentlessly trying to imprint her own peculiarities upon them.

While still young the children must have sensed that her love for them was offset by her indiscriminate hatred of relatives and neighbors, of God and His ministers, and of the injustices perpetrated in Salem and the universe itself. This aggressive, isolated woman could not have long concealed from her children the basis for her "war with the world." Because of her "severe experience of life" she was "at odds with the existing state of society," and was repelled by the "pretensions and conventions of religion." [24] The only portion of the universe which did not deserve her personal condemnation was controlled by herself, and was located at 154 Federal Street. Here her capacity for love was concentrated.

Even though frugality was needed in this household, Lydia Very was prodigal of herself, of her personality, and of her convictions. In this close little world of highly dramatized emotions and nervous energy, where eccentricity was contagious and unrelieved by the moderating influence of husband, relatives, or guardian, she raised her son Jones and her three other children.[25]

The return of young Jones from sea in 1824 had been followed by his return to Isaac Hacker's Public Grammar School. After his father's death his former solitary ways and the massive pressures of his mother were resumed as well. But now he was "unusually mature for his age" and thus better able to endure her overwhelming presence. Now too the contrasting image of his father as a generous but absolute ruler of the shipman's miniature universe was etched in his mind. Although he was unaware of it at the time, being etched even more deeply were uneasy feelings about his father's death and anxiety for the moral and spiritual well-being of his mother. An undefined need for atonement and reconciliation was merging with a vague sense of the mysteries of marriage and wedding. The time was not yet, however, when the tensions set up by the interaction of these longings and fears would generate poetry.

Although the next three years saw him pass "the larger part of his time" in study, time enough remained for frequent rambles over fields and glacial-rock drumlins. He made aimless inspections of wildflowers and sky. He listened casually to songbirds and wind. He took walks to old burial grounds and to the ruins of an old stone cellar near Cedar Pond. And in adolescent fashion, he reflected upon the languid North River and the ruthless rush of the sea. By such means he seems to have been instinctively trying to withstand the depredations of his mother and develop a personality distinctively his own. They were simple attempts to reach out toward freedom amid complex maternal tyrannies. As acts of rebellion, they were significant if not completely successful.[26]

In 1827, when he was fourteen, the patterns on his life were broken again, just as they had been in 1822 when he first boarded the *Aurelia*. Then he had felt pain at the loss of his mother, a feeling balanced by the discovery of his father; now he underwent a similar emotional dislocation, longer in unfolding, at the end of which he discovered himself all alone in the larger worlds of Cambridge and Concord. Consequently, when his mother told him in 1827 that the care of the family had finally "devolved" upon him, he sadly agreed. He left school to work as "errand and store boy" in a Salem auction room, but he did not lose his bookish habit. He read whatever found its way into the shop, borrowing some books and buying those few his purse would allow.

Once, while sorting an auction lot, he discovered a "rare copy" of Shakespeare. He was able to purchase it from his employer for a fraction of its value. After reading, rereading, and memorizing favorite passages, he exchanged it for a small collection of books used by young men preparing for college. His study of these books, and the "kindly assistance" of J. Fox Worcester, tutor of students anxious about Harvard entrance examinations, finally freed him from "distasteful" auction-room duties.

Love for his mother, brother, and two sisters, so necessary for his self-preservation, had resigned him to willing sacrifice of his own ambition for their sake. He scarcely dared think of a college education for himself. Instead, with Worcester's help, he prepared to become paid assistant to learned Mr. Oliver, principal of the Federal Street Academy for Boys, one of Salem's leading private Latin schools. As soon as he had qualified, young Very began to help in the teaching of Latin and Greek, English grammar and composition, arithmetic and geography, and traditional good manners. The school charter also prescribed that students be instructed in "the principles of Christian religion." [27]

The schoolmaster was an admirable man. The "exuberant and

enkindling" Henry Kemble Oliver (1800–1885) had ahead of him a long career as educator, musician, writer of hymns, mayor of Salem, state public official, and organizer of various church, civic, cultural, and charitable enterprises.[28] Few men in Salem at this time were better equipped to have a crucial effect on Jones Very. Although born ten years after Captain Very, Oliver was old enough and energetic enough to exert an influence on the boy comparable to a father's. He was just the man to encourage him to respect scholarship, to keep a journal, to write poetry, to think someday of publishing, and to recognize his moral and religious obligations. Moreover, it was he who continued to direct his studies and stimulate his hopes of eventually finding the means to a college education. Like Captain Very, he was in a position of authority, an authority which tempered the influence of Lydia Very; and, like the Captain, he exercised it with "humanity and benevolence." Oliver offered his assistant a course of study which closely resembled Harvard's freshman year.[29] Very responded with an enthusiasm the equal of his patron's.

At Oliver's suggestion he developed the habit of keeping a record of books read and admired, copying into notebooks the passages he felt to be important, and adding comments whenever appropriate, or whenever he felt the entries needed clarification or qualification. He filled three notebooks during the next fourteen years. The first shows unmistakable signs of Oliver's attempt to help his protégé free himself from the intellectual and emotional domination of Lydia Very. Most of this "Journal for 1833" was devoted to studies undertaken for the classes he conducted at the academy, and to studies intended to be the equivalent of a college course. The "Journal" therefore offers much evidence of Very's involvement with Greek and Latin authors: Homer, the classical dramatists, Plato, Aristotle, Plutarch, Virgil, Cicero, Sallust, Persius, Ovid, Horace, and a number of scholarly commentators. Smaller portions of the "Journal," comprising perhaps one-third of the entries, are unrelated to these classical studies and are devoted to "modern" authors. From these, with Oliver's help, Very drew much which later became basic to his maturity.

His own comments on the readings, both classical and modern, are illuminating but relatively infrequent. Many of the 124 pages he filled in 1833 with small and regular, somewhat cramped script, seem to contain original statements which are actually quotations for which he failed to make clear attribution. Consistent with his own needs, however, the avowed purpose of the "Journal for 1833" was to stimulate intellectual growth. "We should read," he wrote, echoing Oliver's sentiments, "not so much with the design of furnishing our minds with ideas as to test the value of our thoughts and receive hints which may be developed and thus suggest new views and thoughts." [30] Therefore, sources he cited during this period indicate the drift of his thinking, several having a direct and lasting effect. These show that Oliver, who had both a personal and a professional interest in "the principles of Christian religion," specifically tried to counteract the "coarse materialism" and irresponsible "Atheism" to which Very had been so long exposed by his mother. Much of his reading seemed to be specifically addressed to incipient "doubts of another world and of the existence of God."

The first of these corrective influences which Oliver made available to Very was James Mackintosh (1765–1832), the Scottish moral philosopher, from whose *Dissertation on the Progress of Ethical Philosophy* Very frequently quoted. [31] Intentionally eclectic, the work drew heavily upon David Hume, Joseph Butler, and David Hartley. Of the three, the views borrowed from Bishop Butler had special impact on Mackintosh, and through him (as Oliver intended) on Very.

Bishop Butler (1692–1752) had formulated a facile exposition of human aspirations and fears, relating them to man's belief in a "Future Life," a conception to which Mackintosh eagerly responded. Very soon came to share his enthusiasm. [32] Butler demonstrated that natural and revealed religions in common owed their origins to man's intuition of the soul's immortality and his innate sense of moral law. Conscience was derived from this longing for eternal life. Butler concluded that since conscience was natural to man, moral action obtained its sanction simply as a natural and inward fact.[33]

Such views, appropriated by Mackintosh, were transmitted to young Very, who followed Mackintosh even to the extent of subordinating the metaphysical and psychological foundations of morality provided by Hume and Hartley to the practical ethical speculations of Butler. But when the time came for Very to build upon his groundwork inherited from eighteenth-century moral philosophy, he left the plodding Mackintosh far behind, although he never quite obliterated the traces.[34]

While Butler's naturalism may have anticipated certain elements in the Kantian ethics, and while Mackintosh himself was thoroughly acquainted with eighteenth-century German philosophic traditions,[35] it was not the writer of the *Disertation* who prepared Very for his eventual encounter with the pseudo-Kantianism permeating much New England philosophical thinking in the late 1830s. Rather, it was the anthropologist-historian Lord Monboddo (James Burnett, 1714–1799). His characteristically Greek distinctions between body and mind revealed to Very the possibilities of idealism, be it Platonic, Pauline, or Kantian.

Although Monboddo's reputation as an authority on Greek culture and philosophy doubtless prompted Very's reading of *The Origin and Progress of Language* and *Antient Metaphysics*,[36] he took from Monboddo something he valued above classical erudition. His primary importance for Very depended upon an anti-Lockean idea. Rejecting all sensationalist psychologies, Monboddo believed in a "self-moving power" of mind which enabled primitive man to struggle against his animal-like dependence upon material things, and to achieve gradually a civilized condition based upon intellectual rather than physical responses.

The process by which the dominance of mind succeeded that of the body was a natural one, motivated by the necessities of human existence.[37]

From Monboddo's presence in the "Journal for 1833" it appears that he encouraged Very to make sharp distinctions between body and mind, and to recognize the natural superiority of the mind made independent of material needs and physical circumstances. Once having accepted Butler's immortality-conscience thesis as an explanation for moral conduct, Very found that it was not difficult to combine it with the complementary views of Monboddo. While Butler revealed the mechanism for right action, Monboddo defined the conditions under which it might be realized.[38]

From the dialectic of the "Journal for 1833" it is clear that Very was quick to adjust to the naturalistic and idealistic arguments, and soon grew aware of the advantages of a synthesis. "When we use our senses," he wrote in the "Journal,"

we do not think; and so the object of those senses can be turned to no profit, . . .

Man's chief occupation and converse are with nature. . . .

Thunder is the battle, the resistance made by the bad weather in opposing the good, and the good weather takes possession of the atmosphere only after it has vanquished and driven off the bad.[39]

A sobering quotation from William Ellery Channing's "Remarks on a National Literature" followed these far-ranging reflections, and served to explain and corroborate the general direction taken by his own conjectures. Its relevance is ingenious, reinforcing both the epistemology and the moralistic-naturalistic bias of Very's preceding statements.

Literature depends on individual genius, and this, though fostered, cannot be created by outward helps. No human mechanism can produce original thought. . . . The men who are to be the lights of the world, bring with them their commission and power from God.[40]

Channing thus reassured Very's still exploratory method and tentative conclusions. Here, apparently for the first time, Very encountered the idea which within five years completely transformed his life—the germinal idea that human greatness derives directly and personally from God. But in 1833 there was no clear indication that this idea would someday be of special importance to him. It was significant only by contrast with his mother's avowed atheism and "coarse materialism."

In addition to giving a distinctive direction to Very's own thoughts, the presence of Channing's sentiments in the "Journal" clearly looks ahead to Very's own poetry and prose. Since he had not yet attempted any original writing of a formal sort, it is not surprising that after digesting Channing's article he tired momentarily of Mackintosh and Monboddo and thought of his own literary ambition. Or perhaps it was Paley who for a while turned him away from his books.

Along with Bishop Butler, William Paley (1743–1805) was instrumental in alerting Very to currents in eighteenth-century moral philosophy.[41] While emphasizing God's benevolence, Paley's *Natural Theology* revealed how God's attributes may be surmised from the "Appearances of Nature." The existence of such a Deity is demonstrated by the argument from design: "I take my stand," the English churchman wrote, "in human anatomy." The book's mass of morphological evidence supports the claim that an intelligent, designing mind was necessary for contriving the organized forms in nature.[42] While Very found in Paley further spurs to intellectual development and liberation from his mother's doubts about the existence of God, of the human soul, and of the hereafter, almost a year elapsed before he imaginatively applied this naturalistic supernaturalism.[43]

Whoever his author of moment, whether moralist, anthropologist, or theologian, sometime in July 1833 Very's interest wavered from studies, leading him, at Channing's suggestion and with Oliver's encouragement, to abandon his texts at least long enough

[ 17 ]

to write what is probably his earliest extant poem, "The earth is parched with heat." If, as it seems, Very's reading at the time this poem was composed had only casual influence upon his choice and treatment of a poetic subject, a recent reading of Pope's *Odyssey* may have had something to do with his choice of the neoclassical couplet.[44] But whatever the poem's antecedents, its theme of human isolation coupled with sudden destruction seems more romantic and theologically orthodox than Very's taste at this time for eighteenth-century theology required. Apparently other influences, some perhaps non-literary and deeply psychological, were at work on him besides those documented in the "Journal." The liberalizing tendencies of Butler, Monboddo, Paley, and Channing, which were already available to him, were slow in leaving marks on his poetry.

"The earth is parched with heat"[45] is an example of nature-description disguised as narrative. Very obscured the human element and the little action that does occur, leaving the landscape the center of attention. A weary traveler seeking shelter from "earth parched with heat" sinks down in exhaustion beneath "some tall oak" in order to dream "of home, of all his soul holds dear." Nothing more is revealed of his personality or prior circumstances. This vacuity is understandable if, as seems likely, Very had his unfortunate father in mind as he wrote. Since this enfeebled traveler "Dreams not, alas! of fatal danger near," he does not realize the scene is being readied for a lethal nature-drama. Summer flowers "droop and die"; stifling dust clouds the air; the sky grows darker; "A bloody redness v[e]ils the scorching sun"; sluggish cattle silently retreat; a farmer, the only truly human figure in the landscape,

> . . . with terror flies,
> And often turning views the angry skies.

With his departure all action is suspended. The lethargy of the inert traveler dominates the menacing scene:

Hushed is the wind, nor e'en a zephyr blows,
All nature sunk in deep profound repose.

Unlike the nostalgic dreamer, however, a nearby river is unaccountably agitated—"its waves, dark as the shades of night," alone breaking the ominous expectancy of the pastoral setting. The climax is suddenly reached when a tree is torn from its roots and, "startling all around," thunder shatters the uneasy calm:

The lofty hill e'en from the centre shakes,
The bravest heart o'ercome with terror quakes.

But the unruffled poet, from his position somewhere above the action, points knowingly to the scene stretched before him, and addresses the bewildered reader:

See on the ground, by that resistless stroke,
The wretched traveller, the blasted oak,
In equal lot, by equal force o'erthrown:
He sunk in death, he uttered not a groan.

Neither the stranger nor the reader had been alert enough to see the consuming flash. Says the poet, God has decreed the death of one who had failed to recognize the warnings everywhere around him. And so the reader, already uncomfortable, is forced to apply the moral to himself, just as Very had himself done earlier when he wrote in the "Journal" of the conflict between morally good and morally bad "weather" which finally clears the "atmosphere." Very then inquired thoughtfully in the poem, paraphrasing Butler: ". . . why then aught men to mourn," since "From earthly joys to heavenly he was borne?" Was not the storm spent with its one fatal spasm? Nature had indeed survived:

. . . gloomy clouds had fled,
Wide o'er the earth, refreshing zephyrs shed
The sweet perfume of many a laughing flower,
Or sighed with soothing notes through many a silver bower.

The poem closes with this resurrection of more hospitable surroundings, the unfortunate traveler completely forgotten amid gloriously replenished nature.

In spite of technical crudities (and unintentional humor) Very's performance is remarkable as a rudimentary statement of the theme of rebirth. Although the idea of Life-through-Death later assumed central importance for Very, the emphasis here falls not upon human rebirth or upon human feelings, but upon the setting itself. The poem's concern is only for the integrity of nature, for its combination of beauty and remorselessness, for its endurance, and not for any sympathy with the peremptorily dismissed traveler. His death is treated as another natural fact of no special significance. The poet is satisfied with indicating only in passing the contrast between the weary stranger in search of rest and the wary farmer fleeing the storm he knows to be imminent. A brutal (but comic) cause-and-effect relationship is established when the intruder enters the field just as the farmer, unaware of the new arrival and of his urgent need for salvation, leaves in haste. Similar unconscious irony is introduced once the exhausted stranger finally gains a more lasting rest than he had intended.

Human life is thus treated with complete indifference. Very admits that it is of little consequence whether the traveler continues to live: through death he surely will find an existence finer than his meaningless wandering. What is significant for Very is nature's automatic recovery, its instantaneous return to normalcy. This little drama of renewal is his 1833 version of Butler's confidence in eternal life. Just as Butler (and Mackintosh) had removed awareness of sin from the deliberations of conscience, so Very had denied the traveler any knowledge of danger. Salvation was left to the discretion of God (and the omniscient narrator), while nature, independent of the poet's control, seemed to respond to its own self-restoring powers.

These then—the readings and comments, and the ambitious

but defective poem—were the main indications in 1833 that Very had hopes of someday getting beyond the reach of Lydia Very's religious doubts and Salem's devitalizing ways. "The earth is parched with heat" was completed on July 24, 1833 and printed in the August tenth issue of the Salem *Observer*. His second poem, on the subject of Negro slavery, appeared two weeks later.[46] When his accomplishments, circumstances, and ambitions came to the attention of a well-situated uncle, Very found a sponsor willing to augment his savings and whatever his impassioned mother's thrift could spare.[47] Examinations for admission to Harvard College were arranged. Not only did he qualify for the September 1833 term, but he won himself a place in the Sophomore Class. This impressive achievement brought an emphatic and happy end to the first phase of his efforts to transcend the limitations imposed upon him by birth and nurture.

## I I

# *Excursions in Cambridge and Salem*

## 1 8 3 3 – 1 8 3 4

W HEN J ONES V ERY arrived at Cambridge in September 1833
he was twenty-years old, a poet with two poems already
published, and ambitious for further honors and distinctions.[1] Not
only was he "unusually mature" for his age,[2] but he was older
than his classmates. They had entered Harvard a year before as
freshmen, most of them at the more usual age of fifteen or
sixteen. In addition, lifelong solitary habits at first made it
difficult for him to feel at ease. Because he was "intensely self-
conscious," a certain "ungracefulness" was observed in him, a
"solemn not-to-be-trifled-with awkwardness." He was thought to
be indifferent toward his classmates;[3] actually he was "nervously
sensitive," only "bashful and reserved."

With the "long, stately" stride he had acquired by hiking
through the Salem countryside, he daily walked alone from his
room in Holworthy Hall to class. When he encountered fellow-
students, a sweetly forced smile did little to relieve "the seemingly
fixed staidness" of his expression. Corresponding to the tensions
inside him, the lean muscles of his body were stretched too tautly

over his face and tall frame to relax easily. Once in class, he would take his seat and, staring grimly ahead to avoid the glances of the young men around him, wait in silence for the lesson to begin. He was "solemn" during recitations, "taking in with his whole soul" the remarks and questions of the instructor. He spoke his answers accurately in a soft "guttural" voice.[4] Soon he was acknowledged by some of his classmates to be "an intense student," and his academic abilities quickly won their "respect" but not their friendship; by others he was regarded as a "laborious drudge," and was scorned accordingly.[5] Never would this austere figure be popular with the younger and more amiable residents of the Yard.[6]

It was characteristic of him to become acquainted with the college library as soon as he arrived at Cambridge, and to withdraw two volumes on September second.[7] He was not, however, in any sense cut off from "society," forced to take refuge in a garden of his own devising, as his mother had done in Salem. Within three weeks, along with other members of the Sophomore Class, he was nominated and elected to membership in the Institute of 1770, the undergraduate debating club. He paid the two-dollar entrance fee at once.[8] But whatever "intimate associations" he had, other than with books, were slow in developing and were mainly with upperclassmen and faculty members, "all of whom," it has been said, eventually came to esteem him "highly." [9]

The form of education carried on at Harvard in 1833 was still traditional. It made only two demands on students: they must memorize, and they must recite. As a result, professors and tutors alike tended to be "simply drill masters and academic policemen." [10] Professor Beck instructed the sophomores in writing Latin, while they read Cicero's *De Claris Oratoribus* and Horace's satires and epistles with his assistant, a "tutor." [11] With Professor Felton they read Sophocles' *Oedipus Tyrannus, Oedipus Coloneus,* and *Antigone,* and Euripides' *Alcestis.*[12] Very, who had learned his classical languages thoroughly from Worcester and Oliver is Salem, was an outstanding Latin and Greek student. And under Benjamin Peirce he excelled in mathematics.[13] But his best academic work was done for the Boylston Professor of Rhetoric and Oratory. This was the teacher who impressed him most and with whom he was most intimate during his college years.[14]

Twice each week Edward Tyrrel Channing (1790–1856) presided at sophomore "forensic days" when he listened to student "Declamations." Since 1826 his classes had learned of his impatience with "old-fashioned bombastic oratory," and of his insistence upon a less passionate style, more deliberate and reflective, supposedly in the manner of the ancient Greeks.[15] In addition to oratory, Channing twice-weekly "instructed" the Sophomore Class in Robert Lowth's *Introduction to English Grammar* and in Richard Whately's *Rhetoric*. Every fortnight students submitted "Themes" which he "examined" and returned for "correction." Afterward he went over the papers again, this time in conference with the writers, each of whom was expected to benefit from his critique of the revision. Channing's aim was to teach the young men to express ideas "logically and in order, in a natural, lucid style."[16] He emphasized a formal structure and balanced sentences with extended parallelisms, was partial to Latinate diction and an abstract vocabulary, and encouraged topics which resulted in "didactic" and "prosy" writing.[17]

Whenever Very was called upon by Channing to declaim, he would unfold a "bundle of manuscripts"—described by one classmate as "big enough for a Fourth-of-July oration"—and would read in his whispery fashion. Doubtless impressed more by attitude and bearing than by his voice, Channing was soon convinced that Very spoke "conscientiously in earnest."[18] In order to improve his writing style, however, he advised him to "be familiar with the best models," such as the *Edinburgh Review,* and to "compose frequently and with care."[19] Often, in place of the required "Themes," he allowed Very to submit original poetry.[20] Soon even Divinity School students heard of the "peculiar friendship" existing between them. It became widely known at Cambridge that they had "long and earnest discussions" about Shakespeare—and particularly about Hamlet.[21] Channing also introduced him to literary friends who called at his home. Richard Henry Dana, Sr., who in 1834 began to deliver public lectures on Shakespeare in the manner of Schlegel and Coleridge, was one of these new acquaintances who in time made a special impression upon Very.[22]

It was Channing too who encouraged him in 1833–1834 to read more widely than he had under Henry Oliver's tutelage. Soon he was familiarizing himself with Bacon and Scott, the rhetorics of Campbell and Newman, Lord Kames on *Criticism* and Archibald Alison on *Taste,* and biographies of George Washington and Napoleon. Other professors also took special notice of Very. At their suggestion he supplemented required texts by reading some Locke, additional works by Sophocles and Euripides, Aristotle, Horace and Ovid, a life of Cicero, La Fontaine's *Fables,* scholarly articles in the *Edinburgh Review* and *American Quarterly Review,* and various Greek and Latin reference books, including Jacob Bryant's fantastic *Mythology.*[23] His reading preferences clearly were derived from literary as well as more constricting academic ambitions, and served to reinforce his emerging sense of himself as a man whose life would be closely involved with scholarship and literature. His unusual dedication and seriousness meanwhile served to emphasize the emotional and intellectual distance separating him from the boys who comprised the Sophomore Class.

Among students, his roommate Thomas Barnard West was his only "bosom friend." [24] The pair, who had known each other earlier in Salem, were "great walkers," oftenest to Mount Auburn—a "wild tract" of land which fifteen years earlier had been Emerson's almost daily "walking ground." [25] They frequently strolled together during study hours, an untimely indulgence they could well afford because they ranked second and third in their class of forty-six men. At times they were joined in their walks by others. West was a likable, cheerfully pious young man who before his death in 1840 would be a leader in Salem's Sabbath School movement. Judging by his popularity, he apparently needed the diversions of a larger company to relieve the somber conversation of his companion.[26] As for Very, not many students "felt like approaching him as an intimate." [27]

In spite of his friendship with West he preferred to visit Mount Auburn alone, even in winter, in order to fully experience its rugged solitude. The cemetery was an old one. Sometimes, amid thickets and gravestones, the dead seemed to him still alive, and to offer him "instruction." Withdrawing for a time from the "worldly thoughts and worldly cares" (of home and college), he could enter here into what he felt was a "deep communion" with the "honored dead." Here, by himself, in a gloomy setting, he experienced the "chill blast of age," the rush of Time which withers youth just as it deprives spring flowers of fragrance and beauty. From the cruelty of winter, the dead seemed to say to him, he should learn not to entrust his happiness to "Fleeting" things. Only by turning to timeless affairs (things "eternal in the heavens") could he respect the wish of a dead parent and lead a "better and happier" life. Sometimes Very would write solemn poetry while visiting this dreary hillside.[28] Hamlet-like musings, deeply involved with strong feelings for his dead father, and which seemed to demand that he restrain his love for his "worldly" mother, must have also been typical of his conversation during long walks. He tended to discourage all but the most sensitive of his classmates, all but understanding young men like his roommate.

With West, Very was active in the Institute of 1770. At meetings regularly held every other Tuesday evening, members debated in rotation. General discussion after debates, student lectures, and declamations rounded out the program. A system of fines discouraged the absence of non-debaters and the failure of debaters to perform when scheduled. Very looked forward to these meetings. His attendance and reliability were unusually good for he was never fined.[29] In an atmosphere more relaxed than the classroom, though less informal than that of the dormitory and less private than Mount Auburn, the Institute allowed him to know and be known by thirty-one sophomores and the others who belonged to the large membership. Although unlike his classmates a "mature man" and "not a boy," he was reasonably "sympathetic" toward them. He would have preferred being genuinely liked, and not merely "respected" by virtue of being older. He was not at all "dictatorial" toward them, but he was "excitable." A "little opposition" to his views "would cause his long face and neck to redden," more from frustration and impatience with himself than from "anger" at them; however, this would have been a distinction difficult for younger classmates to conceive.[30] His well-known earnestness made him an effective Institute member, as soon as he was able to overcome his "diffidence."

In October 1833 he debated the question of "theatrical entertainments," whether or not they were "an evil to society." The following January he declaimed on whether marriage or celibacy were preferable, probably a topic of his own choosing. In March his scheduled debate on the stability of Monarchies and Republics was postponed to permit the election of officers. That evening he "consented" to become the official "maker of Rhymes" for the Institute. Not only, therefore, was he becoming known at Cambridge for other than academic achievements, but near the end of his first college year he was beginning to find a distinctive place for himself in the student community—and, it is evident from his "consent," on his own terms. The office to which he was elected was especially created for him. He was the only member of the Institute ever designated to fill it.[31]

In April 1834 he spent much of his time reading French, especially La Fontaine. For a course in Natural Philosophy he was studying "Mechanics" and reciting in class on "matter and its properties." Once, apparently dissatisfied with his recitation, he needed to remind himself to "aim at highest." By the end of April he was borrowing books from Professor Beck's personal library. He was also reading *Paradise Lost* and criticizing Richard Bentley for tinkering with Milton's text. He thought Bentley's emendations showed more critical "skill" than "practical judgment." In addition he was finding fault with himself, resolving "to live temperate next week and go to bed early *si posseur.*" [32] In April he also wrote and had printed in the Salem *Observer* "Hast thou ever heard the voice of nature." [33] It was, he must have felt, a reasonable balance between critical "skill" and "practical judgment." Organized by a three-part rhetorical device, its structure was enough to make the poem more thoroughly designed than anything he had so far attempted.

Before writing this poem, Very had tried at least three times during 1833 to control and subordinate the natural scene which had loomed so unmanageably in "The earth is parched with heat," and all but obliterated the insensate human figure lying in the foreground of that poem. In one poem he lamented the misfortunes of Negro slaves. In the second he brooded over the familiar surroundings which he was giving up for his first year at college. In the third of the intervening poems he described a December evening at Peabody's Mills in South Salem. But now, in the spring of 1834, he tried a radical way out of his dilemma, relying upon form and technique to free his poetry from its unfortunate overdependence on the natural setting. The result proved psychologically revealing, interesting perhaps as a prosodic experiment, but not satisfactory as a poem.

The first section of "Hast thou ever heard the voice of nature" introduces eight central images; the second section ascribes and modifies them; and the third enforces a moral conclusion.

However conventional in themselves, these images function dramatically in the poem. Evidently paired contraries, one member acquired masculine connotations, the other feminine. The presence of this repressed but highly sexual charge makes the imagery Very's own, even if not drawn from first-hand observation, and suggests the form taken by the "intemperance" for which he had recently berated himself.

The virile "Whirlwind's roar" has a feminine counterpart in the "zephyr's gentle / Breath," and the "fierce eagle's cry" is juxtaposed with the "soft whispering voice of love with / Which the dove salutes his mate." These two sets of contrasts Very calls "harmonious sounds" in the "voice of nature." In a second group, visual images of "force" in various natural "Forms" are paired in a like manner, completing the introduction.

In the second section of the poem the undirected catalogue of images is surcharged when he inquires,

> Hast thou ever seen such sights or heard such sounds,
> And never thought of Him, . . .

and then Very proceeds to repeat the original series of images with slight changes:

> . . . who rides upon
> The whirlwind, who in the gentle zephyr breathes,
> Who to the dove, the eagle, gave their notes
> Of rage or love, who from his awful hand
> The lightning hurls, the lofty cedars bend,
> And with his nostrils heapeth up the waves,
> Who made the brook to run to quench the thirst
> The cattle feel in summer's sultry reign?

The concluding lines resolve the masculine-feminine counterpoint and bring Very's moral purpose into focus, even though the character of the personal God about whom he speaks is still unclear:

If on thine ear or sight all these have fell
Unheeded, and thou hast lived unmindful
Of a God, who gave thee sight to see and
Ear to hear, and for these thy senses formed
Harmonious sounds, and ever varying
Beauties; learn oft as upon thy sight or
Ear they fall to think of him who made them.[34]

Such a noncommittal conception may unburden God of theological trappings, but it fails to define His precise role in the universe beyond recalling His original acts of creation and generosity. He dimly resembles a vocal and punitive Father, whose omnipresence is here a more-than-adequate substitute for the long absent natural father, Captain Very. The poem moreover, with its concluding direction to "think of him," seems addressed to Lydia Very's "materialistic" beliefs and religious doubts. Both the roar and whisper of nature "speak" of the existence of the Creator.

Logically the poem is incomplete, and emotionally it is unsatisfying. Very ignored the creature man in order to celebrate the procreative God. His appeal thus was aimless: he described a universe which failed to accommodate human beings. Even the insensate figure of the vagrant who cluttered the foreground of "The earth is parched with heat" had disappeared, the masculine-feminine imagery alone faintly suggesting certain nondistinctive human characteristics.

Because the poem penetrated the discordant and destructive forces of nature and tried to reveal the hidden beauty and harmony resident in the elemental symbols of masculine power—the whirlwind, the lightning, the enraged eagle, the storm-tossed sea, and the blazing sun—Very could still urge upon his passive readers their responsibility to accept these harsher manifestations of God as eagerly as they accept the femininely warm and fragrant breeze, the gentle dove, the roseate sunrise, and the refreshment of the brook.

The poem reflected little of the liberalizing influence of Mackintosh, Butler, Monboddo, and William Ellery Channing, although Paley's argument from design is implicit throughout. Something went wrong. It failed to take imaginatively into account the human response to the natural scene, the emotions and thoughts of men actually experiencing nature. It was as if Very himself had never made contact with the human element in life. He only knew that consciousness of God's existence made reverence imperative for all the moods of external nature.

In terms of subject and thematic development this poem did not advance far beyond his earliest. While adequate as newspaper verse, and even noteworthy as a poetic exercise by a Harvard undergraduate with literary ambitions, judged on merit and without regard to circumstances it offered little more than a journeyman's promise of better things to come. Nevertheless, as a result of a recent reading of *Paradise Lost*,[35] blank verse— certainly better suited to metrical experiment—replaced the static, end-stopped heroic couplet he had borrowed from Pope for his first poem. It was as if he had purposely chosen an undemanding subject in order to concentrate on techniques for its expression in a more plastic form.

While "The earth is parched with heat" was without significant metrical variation, he now substituted freely, boldly exploring metrics in various ways, especially in the introductory section. In the first eight lines of this thirty-one-line poem there is a controlled disorder, with metrical patterns oscillating until finally the ten-syllable line with alternating stresses is clearly established. Very's metrics here, with disyllabic and trisyllabic rhythms, clipped iambs, internal anapests and dactyls, amphibrachic effects, catalectic lines, and terminal-initial resolutions, derive in a general way from his familiarity with Greek and Latin poetry, rather than from the more regular English tradition.

His attempts at technical dexterity, however admirable as an experiment or tour de force, did not provide him with adequate substitutes for human values; he could not find a metrical equivalent for feelings or thoughts. He had not yet recognized that his prosody lacked organic relevance. It bore no relation to the meaning he intended the poem to convey. He had designed the prosody independently of the poem's meaning, and so it functioned in an extra-poetic way. His metrical experiments were mechanical, and therefore attracted attention at the expense of the poem's meaning.

The difficulty caused by his apparent lack of feeling for mankind is related to the problems raised by his technical experiments. Rarely in his early poems did insensitivity give way to generous attitudes. This emotional dissociation kept him aloof from the real issues of man's existence in a natural world. Although compassion or love did not have to be explicit for the didactic kind of poetry Very was writing at this time, a humanitarian impulse had not even been implied since it was completely absent from his intention. This deficiency existed because, in spite of being older than other Harvard sophomores, Very still knew little about human nature and the experiences of other human beings. Because he had not yet recognized within himself that world of experience, of emotions and tensions, hopes and fears, loves and hates within every individual, nowhere can tenderness, sympathy, or generosity be detected in the two early poems. Both were failures because imagination and feeling had failed. They had been written while he was holding himself off at an uncomfortable distance from the world of men, and (even more significantly) from himself as well. But he was not completely unaware of his problems and their solutions. Without fully realizing it yet, he had in himself a concealed wildness which had its counterpart in the wild rhythms he heard and reproduced in "the voice of nature."

Only in the slavery dirge, written before coming to Harvard, had Very so far shown real concern for human beings and made an effort to understand their sufferings and learn the sources of their feelings. For this poem, however, he ignored his own observations of slavery in 1823–1824. They had been made possible by Captain Very's last voyage to New Orleans, from which he had returned fatally ill. Instead of recollections closely bound up with intimate and painful associations, he appropriated for his poem someone else's impressions of the rigors of Negro life in the South, those of an English visitor, James Stuart. Thereby he avoided responsibility for his own emotions, and offered instead a gratuitous pity.

Except for the delegated feelings, Very's intentions in "Lines— Written on Reading Stuart's Account of the Treatment of Slaves in Charlestown" were valid. That poem begins with a conventional rhetorical flourish:

> Oh slavery! thou bane of human kind;
> Thou tyrant o'er the body and the mind;
> To all that's just, to all that's right a foe,
> Thou fill'st the world with misery and woe.

Finally, in a couplet at the end of the poem, Very spoke for himself, dropping his assumed "voice" to confess his inability to adapt his own diffused feelings to an appropriate poetic form:

> Would that by me their wrongs could half be told,
> Would that their sufferings I could half unfold.[36]

Four subsequent events showed that the gift he wished for in the summer of 1833 was the consequence of perceptive self-criticism rather than literary pose.

That the concluding couplet was a sincere avowal of failure is first intimated by an untitled and unpublished poem written before coming to Harvard, or just after his arrival. Near the end of the poem, after bidding farewell to "Haunts of my youth" (likening his home to "much-loved Ithaca"), pretentiousness for a moment gave way to honest albeit familiar sentiment:

> . . . there's no winter in my love
> For thee, no age but death. . . .[37]

These few words showed his emerging awareness of the inadequacy of a subjectless poetry, and of his need to discover materials close to him which might be converted into poetry.

About four months later, after Professor Channing had begun to show interest in his work, came the second indication that he was taking his poetic inadequacies seriously. During Christmas vacation he wrote an eight-line poem almost Oriental in simplicity and stylization, and recalling the flat panoramic clarity of folk art.

The silent moon is rising
O'er the hills of purest snow,
The silent river's flowing
In its deep bed below.

The bustle too is dying,
Around the noisy mill;
The workmen home are hying,
All is hushed and still.[38]

What makes this low-keyed lyric memorable is his declared intention. The poem had been "Suggested by Hearing the Beach, December 21, 1833, at F. Peabody's Mills, South Salem." Through visual images, therefore, he had tried to represent his feelings, affected even by the ripple of water against the banks and shore where Forest River flows into Salem Harbor. The natural world was balanced by the commercial world of Wyman's Grist Mill, where men did grinding and mixing for Colonel Peabody's white lead business.[39] Somewhere between the stillness and the animation of the two stanzas Very was trying to locate his own feeling self, a self capable of graphic responses to the sounds heard at the Salem beach.

The third confirmation that he was resolutely seeking appropriate content and attitudes for a poetic career comes from his second commonplace book, begun in May 1834. The "Scrap Book" was begun less than a month after writing "Hast thou ever heard the voice of nature," and on its title page are well-known lines from Milton's *Paradise Regained* (IV, 321–30), reproving the reader "Deep verst in books" who is "shallow in himself."

Finally, additional evidence that he was preparing to set off in directions new to him is supplied on the last page of the "Journal for 1833." In a list of "Books to be Perused" he listed "Hobbes on Human Nature; Shaftesbury's Moralists; Dr. Parr on Education; Godwin." [40] Each of these writers, Very apparently felt, probed the sources and characteristics of human conduct, and in various ways explored the limits of man's intellectual and emotional potentialities. Each seemed to have been chosen as a possible guide to those areas of experience in which Very felt himself a stranger.

Hopeful that his repeated failures of poetic matter and manner would be overcome, he accepted the challenge posed by Milton's rebuke. He undertook a program of study designed to supplement his own limited experiences as well as to familiarize himself systematically with the English poetic tradition. He would try to correct the callousness of his attitudes by making heretofore unsuspected resources within himself accessible to poetry. No longer then, he hoped, would his poems be written by one who seemed remote even from himself.

During the following months the abstract naturalisms of Mackintosh, Butler, Monboddo, and Paley germinated in his mind, re-emerging only when he had become better equipped to use them as his own, and when they could be dramatically employed in prose as well as poetry. But meanwhile, because of the demands of the Harvard curriculum, it seemed he would have to delay preparations for at least several months. In May, in addition to studying "Logic," translating Horace, and writing Latin themes, he was reading Todd's *Milton* and Symmon's *Life,* being impressed most by Milton's study habits. He seemed amazed to learn that Milton had "read over all the Greek and Latin authors in 5 years." [41] Then his own studies were suddenly interrupted.

Seven weeks after his rescheduled debate at the Institute of 1770, the question of the merits of Monarchies and Republics arose on the Harvard campus in unexpected and livelier form. With it came the climax to Very's first year of college, involving him without regard to scholarship, oratory, or poetry, and in spite of limited friendships and restrained participation in the activities of his class—a class subsequently "denounced" as unfortunate.[42]

The "Dunkin Rebellion" erupted on Monday morning, the nineteenth of May, when a freshman in Mr. Christopher Dunkin's Greek class failed to recite to the satisfaction of his instructor. The student questioned Dunkin's judgment. Classmates added catcalls. The rowdiness came to the attention of President Quincy, who of course upheld Tutor Dunkin's authority. The following day the freshmen expressed their disapproval by smashing furniture in the Greek recitation room, and later by breaking dormitory windows. At compulsory chapel the next morning, the Sophomore Class expressed its collective opinion of Quincy's handling of the affair. Sustained groans and the shuffling of feet prevented the Wednesday prayer service from being concluded. President Quincy replied by "rusticating" all but three members of the Sophomore Class, whereupon juniors and seniors destroyed hundreds of dollars worth of college property. Amid student threats to burn Quincy in effigy, Jones Very returned to Salem several days later, protesting his innocence.[43]

The extent to which he actually participated in the disturbances is not known. He was sufficiently involved in sophomore unrest, however, to sign the Class petition protesting the "system of rank" used by the college. The "uprising" finally ended on the second of June when the faculty appealed to the "tribunals of the State of Massachusetts" to restore order. By that time Very was already back in Salem. Officially, though, his first year at Harvard did not end until the faculty committee, on the sixteenth of June, rejected his formal request for reinstatement.[44]

Although feeling injustice had been done him, he was not so

upset that he could not use to advantage the long summer holiday the "Dunkin Rebellion" made possible. He returned to Salem, to the house on Federal Street, and to the physical world which—at least according to his mother's passionate account—was the ultimate existence, irremediably evil, inhabited by creatures who lacked spiritual counterparts to their material natures, some of whom were perverse enough to insist upon a God for whom no corresponding reality was possible. Jones Very found here an extended opportunity for the practice of poetry, his first since the end of August 1833.

In the series of poems he wrote following his return, he reverted to elements already used in earlier ones. Not only themes but even literal images were appropriated and recast in the first of these new poems. It was as if he were beginning his poetic career again, rewriting poems he now knew were defective. From "The earth is parched with heat" he borrowed the river, the oak, the stranger, and provided them with surroundings which elaborated its halcyon conclusion; and from "Hast thou ever heard the voice of nature" he adopted a form of blank verse scarcely less extravagant. To these borrowings from himself he added original elements which gave this untitled composite its distinctive quality and merit.

Most dramatic of the modifications was his descent from the vague height at which formerly he had viewed the natural scene. Now he freely entered the landscape at a familiar level. He inquired at the outset whether there was anything

> . . . more delightful than to wander forth
> In spring, before the sun has chas'd away
> The freshness of the morn; . . .

Very had himself assumed the role of the strangely exhausted traveler who had been destroyed by lightning, but with less disastrous effect. No longer was he aloof. He immersed himself completely in the nature which was his subject. Once within the scene, he recognized that no longer were there anxieties which needed to be relieved by confidence in immortality.

> Nature seems
> As young as when the morning light first broke
> On Eden.

From this intimate perspective no sudden catastrophe threatened the calm.

> Would that my thoughts could speak, my tongue describe
> The pleasure that a scene like this affords!
> No—language is too feeble to give them
> Utterance.

"Pleasure within my breast" had replaced former signs of tension and futile attempts at reconciling the ways of God to man:

> In silent gratitude I raise mine eyes
> To heaven.[45]

Simple notes of piety were justified in such surroundings, and were much more convincing than the solemnities of the 1833 version. Lyric gracefulness, a mark of Very's increasing competence, prevented the discomfiture and uncertainty which had marred most of his earlier poems.

His "Death of Lafayette" showed further signs of poetic awareness. It recorded a patriotic sense of indebtedness to the hero, and boldly exhorted Americans to "lament for him." Eight lines near the end rise to unexpected heights of rhetoric, showing that he had learned Professor Channing's lessons well. Very had given no hint before that he was capable of such powerful if derivative eloquence.

> Ye mountains veil your heads in clouds and mourn
> For him, who around your summits cast glory
> More bright than noon-day sun! Ye waving pines
> Sigh louder in the blast; for he, who gave
> You liberty's fair soil, is now no more.

And thou, O boundless ocean, mourn! for ne'er
Again thy waves shall bear to freedom's coast,
One more worthy of thy lamentation.[46]

The diction, the masculine rhythm, the pattern of breathsweeps, the prosodic restraint, the scale of emotion and its projection into nature, all combine to make this relatively fresh. While the intention of the poem reverts to similar sentiments expressed in the slavery dirge, there is no other common ground. Where one had been hesitant, this is decisive; where one had been apologetic, this is insistent; where "lamentation" seemed too strong a response to the condition of thousands of unfortunates, it was almost too weak for the painless death of an old and much-honored man; where a domestic tragedy seemed remote and beyond reform, the foreign event gained an immediacy requiring action which could no longer be deferred. Very's entire calculus of values, technical as well as emotional, had been revised upward for this poem, and with what for Very were spectacular results. The subdued kindnesses of Professor Channing and the exaggerated intensities of Lydia Very's household were responsible only in part for this.

In another poem written during the summer of 1834 were further signs of change. Very took for his theme the metaphorical pursuit of "true pleasure," and parenthetically revealed a callow idealism while reaffirming his poetic ambitions. After exhausting exotic as well as familiar settings—but deliberately excluding the "domestic hearth" as a likely residence for the "Goddess of Pleasure"—he unexpectedly encountered her in "that inward fount" where the quest had originated. The "mind," he concluded (recalling his readings in Butler, Monboddo, and Channing), "Is its own home." True pleasure may be found only in "the mind communing with itself." Nature, society, love, power, and physical comforts may certainly yield satisfactions, but once the highest form of pleasure—that of the mind and of the imagination—was experienced, all others became deficient. Whoever "seeks thee not within . . . neglects the banquet of the mind." Only by turning inward into himself, Very seemed to be saying, could he find sustenance for life and thus for poetry.⁴⁷

Everything considered, these three imperfect poems were more encouraging than earlier ones. Nature had become a flexible instrument for the poet to use, not merely a two-dimensional canvas before which a poem was attempted. Emotions had been intensified. And nature and emotion in turn had been subjected to imagination. Very was achieving greater precision in expression, and as a result these poems have a clearer purpose and direction.

Although it had been written in April 1834, "Hast thou ever heard the voice of nature" had less in common with the poems of the late spring and summer of 1834 than with those written a year earlier. The changes, including the broadened imagination and more intense manner, came suddenly but not unexpectedly. After his academic work had been interrupted by the "Dunkin Rebellion," Very commenced the new program of out-of-class study he had proposed for himself earlier. He left evidences of it in the new notebook begun in May. The entries he made in the "Scrap Book, 1834" relate chiefly to poets and poetry, and bear intensively upon his efforts to discover the poet's relations to the world and to his art. Hours not spent listening to Lydia Very's seemingly endless denunciations of the injustices authorized or overlooked by society, and of the universal evils which no God prevented or condemned, were spent wrestling with possible answers to the question, "What is a poet?" and in trying to discover the range and function of the poetic imagination. At the same time, and with partial success, he was trying to relate himself to the less abstract matter of living beings making their way in a living world. Both major themes, the poetic and the moral, were represented in his work during the next few years. These self-imposed studies went far to root him in a poetic tradition.

First he painstakingly waded through a long, pretentious, apocalyptic poem written by the Scottish Calvinist poet, Robert Pollok. Disregarding the most typical sections of *The Course of Time* (1827), those in which Pollok affected an archaic diction for his copious flow of words and images about the "spiritual life" and the "destiny of man," Very located the few passages conforming to his own specialized needs. He pored over those seemingly interminable lines which told of the more "Pernicious effects of sloth in the literary man." In view of his earnest ambitions and his resolution to "aim at highest," Very was understandably impressed by this menacing account of a poet in whom "Decision, fulcrum of the mental powers," had "quite worn out." After a good deal of posturing, Pollok's irresolute rhapsodist finally reached the point where suicide seemed the only release. He

. . . drank with desperate thirst the poppy's juice;
A deep and mortal slumber settled down
Upon his weary faculties oppressed;
He rolled from side to side, and rolled again,
And snored, and groaned, and withered, and expired,
And rotted on the spot, leaving no name.[48]

Since the moral had little significance for Very's own situation, he was mainly interested not in the theme of "Literary Indolence," but in its treatment by Pollok. The comparison of the poet's indecision to a "plant up-rooted oft" he thought a "very good description . . . beautiful and natural." However, defects of technique marred the passage. "The word 'even,'" Very noted, "seems to be intended for 'e'en.'" He disliked the words "snored" and "rotted," and was irritated by Pollok's fondness for repeating "and." In one line he found "one syllable too many," and in other lines certain phrases seemed to be ungrammatical.[49]

Although Pollok's lapses did not discourage Very from later copying two additional passages, they were serious enough to make him hesitate before proceeding.[50] With reservations clarified, Very studied the grandiose perceptions of Pollok's "lonely bard" who manipulated "visionary things fairer than aught / That was." As an aspiring young writer looking for directions to his own poetic career, Very was understandably impressed by the sober musings of an ideal poet who was intimate with

> . . . the distant tops of thoughts,
> Which men of common stature never saw,
> Greater than aught that largest words could hold, . . .[51]

The search by the reflective Very for a vocation amid the parochialisms of Salem and Cambridge was stimulated by Pollok's vatic poet. His kind of power, an intellectual and imaginative power, was precisely what Very was seeking.

Pollok claimed to express thoughts differing from those of "men of common stature." Unlike the down-to-earth idiom and concerns of Salem, and unlike the certain strains of living with Lydia Very and her compulsive doubts, Pollok's words and intentions seemed to reflect aspirations which corresponded to something "noble" in Very's own mind, hitherto unexpressed. For the first time, he thought, he was about to share feelings whose value he previously had only suspected, as in the poem "Pleasure." By way of confirming mutual understanding with a thoughtful contribution of his own, Very inquired: "What can prompt us more to acts of charity and benevolence than the remembrance that we partake no more of the morrow's light than the humblest object of our kindness?"[52] Addressed to Pollok, this was his offer of thanks for the help he hopefully expected would allow him someday to break through the isolation which he was feeling so intensely.

In a short time many of Very's contemporaries would also find themselves beset by frustration and yearning. Some, following the lead of Coleridge and Carlyle, were already beginning to respond to influences from the Continent—from Goethe and Kant, from Fichte, Hegel, Schleiermacher, the Schlegels, from Novalis, Schiller, and Schelling, or from Cousin, Fourier, Jacobi, and Jouffroy. However, there was no one in Salem (at least not until

Elizabeth Peabody's return from Boston in 1837) to guide him in such directions. Oliver was too piously orthodox to have helped, while Cambridge professors were either too cautious, as was Channing, or else their European experiences were only just beginning to stir students, as happened with Charles Follen and George Ticknor.[53] Thus, for a time, Very was left to find his way by himself, and he turned to Pollok for what he sought.

While Very thought Pollok would assist him in working out of his isolation, his expectation of finding liberating and germinal influences in the devout Scotsman was disappointed. No matter how often he promised in *The Course of Time,* Pollok never rose above commonplace levels of experience and communication. Nevertheless, Very still seemed to learn something from him. Pollok believed the "mysterious secrets of existence" could be learned through the high powers of imagination which endowed his wizard poet, grandiose powers capable of creating a "wondrous sort of bliss." Very followed this ideal poet until, after surmounting many obstacles, he at last

. . . entered in to Nature's holy place,
Her inner chamber, and beheld her face
Unveiled; and heard unutterable things
And incommunicable visions saw.[54]

By abruptly ending the quotation at this point, Very expressed his annoyance with anticlimactic revelations. Pollok's lines in effect were only a prelude to poetry. Although seemingly poetic, they were only a preparation for a poem which failed to materialize during prolonged writing. The least to be expected from a poet was communication; thus, when Pollok repeatedly tried at the crucial moment to justify his imperfect imagination by claims of ineffability, his pretentions were exposed.

Very's interest in Pollok was therefore symptomatic rather than substantive. He simply wished to become a "true, legitimate anointed bard" himself. But as for the necessary *truth,* the *laws,* the priestly *rites,* and the terms of the office, these were still undetermined.

The passages from Pollok's poem which found their way into the "Scrap Book" indicate that Very had already recognized the need to revise the concepts which lay behind such poems as "The earth is parched with heat," "Lines—Written on Reading Stuart's Account of the Treatment of Slaves in Charlestown," and "Hast thou ever heard the voice of nature." None of these were works like those of Pollok's "reflective poet"—of "faithful memory, vastly stored," and "accurate of observation." Like *The Course of Time,* Very's own early efforts were only on the verge of poetry, depending upon bare, stiff statement or mawkishness for their distinctive effects. Very's awareness of his own deficiencies through those of Pollok was a step toward remedying them. However, the problem of furnishing an outwardly uneventful life with the materials for poetry still remained.

Pollok's poem and the conclusions Very drew from it and applied to his own poetry still do not fully account for the differences between the early poems and those written during the summer of 1834. Other influences had been brought to bear, either before Very's leaving Harvard or shortly after his return to Salem. The series of quotations from Byron which immediately followed the excerpts from Pollok showed him what might be done with a poet's intimate reactions to the natural world.

When Very occupied himself with Byron in the late spring and early summer of 1834, he retained the same principles of discrimination and selection he had applied to Pollok: he included in the "Scrap Book" only passages relevant to his own situation. He was not particularly concerned with illustrating all or even the most representative aspects of Byron and Byronism, just as the record of his reading of Pollok gave little indication of the prolixity, the dripping sentiment, and the more foolish vagaries which are so integral a part of Pollok's poem.

Very's selections betray his distrust for the more demonic side of Byron. He did not sympathize with any of Byron's moments of tortured despair or of vigorous cynicism. The ironic view of reality, which at times threatened to transform Byron's love of freedom into revolt for its own sake, to convert skepticism into moral anarchy, melancholy into misanthropy, was barred—perhaps because these were characteristics too close to those of Lydia Very. In any event, the funereal mood failed to impress him, just as he ignored the blasphemy and obscenity, and for different reasons disallowed the satiric elements, the mysterious, amorous adventures, the terrible arrogance, and the pervasive guilt and doom which animate so much of Byronic romanticism. Echoing John Gibson Lockhart, Very acknowledged that perhaps Byron "flowed best at midnight." [55] But since he was trying to stimulate what he believed was best in himself, and did not necessarily want to learn from what was "best" in Byron, the darker elements were omitted without apology. In short, the romantic intensities of *Childe Harold's Pilgrimage* rather than the perverse nobility of *Don Juan* attracted him.

The first stanza impressing him enough to be entered in the "Scrap Book" was the familiar one in which Byron energetically established the romantic dichotomy of nature and civilization (II, xxv). Preferring isolation to society, the life of the observer to that of the participant, Byron's persona reflected upon nature for the antidote to his feelings of loneliness. "To sit on rocks, to muse o'er flood and fell," to examine the brightness and shadow in nature's scene, to make archetypal discoveries in nature for oneself,

> This is not solitude: 'tis but to hold
> Converse with Nature's charms and view her stores unroll'd.[56]

Nothing in Byron's world was mawkishly spiritual. It was all hard, physical, material. Yet in his hands it somehow became connotative, finely responsive to psychological probing. From somewhere within the hero-outcast, self-conscious and inward-looking, he evoked whatever sanctity was latent in his experiencing of nature. Thereby he gained salvation, or what passed for salvation with Byron.

Part of this formula for a ritualistic redemption was already familiar to Very from his own wanderings about the rugged Salem countryside and along the gloomy slopes of Mount Auburn; part was familiar to him through Butler and Paley; part he may have extrapolated from William Ellery Channing and Pollok; much of the remainder, however, and the peculiar intensity in particular, was new. Byron again and again made plain to Very that, regardless of nature's "features wild," and even though he may have "loved her best in wrath," the sentient individual can be redeemed only through his dedication of mind and heart to

> Dear Nature . . . the kindest mother still,
> Though always changing, in her aspect mild.[57]

This total dependence did not conflict with Very's own conclusions about the efficacies of nature so much as it dramatized the weaknesses in his own formulation of it in poetry. Whereas Very had postponed the rewards of a moral life until a remote future time in "The earth is parched with heat" and the poem on slavery, Byron—like Lydia Very—seemed to be impatient with Christian submissiveness. Byron, as he was projected in the "Scrap Book," insisted upon redemption *now*. It was to be enjoyed in the very process of seeking it. Being inseparable from the quest, redemption could only be perpetuated by continuous renewal of the search. Hence, eternal restlessness and yearning paradoxically became the price for Byron's redemptive program:

> There is a fire
> And motion of the soul which will not dwell
> In its own narrow being, but aspire
> Beyond the fitting medium of desire;
> And but once kindled, quenchless evermore,

Preys upon high adventure, nor can tire
Of night but rest; a fever at the core,
Fatal to him who bears to all who ever bore.[58]

While Very hoped to experience, at least vicariously, comparable excitements himself, he disapproved of Byron's categorical endorsement of such burning emotions. He questioned the self-serving satisfaction to be found in Byron's agitated feelings; and he also doubted the wisdom of temporary deliverance from the crass world. He counted Byron among those "whose religion, at best, is an anxious wish like that of Rabelais, 'a great Perhaps.'" By way of further reproof he claimed that "True glory, like the celestial fire, is kindled from above." It does not spread "like the wave dispersed to nought, but rises in a pure and sacred flame, pointing upward to its divine origin."[59] To cautious Very, following the more conservative preferences of Butler and Monboddo as well as of Professor Channing, physical passion remained suspect, even when recognizing its importance to the poet and to poetry.

His specific disagreement with the Byronic indulgence of passion he registered in a poem, "Lines: Suggested by Seeing a Butterfly Sculptured On a Tomb," written in July 1834.

> . . . Passions fierce attack, attack most
> Direful; . . . these and thousand nameless foes,
> That strive to fix thy thoughts on things below
> Thy noble destiny, repel; then, like
> The Phoenix, thou shalt rise triumphant from
> Thine ashes . . .[60]

Here Very is critical of ignoble passions and those worthy in themselves but turned to questionable ends. The passional principle itself, what he called the "eager flight," he upheld, challenging only its misuse. His poem "Lines" supplemented "Pleasure" in emphasizing the non-physical, introspective aspects of the true gratification. The essence of Byronism as Very understood it, the

[ 47 ]

symbolic atonement through passion, thus received qualified endorsement, extended for "flight," withheld from the "dark and loathsome mansion" inhabited by "creeping," "worm"-like man. Beyond this, Very was unyielding.

*Childe Harold* thus helped him write his poems during the summer of 1834. More than Pollok, it was Byron—whose energies and outlook seemed to have much in common with those of Lydia Very—who carried him for a time out of the "false, hollow world," [61] and brought him closer to the realization of his own poetic art. Without Very knowing it at the time, Byron had also brought him closer to his fulfillment as a man, a process begun in Salem and completed at Cambridge by his own later efforts.

# The Expanding Field

## 1834–1835

W H A T E V E R   V E R Y ' S  lingering bitterness over the outcome
of the "Dunkin Rebellion," he forgot it at least temporarily in his
excitement over Byron and the discoveries about himself and his
poetry that Byron was making possible. By the time his return to
Cambridge near the end of August 1834 was authorized, he was
anxious to leave Salem and was again looking forward to college
studies. On the thirtieth, after passing a special examination and
obtaining a certificate of good conduct, he was placed on proba-
tion as a requirement for readmission with Junior standing.[1]
Before resuming classes in September he received permission to
take the course in Spanish literature given by the Chairman of
the Department of Modern Languages and Literature. George
Ticknor was the one professor at Harvard who had personal
knowledge of Byron.

Although the Boston-bred, Göttingen-trained Ticknor was
reputed to be "cold" and "distant" toward students, and to have
an unusually formal classroom manner, he was known to inter-
rupt his lectures with reminiscences about the famous people he

had met during his 1815-to-1819 *wanderjahre* abroad. Ticknor, Harvard students knew, had been Byron's close friend and had heard the story of his life and love affairs from Byron himself. He had also traveled widely in England and the Continent, visiting Wordsworth and Sir Walter Scott, and for a time belonging to the literary circle which included Hazlitt, Lamb, and Leigh Hunt. In Rome he had been on familiar terms with Napoleon's family and Mme. de Staël; in Paris (and elsewhere in Europe) he spent time with Washington Irving, and had seen Lafayette; and in Germany he called upon Goethe several times. Therefore there was much about Ticknor besides his reputation for thorough scholarship to recommend him to Very. Moreover, it is probable that Professor Channing had introduced him to Ticknor during his sophomore year, for it seems to have been at Ticknor's suggestion that Very expressed the desire earlier in 1834 to "peruse" certain books. Of the four on his list, two were by men Ticknor had known, Samuel Parr and William Godwin; the other two, Hobbes and the Earl of Shaftesbury, were men of the seventeenth century, a period for which Ticknor was then Harvard's foremost scholar.

Apparently then, since Ticknor was acknowledged to be a great teacher from whom much might be learned about recent and non-recent literary history, Very's purpose in electing the course was not merely to learn something about Spanish literature. He wanted to find additional directions for his own writing and special studies, and the celebrated Ticknor must have seemed just the man to make this possible. His coldness, distance, and formality could not prevent him from encouraging students with literary ambitions.[2] Very responded accordingly, and made detailed notes for each of the nineteen lectures in the series.[3]

He was properly impressed with Ticknor's showing how an epic like the "Poema del Cid" remained so "full of life" and "vivacity" that even after seven hundred years it continued to evoke "the feelings of the age in which it was written."[4] He was impressed too with Ticknor's intricate knowledge of Provençal poetry, of sonnets, canzones, terza rima and ottava rima, canzonets, pastorals, and eclogues.[5] At times, however, as when Ticknor discoursed rapidly on the great literature of the Golden Age ("This period follow[e]d the time of wars as in other countries"),[6] he had to be satisfied with such an observation as, "We first have a general view of many writers then fix on some favorites so stars at night."[7] The nocturnal luminaries seemed Very's own. In the midst of scholarly remarks on Cervantes, Very thought it "somewhat remarkable" that a people "so given to war" as were the Spanish, "still turned from its turbulent scenes to pastoral forms of life." It was as if Very thought that peace and joy could emerge only from struggle and pain.[8] The "whole series of epics" from the reign of Philip II were failures; they "seem[e]d to be nothing but chronicles and but little differ from histories"; they were "too much concerned about facts rather than feelings and invention." [9] Obviously for Very emotions and imagination, not the antecedent "facts" of war, were the means by which the peaceful, joyous life was gained.

Finally in November, when the course was almost complete, Very understood that "national character always prescribes the limits to literature." [10] This idea, original with neither Ticknor nor Very but evidently derived by the former from A. W. Schlegel's *Lectures on the History of Literature,*[11] Very remembered along with other remarks on epic poetry, his professor's and his own. A year and a half later, in April 1836, he used them to explain why it was unlikely that a "Great Epic Poem" could be written in modern times. He said that the character of "modern man," which was based on non-epical principles, precluded it.

Most of what Very was finding out about the modes of heroism and its expression in the nineteenth century was not taught him in Harvard classrooms. Encouraged by the insights bred by Ticknor's scholarship and eloquence, Very resumed his private literary studies in the autumn of 1834, and continued to fill his mind and commonplace book with materials relevant to his work of the summer. Having learned from Ticknor's historical and comparative method for approaching literature, Very soon was acknowledging Byron's indebtedness to Spenser. He felt Spenser surpassed Byron in both "Genius" and "Taste." [12] It took but a single allusion to the *Faerie Queene* to make him quit Byron's poetry for a time, and recall in its place lines from the "sweet madness" of Milton's *Comus:*

> Can any mortal mixture of Earths mould
> Breath such Divine inchanting ravishment?

Spenser was closer to Milton than to Byron. Very noted that Milton's rich soliloquy ended far differently from any Byronic climax:

> . . . such a sacred, and home-felt delight,
> Such sober certainty of waking bliss
> I never heard till now. [13]

This lovely digression was a circuitous introduction to the Coleridgean distinction between Fancy and Imagination, a distinction Very had discovered during his most recent sojourn in Salem. The course ran from Byron's robust introversions in rough-hewn poetry, to the dream-like images of Spenser, to the etherealized but domestic responses of Milton's *Comus,* arriving finally at Colerdige's psychological and aesthetic speculations. All this required brief space, four pages in the "Scrap Book." Very's readiness to leave *Childe Harold*—even if it proved a temporary removal—further indicated his uneasiness with Byron. In spite of the extent and quality of his admiration for Byron's energy, Very rested more comfortably in the presence of less tempestuous spirits.

His interest in Coleridge at first was only a reaction to Byron. An uncommon emphasis upon feelings ("Passions fierce attack, attack most / Direful") [14] had raised doubts concerning the validity of Byron's method and purpose. A fuller investigation of psychological fundamentals relating to the poetic process therefore was indicated by the dialectic of Very's previous studies. He reflected at this point: "Memory seems given us to reap instruction from Nature and its field is ever extending." [15] With this observation the several strains converged, Byron representing Nature and Coleridge the operative mind.

The function of Coleridge's theory of imagination for Very in 1834 was almost identical with that of the "ideal poet" from whose trafficking in rarified things Pollok had tried to make so much. In contrast to Byron, whose poetry Very thought too firmly grounded in "materialism," Pollok and Coleridge had dealt with a more delicate commodity. But Pollok called for capricious daydreaming which resisted artful expression, was really an evasion, and was wisely rejected by Very. Coleridge's insights he found more substantial and congenial. Ultimately they placed Byron's achievement in a favorable light.

Although Very had begun to acquaint himself with James Marsh's Vermont editions of Coleridge's prose works during the 1834 summer recess,[16] what interested Very most at the time he was taking Ticknor's course was not the *Biographia Literaria* or any of Coleridge's other books. A popularization of his ideas by his nephew and disciple Henry Nelson Coleridge more closely suited the problems uppermost in Very's mind at this point. Very however acknowledged indebtedness to the elder Coleridge in ironical fashion by ending the passage in the "Scrap Book" with an abrupt statement from *The Friend:* "In wonder, says Aristotle," according to Coleridge, "does philosophy begin: and in astoundment, says Plato, does all true philosophy finish." [17]

The section which engaged his attention came from the younger Coleridge's *Introductions to the Study of the Greek Classic Poets* (1831). Having nothing whatever to do with the Greeks, the passage suggested that Mercutio's description of Queen Mab (*Romeo and Juliet*, I, iv, 53–69) was "an instance of Pure Fancy, as contradistinguished from Imagination"; while the "mode and direction of the profound madness of Lear" during the phantasmic trial (III, vi, 23-87), "flow from the Imagination of the Poet alone." In a manner related to the distinction Very had drawn in the midst of Ticknor's lecture between "facts" and "feeling" combined with "invention," Henry Nelson Coleridge demonstrated how the two faculties of mind differed.

In the first of these passages, the images taken from objects of nature or art, are presented *as they are;* . . . without any connexion with the being and feelings of the speaker or the Poet impressed upon them; . . . In the second, the images are transfigured; their colors and shapes are modified; one master passion pervades and quickens them; . . . The first is Fancy; the last is Imagination. . . . That presents a spectacle, and presents it only; this projects the man into the object, or attracts it to the man, with a vivifying, humanizing, impersonating energy. . . . Fancy collects material from the visible world, and human interest; Imagination takes the moulds the objects of nature at the same moment; . . . renders them instinct with the inspired breath of human passion.[18]

In addition to its shaping and modifying power, the Imagination finally transcends sensational material altogether and brings the mind into direct contact with supersensuous reality. As Very had already phrased it, the "facts" were left behind because of the mind's "ever extending" field. Once the "vivifying, humanizing, impersonating" capacity of the Imagination was linked to the poet's ability to impregnate facts "with the inspired breath of human passion," Very's return to Byron was assured. He could now try to perceive what Byron had seen with his "mind's eye."

This same purpose of redirecting him to Byron was served by an anonymous "Review of Coleridge's *Poetical Works*" in the current (October 1834) issue of *Blackwood's Edinburgh Magazine:*

Imagination is no liar—a veracious witness she of events . . . invisible to sense—and incredible to reason—till she pictures them in her own light—and then . . . the miraculous creates its own faith.

The ordinary rules of evidence are set aside—and there is felt to be no limit to the possibilities of nature. . . . Nothing is unnatural that stirs our heart-strings—her voice it is, if from some depths within us steals a response. The preternatural—and the supernatural— . . . is an empire bounded only by the soul's desires—and what may bound the soul's desires? [19]

His oblique comment on the article disclosed his understanding of the effect of a shaping imagination. "The circle of the natural," he said, "is every day widening into the supernatural." [20] Byron's use of emotion for the purpose of transforming "facts" Very thought worth reconsidering once it could be rephrased as a function of embracing imaginative power which went beyond nature and facts. Even in Salem and Cambridge such operations of mind were possible. He made this explicit by remarking at "the infinite number of Images or Forms" found in nature which could be carried over into poetry. [21] With this affirmation the long but necessary digression was complete. Very was now prepared to reread and reconsider Byron's work in an effort to see what more of use to his own life and poetry could be learned from it.

Sixty-five lines from *The Giaour,* unlike those which had impressed him before, testify to his renewed interest. These constituted the extent of Very's concession to the demonic Byron. That he copied out two long passages (lines 832–82, 958–71), was because of the preceding discussion of poetic capabilities. To "the close observer," Byron revealed "brighter traits with evil mix'd." [22] It was Byron's expansive imagination which dared to suggest good in the midst of evil, signs of grace (if not of righteousness) in spite of seeming apostasy. Fancy could not conceive so complicated a state, no more than Lear's madness could have been sustained without the intervention of Shakespeare's imagination.

The second extract from *The Giaour* struck Very as a virtual challenge to join in "high adventure" of an imaginative order. Heroism, Byron was saying, while psychological, in no way leads to consequences which are illusory. Actually few actions are more substantial or require greater courage than the exercise of will.[23] Therefore, aided by Coleridge's doctrines of the "vivifying" imagination, Very no longer found himself on the defensive when confronting Byron's dark passions.

His subsequent selections from *Childe Harold* incorporated the poem's earlier emphasis on nature and emotion with newer elements from *The Giaour*. A stoic acceptance of the inevitable spiritual unrest, coupled with self-immolation, had replaced overconfidence in the natural birthright of Byron's sensitive persona. Very scattered eight stanzas through twenty-five pages of the "Scrap Book."[24] The first alone was taken from Canto II, and this was the single stanza recorded during the autumn of 1834. The remaining seven were from Canto III and were entered early in 1835, with the last entry made almost a year after Very had begun examining *Childe Harold* closely.

During this period, from the spring of 1834 to the spring of 1835, he was reading widely, in addition to devoting himself to college studies and writing poetry upon occasion. However, the "Scrap Book" suggests that his thoughts repeatedly returned to Byron, even as he read James Beattie and Thomson, John Gibson Lockhart, Burns, Samuel Butler, Cowper, Samuel Rogers, Scott, Prior, Goldsmith, and Bulwer-Lytton. While most of the quotations were randomly chosen and not extensive, and reflected an interest weighted heavily with sentimentality, several had special bearing on Byron. Indirectly they also revealed how significant Ticknor's influence was upon the rationale for Very's commonplace book. Throughout these months he was making a systematic but unhurried study of Byron's poetry, especially of his treatment of nature. Beattie and Thomson in particular supplemented this examination since Very's selections from these eighteenth-century poets shared poetic matter, form, and manner with Byron.[25]

The final series of extracts from *Childe Harold* shows that

Very was examining not only some of its antecedents but also Byron's evolution as a poet. He carefully preserved the chronology: since Cantos I and II were composed before *The Giaour,* while the third Canto appeared several years after it, this was the order of passages in the "Scrap Book."

Made while Very continued to be saturated with Ticknor's personal sense of literature, these entries revealed the changed character of Byron's hero and his expanded activity in the natural setting. Although other entries intervened, the quotations all related to a single unifying theme. Its best expression came in a hyperbolic credo:

> Could I embody and unbosom now
> That which is most within me,—could I wreak
> My thoughts upon expression, and thus throw
> Soul, heart, mind, passions, feelings, strong or weak,
> All that I would have sought, and all I seek,
> Bear, know, feel, and yet breathe—into one word,
> And that one word were Lightning, I would speak;
> But as it is, I live and die unheard,
> With a most voiceless thought, sheathing it as a sword.[26]

Once expressed, this logos would reveal the unity of intimate, personal longings and the elemental forces in nature. The new form of heroism Very was discovering during 1834–1835 consisted of this act of expression. By coupling imagination with feeling, the circle of natural facts could be extended until it passed imperceptibly into the realm of spiritual truth.

As justification for this interpretation of Byron's Word, Very carefully arranged a group of three stanzas, imposing upon them his own order. (III, lxxv, xiii, xiv.) The resulting structure revealed as much about Very's aspirations as it did about his insight into what he believed were Byron's intentions.[27] Very considered these stanzas illustrative of Coleridge's vitalizing imagination. When most successful, as here, Byron's poetry was not "too much concerned about facts rather than feelings and invention." [28] Very now recognized that even at his most rhetorical Byron provided a consistent depiction of nature emotionalized. He went beyond the circle of natural "facts." By willful acts of imagination, by heroic acts of epical proportion, he had made nature coincide with a complex series of inward experiences, almost converting topography into human thought and feeling. Since the later poetry by Byron which found conspicuous place in the "Scrap Book" was humanized, it could be accepted by Very without qualification.

Although the grouped stanzas provided the climax to Very's investigations, nine pages and about a month later Very repeated the last five lines by themselves as the final citation. In so doing he adapted them once again for his own purposes, this time as a general judgment of Byron, more sympathetic than a later reference to Byron's "discolored and passion-stained bosom." [29]

> Could he have kept his spirit to that flight
> He had been happy; but this clay will sink
> Its spark immortal, envying it the light
> To which it mounts, as if to break the link
> That keeps us from yon heaven which woos us to its brink.[30]

This final tribute to Byron marked Very's victory, with the assistance of Coleridge, over the earthbound poet of Cantos I and II. Thereby Very showed signs in himself of that same inward heroism which he thought distinguished the age in which he was living, and which gradually was obliterating the differences between natural fact and spiritual truth.

Although his own heroism had not yet found completed form by this time, Very did publish three poems in the Salem *Observer* in his Junior year, none however between September and December 1834 while he was taking Ticknor's course. These poems, written during the last phase of his study of Byron, showed the effect of his extracurricular interests. In "The New Year" he disclosed qualities distinctly superior to those of his earlier poems.

An undercurrent of Byronic restlessness made all the more convincing the un-Byronic contentment which finally resolved the tensions of the poem. Unlike those composed before it, it was emotionally realistic in objectives and more disciplined in prosody. Within the scope of less than a dozen lines he found an external representation for his inner feelings; and simultaneously he discovered the external world conforming to the complex patterns of emotion within himself.

He greeted as a "welcome guest" the arrival of the storm-clad year 1835. He thought:

'Tis sweet to struggle with the wintry blast,
And, as the cruel storm is raging round,
To feel within the breast a calm as soft and sweet
As summer's eve; to see the snow whirling
In eddies, like the wide world in passion's
Eddies mingled, to see and smile is sweet.
To feel the breast as snow-flake pure which falls
Upon the cheek; or, if within anger
Should rise, to know 't will melt as soon into
The tide of warm and ever-flowing love.

The meaning of this low-keyed fragment from the poem, however much it drew upon complex energies within him, is neither intricate nor abstruse. His conception of the relation between the individual and the worlds of nature and men, between feelings and events, was transparent. But the prosody was remarkable because it consciously reinforced the meaning, something he had been unable to manage before. Trochaic substitutions dramatically heighten the emotion by isolating and emphasizing "whirling," and by contrasting it boldly with the placid "summer's eve." The trochaic linking of "snow whirling" to the "wide world" sustains the sensation of a dizzily spinning vortex. Momentarily everything is twisting visually and metrically, the snow and the larger world caught up together by the force of wind and passion. With the emergence of sobered thought—"to see and smile is sweet"—the regular iambic rhythm is restored, preparing the way for the satisfying calm of "The tide of warm and ever-flowing love."

Tender sentiments succeed "anger" in much the same way as Very believed the "turbulent scenes" of war (to which Ticknor had alluded in his lectures) made possible the peace and joy of ensuing "pastoral forms of life." Like "whirling" and "eddies," trochaic "anger" is identified with the winter storm. The external "struggle" against the snow consequently is given an emotional resolution "within," as well as an organic metrical relevance that leads to the inevitable homely scene indoors.

By applying "invention" to the "ever extending" field of "Memory," Very provided an idyllic domesticity for the poem's conclusion.

> Oh this is sweet: come, let us look where streams
> The cheering light, . . . round the evening fire.
> See the fond mother, as with looks of love
> She turns now here, now there, now her children
> Smiles upon, and now their sire; and see him,
> As the laughing boy he raises, imprint
> Upon his lips a father's kiss; . . .
> Hadst thou a human heart, thou savage blast;
> 'Twould melt at such a sight, and thy rough voice
> Would whisper soft in gentle zephyrs round
> That dwelling.[31]

Transforming "facts" into a higher form of truth, his imagination purged the actual Lydia Very of her turbulent intensities and restored to life his long-dead father. These realities, perfected by the shaping mechanisms of Very's mind, temporarily relieved the anxieties building up during his years of coming into maturity. The painful knowledge that his mother possessed a "heart unchanged," a heart still a "slave of sin" and not yet "alive to God," a heart which therefore "clouded e'en our home" and dimmed the domestic "light"[32] was knowledge transformed.

However transiently and fictively, he thus created out of neo-Byronic yearnings his own imaginative counterpart to Milton's "home-felt delight." The "simple vehemence" of his mother's "passion," and her atheism and "course materialism," were momentarily forgotten. Even the taint of illegitimate birth was temporarily removed in order to ensure a glorious reconciliation with his father.

The transformation in the second published poem of 1835 tapped resources not so profound as his relationship to his parents or feelings associated with them. Nevertheless it revealed an aspect of himself he had never before utilized in poetry. Seeing from a distance a group of gay young people swiftly dashing through the darkness in a sleigh—"Hurra, hurra, away *they* go"—he was certain he saw laughing eyes

That glance from under the brow of night,
And kindle the heart with soft delight.

By an act of the imagination which crossed the bounds of fact, he transcended his loneliness and found himself amid the happy company: "Away *we*'ll fly like a bird set free." [33] Although this lyrical and refreshing release from the actualities of life in Salem scarcely constituted the intellectual heroism he was predicating for himself, it was a striking symptom of personal dissatisfactions, and of his continuing desire to overcome them by operations of mind. Guided by feeling, his will had enabled him to shape events so that they gained a significance they lacked in their natural form.

The third poem required additional variations on a self-centering process of composition. Written in Salem during Easter vacation, it celebrated the "Snow-Drop" as an "early harbinger of Spring." It also celebrated Very himself since he was reflected in the flower, and the work of feeling and imagination consisted of rapidly developing an image which mirrored in a few lines the essence of his own life, from ambiguous origins and upbringing to newly won sense of his own capabilities. Very recognized himself in the "Sweet snow-white flower" of modest appearance, nurtured by "blasts of winter," which never found its way into "ladies' bowers." Since he could "feel" its "power" as never before, the snow-drop brought him "new joy." The self-revealing flower signified the resurrection of life-giving forces both within and outside himself.[34]

Despite these excursions of feeling and imagination which Byron, Ticknor, and Coleridge were making possible, and despite the "instruction" which Memory was reaping from the "widening circle" of Nature, the external world of Harvard continued to impose demands upon Very. Two weeks after his reinstatement as a student in 1834, and after formal prompting, he finally fulfilled an obligation he had assumed nearly six months before. At the end of the first week in September the Institute of 1770 designated three of its newest members a special committee to invite "the poet of last year" to deliver his long-promised poem at the next meeting. Henry Thoreau, who had been elected to Institute membership in July while Very was still lingering in Salem, was one of those who called at the room on the top floor of Holworthy Hall to extend the invitation.[35]

Apparently the poem had not yet been written. Soon after Thoreau's visit Very undertook certain "researches" requiring him to withdraw from the college library more than the number of books ordinarily allowed the juniors. Professor Felton intervened at Very's request, and arranged with Librarian Harris for Very to charge books to his name whenever necessary.[36] By September fifteenth his work was completed, and that evening "Occasional business" of the Institute was postponed for the recitation.

The text of the poem has not survived. Presumably it was a mock epic, perhaps a Homeric or Byronic rendering of the "Dunkin Rebellion"; in any event the delighted audience greeted it with "much applause."[37] The conventional gaiety of such occasions, however, was shortlived because his leisure soon was devoted to other matters.

Since freshmen and sophomores active in the Institute automatically became honorary members in the Junior year, the delivery of the poem marked the end to his participation in the affairs of the organization.[38] This was the time, consequently, that along with his roommate Thomas Barnard West he joined a "small Society" meeting weekly for "religious improvement." [39] Except for twice-daily compulsory chapel services, at which faculty members and visiting clergymen presided, this apparently was the first experience Very had with any group whose purpose was avowedly religious. Because Lydia Very rejected Christian beliefs and tried to impose her idiosyncratic views upon her four children, Salem records do not show members of her family belonging to any church until 1836, when her eldest son joined Salem's North Society.[40] However, by the autumn of 1834 he had already won a measure of independence from her fierce affections and intensely held convictions. From Thursday evenings at Cambridge devoted to religious discussion, group study and prayer, and private instruction, he received "great satisfaction." He thought such hours, directed by Professor Ware of the Divinity School, "well and happily spent." [41]

Henry Ware (the Younger, 1794–1843), was a devout, conservative Unitarian who in 1829, as minister of Boston's influential Second Church, had cautioned his young associate, Ralph Waldo Emerson, about "unorthodox tendencies." [42] Now a rather sickly man with ascetic tastes and more cautious than ever, he was still skeptical of the judgments of men unaided by scriptural authority and not confirmed by enlightened Protestant learning. A fundamentalist, he insisted upon resolving all apparent "contradictions" between human reason and "the letter of the Bible" by following the "written word." The revelations of the Bible, he told all seeking "religious improvement" from him, were the only certain guides to "correctness" in thought and action.[43] He was "passionately interested" in what he called "the saving of souls," and was as "aggressive as any fanatic revivalist in his Christian enthusiasm." He gave to students "books of the church mystics" and biographies of missionaries, which he believed "quickened" them in "evangelistic zeal" and "led them into close personal communion with God, and into a sense of the power of the Spirit." [44]

Since students in the Junior year were required to read the Greek Testament in addition to ancient classics, and since Very was jealous of his reputation as a scholar, his interest in Ware and the "Society" may in part be explained by academic ambitions. However, even before he came to Harvard in 1833, a fundamental shift in his outlook had been initiated, which now gave his membership in the "Society" a somewhat different significance. The serious concerns of Henry K. Oliver, and the solemn readings which he recommended, had already undermined the basis of Very's relationship with his infidel mother. At the same time they encouraged recollections of his father and of his father's Masonic-deistic faith in God. By now his attitude toward Lydia Very must have become ambivalent. If so, it would have been compounded of conflicting feelings and contrasting inventions: filial love in response to her unfailing devotion to him, and hatred for her persistent denial of the Christian God and moral order; pride taken in her spirited denunciation of injustices she believed had been done her and her family, and shame for the unsanctified birth which alienated him from both God and society; and his wish for reconciliation with a father whose powers of command had been exercised with benevolence, even if this reconciliation meant estrangement from a mother who believed that the universe was a mechanical system of blindly destructive forces.

Once his intellectual growth had been ensured, and an incipient reaction against his mother's noncomformity and its unnerving consequences had occurred, it was only a matter of time before Very developed an acute interest in religion. The moralizing of such Harvard teachers as Edward Tyrrel Channing (toward whom he felt a special affection), was distinctively Christian and specifically orthodox Unitarian. Moreover, fellow-students like Thomas Barnard West exposed him to the conventional pieties of home and church which they had carried to Harvard. All these combined with the "improving" tendencies of Henry Ware's "Society" to stimulate Very's evolving concern with religion. And concern about his own present moral values was stimulated as well.

Notwithstanding scholarly habits during his first two years at Harvard, he had managed to gain the surreptitious reputation among classmates for being a man of "unbridled passions." His extended involvement with Byron may have contributed to his surprising notoriety, since these immoderate passions had to do with his being "so given to women." [45] Even if exaggerated by the delicate sensibilities common in this rather prudish era, such a report is credible. Very himself, now twenty-one years old, shortly was to become quite concerned about longings which went beyond writing sentimental and fanciful verses in ladies' "Albums." [46] Earlier he had berated himself for not being sufficiently "temperate" and for keeping late hours, and had pledged himself to reform, if possible. [47] But not until the beginning of his Senior year, when thoroughly exposed to the instruction of Professor Ware and the other "improving" influences at Harvard, did he finally decide to do something dramatic about restraining natural instincts. Until then he postponed a direct confrontation with the natural man within himself. He was satisfied merely with repeating the platitudes he was hearing around him, but in a manner which frequently gave them veiled meanings quite different from those intended by less ingenious speakers.

In the spring of 1835, when he rediscovered the lonely snow-drop, tensions and feelings of guilt seemed to take less personal form than later, and were directed away from himself. In April he appeared for a time to be entirely unaware of them as he translated into Greek passages on "the true pride of ancestry" from Daniel Webster's "Plymouth Oration" of 1820 for the Harvard Scholastic Exhibition.[48] In May, however, he undertook a more ambitious project, one in which he could not ignore his personal anxieties since he was summarizing in a twenty-four page essay the public and private influences at work upon him since 1833.

"The Practical Application in This Life, by Men as Social and Intellectual Beings, of the Certainty of a Future State" purported to be his entry in the competition for the Bowdoin Prize. Actually it was more than this, more perhaps than even Very realized. Signed with the pseudonym "Athanatos," it was tacitly addressed to nonconforming and non-believing Lydia Very—even while "inscribed" to a friend, surely one of the pious young men, Horace Morison, of the class graduating next after his own. The "immortal one" who wrote the dissertation spoke of the "internal consciousness of right" which "human reason" may reach without the aid of scriptural "revelation" and unaccompanied by belief in life after death. (These, along with a radical conception of marriage, were essential components of his mother's "coarse materialism" and "Atheism.") He concluded that such a sense of right was pitiful, exercising at best only a feeble influence on human motives and actions.[49] Seeming to rely primarily on the orthodox ideas of Bishop Butler and Professor Ware, but with overtones from Very's reading and criticism of Byron, the essay was the first of a series of formal and reasoned arguments which were privately directed to Lydia Very, designed to impress upon her the errors of her disbelief in the Christian God and afterlife, and the fallacy of her rejection of social conventions.

The essay is remarkable for other reasons as well. Not only did it disclose that Very, like generations of other Harvard-men-turned-writers, had mastered the Channing style of writing, but more importantly, it showed the interplay in his mind of classical and Christian traditions, both serving as background for the unfolding of his own life. The essay was a covert confession of the directions his life was taking, and a forecast of what, emotionally and religiously, still awaited him. In places it now reads almost like an allegory of his own and his family's circumstances.

Among the ancients, he wrote, belief in a hereafter was considered a childish superstition. The desire for glory (an earthborn immortality) moved the few great men of pre-Christian times to noble deeds; but people who were incapable of responding to such abstract motives "exposed" themselves "to the open attacks of sensual pleasure." With no guide other than "the sentiment of his own conscious mind," a person was likely to succumb to "the sublime errors." Since the Greeks and Romans had ignored the rewards and punishments of an afterlife, their "intellectual might" came from minds "fixed to this earth." Consequently the only cultural "mission" they could perform was to leave "the beauty of materiality" as a heritage for succeeding generations. (Pp. 4–7.)

In contrast with the ancients, "there remains for *us*" something finer:

a higher destiny—to develop the sublimity of the world of thought—to rise from that which is seen and temporal to that, which is unseen and eternal. The revelation of another life has opened new regions in the world of thought, and infinitely extended and adorned those already entered. [Pp. 7–8.]

This, however, did not mean that Very thought the Christian revelation of an afterlife had suddenly revolutionized human personality. On the contrary, he found its influence still working slowly in the nineteenth century.

It was not intended that the reality of another life should so press upon our senses, as to render us indifferent to this. It is no longer a certainty of outward sense; but may become a certainty to the "senses of the mind." It is a truth to which reason, illuminated by faith, must lead the way; and to which we must ascend by tracing the steps of thought. Obtaining thus a seat in the depths of the soul, it becomes a quickening spirit to all our motives,—transfuses itself through our whole being—inspires us with the most generous feelings, and prompts to the most noble actions. [Pp. 11–12.]

Very went so far as to suggest that the Future Life was a "continuation" of this; earthly existence was "in fact, a part of the other life"; were it otherwise, were it considered to "embrace but a diminutive portion of time," it would violate the "scheme of existence" itself.

The idea of Eternity is not, as many seem to suppose, something which is to act upon us independent of time; but to mingle with it, . . . saving the mind from polluting and impoverishing the sources of its strength, to direct its energies to nobler objects. [Pp. 12–13.]

Following the intellectual acceptance of these truths (which were specific instances of the widening of the natural circle into the area of the supernatural), there comes an unexpected "feeling":

This is a feeling the direct result of the deep conviction of the certainty of a future state, . . . It is one pervading this whole being—purifying from self—at which having once arrived we become living souls—things, that before appeared discordant, become harmonious—the low motives, to which, . . . we have become subjected, give way to nobler and more permanent ones—and the soul, freed from its shackles, concentrates all its energies for the accomplishment of its mighty work. . . . How long must it be before men learn to look within . . . and see the inworking spirit, the soul infused through all, that gives to the eye its intelligence, to the hand its power? [Pp. 14–16.]

With this growing conviction in man of his own immortality, heroism gains new meaning. "Conquerors of the world" are "animated by a nobler aim" than the domination of men and women by physical forces. The modern hero is a man of sensitivity, a poet who wishes not to subdue, to crush the spirit of man—but to elevate it to a con[s]ciousness of its own worth, . . . He needs no mighty physical power to effect this—no sword, no sceptre. He seizes the quill, the mere toy of a child; and stamps on the glowing page the copy of his own mind, . . . and sends them forth, wherever the winds of heaven blow, or its light penetrates, . . . [Pp. 18–19.]

The thought of immortality then is a "quickening spirit" to the man (or woman) fully apprehending its significance. It mingles

with all the creations of the mind, breathing into them a divine life and energy; . . . Where can imagination find so large a field for its exercise, as in the boundless regions of a never-ending existence? . . . By awakening the soul to its high destiny, by turning man in upon himself to the cultivation and improvement of what in him survives decay; it has opened to him new and more satisfying sources of enjoyment. [Pp. 20–23.]

The result is that "this life is no longer a barren waste." (P. 23.) The man unenlightened by "revelation" may consider misfortune "the mark of some vindictive divinity," and is thereby led to a "dark view of life"; but by the enlightened man misfortune is recognized as a "trial," through which he can "rise to higher degrees of purity and happiness." (P. 5.) He overcomes his suffering by an exercise of will, and thus

seems to dwell in a living temple of beauty, . . . whose holy of holies is the chamber of the soul, the fit abode of the shadowed image of the Deity. In fine, it has operated with a power, . . . rendering man superior to mere external impressions, by leading him gradually to prefer interest to the original gratifications—honor to interest—mental enjoyment to that of sense—the dictates of conscience to pleasure, interest, and fame—benevolence to his own indulgences—tending, in short, to elevate him to that state, where . . . he is made capable of the highest enjoyment, of which his nature is susceptible. [Pp. 23–24.]

Had the Bowdoin Prize judges realized that behind the impressive rhetoric and sentiment of the essay lay autobiographical truths mixed with private fantasies, a form of Byronism adjusted to the outlooks of Coleridge and Henry Ware, and concealed promises of marvelous events to come interwoven with secret desires, they might well have hesitated before awarding Very the forty-dollar first prize in the July 1835 competition for Harvard juniors. The Greeks, the Romans, the Stoics, and the poet-hero whose reason was enlightened by Christian revelation were all projections of Very's own intricate personality, reflecting private fears and repressed urges, ambitious hopes for himself and ambivalent feelings toward his unrepentant mother. Much that was relevant to full comprehension of the essay and the essayist, therefore, remained unsuspected by the judges. The heroism, the "god-like" struggles against vice, the soul "retiring into its own depths," were his own; the world-rooted materialism of "the ancients" and the "dark view of life" brought on by misfortunes were also those of Lydia Very; the continuity of "this life" and the afterlife soon would make possible the communion of Jones Very (the Son) with Jones Very (the Captain Father). The arguments so methodically unfolded, filled with quotations from Shakespeare and Paley, paraphrases of Butler and Monboddo, and references to Milton and Newton, were really brilliant translations of private realities. As such they were beyond the academic grasp of Edward Tyrrel Channing and the other Bowdoin committeemen, and of course they eluded the orthodox pieties of "friend" Morison.

This doctrinally unobjectionable essay contained the seeds of a heresy which within three years would shock the complacent gentlemen of Harvard, both professors and students. While he was rejecting his mother's nonconformity, he was gradually cultivating his own, even more startling and disruptive than hers. Nothing was impossible to a passionate young man who was confident that facts might be transfigured by strength of will and imagination, and that the world of nature was literally contiguous with eternity. Only the heroism of a disciplined mind was needed to effect wonders. The content of that mind, and the principles of the discipline which would control it, were on the verge of finding appropriate forms. These in turn would determine the class of wonders which would someday be achieved.

# The Composition of Greatness

## 1835

J u s t   a s   the Byron of *Childe Harold* dominated Very's extra-curricular studies from the spring of 1834 until early 1835, the Wordsworth of *The Excursion* was the primary focus for subsequent studies in 1835, and the tone of the "Scrap Book" was affected accordingly. For his poetic vocation, however, during 1835 and 1836 readings which supplemented his interest in Wordsworth—covering the expanse of English poetry from Chaucer to Sidney and Shakespeare, to Coleridge, Shelley, and Keats—were more impressive. These, moreover, were reinforced by study of Goethe, the Schlegels, Mme. de Staël, Carlyle, and Sismondi, whose writings implemented George Ticknor's lectures and classroom digressions in opening up for Very the range of European literature, ancient and modern.[1]

While Byron had articulated views which caused Very to adjust his outlook because they were new to him or were presented with unfamiliar emphasis, by contrast the later Wordsworth expressed less radical attitudes, and thus he supplied Very with moral and intellectual norms for studying life and poetry.

Wordsworth provided a frame of reference within which familiar ideas were recognized in 1835 and new ones contrasted. Therefore he became the measure of Very's developing views, although the progress itself came primarily through other sources.[2]

Ten lines of the more than two hundred he transcribed from *The Excursion* indicate the chief qualities which impressed him. Moral and moralizing, reflecting the subtitle "Despondency Corrected," solemnly prosaic lines typical of the older, effete Wordsworth filled pages of the notebook:

> 'Tis by comparison, an easy task
> Earth to despise; but, to converse with Heaven—
> This is not easy:—to relinquish all
> We have, or hope, of happiness and joy,
> And stand in freedom loosened from this world;
> I deem not arduous:—but must needs confess
> That 'tis a thing impossible to frame
> Conceptions equal to the Soul's desires;
> And the most difficult of tasks to *keep*
> Heights which the Soul is competent to gain. [IV, 130–9.]

In 1835 Very thought of Wordsworth as the poet who gave emotions a conventional religious outlet in poetry, contrasting with the secular expression Byron had given them. Therefore Very was absorbed by those reflective and speculative sections of the poem which described Wordsworth's satisfactions with the promise of heavenly recompense for earthly sufferings (Bks. II–IV), and were consistent with the aims of Professor Ware's Society for "religious improvement" and with the tone of "The Practical Application."

He left no doubt about his preference for eternal glory when he prefaced his first quotation from *The Excursion* with a monitory excerpt from the eighth stanza of the *Immortality Ode:*

> Full soon thy soul shall have her earthly freight
> And custom lie upon thee with a weight,
> Heavy as frost, and deep almost as life! [3]

Throughout 1835 the "Scrap Book" reverberated with the impact of Wordsworth's anticipation of divine rewards: the prospect of "freedom loosened from this world" recurred often.

Near the end of the year, in response to Goethe's observation that "Feeling is all in all," Very wrote by way of confirmation: "The Images of *The All* written on every single thing." [4] With this assertion, which reverted to his readings in Monboddo, Paley, Channing, and Coleridge, and anticipated many of the notebook entries which followed, Very's conception of a poetic theory began to take form. Meanwhile additional sources were contributing to the shaping process.

Before he undertook the series of entries from *The Excursion,* Very was committed to finishing his study of Canto III of *Childe Harold,* deferring the Wordsworth passages until the spring. The first appeared immediately after the last full stanza from *Childe Harold* (III, xiv). [5] The transition from Byron to the later Wordsworth was effected by other writers and poets who engaged Very from January to April. Here, through the secondary sources which preserved the continuities of his extracurricular studies, rather than through the extensive quotations from Wordsworth, came the stimuli to which Very was responding, clarifying his emerging conception of himself as a poet.

The first substantial indication that the burden of Very's interest was shifting from Byron came through a book of travels published the preceding November. In Francis Lieber's *Letters to a Gentleman of Germany* (1834), were ideas which contributed to Very's understanding of the relationship between nature and poetry, and the function of the poet with respect to both. [6] Here he found variations on themes he had begun to follow in 1833 with Monboddo and Channing, and which by 1834 had led him through Pollok and Byron to Coleridge. Lieber touched upon matters relevant to each, but especially to Channing's dictum that "men who are to be the lights of the world, bring with them their commission and power from God." [7] By other means as well,

Very was already acquainted with this account of inspiration. In 1834, while reading *Paradise Lost,* he had noticed that Milton made a similar observation in connection with his "Celestial Patroness" (IX, 21–24).[8] Early in 1835 he was again reading *Paradise Lost,* and he thought that Milton's phrase, "to the highth of this great Argument," was related to Shakespeare's "Rightly to be great, / Is not to stir without great argument."[9] Not only the "Scrap Book" context but also the original settings of these lines relate to the idea that the great works of men come from God. The passages from Lieber therefore expressed ideas for which Very was adequately prepared, and which easily found their way into his notebook.

Lieber's relevant ideas were based on a principle of inclusion more stringent than Very's casual remark in 1833 that "Man's chief occupation and converse are with nature."[10] Lieber was unequivocal in his insistence that "like the rest of creation," man is "wrapt up in the all-enshrouding spirit of the Creator." Man's mind, he explained, is as much a "work of God" as a plant or mountain. Great art—and by this he meant art whose "grandeur" was of a "more spiritual cast" than the "sublimity in the great works of nature"—may be the realization of man's imagination, but God is ultimately the artist. And since man's actions obey God's laws (natural laws were actually divine laws, according to Lieber), His will is revealed through the artist who is His particualr agent. True artistic creativity, therefore, is possible only to the extent the will of the artist corresponds to that of the Creator.[11]

In the presence of such grandiose thoughts Very could not long remain unmoved. Instead of merely copying a sensitive observation by Lieber he expanded upon it, providing some of his own answers to questions Lieber had raised, somewhat in the manner of the poet of *The Excursion.*

The reason of people's requiring some great and powerful phenomenon to lead them from nature up to nature's God, their adhering to

matter and not elevating themselves to a contemplation of the principle of Life, results, . . . from having their thoughts so much engaged
in worldly pursuits that they have no time for meditation—abstract
their attention from these—lead them to contemplation, lead them to
know the feeling infinite.[12]

Prompted by Lieber, Very implied (as had Pollok and Wordsworth before him), that the artist shares with the saint the
responsibility for the spiritual awareness of mankind generally.
As God's minister, the poet is involved with the state of human
souls as much as he is with representing truth and beauty.

Meanwhile, evidence of Very's concerns with poetry and artistic activity in general rapidly accumulated in the "Scrap Book,"
giving additional weight to passages he read in Lieber's book.
From John Gibson Lockhart's *Life of Robert Burns* he recorded
that poet's account of his procedure for lyric composition, consisting of "cursed egotism!" [13] He copied out Cowper's invectives
against music: like wine it "weakens and destroys the spiritual
discernment." [14] He thought several lines from Samuel Rogers'
*Pleasures of Memory* (I, 339-341), "might have given rise to
Bryant's 'Water-Fowl.'" [15] He read Coleridge on the "Organic
Principle," according to which words were construed as "living
growths, aspects, and organs of the human soul," and he summarized the idea: "There are cases in which more knowledge of
value may be conveyed by the history of a word, than by the
history of a campai[g]n." [16] He also noted Coleridge's proposal
for an essay about a man "who lived not *in time* at all, past,
present, or future but beside or collaterally." [17] From *Woodstock,*
Scott's scrupulous novel of the English Civil Wars, he entered a
reference to *"Animus Mundi,* or Creative Power in the works of
nature, by which she originally called into existence, and still
continued to preserve, her works." [18] And following the last
citation from Lieber, he set down two additional fragments about
inspiration and imagination, taken from Washington Irving's
sketch, "Stratford-on-Avon." [19] Clearly then Very was continuing

to press his inquiry. But something more was needed to complete his own conception of poets and poetry, of art and nature, and of the relationship between man and God, matter and spirit.

He found what he needed near the end of March 1835 in William Ellery Channing's *Tracts,* which he had borrowed from the college library. In his notebook he summarized a section of the "Life and Character of Napoleon Bonaparte" which distinguished between "moral greatness, or magnanimity," and "intellectual greatness, or genius in the highest sense." [20]

Channing defined both kinds of greatness in terms of intuitively perceived rather than logically reasoned functions. By "moral greatness" Channing meant

that sublime energy, by which the soul, smitten with the love of virtue . . . hears in its own conscience a voice louder than threatenings and thunders; withstands all the powers of the universe, which would sever it from the course of freedom and religion; . . .

As distinguished from this "magnanimity," "intellectual greatness" was

that sublime capacity of thought, through which the soul, smitten with the love of the true and the beautiful, essays to comprehend the universe, soars into the heavens, penetrates itself, . . . rises from the finite and transient to the infinite and the everlasting, frames to itself from its own fulness lovelier and sublimer forms than it beholds, discerns the harmonies between the world within and the world without us, and finds in every region of the universe types and interpreters of its own deep mysteries and glorious inspirations.

This was the greatness achieved by philosophers and "the master spirits in poetry and the fine arts." [21]

Very worked out his own variations on Channing's views, modified by elements from Paley, Coleridge, and Lieber, in a statement of poetic principles prompted by observations Wordsworth had made in the 1800 "Preface to *Lyrical Ballads.*" More than denying Wordsworth's claim that it was necessary for the poet to give "immediate pleasure," Very set forth a prospectus for his own poetry, and in doing so incorporated elements from *The Excursion*. He wrote:

The true poet is in my opinion under no restriction whatever. . . . Nature does not assume a more beautiful form under the plastic influence of his mind merely because he wishes to give "Immediate pleasure to a human Being" but because his soul has been framed [so] that it cannot act upon anything without stamping it with its own impress, . . . A higher motive, a something within him . . . prompts him to awaken in man a consciousness of his high destiny by exhibiting the almost creative power of the human mind when exerted on Nature.

He cannot . . . look about Nature without feeling the relation which exists between it and his own mind. . . .

Besides, the view of the various fluctuations of the human mind, as exhibited . . . in the poetry of successive epochs, is more interesting and less liable to convey erroneous impressions, than any record of man's events. . . . Historic facts are chiefly valuable, as exhibiting intellectual phenomena. And as far as poetry exhibits this phenomena more perfectly and distinctly than history does, so far is it superior to history.[22]

When he spoke of the "true poet" being "under no restriction whatever," he meant that great poetry does not result from the same order of motivations that determine the actions of ordinary men. The desire "to please others, to acquire wealth, fame and earthly prosperity," all familiar explanations for human endeavor, are not relevant to the poet's circumstances. Very had learned from *The Excursion* that it was the duty of the poet to try to "converse with Heaven," and thereby "frame / Conceptions equal to the Soul's desires." He believed, as he said in reply to Lieber's similar reflections, that the poet's obligation is to "abstract" the "attention" of men from their "worldly pursuits" and lead them to contemplative knowledge of "the feeling infinite." In view of the special relationship between the "true poet" and God, it could scarcely be otherwise.

Between 1833 and 1835 the notion that God was the source of the poet's inspiration was gradually being clarified in his mind. Beginning with the specific hint by Channing in his "Remarks on a National Literature," made all the more meaningful by his understanding of Butler, Monboddo, and Paley, it was traced and nurtured through the works of other writers. The idea was modified by coupling a Coleridgean conception of the imagination to the sensibilities of Byron's persona, and it was consummated by Lieber's statements. Very went from him to other sources for confirmation and subsidiary evidence, eventually returning full circle to Channing, and finally expressing the idea in the retort to Wordsworth. There he incorporated all the contributing influences, religious as well as aesthetic, stamping the resulting synthesis with his own sensitivity and bias.

By the summer of 1835 his romantic view of the poet and the poet's art stretched far beyond his ability to act according to such abstract and rarified principles. The external pressures and inner tensions to which Lydia Very subjected her son (she vehemently denied all claims that mankind had a "high destiny") prevented him from receiving any divine imperatives which might be transferred to poetry. While he would never write precisely the exalted kind of poem he was formulating in theory, capable of elevating men "to a contemplation of the principle of Life," within two years, when he wrote the sonnet "Beauty," he at least came close to balancing poetic vision with the practice of poetry. The four poems published in the Salem *Observer* in August, after his "Scrap Book" pronouncement and after his return home at the end of his Junior year of college, indicate that he still had much to learn during the ensuing two years before maturity and skill could consistently enlighten his work.

In the first poem, saddened by his inability to revive "beauty" which had been crushed by nature's "cruel teeth," he mourned a dead hummingbird whose return to the nest was awaited by her anxious mate and brood of young.[23] In "Eheu! Fugaces, Posthume, Posthume, Labuntur Anni," he overcame vapid sentimentality by making "Beauty" a woman, and continuing the prosodic experiments which marked "Hast thou ever heard the voice of nature" and "The New Year." Signs of mastery of trochaic and anapestic meter finally began to show in three of its five stanzas.

> Beauty's cheek but blooms to wither.
> Smiling hours but come to fly;
> They are gone! Time's but the giver
> Of whate'er is doomed to die.
>
> Thou may'st touch with blighting finger
> All that sense can here enjoy;
> Yet within my soul shall linger,
> That, which thou canst not destroy.
>
> As the years come gliding by me,
> Fancy's pleasing visions rise;
> Beauty's cheek, ah! still I see thee,
> Still your glances, soft blue eyes! [24]

But even where prosodically sound, the more successful portions of the poem were undermined by the pervading thought that life's present pleasures are transient, memory alone giving permanence to external events. Although his own fears and guilts were responsible, Time was blamed for his inability to fix the original experience—actual or imaginary—in poetry.

The third poem told how, withdrawing from "silent depths" to a high hill, the poet lost all sense of his distinctive self and personality. He flew with the "beach birds" over winding streams, and skimmed the calm sea and white-sailed boats with the gull. At last even this "waking dream" passed as stars called him away

To groves, fields, where flowers of deathless bloom
Breathe o'er a land unsullied by a tomb.

Refreshed by draughts

     from far purer streams of bliss
Than flow near the dusty paths of life,
Uptost by madd'ning passion and strife;

he returned from celestial heights

To join in the world of care again,
And look on the struggles and strife of men,
With an eye that beams with as pure a ray
As call'd my soul from these scenes away.[25]

The last of the poems of the summer of 1835, "Religion,"
reported the lessons supposedly learned during such flights
beyond painful realities into "heavenly light." Only the soul's
"calm rest" and God's "dread might"—neither of which Very had
as yet experienced in any meaningful fashion—bring comfort
capable of withstanding life's strains. Death, the passing of
Beauty, and the other sorrows wrought by nature's cruelties,
relentless Time, and the "madd'ning passion and strife" of men,
can be endured only if "treasures" of an inward sort are gained.[26]

For the "true poet" these take the form of God-derived inspirations—gifts, Very well knew, not yet proffered him. He was
aware that his intentions were more finely developed than either
his craft or the material out of which he might make a poem with
sustained merit. In Salem during the summer of 1835, he was still
standing irresolutely on the verge of "true" poetry, anxious to
move beyond but frustrated by lack of means for the attempt. He
therefore returned to Harvard at the end of August and began
his Senior year in a frame of mind different from any he had
known before.

Neither despondent nor hopeful, he was haunted by memories
from the past which had gained the status of present realities.

Lacking the "calm rest" spoken of in his recent poem, he continued to be troubled by feelings he was sure must be overcome if ever he were to receive from God the currents which flow from His "far purer streams." In spite of what seemed his poor prospects, he yearned for those life-giving waters since they made possible both the "magnanimity" and the "intellectual greatness" described by Channing. More than anything else he wished to join the exclusive company of saint and artist. He wanted his to be the soul so "framed that it cannot act upon anything without stamping it with its own impress." He wanted his to be the mind which could awaken men by exhibiting its "almost creative power . . . when exerted on Nature."

With the autumn of 1835 a three-year period of crisis began, only indirectly due to dissatisfactions with his poetry. A period of emotional rather than intellectual strain, it was brought about because he continued to be tormented by "unbridled passions" of a sexual nature.[27] They became an increasing problem until even his studies suffered during his third Junior term and throughout much of his Senior year.[28] After months of distress he no longer could endure, he experienced a *"change of heart."* [29] Occurring in September or October, it marked the beginning of his emotional estrangement from his mother, and paralleled the intellectual break from her which Henry K. Oliver had instigated earlier.

In bringing this "change" about, Professor Ware and his "small Society for religious improvement" played as decisive a part as his own revulsion at the morally irregular circumstances of his birth, circumstances for which his mother's "free-thinking" was to blame. As a result, he was now painfully aware of the need for a radical transformation of his character and way of life. That is, he at last was "spiritually regenerated." (This inward change reminded a perceptive classmate, a liberal Unitarian, of the "new birth" of the Calvinists.) [30] Very now knew, with a certainty more compelling than was usual at Harvard, that "all we have belongs to God and that we ought to have no will of our own."

This knowledge was a felt experience, something strongly sensed as much as it was cognitively known.

While itself constituting a "great happiness," this religious experience left him still uneasy about what he believed was his immense capacity for carnal sin.[31] Earnest resolves to "live temperate," even abstinence, were not sufficient. Repression of sexual desires only reminded him of what he considered his fatal weakness. His yearning "to do ill," even when controlled, indicated to him that something more was required. Love-longing had to cease entirely, not merely be resisted. His solution: "he had made himself a law not to speak (or look at) women." Because of this "sacrifice of Beauty"—announced to friends with a sense for the dramatic learned from Lydia Very—he was becoming known in the Harvard yard for "monkish austerity and self-denial."[32]

Nevertheless, he worried about his continuing need to discipline what seemed to be a satanic impulse. He "could not," he confided to a friend, "rest in it." When he still was plagued by wordly "temptation" in spite of his resolves, he felt such guilt and shame that he began to despise himself with a ferocity which terrified him. His every thought seemed unworthy of his reverence for God. He was wretched because it was his "constant work" to "justify" his soul. Love of God had grown so quickly and so painfully intense that at last it had driven him to hatred of his unmistakably evil self.[33]

Sometime during his Senior year, probably early in 1836, he finally discovered what he believed was the truth about his anguish: since only through thought could evil come into existence, temptation (in part at least), was a function of the "will"; it was inseparable from the commission of sin. Temptation was a thoughtful act. Therefore, with a reckless determination reminiscent of his tough-minded and thoroughgoing mother's, he concluded that the only way to relieve his misery would be to attempt the ultimate heroic act. He would dismiss all thoughts from consciousness. That this conclusion could not be reconciled with his college and literary ambitions did not trouble him. He had reached the point of anxiety at which the demands of logical consistency no longer posed any obstacle.

His demonic nature continued refractory however, and seemed the product of a completely un-Godlike private self. He therefore feared he was incapable of implementing his conviction that God is all, and that His will alone must be done. So long as he had a "thought" of what he "ought to banish" from consciousness, he was alarmed. "I felt," he said, "that some of my will remained. To this I was continually prone and against it I continually strove." [34] Meditation and solitary sessions of prayer, and hymn singing in which he was joined by roommate West and another classmate, filled out waking hours not devoted to study and poetry. Although religion was now a "central life" for him, and he had become a "kind of emblem of uprightness" to those who understood what he was undergoing, the relief he so anxiously sought failed to come.[35] Nevertheless, in spite of an avowedly obdurate spirit and the willfulness it produced much to his torment, he decided to enroll in the Divinity School upon gradua-tion and prepare himself for a career as a minister. His unqual-ified commitment to God's presence left him no alternative but to dedicate his energies and talents to God's cause. This selfless service, he thought, might destroy his capacity for sin and bring the spiritual "rest" so essential for greatness as he understood it. He knew of no other way by which he might—as Wordsworth phrased it—"converse with Heaven."

V

# *In Private*

# 1835–1836

WHILE INSIGHTS into himself continued to generate new
anxieties for Jones Very, they did so without preventing his
undergraduate record from finally being brought to a brilliant
climax. Throughout 1835–1836, his Senior year at Harvard, the
"individual research and thought" which had distinguished his
presence there since September 1833[1] was further displayed,
publicly as well as privately, and several times was suitably
acknowledged. On October 20, 1835, as an honor student in
Professor Peirce's advanced mathematical course, he participated
in a special demonstration of the "Barometric Method" for calcu-
lating heights, witnessed by the Board of Harvard Overseers and
invited guests. Two weeks later the college faculty gave formal
recognition to his academic achievements and his financial need
by awarding him a scholarship, the income from Madam Mary
Saltonstall's "donation"; in February 1836 the stipend was renewed to his advantage.[2]

Besides prescribed studies (Dugald Stewart's elementary
philosophy and William Paley's moral philosophy were among

the required subjects), he was busy with a number of the "improving" books suggested by Professor Ware: Southey's *Book of the Church,* the *Natural History of Enthusiasm,* Charles T. Beke's *Origines Biblicae,* a volume of Jeremy Taylor's *Works,* a *Life of Thomas More,* and Bishop Whately's book on St. Paul.[3]

During his Senior year he was also reading books likely to have been recommended to him either by Professor Channing or by Professor Ticknor: a volume of Lamb's *Essays of Elia;* Hazlitt's *Characters of Shakespeare's Plays* and *Lectures on the English Poets;* Chaucer's *Canterbury Tales* as well as a *Life of Chaucer;* Sidney's *Defense of Poesy;* a volume of Milton's *Prose Works;* poems by Ben Jonson, Donne, Coleridge, Shelley, and Keats; Isaac D'Israeli's *Essay on the Literary Character;* Oliver Goldsmith's *Inquiry into the Present State of Polite Learning in Europe;* Samuel Butler's *Hudibras;* Sir Humphry Davy's *Consolations in Travel;* Dr. Parr's *Discourse on Education;* Scott's *Ivanhoe* and *Guy Mannering;* Lamartine's *Pilgrimage to the Holy Land;* and the tragedies of Vittorio Alfieri.[4]

At this time he was also reading books which were "improving" neither in Ware's sense of the word nor in Channing's nor in Ticknor's. Nevertheless, these were completing his education by preparing him for his eventual participation in the world of New England intellectuals, writers, and radicals who functioned outside Harvard's academic walls: Coleridge's *Friend, Aids to Reflection, Stateman's Manual,* and *Biographia Literaria;* Carlyle's *Sartor Resartus* and "Characteristics"; William Taylor's *Historic Survey of German Poetry;* Goethe's *Wilhelm Meister, Faust,* and *Memoirs;* Schiller's essay "On the Sublime"; Friederich Schlegel's *Lectures on the History of Ancient and Modern Literature;* August Wilhelm Schlegel's *Lectures on Dramatic Art and Literature; Christian Examiner* articles by Charles Follen and Orestes Brownson; and Mrs. William Minot's article on "Cousin's Philosophy" in the *North American Review.*[5]

Whatever doubts Very had about the well-being of his soul,

they were only indirectly reflected in these readings, and they did not extend to his conception of himself as a poet or to the poetry he meanwhile was writing. He was sure enough of his literary ambitions in January 1836 to compose a short statement of principles, reaffirming his belief in his abilities and their continuing development. It also revealed that his preferences and self-imposed studies still were taking an inward direction. "The poet writes," he said,

in the confidence of his power to impart interest to the realities of life, deriving both the confidence and the power from the deep interest which he feels in them. It is an attribute of great susceptibility of imagination to need no extraordinary provocations; and when this is combined with intensity of observation and peculiar force of language it is the high privilege of the poet so endowed to rest upon the common realities of life and to dispense with its anomalies— . . .[6]

Elsewhere in his notebook he identified this "power to impart interest to the realities of life" as the special quality of "genius": "It neither distorts nor discolors its objects, but, . . . brings out many a vein and many a tint, which escape the eye of common observation."[7] Additional passages in his "Scrap Book"—most of them originally written by others but adapted by Very for his own purposes—clarified the meaning and consequences of the poet's "great susceptibility of imagination," his "deep interest," "intensity of observation," and "peculiar force of language."

He recently had been reading Coleridge and had recorded passages relevant to the "office and duty of the poet," and specifically to the poet's self-generating powers and oyster-like capacity to almost "secrete" poetry from "resources" within himself.[8] As a result of his growing conviction that God is the origin of the poet's inspiration, Very now was thinking of poetry and the "realities of life" (which intrude upon consciousness), in terms which tended to obscure the distinction between poetry and religion. Although it was not evident either in his statement or in the quotations from Coleridge, other texts he was reading at the time made clear that God was involved in the poetry of "genius." Bulwer-Lytton, who for this purpose accepted Coleridge's conception of poetry as an "earnestly sincere" and total inward response to external stimuli, suggested the desirability of reconciling poetry and religion, of adapting them to each other by having poetry absorbed into religion. "Religion wanes," wrote Bulwer in *England and the English,* "as Poetry vanishes from Religion." [9] Wilhelm Meister's "prayer" (which Very soon after copied into his notebook), urged a similar result by proposing instead that poetry exercise a distinctively religious function: he prayed to God for the "power to write a poem according to my heart and his own—a visible, living image animated and coloured with his visible and invisible creation." [10] The intentions of this prayer, so far as they concerned poetry, were further illuminated by Goethe's conception of "the infinite poetry of double creation." This too found its way into Very's growing collection of statements personally significant to him.

There are harmonies between all the elements, as there is a general one between material and intellectual nature. Each idea has its similitude in a visible object which repeats it like an echo, reflects it as a mirror and renders it perceptible in two ways: to the senses by the image, to the mind by the thoughts; . . . [11]

The relevancy to poetry and religion of Goethe's recognition of the "harmonies" existing between "material" and "intellectual nature," between "visible object" and "idea," between "senses" and "mind," and between "image" and "thoughts," in turn was clarified in another passage, one which extended Very's developing theories about poetry by introducing him to the special usage of the terms "instinct" and "reason." Goethe related them both to inspiration from God, and to the fundamental connections between religion and poetry. "Instinct" was

reason itself, innate reason, reason unreasoned upon, reason such as God made it, such as mind finds it. It strikes us like a flash of

lightning, without the eye being at the trouble of seeing; it illumi-
nates at once. Inspiration in all the arts . . . is also this instinct, this
innate reason. Genius also is instinct, and not logic or labor. . . . All
that is supremely beautiful comes from nature and God.
Christianity . . . has comprised it from the beginning. The first
apostles felt in them that immediate action of the divinity and
exclaimed at once, *"Every good and perfect gift comes from
God."* [12]

Therefore, when Very early in 1836 was resolving to surrender
*"all* thoughts" in an effort to avoid "temptation" and evil
thoughts, he was proposing a course of action which promised to
affect more than his prospects for heavenly glory. Although
religious feelings and personal anxieties rather than poetic necessities prompted him, his poetry was not immune to the consequences of his decision. A number of quotations from *Faust,* of
which the following is typical, indicate that Very was finding
material compatible to the inward transformation he desired, and
to his understanding of the "peculiar force of language" by which
"genius" is expressed:

Be no tinkling fool! Reason and good sense express themselves with
little art. And when you are seriously intent on saying something, is it
necessary to hunt for words? Your speeches . . . which are so highly
polished, are unrefreshing . . .[13]

A quotation from Schiller made another allusion to that mental
attitude of "genius" which generated religious and poetic sentiments. It also explained the "deep interest" the poet required in
the "objects" proper to his art.

The mind which has so far ennobled itself as to be more affected by
the Forms of things than their material substance . . . bears within
itself an inward and abiding Fulness of Life because it has no need to
appropriate to itself the objects among which it lives, . . .[14]

An analysis of "Cousin's Philosophy" finally provided an
element of French idealism which had obvious philosophical

connections with Coleridge's ideas, and even more with those of Goethe and Schiller. In addition it contributed to the religion-and-poetry theme by supplying further justification for Very's decision to forego conscious thinking as a means of achieving the "abiding Fulness of Life."

The human mind, says Cousin, contains in a latent state those divine rays which . . . are the truths of spontaneity, and are the same to all. The vast variety and differences of mankind, . . . arise from *reflection*. Spontaneity is uniform, but reflection is an element of difference. The condition of reflection is time, that is, succession. As reflection can only consider the element of thought successively, . . . Error does not consist in false, but in incomplete ideas; and every conception, . . . is true excepting so far as it is taken for the whole truth.[15]

Very's assertion that he would no longer entertain conscious thoughts therefore seems to have meant he was renouncing consecutive thinking, the logical and labored activity of mind which Bulwer had called "Rationality" and had contrasted with Poetry and Religion. Hereafter he would try to rely entirely upon non-reflective thinking, the spontaneous and instinctive thought which Goethe called "reason," or the faculty of genius. This nobler form of mind, although discoverable within the individual, "comes from God" rather than from some selfish source peculiar to him. Differential thinking, on the other hand, is susceptible to "Error" according to Cousin, even when not "false" because it is necessarily partial and fragmentary. Thus, Very's renunciation of *"all* thought," and his denial of his private "will," meant he would strive to release his "noble energies" and seek salvation and the "means and materials" for poetry within himself. There, in the inmost recesses of his mind, he expected to find spiritual "rest" as well as God's "good and perfect gift" of poetry, the "whole truth" which needed no "highly polished" art in order to evoke the highest religious responses in others.

According to an observation Very made in April 1836 (after he had already decided upon the radical program for transforming himself), "One thought includes all thought"—evil as well as good and neutral thoughts—"in the sense that a grain of sand includes the universe." [16] Instead of taking a moral risk and accepting the "universe" for good or evil, he chose what he considered both a wise caution and the more heroic course, and attempted to relinquish the world of thought in its entirety.

So long as he was in this negativistic state of mind he could not trust the motivations for his thoughts. Since he believed that whenever "Pleasure and Sin" stimulated actions the result necessarily was "Absolute Evil," and since "Pleasure and Sin" were thoughtful pursuits, he concluded that deliberate thinking was morally dangerous.[17] (Cousin had less emphatically designated the opposite of "truth" not "Absolute Evil" but "Error.") As justification for his drastic campaign to curtail conscious thought, but in a moment of noticeably less terrifying anxiety, Very wrote: "Our relations, are to *beings* (is a personal one), and not merely to *ideas* (an intellectual one.)" [18] By considering himself and his actions in terms of existence rather than concept, in terms of his person rather than intelligence, and in terms of feelings rather than cognition, he was trying to redefine his nature in a non-rational way, in a way which excluded whatever might jeopardize his "soul." "Intra et extra = whole," he wrote, intending by this cryptic formula to indicate the magnitude of the work he had undertaken.[19] He was sure his "relations," in their totality as objects of thought, embraced everything—both within him and outside him. The "whole truth," in its non-rational aspect and as it was perceived by the Goethean "reason," had a dual location. It was to be found concurrently, in the measureless depths Very contained in himself, and in the infinite expanse of nature's existential world. It had its center in him, but stretched out far from him and beyond him.

Although by early 1836, with the assistance of the sources filling his "Scrap Book," Very had completed specifications for a radical program of self-conquest satisfactory to his restless spirit, two years were to elapse before his conduct of life was outwardly affected by it. An interim period of inner struggle with his demonic self, not concluded until September 1838, still was required even after the intellectual formulation. He believed that the difficulties to be overcome before his thoughts and actions would please God were proportional to his infernal urges and the intransigence of his private will. Because of his conviction that his capacity for sin was immense, the discipline (which was necessary before he could act in conformity to God's will), required heroic efforts for which his own will was not yet prepared.

However, only another year was necessary before spontaneous reliance upon his "instincts" consistently affected his writing of poetry. Even though additional development took place in his poems after 1837, a shorter gestation period was needed until his poetry was significantly transformed. While his *change of heart* had preceded the decision to alter his mode of thought by only several months, for almost three years he had been conscientiously trying to find within himself materials out of which he might make poetry. Therefore his poems during 1835 and early 1836 showed no drastic changes, only continuation of the lines of development begun in 1833.

The theme of the mind's journey beyond Strife and Time—important for his poems of the summer of 1835 and for the *change of heart* which followed them—recurred in the poems of the autumn and winter. Close examination of a withered leaf placed on a study table (one of the qualities Very had attributed to "genius" was "intensity of observation"), led to discoveries which penetrated the ugliness apparent to the "outward eye." When seen not as a botanical leaf but as a spiritual page inscribed by "Love Divine," it has "beauty for the soul," its "learned lore" dwarfing the wisdom of *"man's* vain words." Recollection and meditation supersede the books on the poet's table, and the poet's soul detects contrasting sounds, the beautiful strains of "Distant music of the Past." By means of the withered leaf and the memories it triggers, the poet "soars" high above

Realms of Death and pale Decay;
And before God's throne adores,
Mid the spirit's native day.

Thus the poet was enabled to move out of his troubled present into the painless, remembered past of summer, and then into the certain "Future State," the soul's eternal springtime, from which—in this poem at least—the poet never did return.[20]

While "A Withered Leaf—Seen on a Poet's Table" permitted Very an imaginative removal from the reality of his torments, "The Stars" (written a month later, in December), reversed the effect and returned him to the depths of anxiety. Hanging above him with "angel look so bright," and looking down upon him "Like mother o'er her child," the stars reminded him of his estrangement. "Why hear I not that seraph voice," the speaker of the poem inquires, "That woke with earth's first morn?" The answer, implicit in the lines which follow, is that his life was paralleling "earth's wayward course." Nevertheless, because "love divine can never die," the stars still turn hopefully and look down upon him, encouraging him to overcome his waywardness.[21]

The confidence that God had not abandoned him, no matter how horribly he may have sinned, was reaffirmed in "The Snow-Bird," a poem about a "White wandr'er of the air" who was able for a while to love even winter's "savage form."

I bless thee bird—for He, who lent
    Thee love for one so rude;
Hath bid thee seek my tenement,
    To wake my gratitude.

Before departing, the snow-bird had imprinted its "image" on his troubled mind,

And bid me feel that He, whose eye
    Thy wants doth pitying see

And through the wintry time supply,
  Will surely succor me.[22]

More complex conceptually and more skillfully executed than
these related poems, "The Painted Columbine" (written in January or February 1836) not only brought this series of memory-
poems to a climax, but since Very had learned from his experience with the preceding poems, it effectively superseded them. He
reworked the themes and images he had already used, in an effort
to balance off spiritual malaise with hopes for permanent relief.
Seeing a picture of a columbine colored too brightly (painted
probably by his sister Lydia Louisa Ann), Very was reminded
that "swift-winged shadows" no longer were passing by him. The
painted "image" of the flower, "Robed in mimic tints of art," was
easily replaced by the fairer-hued picture left upon his "heart" by
"Nature's hand" when he was a child. His heart's representation—not the contrived "painter's page"—recalls "fond-
remembered" scenes of his outwardly untroubled youth before his
father's death. But in spite of pleasant memories, harsh reality in
the form of the gaudy painting intrudes on the "loved flower":

Fair child of art! thy charms decay,
Touched by the withered hand of Time;

. . . . .

But on my heart thy cheek of bloom
Shall live when Nature's smile has fled;
And, rich with memory's sweet perfume,
Shall o'er her grave thy tribute incense shed.[23]

The columbine's three forms—as painting, natural flower, and
happy recollection—interacted to charge the poem with restless
feelings and delicate sensitivity. To the extent lines were
informed by "susceptibility of imagination"—as in the refined
fragrance which pervades the last two lines—sentimentality and
stereotyped language were avoided.

Latent, but nevertheless basic to each of these poems, were
operations of an anxious mind. Apprehensions would shortly be

made more explicit than they were at the beginning of this period of intense psychological crisis. But at least once during the spring of 1836 he wrote a poem while his mind was being choked with those "unhallowed" thoughts he was struggling to overcome by repressing all deliberate thinking. He imagined, according to this poem, that he heard his mother speaking to him. The "sweet deceptive song" he heard—"My mother's voice! I hear it now"—was the creation of a mind given temporary freedom to wander without imposed direction. The result was a mixture of near-accurate recollection and dreamlike reconstruction of the mother he yearned for but did not have, a God-loving and God-fearing woman of gentle and warm nature, with none of the intensity and near-hysteria with which the actual Lydia Very conducted her daily affairs. Interwoven with feelings and visions which subsequently increased his sense of sin and guilt, the voice of the imagined mother seemed to sweep away the thoughts he knew must not be entertained if his spirit was ever to be at peace. Fanciful distortions of remembered incidents—involving a "hymn of praise" she had never sung, pious "blessings" she had never bestowed, tales of "holy men" and "Patriarchs" she had never related, and prayers she had never uttered—blended with his more accurate recollections of her possessive love, her worry during his childhood injuries and illnesses, the touch of her hand on his feverish forehead, her eyes "gazing downward" (like "The Stars") into his face, and her attempts to comfort him as he lay "soft pillowed on her breast." [24]

At such times as this, when half-invented, half-remembered visions swept aside his despair, he felt as if he were a child again, as if the voices of "Friendship" and "Love" had not been silenced, and as if the painful realities were only unpleasant nightmares having no basis in fact. However, such moods were transient. They soon released him to confront the grim truth about himself, now grown even more intolerable because of the contrast with the idyllic dreams. He was even more determined now that "unhallowed" thoughts must cease.

# *Public Exhibitions*

## 1836

IN ADDITION to required classroom studies and extensive readings of his own choice which left their marks in his notebook and on his mind, and in addition to poems which sometimes strongly (sometimes lamely) reflected these readings as well as his tensions and aspirations, the months before Jones Very's graduation in 1836 were distinguished by some of the most remarkable prose he would ever write. Apparently the qualities of "genius" as Very understood them—consisting of "deep interest," "intensity of observation," and the "peculiar force of language" achieved by the "artless" words of God-given "reason"—were not restricted to poetic forms. In March and April 1836 he worked on an "Oration" he had been invited to deliver at the Public Exhibition early in May. Also in April he completed a dissertation on epic poetry, and after revising it (probably in the latter part of May), submitted it to President Quincy sometime before June first.[1] In July this most impressive of his college essays was awarded a Bowdoin Prize. Also in July, probably as part of an arrangement enabling him to follow the

Divinity School course of studies in the autumn, he was appointed Tutor in Greek. A week later the Class of 1836 performed a suitably sentimental song he had written for "Valedictory Exercises." [2] And finally, on the last day of August he graduated, second in honors to Robert Bartlett (recently appointed Tutor in Latin), and delivered a commencement address, better than most and appropriately entitled "Individuality." [3]

Now only twenty-three years old (but the oldest of the graduates), and ambitious for himself, he possessed a hard-earned reputation as a scholar. He therefore had every reason to be confident of the life he believed awaited him as teacher, poet, essayist, litterateur, and eventually Unitarian minister. However, the doubts and dissatisfactions with himself, constantly intensifying in spite of his efforts to overcome them, were not to be dismissed by rational means. Tendencies Henry Ware would have condemned as wicked if not "Absolute Evil" had he known of them, had to be exorcised. The remarkable prose he wrote in his Senior year made this clear to himself, but not to those who lacked full knowledge of the mounting pressures building up inside him.

For the May 3, 1836 Exhibition Program, Very reworked his prize-winning Bowdoin Essay of July 1835 ("The Practical Application in This Life, by Men as Social and Intellectual Beings, of the Certainty of a Future State"), transforming it into the disciplined and symmetrical kind of "English Oration" acceptable to Professor Channing, and retitled it "The Heroic Character." [4] In spite of the studied rhetoric, traces of genius remained. He retained without change the main point of "Practical Application," that the accomplishments of the Greeks and Romans, however admirable in a "material" way, were restricted by the classical conception of immortality as earthly fame. The "heroic character" of the ancients thus was imperfect because it was a "development of the mind acting under limited motives," motives which were "worldly" and therefore "incapable of calling forth the strength of the soul." (Pp. 1–3.)

Once Very's guarded and abstract language is scaled down it becomes apparent that the argument, as before, was relevant to his own predicament. The men of Greece and Rome need to be understood as archetypes of Very before his *change of heart;* the men of post-classical Christian times, as counters for Very "regenerated." The implications of the address then converge in spectacular fashion to illuminate the emotional strain under which he composed it.

While the "mere instinct of life" had prompted the heroism of earliest times, modern man, aware of what he is and what he "may become," must learn to "restrain" his momentary passions. Classical man, "fettered by his senses," could make his experiences meaningful only by locating them "within the sphere of his rational views"; but rationality cannot provide adequate motives for man in the nineteenth century. This is so because the

principles of action are ever changing, . . . and manifesting themselves in new and more noble forms—forms not seen indeed like those of former days by the outward eye, but which, perceived by the soul, fade not when the faint glimmerings of sense are extinguished, . . . [P. 2.]

Were modern man to pattern his life after the ancients, "however long, or however high" he might "soar on worldly motives," he would in time "feel the attraction of earth; and, exhausted by the vain struggle, be compelled to descend, to seek other pinions." What he needs is a "nobler spring of action, than has yet been brought to operate upon the mind," a motive not grounded in the pleasurable gratification of the physical senses. This new incentive to action is "consciousness of our immortality," an awareness which as yet has "scarcely begun to manifest itself." This alone may bring a "higher and nobler character" to heroic action, and make "the face of nature beam with a more divine radiance." (Pp. 4–8.)

If after almost a year Very was still contemplating the impact of the certainty of the next world upon his own and other men's conduct in the present, neither this concern nor his recent decision to blot all rationalistic thought from consciousness prevented him from developing a secondary but related theme in the "Oration." He had referred in "Practical Application" to the contrast between classical and modern literatures. In "The Heroic Character" he began to work out the differences in detail, completing the task in his second Bowdoin Prize essay.

When he was writing this part of the "Oration," however, probably in March, he limited himself to criticizing such "sickly strains of false poetry" as he found in Byron, citing lines from *Childe Harold* (III, lxvii). (P. 2.) Now Very showed the effect upon his critical judgment of his *change of heart*. Byron had given a "wrong impression" about the "forms of the heroic character":

there is no man, perhaps, who deserves more of his age for having pointed out so strongly the wrong influence, which heroic poetry must have on the mind not guarded by Christian principles. His words should be sounded with trumpet voice through every part of Christendom, until men shall learn to build up the[ir] character on a foundation, which shall render such influences harmless—until they shall learn that there is a nobler element in Christianity, than has yet been developed; . . . than has yet been brought to operate upon the mind. . . . It is in vain we echo the language of other days, and call it poetry—[Pp. 7–8.]

Byron's "energies," like those of the Greeks he reverenced, "lived and moved in their visible effects," and "the beauty and grandeur" which delighted him and which he embodied in his "creations" were those of "the material world." (P. 3.) According to Very, Byron was incapable of raising men's minds "above the dominion of sense." (P. 8.)

After contrasting Byron's outmoded and therefore dangerous "heroism" with what was presently needed, Very concluded that "evil is not to be overcome by shunning it, but by meeting and resisting it." Byron had ignored this challenge—as had Very before his *change of heart*. Since then he had himself taken it up. His own times demanded heroes who could

resist the deluge of other men's thoughts, and stand forth in the strength of [their] own individuality . . . [and] go forth with the strength of an eternal motive, with the spirit of the puritan fathers bright glowing within their bosoms, and the light of God's countenance resting on their brows. [P. 13.]

What Very's "Oration" neglected to make explicit was that in its highest form "heroism" in the nineteenth century involved not only suppressing one's own Byronic thoughts, but resisting all earthbound thoughts, including those of Lydia Very. Physical passions (sexual or not), motivations and actions which ignore the needs of the spirit, reliance upon the senses while denying the perceptions of the soul, equating nature with matter and attributing events to material causes without taking the will of God into account, refusing to admit the existence of the soul and of a loving God, questioning His goodness and mercies, and insisting upon the importance of self to the detriment of one's soul and of society—all such ideas and attitudes, and their rational-logical-empirical justifications, had to be overcome. The "heroic character" of modern times was called to this task; its accomplishment provided the only means for winning inner peace now and salvation hereafter.

Several months later Very used another formal occasion to make a further statement of the complex system of tensions within him, and once again his fears and hopes—so real and critical to him—were veiled by impersonal abstractions and academic requirements. In July he won his second Bowdoin Prize, fifty dollars awarded for the best essay by a senior on the subject of epic poetry. It was a special honor for him since for the first time the same writer had gained both Junior and Senior Prizes. The long essay, forty-six pages of manuscript, had been completed in April but was revised before being submitted by the addition of several clarifying sentences, by several deletions, a number of minor verbal changes, and the insertion of a short passage from "Heroic Character." (A passage from "Practical Application" had been introduced into the original text.) [5] The presented version was dedicated "As a tribute of love and esteem" to Samuel Tenney Hildreth, a member of the Junior Class and friend of Henry Thoreau.

With the help of his reading of works by A. W. Schlegel, Coleridge, and Goethe, he worked out a synthesis of his immortality theme and a theory of literature which took into account his own experiences as a Christian and poet. The essay was a further development of ideas first publicly broached in "Practical Application" and in "Heroic Character," and consequently represented another attempt to provide an objective rationale for his own emotional growth. The framework of the essay is the distinction he drew between classical and romantic attitudes, one being essentially epic and the other dramatic when seen from the perspectives of cultural history. He assumed that all literature is a product of cultural forces, and that whenever changes in the conditions of a culture occur, men of genius produce different types of literature. Accordingly, he examined a number of major poems in relation to the times during which they were written, and particularly in terms of the religious orientations of the respective periods.

The "classical spirit," as he understood it, was characteristic of the "childhood" of civilization, when societies were, by contrast with subsequent developments, still "primitive," and man was limited by his physical capabilities and the capacity of his senses for experiencing the natural world. During this stage of man's progress—which Very recognized not only in Greek culture but in that of the "Israelites" and "Hindoos" as well—man customarily viewed himself in terms of the natural world outside himself. Heroism involved outwardly visible action, and literature accordingly was faithful to the senses and glorified the physical universe. Its most perfect embodiment was in the epics of Homer, whose characters bore "nature's own image and superscription." (P. 10.) Like the *Iliad,* the classical epics of Virgil and Lucan depicted heroism as a visible event, as an external conflict between men in the presence of visible gods. The epic form was essentially simple and objective, sculpturesque in effect, descriptive in technique, and was set in the outward world of physical impressions collected by rational intelligence. Heroism, in poetry as in life, was therefore time-bound, finite, and involved the physical struggles of men in search of material values.

At the opposite extreme from this initial stage in the development of human culture was the contemporary romantic tendency, with its psychological, inward probings, its "incursive" rather than "excursive" movement. (P. 2.) The present time, as Very understood it at its characteristic best, was a subjective age, self-centered to the extent that man viewed the world in reference to himself—a world which was complex and, by contrast with that of the classical period, non-rational. The refined heroism of human greatness now centered around the inward struggle of man's will for control of the "springs" to his action, not in the resultant action itself. As a result of the "expanded mind and cultivated affections" of the modern age, "a stronger sympathy with the inner man of the heart is more and more felt, and becomes more and more the characteristic of literature." The distinctive expression of this historical period came from dramatic poetry—or as Very also called it, by way of explanation, the "poetry of sentiment." The "interest" of the dramatic arose not from the "contemplation of certain *objects* grand and beautiful in themselves," but from "sympathy with the passions and feelings of others awakened by such objects." (P. 15.) Its setting was the world within, the human consciousness itself, the mind where thoughts are deeds and ideas are indistinguishable from natural facts, the inner world of moods, of feelings, and motives. In its latest manifestation heroism consequently could be depicted only by invisible forms, through internal conflicts witnessed by an invisible God. The modern hero therefore was not limited by his physical capabilities. His sensibilities, his imagination, his perceptions of the subtleties in an infinite world of invisible nature, freed him from the limitations of time and space. Given the "pure spirituality of the present day," his instruments of power had become intangible extensions of his intellectual and spiritual being. (Pp. 3 ff.)

Separating the earliest and latest stages of human development was an amorphous period, an intermediate stage covering most of post-classical time until the "present age," when, under the influence of Christianity, attitudes oscillated between outward and inward forms of life and action. Then there were no exclusive commitments to "the material or the immaterial systems." (Pp. 31 ff.) To varying degrees, depending upon the particular mood of their times and upon individual temperaments, poets of the second stage, such as Dante, Ariosto, Tasso, and Milton, used epical means for dramatic ends, and thereby gave concrete shape to actions which were essentially abstract and intellectual. This then was a transitional period, a "new development of the Homeric spirit modified by Christianity." (P. 24.) As the decisive fact in human history, Christianity had gradually "rendered every finite subject unsuited for an epic poem." (P. 21.) Its effect

was to make the individual mind the great object of regard, the centre of eternal interest; and, transferring the scene of action from the outward world to the world within, to give all modern literature the dramatic tendency—and . . . to make man the great centre of interest, . . . [P. 26.]

Within this three-part structure Very tried to find answers to the question posed by the title of his essay, "What Reasons Are There For Not Expecting Another Great Epic Poem?" He considered the problem from the point of view of the "principles of Epic Poetry, and the human mind," and concluded that poetic and psychological developments presented "an insuperable barrier to the choice of a subject" by which to show the "present development of the heroic character in action." (P. 5.) He discussed Coleridge's statement that "the destruction of Jerusalem was the only subject now remaining for an epic poem," and referred to Schiller's plan to treat Frederick the Great as an epic hero. He was familiar enough with William Wilkie's *Epigoniad* and Pollok's *Course of Time* to dispatch them quickly. He was disappointed in Vincenzo Monti's *Bassvilliana,* and irritated by Lamartine's complaints "at not being able to give to the world an epic embodying the present development of the heroic character." However, Very "rejoice[d] in this inability," considering it "the highest privilege of our age—the greatest proof of the progress of the soul—and of its approach to that state of being where its thought is action, its word power." (Pp. 43–46.)

Very's remarks about specific works, particularly for the first two periods, often are full of insight, as when he looked beyond obvious differences to recognize the fundamental connections between Homer and Shakespeare, and discussed the relation between the "moral sentiment of the artist" and his "imagination." (P. 18.) However, his most brilliant comments deal in a general way with the status of poetry in his own times. These observations have an authority derived from his own experiences as a poet and as a serious reader of contemporary poetry and criticism, and therefore are not burdened by displays of classroom learning likely to impress Professor Channing. Mainly obiter dicta and unsystematic, they constitute a manifesto for his own poetic objectives and techniques, as he understood them in 1836; and they were so interpreted by classmates, who began to repeat "strange stories" among themselves about how Very "considered himself born for a great poet" and how he had promised to "restore epic poetry" to its former greatness.[6]

With the confidence born of experience, and which he alone of the Class of 1836 commanded, he proclaimed that poetry should follow only the "voice of nature herself speaking through her interpreter," who was the inspired poet. If a "true poet," he must not look to others for the rules of his art: "he feels within himself the living standard of the great and beautiful, and bows to that alone." But only if he also "has felt more strongly than any other the great moral wants of his age" and has felt the "harmony of his own soul," can he hope to "stamp" his soul "upon the creations of his mind." (Pp. 15–17.)

As for the structure of a poem, to be effective it cannot be "studied or mechanical"; it must be "as much the effect of inspiration, as the images or sentiments"; its unity must be one already "existing in the subject and revealed to the mind in harmony with that subject by its own consciousness."[7] Indeed, the modern poet has been left "unrestrained from prescriptive forms" and has even been exempted from the "bonds of history." (P. 27.) Nevertheless, his freedom is accompanied by a high duty: his soul, "feeling itself contending with motives of god-like powers within," is obligated to "express that conflict in the dramatic form, in the poetry of sentiment." (P. 26.) The origin of "sublime works of genius," modern and ancient, was that "desire"—indistinguishable from the moral duty of the artist—which drives the "greatest minds" to leave behind a "copy of their own souls," representing the "vague but universal spirit of the times when it was written." (P. 29.)

Observations of this sort indicate that by 1836 Very had absorbed more than a few of the basic ideas of contemporary romanticism, including the rejection of "common sense" experiences of the phenomenal world, rationalism, and the classical rules of composition, and the assertion instead of the claims of instinct, emotion, sensibility, and the imagination. His frequently militant tone suggests that as far as he was concerned, the essay was something more than an academic exercise. He made it clear that as a poet himself he held these views as strongly as he held any. And to make his arguments even more convincing, he reworked the text of the essay at least four times between April 1836 and May 1838, and three different versions have survived.[8] The last contains sections devoted to Carlyle's *Sartor Resartus* and Wordsworth's *Prelude,* neither having been mentioned in the April and July 1836 versions although Very was already familiar with both works. Near the end of the Bowdoin essay (both versions), however, he made a partisan apology for the romantic poets as a group—the poets of "imagination" rather than "fancy"—which of course would include himself, perhaps at the expense of Byron.

We cannot sympathize with that spirit of criticism, which censures modern poetry for being the portra[i]ture of individual characteristics and passions; and not the reflection of the general features of society, and the outward man. If we want such poetry as Homer's, we must not only evoke him from the shades, but also his times. . . . But that page of the heroic character is turned forever— . . . To stir the secret depths of *our* hearts writers must have penetrated deeply into their own. Homer found conflicts *without* to describe; shall the poets of our day be blamed because they would exhibit to us those they feel *within?* . . . What indeed are the writings of the great poets of our own times but epics; the description of those internal conflicts, the interest in which has so far superseded those of the outward world. [Pp. 41–43.]

Of the remarkable aspects of this essay—unquestionably the most important he wrote as an undergraduate—the pseudonym he adopted for the occasion, "Epictetus," is especially illuminating. It establishes once again how intimately his college writings functioned and that they were not merely academic exercises. This first-century B.C. Stoic provided him with suggestions and confirmations for some of his own developing ideas. The Phrygian philosopher had taught that man's body is not really his own; that it belongs to the world of things outside consciousness; that the only thing man fully possesses is his will; that God, not man, is responsible for the ideas that present themselves to consciousness; that each man has God within him, and consequently all men are in a sense "sons of God"; that God's will is the same as the will of nature; that man can learn what that will is; and that man's highest aim therefore is to grow into the mind of God, and thereby make the will of nature his own. Within two years Very was using these and similar ideas as guides to his own romantic and dramatic actions, ideas which helped transform his life, for a while at least, into the kind of modern epic which could be rendered through the "poetry of sentiment."

Before that time, graduation ceremonies provided Very with the opportunity for an epical action requiring heroism of modest proportion, expressed in the language neither of sentiment nor of poetry, and set in circumstances none too promising. August thirty-first was an unseasonably cold day, and so windy and dry that streets near the College had to be sprinkled with water in order to keep down the dust. The academic procession passed slowly from the library to the meeting house, and the exercises began at 10:15. After the band played a "voluntary," Henry Ware offered a "short and devout prayer." Very's remarks on "Individuality" came twelfth on the four-hour program, and showed him in an Epictetian mood.

Among the distinguished guests were Presidents William Alexander Duer of Columbia, Heman Humphrey of Amherst, and Francis Wayland of Brown University. Another visitor, the Rev. Dr. John Pierce, who had attended every Harvard commencement since 1803, could not recall when fewer persons were present for the occasion. He thought the exercises "below mediocrity." In general, with few exceptions, the "speaking" was "tame and monotonous." He considered the best exercise William

Minot's dissertation on famous places. This commencement was exceptional according to Pierce for one reason alone: it was the first he had attended at which he saw "not a single person drunk in the hall or out of it." [9]

Lack of high spirits and Pierce's judgment about Minot's set piece to the contrary, Very's address was intended as a stirring attack upon complacency. Even if delivered in the "tame and monotonous" fashion usual for Very's public performances, the substance of his oration could not be so characterized. It was symptomatic of the unrest current among a few sensitive New England intellectuals of the time. Growing uneasy amid prevailing optimisms, they belonged to a protestant movement which was still undefined and unled, and would remain so for at least ten days longer—until after the publication of Emerson's *Nature*, first advertised for sale on September 9, 1836.

What set Very apart from them and from Emerson was the underlying basis of his protest. His originated in private dissatisfactions with himself. These so engulfed him that fear and anger easily overflowed the limits of self, and the excess was directed away from him, and away from the mother he held ultimately responsible for his own feelings of guilt and shame. Only then, at an impersonal remove from what prompted it, did he apply his indictment to American society, including even the academic world of Harvard—unwittingly represented by the meticulous but unperceptive Rev. Dr. Pierce.[10]

At the start Very told the distinguished gathering that a "fatal disease" has been working upon every one of them and upon their "social system." As men are made "physically dependent" upon each other by "science and civilization," Very explained, they are subjected to "moral evil." Most of them have already succumbed to the three chief evils of modern civilization: the "mechanical spirit of our age," the "all-pervading selfishness," and the annihilation of "individuality." [11] His address then was a traditional New England jeremiad of the sort Harvard audiences

had regularly listened to since Puritan times. But however familiar it was in tone, the terms of Very's complaint posed a strikingly modern paradox. He recognized that "progress" in the
human community is gained at great expense: as society
advances, the integrity of the individual is eroded until his moral
nature as well as his personal identity are destroyed.

After having discomforted his audience, Very further unnerved
them by recalling what he was sure they had forgotten. While
civilization tends to limit freedom of action by destroying independence of a primitive sort, it creates a "higher and nobler"
form of individuality, that of "our moral and intellectual being."
The annihilation of this individuality Very found unfortunate.
(P. 1.) The evils of modern civilization, he said, arise from the
failure of the "law of necessity" to act on the "rich in this world,
in goods and the wealthy in intellect." Ignorant of the moral and
intellectual dimensions to their existence, men "confine their
god-like vision to this narrow span of earth," preserving a "notion
of action" they inherited from the "semi-barbarism" of the past.

Unfaithful to themselves . . . their individuality, the highest gift of
God to man, is, with suicidal hand, sacrificed on the altar of their
worldly ambition. . . .

This is the state of things in which we exist. . . . Goodness,
instead of being regarded as a common world of everyday action,
seems a shining far-off sphere, . . . [Pp. 1-2.]

If men continue to acknowledge the "supremacy" of their own
"pleasure" as the sole motive for action, the death of their moral
nature inevitably follows. "The great law of our moral nature is
the law of duty, and this is the great antagonist principle, which
can alone resist the evils with which we are threatened." (P. 3.)

He explained what the "law of duty" required in order to
overcome the three great evils of modern civilization. Society
cannot be "regenerated" through "forms of polity or worldly
wisdom," but only "by awakening men to a consciousness of the

*reality* of their *moral* life." They must accept the "guilt" they bear for "sacrificing" their moral life to "physical pleasure." This obviously is a matter requiring individual rather than collective remedy, and therefore governments cannot "take cognizance of that guilt." Only as men accept their individual guilt will they be able to resist the "injurious influences" brought about by society. "We," the speaker himself included, must learn to see "our physical enjoyments in their true light." (Pp. 3-4.)

Very was hopeful. He had "faith" in the "counteracting influences" of the soul, in the soul's "being destined to give a new birth to society, by strengthening its bonds of union and unfolding new principles of action." He rejected the mystical idea of Lady Stanhope and of the writer of the *Natural History of Enthusiasm* that "this change will manifest itself in any sudden or striking manner"; rather, it will accompany "the gradual recognition and assumption as a motive of action, of the great truth which is the foundation of our religion, the belief in our own immortality." (P. 4.)

While society makes us dependent upon one another for the "common [material] wants of our nature," he concluded, it simultaneously has developed "another part of our being," previously unknown, which has given us an individuality far greater than that of uncivilized men, a "spiritual freedom which is superior to that of the body." Men

should learn to contend for it as their fathers did for civil rights. Let them look upon it as something to be won by their own free exertions—something which no father's hand can bequeath. . . . Let them look upon their moral nature as something which is to be divested of this robe of earth thrown around it; and in a few years, to stand forth in a living consciousness of its own being. . . .

Acting from a consciousness of our own immortality, we shall be able to resist all that is hostile to our progress in civilization. We should not, we cannot resist that physical dependence on others which society imposes upon us; but we would guard, as our most sacred trust, that nobler independence which she gives us in its stead. Our land of freedom is the world of thought; let us guard it as the dearest birthright of the soul. [Pp. 7–8.]

To those unacquainted with Very and his earlier compositions, the talk about "moral evil" and "guilt," "selfishness" and "sacrifice," "physical pleasures" and the "law of duty," a "nobler individuality" and "spiritual freedom" not bequeathed by a father, must have been largely incomprehensible and seemed strange terms for a graduation address. Those familiar with him would have recognized "Individuality" as an adjunct to aspects of "Epic Poetry," to the view stated there that the present constituted the highest stage in the development of spiritual and intellectual powers. Here he commented on the widespread materialism; there he had emphasized the idealism. Taken together, they are an index of Very's own present, of a nature torn between mysterious sins and glories, of moods alternating between self-accusation and self-exaltation. No one, not even Very himself, knew that the instability would continue until 1838. At that time his own nobler individuality would exert itself dramatically, bursting willful restraints, and gaining spiritual freedom and reconciliation with "the Father." Much to the dismay of fellow members of the Harvard faculty, including Henry Ware, who little suspected the kind of "religious improvement" Very had achieved during the intervening years, his actions would be manifested in the "new and more noble forms" announced in "The Heroic Character"—forms perceived not by the "outward eye," but by the soul.

# PART TWO: PERFORMANCES

"I feel as I never felt before that to be true to one's self is the first thing—that to sacrifice the perfect culture of my mind to social duties is not the thing—that what we call disinterestedness of action is often disobedience to one's *daimon*—that one's inward instinct is one's best guide—that selfdenial may encroach on the region of the spiritual— . . . I have often . . . acted selfishly—because I knew I could not act disinterestedly in the instance without a certain falseness.—But this was always painful to me—because it argued a great infirmity to be selfish in order to be true—But I see now that to the *imperfect* this must be—the duties will clash—and if we act selfishly on a high principle—it becomes a different thing. I hope you understand me."

—*Elizabeth Palmer Peabody, July 31, 1838 letter to Sophia Peabody, in the Berg Collection of the New York Public Library.*

# Gladly Would He Learn
# and Gladly Teach

## 1836–1837

AT THE SAME time, following his college graduation in 1836, as the latest company of Harvard freshmen were beginning to address him in the Greek recitation room as "Mr. Tutor Very," Jones Very began his studies at the Divinity School, under the direction of Dr. John Gorham Palfrey and the Henry Wares, father and son. The course leading to approbation of candidates for the Unitarian ministry usually required three years to complete. It entailed study of Hebrew, Biblical history and criticism, the content of natural and revealed religion, and the details of Christian theology, institutions, and "ecclesiastical powers." Students were also instructed in the "rights, duties, and relations" of ministers, and were given exercises in extempore speaking, in writing and delivering sermons, and in conducting public worship. The professors stressed critical reading of the Bible in Hebrew and Greek. They believed they would have an "all-sufficient" answer for every modern question if only they could discover by their scholarship "what Jesus Christ wanted done to-day." John Winthrop and John Cotton, it was said, were not more certain that the "details of Mosaic legislation" applied to Massachusetts Bay Colony, than were the Divinity School faculty in the 1830's that the Gospels contained "detailed direction for the exchange, the market, and the factory." [1]

First installed at Harvard College early in the nineteenth century as "liberal Christianity," Unitarianism had become "moribund" and "dogmatic" by the time Very enrolled in the Divinity School.[2] Ever since 1814 the doctrinal terms for admission to the "Church in Harvard University" had been formally stated. Members agreed to articles of faith which precluded views held by men like Jonathan Mayhew, James Freeman, Charles Chauncy, and William Bentley, and made clear that the influence of such "liberals" as Joseph Priestley and Hosea Ballou was intolerable. In the "Form of Admission" members announced "faith" in Jesus Christ, accepted "his religion" and "his laws" without reservation, and expressed "earnest desire to obtain the salvation proposed in the Gospel." Moreover, each member had to acknowledge "humble and grateful reliance on God for the pardon of sin," and agree to seek "the riches of divine favour" in our Lord Jesus Christ.[3] Although subject to interpretation, these general principles reflected the increasing demand by ministers and congregations alike that Unitarianism adopt creed, offices, and the other institutions of a conventional Christian denomination.

Originally, as understood by men like William Bentley (1759–1819), of Salem's East Church, Unitarianism was rooted in the eighteenth-century concept of natural religion. Bentley believed that the ceremonies and dogmas of Christianity were incidental to salvation, and that whatever was distinctively Christian in Unitarianism supplemented rather than supplanted natural religion. But by 1836 most of the original impetus of such liberal ideas, carried over from the Enlightenment and from Arian and Arminian heresies, had been spent. Under the direction of the professors an establishment developed. Unitarianism became inflexible, and Harvard was no longer latitudinarian.[4] But even then, unlike the Congregationalism which had spawned it, Unitarianism did not endorse any of the modifications of the Westminster Catechism; nonetheless, it did encourage a body of unofficial dogmas, the creation of scholarly men who were trying to teach clerical aspirants a systematic corpus of belief. They denied the traditional versions of Trinity, rejected the old orthodox conceptions of atonement, and did not consider the crucifixion a special Christian mystery. The resurrection was construed primarily as the glorification of the human but godlike powers of perfected man, the son of Joseph and Mary, and not as the completion of a sacrificial act designed to reconcile God to imperfect men. However, the distinction between God and the godlike man Jesus was obscured; the communion ritual was retained; and the confirming sanction of biblical authority was necessary for discriminating between probity and sin, defining them in social and ethical rather than sectarian terms.

The learned members of the Harvard faculty who implemented such ideas "looked without for knowledge, rather than within for inspiration," and consequently were easily disquieted by varieties of "mysticism, enthusiasm and rapture." While claiming to emphasize "rational theology," they were cool toward the higher criticism of the Bible undertaken by recent German theologians; they made "increasingly smug use of reason at the expense of liberality"; and they insisted upon the historicity of the miracles of Jesus. Because their convictions were based on what they said was the "cold light of reason and nature," their new orthodoxy was marked by emotional reserve—a "frigid" and "empty theism" thought its critics. The Divinity School faculty in turn charged Calvinists and revivalists with lacking all sense of human dignity, and the more liberal and radical Unitarians with being outside Christianity entirely.[5]

By 1836 it had become evident that a significant division existed in the Unitarian community. As early as 1832 the *Christian*

*Examiner,* the journal of informed Unitarian opinion and scholarship, was occasionally printing articles which in effect were urging a contemporary equivalent of the liberal religious outlook which had originally spawned Unitarianism. Contributed by men like George Ripley, Convers Francis, Frederick Henry Hedge, and Orestes A. Brownson—all of whom were responding to the romantic currents of nineteenth-century European literature and philosophy—these articles expressed an influential but nevertheless minority point of view, one which was primarily a reaction against the orthodoxy expounded at the Harvard Divinity School.[6]

John Gorham Palfrey was Dexter Professor of Sacred Literature and "Dean" of the Divinity School from 1830 to 1839, having replaced Andrews Norton who had retired to devote himself to scholarly writing about the Bible and to theological controversy. A man whose "acute conscience" combined with a highly developed sense of History, Palfrey retained the conservative character his predecessor had imprinted upon the School. With Palfrey as nominal head, Norton therefore maintained his hold on the theological world of Cambridge for an additional decade, continuing his domination (said his critics), ex cathedra "Unitarian Pope." [7]

Henry Ware, Sr. (1764–1845) had been elected to the Hollis Professorship of Divinity in 1805, gaining distinction thereby as the first faculty member of Harvard College who was not an avowed Trinitarian and Calvinist. His views concerning the original goodness of man were so repugnant to the "Hopkinsians" and "Old Calvinists" that loss of this citadel of God compelled them to establish Andover Theological Seminary in 1808. By 1836 he had long been a leader with Norton of what was then the conservative Unitarian faction. His conception of man's "natural affections" (they occasioned "error and sin" because they were susceptible to corruption by a "wrong direction," not by

native depravity) had not substantially changed in the intervening years. His long-standing practice was to cite biblical text as
well as "human experience" in support of dignifiedly optimistic
beliefs, now well established in Boston and vicinity.[8]

Henry Ware, Jr. (1794–1843), the Professor of Pulpit
Eloquence, was a less tranquil version of his celebrated father. He
followed the moderate Unitarian principles developed at
Cambridge by Norton and the elder Ware, but was more evangelical than they, more anxious about the urgency of winning a
state of grace. He encouraged long sessions of private devotion,
and worried over his cautious estimates of the spiritual improvement made by students. An energetic teacher, his understanding
of the need for "close personal communion with God" spread
among Cambridge students, undergraduate as well as graduate,[9]
and as early as 1834 had already reached the new Greek tutor.

Very was not regularly enrolled in the program offered by
Palfrey and the Wares. By custom or special arrangement, since
he conducted fifteen periods of freshman classes for the Greek
Department each week, he was allowed to carry in addition a
"full load" of divinity courses.[10] Therefore the records of the
Theological School which have been preserved do not once
mention his name, nor was his presence at classes ever noted in
faculty minutes.[11] This was not unusual. Persons not officially
enrolled often were permitted to attend lectures and recitations
for an unspecified number of terms. But the silence of surviving
records raises the question of how diligently Very applied himself
to such obligations as lectures and recitations. His dual status as
Greek Tutor and unclassified student led to some confusion even
among his friends. While Robert Cassie Waterston, a member of
one of the more advanced classes, said he knew Very "intimately"
when Very "was at the Divinity School," [12] another friend who in
September 1836 was also a first-year divinity student, George
Moore, failed to include him in his diary listing of classmates.[13] In

addition to this omission there appear to be other indications that he was a desultory student of the systematic theology being taught at Harvard.

His newly sharpened religious and moral sensitivities found little outlet in the bland program administered by the stolid professors. They moved him to borrow from the library only three volumes relevant to the divinity course during the 1836–1837 academic year, and these may rather have been readings prompted by the younger Ware's Society for Religious Improvement: Wall's *Christ Crucified,* the second volume of Southey's *Book of the Church,* and once again Bishop Whately's *Essay on St. Paul.* Matters other than formal divinity as practiced at Cambridge were most important to him at this time.[14]

He undertook instead his own investigations, replacing or supplementing the graduate course he was expected to follow. He read or reread Mme. de Staël's *Germany,* A. W. Schlegel's *Lectures on Dramatic Art and Literature,* an edition of *Hamlet,* a Blackwood's article on Shakespeare, volumes from Edmund Malone's *Shakespeare* and Lamb's *Works,* Carlyle's "Signs of the Times," *Wilhelm Meister* and several essays on Goethe, including one by Novalis, Burke on the French Revolution, Lockhart's *Life of Scott,* Bulwer-Lytton's *Pelham,* and various contemporary periodicals. Moreover, just as indicative of his refusal to allow the Divinity School to arrange his immediate interests were readings for his own freshman classes. He withdrew from the library various editions of Herodotus and Thucydides (and translated passages from them, and also from *Medea*), Greek lexicons, two volumes of Potter's *Antiquities of Greece,* Cowper's *Homer,* Karl Otfried Muller's monumental study of Dorian culture, a half-dozen volumes on *Ancient Marbles* and *Ancient Terracottas,* and a volume of *Athenian Letters.*[15] Therefore, whatever his attitude toward the Divinity School curriculum and the conservative beliefs of the faculty, he appears to have taken his own independent studies and teaching duties quite seriously.

His disenchantment—if indeed this is what it was—with divinity courses and divinity professors so soon after deciding to prepare for the ministry at Harvard, is scarcely puzzling. The Divinity School faculty, as Very had known for several years, had much to do with setting the moral tone throughout Harvard. As a College graduate he therefore would have expected more of the same from Palfrey and the Wares. In part his indifference may have been apparent, or temporary, due only to the conscientiousness of a young instructor confronting his first group of students. In part though, it must have been due to his concern for his own spiritual needs, which were not identical with the needs of other students because they stemmed from his own peculiar anxieties and temperament. Moreover, the unofficial education he had been providing for himself since 1833—and a form of which he soon would be making available to his freshman students as well—imposed special intellectual and emotional demands upon him which could not be readily satisfied by the orthodox studies supervised by his professors. The most comprehensive explanation, however, is to be found in his personal copy of a small blue book with covers decorated by tree-like vines. Mr. Tutor Very purchased it in September 1836, only a few days after it was published. The timing of its acquisition at once suggests that he was already familiar with the latest modes of nonconformity, and perhaps was even anticipating the book's publication. At the end of August, in his Commencement Address, had he not expressed his confidence in the power of "new principles of action" to resist the "mechanical spirit" of the times, which he felt was suppressing the more heroic and precious forms of individuality? Now the opportunity arose for him to study the detailed grounds of another man's affirmations and dissents, a man somewhat older than he, and more knowing in the ways of spiritual heroism, about which the Divinity School evidently could teach him nothing.

He may have first learned of Ralph Waldo Emerson during the

winter of 1835–1836, when the latter delivered a series of ten lectures on English literature, from Chaucer to Shakespeare, to Byron and Coleridge, at Boston's Masonic Temple. Or, as was perhaps more likely, when Very visited Boston that winter to listen to sermons (as he must have done, following his *change of heart* and recent choice of a ministerial career), he may have heard Emerson in one of his church appearances, since he preached usually twice a week during the run of his lecture course.[16] Or, between January and May 1836, after walking the seventeen miles of turnpike linking Cambridge with his home, he may have attended one of the approximately fifteen lectures on biography and English literature Emerson delivered at the Salem Lyceum in two series.[17] (In view of the attitudes Very was cultivating at the time, the Martin Luther, John Milton, and George Fox lectures might well have tempted him.) But whatever the way he discovered Emerson—and there were sufficient opportunities for him to have at least heard about him as early as 1835—it is certain he read *Nature* eagerly in 1836, with pencil in hand, scoring margins, underlining sentences, and making written comments.[18]

Most striking about Very's markings and marginalia is that they indicate he was not at all surprised by Emerson's aerial prose poem; instead, he apparently found what he expected—and this neither confounded nor offended him, as it did most readers. Several times he questioned what he read, but never did he challenge Emerson: his mood seemed respectful throughout. It was as if his reading confirmed suspicions that the author was a thoughtful man whose reflections repaid close scrutiny. (Though a minor aspect of Very's use of *Nature,* it is indicative of his attitude toward it that he treated it incidentally as a source book for the compatible ideas of others, of Coleridge for example, and of Shakespeare, Michaelangelo, George Herbert, and even of the unnamed "orphic poet.")[19] He read *Nature* then as a literal rather than figurative testament about the nature of God, and about the relationship between God and man. He read it as if it were a conduct-book filled with supernal imperatives. While certainly not a usual approach to the book, it still was a valid one, given the disposition of the reader in September 1836. He was looking for certain information, and believed it might be found here rather than in the Divinity School.

Very was particularly curious about the effects of nature upon Emerson, about his emotional and artistic responses to the natural world. Moreover, Very seemed interested in external nature as the basis for communion with God, and this accorded well with the viewpoint Emerson developed. (The professors would have shouted Very down had he suggested such an idea in the classroom.) He was concerned too with the relationship between personal morals and the morality of art, and specifically of literary art. But he seemed not so interested as Emerson in attempting to explore the philosophical middle ground between idealism and materialism. Several of the statements recalled to him verses from the Book of Revelation, and several others reminded him of the corrosive powers of sin. Emerson's book therefore generally served to stimulate his own distinctive thoughts in an original way, one which at times was inconsistent with Emerson's intentions; that is, from the marginalia in his copy, Very's *Nature* seems not quite the book that Emerson wrote. But this does not mean that his comments and markings conformed to any viewpoint even remotely acceptable to the provincial orthodoxy maintained by Andrews Norton and his colleagues.

When Emerson discussed the relationship of words to natural and spiritual facts in the chapter on "Language," Very wrote at the bottom of the page that "the lip is the parcel of the mind." (P. 33.) By this he meant that words are related to ideas in the sense that words are a small portion of the mind. Since they are the extensions of thoughts, they reveal the state of spiritual health within. While this is not quite Emerson's meaning here, it is still an Emersonian idea, and is confirmed by Very's scoring of the entire margin of another page. There Emerson observed that one of the results of the corruption of men by such secondary desires as riches, pleasure, power, and praise, is the corruption of language. The "simplicity and truth" of words are replaced by "duplicity and falsehood." When this happens, "words lose all power to stimulate the understanding or affections," and "new imagery ceases to be created, and old words are perverted to stand for things which are not." It is therefore an indication of personal and cultural disintegration if language is not derived directly from "nature" but still manages to convey the illusion that the speaker has seen and uttered truth. (P. 38.) As he read this Very must have been reminded of the empty rhetoric of the Divinity School Unitarians. And to complete the meaning of "the lip is the parcel of the mind," Very marked the margin opposite Emerson's observation that the poet or orator who uses natural images instinctively as symbols makes language an automatic instrument of power since he draws upon spiritual energies. (P. 40.) He immediately would have recognized this as being perfectly consistent with his determination to repress all deliberative thought while continuing such activities as writing poetry, preparing for the ministry, and instructing students in Greek.

He did not mark what Emerson said about "the moral influence of nature" in the chapter on "Discipline," undoubtedly because it was already familiar to him. He did note, however, the one sentence in the chapter which spoke of "tranquilty," the inner rest which comes to man "from the azure sky, over whose unspotted deeps the winds forevermore drive flocks of stormy clouds, and leave no wrinkle or stain." (P. 54.) Very was seeking such "tranquility" for himself. It would continue to be a "parcel" of his mind throughout his reading of the book, even when not to Emerson's purpose.

Almost half of Very's marking and all but two of his comments appear in the famous chapter on "Idealism." When

Emerson spoke of the "noble doubt" about the outward existence of nature, and asked what difference is made by "my utter impotence to test the authenticity of the report of my senses, to know whether the impressions they make on me correspond with outlying objects" (p. 59), Very grasped the epistemological issue which Emerson had raised. He restated it in somewhat different terms in a comment at the bottom of the page, introducing the element of *will:* "We do not doubt the senses or the authenticity of their report, but we reject and refuse the impression which they make." Very undoubtedly meant that while he did not question the camera-like accuracy of the senses, if given a choice he preferred reality to the photographic record it left. He seemed to feel that this reality might be apprehended by means other than the senses. How, exactly, "Nature is made to conspire with spirit to emancipate us," he was not sure; but he apparently thought a clue might be found in Emerson's observations on the effect of changing one's point of view toward external nature, thereby giving a "pictorial air" to the "whole world." (P. 63.)

Emerson said that the world can be made to seem like a marvellous picture, more like an appearance than a substance, by shifting one's physical perspective. (P. 63.) Therefore an alteration in the distance between the observer and the spectacle, or any other "mechanical changes" in the relationship of man and nature, bring about a mixture of "pleasure" and "awe," and "a low degree of the sublime is felt from the fact . . . that man is hereby apprized, that whilst the world is a spectacle, something in himself is stable. . . . In a higher manner, the poet communicates the same pleasure." (P. 64.) After scoring the last sentence and the two clauses preceding, Very wrote at the bottom of the page:

Rev xx:11
The same effect is produced by looking steadfastly at Nature or a scene in it.

What Very intended by distinguishing between "Nature" and a "scene in it" is not clear, unless by the former he meant a broad, inclusive landscape consisting of many component "scenes." The effect of "looking steadfastly" (a "mechanical change") and the order of experience he had in mind are indicated by the verse from the Revelation of John: "And I saw a great white throne, and him that sat on it, from whose face the earth and heaven fled away; and there was found no place for them." This then is the kind of "scene" missed by the "report" of the senses but caught by intense reflection, and which brings "tranquility." For his "emancipation" Very was prepared to go beyond the more cautious pantheism pervading *Nature*. By citing biblical text, however, he had forgotten or did not realize that he was himself in danger of ceasing to create new imagery and was on the verge of perverting old words.

Emerson traced unquestioning belief in the solidity of the external world, and belief in no other, to the universal confidence children have in the existence of whatever appears. This, he said, is the "popular faith" even of adults, until it is replaced by an "afterthought" to the contrary, or until it is corrected by "culture." (P. 74.) For Very this naïve confidence in the "report" of the senses, if persisted in beyond the innocence of childhood, arouses "two evil desires." These he did not further identify in the marginal note mentioning them: apparently they were so familiar to him that further specification was unnecessary, or perhaps they were so repulsive to him that he dared not even hint at (or think of) what they involved.[20]

When Emerson differentiated between ethics and religion, Very used double margin lines to emphasize the passage:

. . . the one is the system of human duties commencing from man; the other from God. Religion includes the personality of God: Ethics does not. . . . The first and last lesson of religion is, "The things that are seen, are temporal; the things that are unseen are eternal." It puts an affront upon nature. It does that for the unschooled, which philosophy does for Berkeley and Viasa. [P. 72.]

The significance of the markings, and his reaction to the claim that "religion" entails the denigration of the external world, were concealed for several pages. After placing a question mark opposite the statement that the Soul "accepts from God the phenomenon [of nature], as it finds it" (p. 75), he wrote: "The greatest men always believe in the stability of Nature and truth of its law." The kind of "religion," then, which "puts an affront upon nature" by depreciating "things that are seen," was not for Very. The "great white throne, and him that sat on it" were, after all, made visible by "looking steadfastly" at Nature.

While idealisms which affirmed spirit at the expense of the phenomenal world were impossible for both Emerson and Very, their reasons for rejecting them differed. Emerson recognized the peculiar risk run by ecstatic visions. If not anchored in nature they ended in self-delusion or something worse, madness. And Very knew of this danger. He underlined the sentence relating how Emerson avoided it by being simultaneously in and out of nature, and therefore could "expand and live in the warm day like corn and melons," without peril. (P. 75.) Nevertheless Very was more concerned himself with danger of another sort: the moral danger arising from the attempt to adapt nature and spirit to each other. "Vice," he wrote at the bottom of the same page, "crushes some mans ideal in spite of [the Soul]." And, thinking possibly of the two unnamed "evil desires," he added the ominous word, "Vices." These then also belong to the substantial world. "Vices" prevent the Soul from accepting the natural "phenomena" offered by God, and thereby prevent "tranquility." Idealism, according to Very, must take them into account since evil as well as good exists in the natural world, or at least in the world as it is known by men.

In the chapter on "Spirit" Emerson also rejected that idealism which denies the "existence of matter" because it "leaves God out of me. It leaves me in the splendid labyrinth of my perceptions, to wander without end." (P. 78.) Very scored the margin and reinforced it with an "X," indicating his qualified agreement. For him more than God was in man: "evil desires" and "Vices" were there, introduced by the "existence of matter." Until these were overcome by application of will, "tranquility" was impossible. Un-Godlike elements in man had to be destroyed, else the soul was doomed to endless wandering in the "labyrinth" of self.

Very marked with a broken line the passage in which Emerson asked, "Who can set bounds to the possibilities of man?" Next he marked the one which discriminated between two related aspects of nature:

The world proceeds from the same spirit as the body of man. It is a remoter and inferior incarnation of God, a projection of God in the unconscious. But it differs from the body in one important respect. It is not, like that, now subjected to the human will. Its serene order is inviolable by us. It is therefore, to us, the present expositor of the divine mind. [P. 80.]

The key ideas to which Very was responding here were the likeness of man and nature, both being material projections of God; the difference derives from nature being subject to God's will, while the body is subject to man's. Man's task then, as Very understood it, was to make human nature also the "expositor of the divine mind." One way of achieving this was by shaping the "world" into a less remote and inferior "incarnation of God," by transforming it into a conscious rather than "unconscious" projection. The human will might then operate in the external world in much the same way as it now does in the personal world. Through his will man possesses the means to affect his relationships with both God and nature. His "possibilities" are therefore unlimited.

After reading the "orphic saying" in the last chapter, "Prospects," about man being a "god in ruins," he scored the conclusion to the passage: "Infancy is the perpetual Messiah, which comes into the arms of fallen men, and pleads with them to return to paradise." (P. 88.) In the margin he added a cryptic "R12." The twelfth chapter of the Revelation of John describes a vision in which a woman is seen gloriously arrayed: "clothed with the sun, and the moon under her feet, and upon her head a crown of twelve stars." In the threatening presence of Satan, who has appeared in the form of a "great red dragon," she gives birth to a male child. The infant is "caught up unto God, and to his throne" while the mother flees into the "wilderness." Thereupon the Revolt of the Angels occurs, ending in the defeat of Satan, cast out from Heaven with his band. The child is then revealed as the Christ: a loud voice calls out from Heaven, saying, "Now is come salvation, and strength, and the kingdom of God."

The connections between the orphic passage and John's vision are clear. To use Emerson's terminology, one speaks in the "ethical" accent, the other in the "religious," of the prospect of godlike innocence not yet "in ruins." The connections, however, were not yet so clear that Very could recognize himself in the role of the wondrous son destined to save the outcast Queen, Lydia Very, by bringing her back to paradise from the wilderness of her disbelief. Above the first sentence of Emerson's next orphic saying, "Man is the dwarf of himself," Very placed a question mark. Emerson described men as being no longer "permeated and dissolved by spirit." Very was less sure that the time had really passed when *he,* at least, "filled nature with his overflowing currents."

Very's final markings in the book reinforce the conclusion that he saw a personal significance to much of *Nature.* He noted what Emerson said about the "faithful thinker" able to "detach" himself from external objects. If he could also see them "in the light of thought" and at the same time "kindle" the knowledge of natural facts "with the fire of holiest affections," a miracle would occur: "then will God go forth anew into the creation." (P. 92.) Very identified this mythic thinker full of "faith" with the God walking the earth. Soon he would identify himself with both, as the "perpetual Messiah," the man whose "possibilities" were without bound.

Emerson, therefore, was unintentionally helping Very to understand the strange role he would shortly assume. Facts, Very learned from Emerson, disintegrate in the presence of an "idea," and the "real higher law" concealed by them is apprehended. (P. 92.) What impressed him most in *Nature,* as indicated by his markings and comment, suggests that the time was approaching when he would penetrate the "facts" about himself and reach the "truth" which brings tranquility. (Who at the Divinity School in September 1836 could have possibly helped him to this "prospect"?) As for Emerson, in 1838 and 1839 he would witness in Very a part of the process he had unknowingly encouraged following Very's graduation.

Neither the ideas of Emerson nor their variants occurring to Very as he read *Nature* could be tolerated at Harvard. Very's comments as well as the implications of the passages which impressed him most constituted a tacit indictment of orthodox Unitarianism. Taken together, they challenged the complacent world in which he had set himself, and constituted a subtle attack upon its elegant but devitalized theology.

Speaking for the establishment in a review of *Nature* in 1837, Francis Bowen (Very's predecessor as Tutor, and now instructor in philosophy, and later Alford Professor), thought the book arrogant and absurd. However, he took Emerson seriously, and recognized him as a dangerous man.[21] Were Very to indicate even qualified acceptance of such "new views," his own position as Tutor and candidate for the ministry might be jeopardized. In order then to reassure Harvard authorities that however heterodox his own beliefs might seem, he was still no infidel, he made a dramatic gesture. Perhaps this was after he had been questioned by the younger Ware, the professor who was so solicitous about states of grace. Whatever the circumstances, Very subscribed to the "Form of Admission to the Church in Harvard University" on May 17, 1837.[22] Therefore, eight months after his stimulating reading of *Nature,* he added his name to a register which had already been signed by William Henry Channing, Cyrus A. Bartol, John Sullivan Dwight, and Harrison Gray Otis Blake, among others, each of whom had already or would soon express his own dissatisfactions with conservative Unitarianism.

In 1837 Very had additional reasons to be concerned about his status at Harvard. By then he had made himself conspicuous by the manner in which he conducted classes and established unusual relationships with students. Even in his daily academic behavior he implied a criticism of the Harvard proprieties. Although as an undergraduate he had enjoyed a close association with Professor Channing and others among the faculty, he knew such privileges as he had managed were exceptional, and indeed had further served to isolate him from most of his classmates. The aloof manner of Professor Ticknor was more typical of the faculty bearing toward students. Now that Very was himself a teacher, he tried not to adopt the traditional cold and distant academic attitude.

His recitation course for freshmen was divided into three customary sections. According to the abilities of each group, students were required to read from Herodotus and Thucydides, Cleveland's *Greek Antiquities,* and portions of Buttman's *Greek Grammar;* to write twice-monthly compositions in Greek, or translations from the Greek; and to write occasional essays on the assigned authors or on themes otherwise related to their study of the language.[23] This rather unimpressive program, over whose academic substance Very had no control, was transformed into the most popular freshman class by a teacher with an extremely relaxed sense of routine who did not know how to be dull. Frequently he would digress from the assigned lesson to "rhapsodize" animatedly over matters having apparently nothing to do with the study of Greek. His "profound" love for the great English poets led him to include Shakespeare and Milton among his favorite topics for classroom discourse. This practice endeared him to students affected by what he had to say, as well as by those who preferred any conversation to the severities of Greek roots. He spoke to them, not about the "thought" and "beauty" to which only men of remote times could respond, but about the "thought" and "beauty" which still possessed "vitality," and which would be meaningful to these young men.[24] Quite likely he also found occasion to speak to them about Wordsworth, Byron, Coleridge, Goethe, and all the other writers to whom he had himself been responding. And if so, he certainly must have found time to talk about Emerson's *Nature,* and about his understanding of its implications, both personal and philosophical.

Regardless of the particular subjects discussed and however frequent these digressions, they were never trivial or stuffy. The Cambridge traditions of respectability and decorum meant little to him. He was known as one of the few faculty members who was unimpressed by wealth or social standing, and who did not discourage students' literary ambitions or belittle their enthusiasms. Unlike other Harvard teachers (George Ticknor for one), he never entrenched himself "behind the dignities" of his position, or tried to escape the "irksome routine" of academic Cambridge by isolating himself from students. Instead, he visited them in their rooms, and they were welcomed in his.

Further distinguishing him from his peers and superiors at Harvard were his honest efforts to stimulate self-improvement in the young men with whom he daily came in contact.[25] He was convinced, as a matter of pedagogical principle, that

there are moral lessons to be learned from the Homeric poems, not because the characters exhibited or the few maxims uttered ar[e] moral in our sense of the word, but because whatever gives a true representation of human nature in any state may be *made* morally instructive to those who look from the vantage ground of a purer and nobler system.[26]

His classes were small enough for him to become personally acquainted with all his students, and he was so interested in them that he gave them "more than the usual attention." He even wrote original verses in letters on the backs of the Greek exercises he corrected and returned, doing so "whenever he was moved" to encourage some friend to reach for a "higher ideal." [27]

Since he was personally involved in the lives of his students, his attentions often led to afternoons and evenings of purposive talk with groups of young men. With this objective he often invited them to join him in otherwise aimless rambles through nearby meadows. He was obviously one of those rare moralists whose sincerity avoided becoming tiresome. His seriousness was flavored by his gift for dramatic utterances and actions. He spoke with them about the "wonders of Nature" as presently seen in the "Heavens and the Earth." He spoke too about the "deepest spiritual subjects" and employed the "most devout tone." Yet what he had to say, and the intensity with which he said it, were found "so interesting" that students considered it a "great privilege" to be invited to walk with him, especially to his favorite retreat, the cemetery at nearby Mount Auburn.[28]

If the passing thoughts he recorded in his commonplace book are any indication of what he was telling his students during moments of serious reflection, then he did not repeat the usual platitudes. He was as worried about their spiritual well-being as he was about his own. "Let us tremble," he said, "at the approach of that day when time for *us* shall be no longer—You whom the follies and fashions of time save awhile from a crushing [death]—tremble least when the idea of Eternity open[s] upon your minds." He prayed that "it may not crush you with a weight heavier than the burthen of piled up mountains on your breasts!" [29] He also might have discussed with them "certain views" about which men often ask, "what more do they mean than such and such abstract propositions?"—and he would have explained the difference between meaning and being: the "views" (details not given) do not "mean more than these [abstract propositions] but they are more for they are those abstract[ions] as formula drawn out and made real by the life—in the one you see the abstract, in the other the concrete." [30] And perhaps he discussed with them the question he pondered near the end of the 1837 academic year, whether it were really true that "knowledge is power." [31]

Whatever the specific topics and attitudes developed by his conversations, these hours were not soon forgotten by the participants. Emotions were touched and deep attachments forged as "Heart answered to heart and mind to mind." He himself said that at such times "thoughts and feelings were freely interchanged and our lives, as it were, blended in one." It was a "delightful communion" he so much looked forward to. Elizabeth Peabody was impressed when she learned from students that his talk was "so free from cant as to command their reverence." She thought this "wonderful proof" of his "power." From her own experience as a teacher she knew that young people will never tolerate "sanctimony." As he transacted it however, the business of improving character and "saving souls" was exciting. [32]

Very's spontaneity in the classroom and informality outside it—both stemming from his decision to repudiate the mechanical processes of thinking and rely upon his higher faculty of Reason—did not mean he neglected his academic duties. On the contrary, he was widely recognized as a "thorough scholar" and an "able and acceptable teacher." Even though as a student he had been shy and withdrawn, he had become the "ideal instructor" according to one former pupil. Another was so taken by his "manner of instructing," so different was it from what was usual at Harvard, that it "produced a leaning" to Greek which lasted more than forty years. [33]

He gained the campus reputation for being the only teacher of classical languages at Harvard who insisted upon accurate translations. He was "unwearied" in drawing attention to tenses and requiring literal translations, "two important points in learning languages, of which Mr. Felton quite lost sight." Compared to Very, Cornelius Conway Felton, the Eliot Professor of Greek Literature, was "superficial and heartless" in his conduct of the course. Moreover, Very was said to have truly felt and always communicated the essence of Greek civilization: he "fairly breathed the spirit of the Greek language and its literature." He himself modestly claimed that he "only let the Greek grow"; but it was recalled by one who knew that he "surrounded" the language with a "charm" which disappeared from Harvard when his teaching career ended.[34]

While it is hardly likely that Professor Felton would have shared these glowing estimates, he did acknowledge that the accomplishments of Very's students indicated he conducted his classes in an "able and satisfactory manner." [35] And Very's reputation for exercising a wholesome influence on the young men of Cambridge reached beyond the limits of Harvard, eventually impressing even that peripatetic pedagogue, Bronson Alcott.[36]

Very did not attempt to conceal from authorities that classroom time regularly was devoted to informal discussion of matters related remotely if at all to classical pursuits. He announced as much himself, without giving the details, in remarks about his students appended to the formal semi-annual report he submitted to the Harvard Overseers: "Their attention to these several studies has been generally such as to make their instructor's duties rather a pleasure than a task; and leads him to look forward with a degree of confidence to the fruits of their exertions in their own best happiness and in the advancement of that of their fellow men." [37] For others at Harvard the past may have been dead; for him it was still vital. But even more vital was his sense of the present moment, in all its delightful or terrifying intensity.

Consequently his attitudes were infectious and his influence, on some at least, lasting. Forty years later, the hilarity of a class reunion was interrupted while former students gave "hearty, loving testimony" to his memory: "one after another attested [to] his individual sense of obligation to Jones Very." [38]

His success as a teacher depended largely on his craving for an audience and his ability to find one. He performed before the young men of Harvard, using them as the targets for his most intimate ideas about himself. The classroom digressions, the verses he addressed to students, the spontaneous conversations in dormitories and fields, all were disguised self-dramatizations or self-dissections, parables which allowed him to exorcise his anxieties in the same ingenious and impersonal way he had developed for prize-winning essays and orations. This meant, however, that the distinctions between private and public, between thought and act, between his own self and other selves, between inner consciousness and external will were all being broken down at the same time as the formal distinction between teacher and pupil was being eradicated. In other words, the kind of "communion" he sought from the Divinity School and which it could not possibly provide, he found through the medium of his duties as Greek Tutor, with Emerson's *Nature* serving as instrumental catalyst. During his years as a teacher he urged upon others what he was urging upon himself, recognizing in them his own weaknesses, fears, loves, and ambitions. He was therefore developing the habit of conducting a dialogue with himself from a public platform, directing his words to others but addressing himself nevertheless, and finding them responding as his own self did. Apparently the dialogue made sense not only to him but to the students who participated, and who forty years later remembered their indebtedness.

# VIII

## *A Poet Steps Forth*

### 1837

JONES VERY managed to maintain his status as a non-matriculated divinity student in 1837 even though he continued to avoid Divinity School dialectics. Since the faculty discouraged enthusiasm on grounds that it was unscholarly, unseemly, and un-Christian, Harvard theology seemed scarcely relevant to his special religious and moral dilemmas. The anxieties he sought to relieve stemmed from self-confessed inclinations to sin, and from his assumption of a complex guilt involving a dead father and an infidel mother. In 1837 he referred to his parents as "blighted flowers," and said that everything connected with them remained in his heart, "as if possessed by some secret undefined power, the witness of some covenant broken with the Lord."[1] The resolution he envisaged for his difficulties was radical, an emotional purification extending to the depths of his troubled soul.

Harvard's pallid intellectualism excluded every kind of ecstatic religious experience. The Unitarian establishment was not at all inclined to deal with such obscure and intimate problems, nor was it disposed to encourage such non-rational solutions, however urgently needed. Therefore, amid self-consuming loneliness and mounting strain in his contacts with friends, faculty, and students, he resisted feelings and memories which had become more and more disconcerting ever since 1834. By shunning academic discipline he intended to avoid whatever was likely to be desensitizing, and whatever might impede an heroic confrontation with his anxieties. Consequently, to the extent he was successful in focusing his attention exclusively upon himself in 1837, the felt presence of God became increasingly important. His consciousness of himself and of the existence of God gradually became the two central facts of his life, in light of which all subsidiary facts were to be understood.

Instead of actively pursuing the systematic but abstract program designed to prepare divinity students to bring spiritual comfort someday to others, he was working out the terms for his own salvation—now, privately, and in a concrete way. Abstract ideas, even those which may have been God-inspired, he considered deficient unless consummated by action: "they are but Revelations which the will alone can render permanent." [2] A month after stating this position, while contemplating in December 1836 the devitalization of religious sentiments which official Harvard sanctioned, he complained, "What a world is this where men must have their duty served up in dainties!" [3] His rigorous sense of the truly religious experience made him impatient with the decorous but ineffectual dogmas espoused at the Divinity School. "We learn from the Testament," he said (citing against the professors their own favorite authority), "that knowledge is never to be separated from duty and that alone is truly interesting which is of use and not a possession." Orthodox Unitarianism was attenuated and enervating, easily professed but a doubtful basis for communion with God. "The true way," he said (and this excluded the Harvard way), "to get rid of old and false laws is to live them down—a new spirit will soon require a new body—and false practices will fall off from the living growth as the bark of trees when useless and decayed." [4]

In an organic fashion therefore, without any guidance except what he believed were his native intuitions (as confirmed by his understanding of Emerson and the Anglo-Germanic romantics he had been studying) he engaged in a "conflict" in 1837. The battle, according to Very, "began with the day and continued to the night." [5] Set within himself, its objective was the suppression of his individual will. At issue, he was convinced, was the supremacy either of a receptive self, sensitive to the will of God, or of an operative self whose power derived from the conviction that one's own actions are self-generated and discretionary. "We cannot predict our actions as if we were machines," he said. "If we are growing in virtue we shall not say what we should do in any particular case but say if the case comes I will do something then which I do not know now. The spirit will tell us in that hour." [6]

His freshman students at times became innocently involved in the struggle within his divided self. Attempting to hear and obey the God-endowed "spirit," he wrestled with a perversely assertive nature even in the Greek recitation room. During such moments, which became increasingly frequent as the year progressed, students were the nominal targets of his pietistic zeal. However, they did not realize that his energies were actually retroflected. What prompted his dramatic exhortations was not so much *their* defective wills as the failure of his own to conform to a rigid sense of "duty," also peculiarly his own.

A decisive stage in the unfolding of his *egomachia* was reached during the summer of 1837. Then for the first time he felt his inward "enemy" weaken. But the disabling process was slow. Although the outcome now seemed certain if only he would not relax his concentration, the remaining strength of the "enemy" was still considerable in 1837. Not until the spring of 1838 was he prepared, in his own words, to go on "rejoicing to the close." [7]

But even then scars remained to remind him of the expense of victory. Recollections of his struggle would continue to haunt him long after the conflict had subsided.

Two of his poems were printed in the Salem *Observer* near the end of 1836. In different ways each reflected the self-created tensions he was living with, and each prefigured their resolution. The first, "The Autumn Leaf" (printed in October), was more explicit, if still somewhat guarded toward the underlying substratum of anxieties. In it, a "fair yet lifeless" red leaf, which seemed beautiful without actually being so, is gently plucked from its "parent vine," in whose "fond Embrace" it would otherwise have been held until torn away by the "rude wind." This maternally bound leaf—"Brief monitor of frail humanity!"—had already felt the withering "touch of autumn's hand." Its "glowing color" at once is recognized by the poet to be in reality the signature of death, and the leaf itself a "tablet" on which are mysteriously inscribed the poet's own "thoughts," which "now are gushing fresh." He feels as if his "soul"

> Had drunk a new life amid these lofty shades,
> And felt its being moved by sympathy
> With unseen power.

He now knows why "decay" has brought about "so fair a change," and why the leaf's "form" has been robed "in tints of beauty" exceeding those of its "vernal prime." Its death is marked by "gayest hues" because, as a "thing of outward sense," the leaf had been "born to live but on the eye." This is the intrinsic difference between it and the poet contemplating its "splendor": the leaf was *not* born "To light a hidden soul with brighter hues." In the poet's particular circumstances, by contrast, "decay Deals rudely with his outward life." "Gloomy clouds" hover menacingly around him to "obscure" the "glory" of his visible presence. But this ugly process of dissolution and derogation, so different from the leaf's brilliant transformation, has more than outward significance at the level of sense. Perhaps because his is a "humble heart," it also is the means of inner coherence and glorification, by which—"from out a world of change"—is simultaneously being shaped

A spirit into those eternal forms
Of Love, and Majesty, and Beauty, which
The all-holy eyes of God approve.[8]

In surface meaning and initial situation the poem resembles "A Withered Leaf—Seen on a Poet's Table," written a year before. But whereas the leaf in the earlier poem set off a series of innocent memories, lacking emotional focus and culminating in a curious flight heavenward, the "Autumn Leaf" related physical and spiritual beauty in an integral way, based not upon vague "thoughts" which were merely abstract ideas, but upon feelings, abstractions made vivid and "concrete." Moreover, verbal ambiguity added meaning which drew freely upon the mounting tensions within him, and combined allusion to the possessive mother, with exertions of "rude" and disabling pressures. The "hidden soul" which the poet is destined to "light" was as much Lydia Very's as his own, the illumination of the former being contingent upon the latter. Thus moral apprehensions were delineated in the "Autumn Leaf," distinguishing it from the earlier poem to which it was related.

The only poem he published during the winter of 1836–1837, "The Winter Bird," also had a counterpart in a poem of 1835, "The Snow-Bird." Unlike it, however, "The Winter Bird" was an attempt to exclude all but the actual confrontation of an experience. Required was a sensitive being whose mind was free to move backward and forward in time. Relying upon iambic-substituted anapestic meter and transparent rhymes, language as bleak as the winter countryside of the poem's setting, and a seemingly effortless mixture of reminiscence with present event, Very constructed a demonstrative poem with an emotional content near zero. The concluding couplet, though personally relevant, was not enough to redeem the poem from twelve meter-padded, rhyme-slanted lines which preceded it.

> Thou sing'st alone on the bare wintry bough,
> As if Spring with its leaves were around thee now;
> And its voice, that was heard in the laughing rill
> And the breeze as it whispered o'er meadow and hill,
> Still fell on thine ear, as it murmured along
> To join the sweet tide of thine own gushing song:
> Sing on—though its sweetness was lost on the blast,
> And the storm has not heeded thy song as it passed;
> Its music awoke, in a heart that was near,
> A thought whose remembrance 'twill ever hold dear—
> Though the brook may be frozen, though silent its voice
> And the gales through the meadows no longer rejoice,
> Yet I felt as my ear caught thy glad note of glee
> That my heart in life's winter might carol like thee.[9]

If stereotyped, unimaginative language proved an insupportable burden for such a short lyric, as a formal exercise—form alone sustaining the simple idea of rapport between man and bird—the poem was instructive. While not an especially significant exposure of Very's "life's winter," the "Winter Bird" was important in determining further developments in his poetic outlook. Quantitatively and qualitatively it foreshadowed the emergence of the Shakespearean sonnet as the means best suited for Very's characteristic expression in the poems of 1837 and thereafter. At the end of 1836, although convinced that art and character were mutually dependent, Very was still unsure of himself as an artist and a man. He was uncertain "whether man here below ought to ascend into that region where fictitious and real life become one to his perception, where the light shines but does not warm nor quicken, and . . . [might] lead to a general want of character." [10] Within four months, by April 1837, the indecision had begun to

pass. The province of the artist, however, was clarified before that
of the man. Several months still were to elapse before he felt his
inward "enemy" weaken.

In his first published sonnet (almost certainly not the first he
had written), crossed quatrains and iambic pentameter replaced
couplets and anapests ill-suited to meditative lyrics and delicate
shifts of emotion and meaning. The easy transitions from the
"Winter Bird" to the form and feeling of "To the Canary Bird"
were achieved through painful introspections and critical discernment in April 1837.

> I cannot hear thy voice with others' ears,
> Who make of thy lost liberty a gain;
> And in thy tale of blighted hopes and fears
> Feel not that every note is born with pain.
> Alas! that with thy music's gentle swell
> Past days of joy should through thy memory throng,
> And each to thee their words of sorrow tell,
> While ravished sense forgets thee in thy song.
> The heart that on the past and future feeds,
> And pours in human words its thoughts divine,
> Though at each birth the spirit inly bleeds,
> Its song may charm the listening ear like thine,
> And men with gilded cage and praise will try
> To make the bard like thee forget his native sky.[11]

Iambic meter, end-stopped lines, masculine rhythms and rhyme,
and a concluding Alexandrine possibly derived from Byron's
Spenserian stanzas, were adapted to reflection, explicit and
implicit analogies, and compassion. Simplicity and sincerity
indeed mustered an eloquence, as Goethe had observed they
would. Now, a year after promising to avoid the hazards of
deliberate and consecutive thinking, Very was beginning to
achieve an artistry which appeared effortless, unstudied, and inevitable. Not only had he finally wrought a measure of self-

confidence lacking in his earlier poems, but he had assumed full responsibility for his poetry by electing to remain faithful to his own "native sky."

The poet of the "Canary Bird," following his cultivated instincts, deliberately isolated himself from common opinion, and proceeded to expose the moral insensitivities surrounding him. He alone, in the poem, is not given pleasure by the beautiful song of the captive; he alone realizes that the canary sings because of sorrow at its "lost liberty." While the outward senses of others are ravished, Very is saddened by the frustration and anguish revealed by the song. He knows, as they could not since they ignored the inner perceptions of the "heart," that the poet's own song originates in such struggles of the spirit for freedom and "tranquility." His song also charms an audience which mistakes the nature and sources of the expressed emotions. This audience tries to domesticate the poet, as it had the canary, but he resists this attack and elects instead his own true element, preserving his integrity at risk of being cut off from the world which long had nurtured him. "Our land of freedom," he had said in his oration on "Individuality," is the "land of thought," and it must be defended as the "dearest birthright of the soul."[12] Just as freedom's poetic form was being achieved for the first time in "To the Canary Bird," so too was a valid intelligence being consummated in one of his poems for the first time. Poet and imprisoned bird each illuminated the other's deepest sorrows. The song of the "Winter Bird" had taken its place among the phenomena of nature without affecting the poet in any integral way; that of the canary was more strongly motivated (being the product of inner conflict), and belonged to the precincts of the spirit, where the poet sought to install himself. Therefore, while one poem expressed the wish that the poet might rise above "life's winter," the other attempted it. Both poems spoke of the poet's song as coming from the "heart"; however, "thoughts divine"—which alone justify the existence of the "true poet" who feels within himself the "living standard of the great and beautiful," and who "bows" only to that "standard"—emerge from the soul which "inly bleeds." Very had written in 1836 that before the "secret depths of our hearts" can be stirred, "writers must have penetrated deeply into their own." [13] In "To the Canary Bird" he showed he was becoming increasingly convinced that as a poet he needed no stimulus more than the compelling urge to dissect his own sensibilities.

In his capacity as a man rather than as a poet, Very in the autumn of 1835 had identified publicly one of the conflicts which prevented his inner "tranquility" from being realized. To the consternation of some of his friends in whom he customarily confided, and to the amusement of others less kindly disposed than they, he declared his intention not to indulge his strong feelings for "women" any longer. Attendant upon his *change of heart,* but before his decision to forego reliance upon conscious operations of mind, he dramatically designated this quixotic pledge—requiring that he neither speak to women nor even look at them—his "sacrifice of Beauty." [14] This solemnly announced monastic rule quickly became public knowledge in the Harvard Yard, giving rise to rumors and often to unkind jokes about the extent of his austerity and self-denial. Truth was, however, that such asceticism as he practiced led him to find indirect means for releasing his energies; first in studies which kept him near the head of his class during a period of mounting strain; then in a notable career as a teacher during which he established intimate relationships with young men seven or eight years his junior; and later as a writer of short but brilliant poems which impressed many of the sensitive men and women of his generation.

Occasionally, as in "The Tree," one of his earliest sonnets (written a few days after "To the Canary Bird"), overtly sexual overtones blended with innocent sentiments to distinguish a poem otherwise no more remarkable then similar ones he had already written. In it, without trace of embarrassment at the possibility his intentions might be misconstrued or considered absurd, he straightforwardly confessed his "love" for the tree, beginning at the time "thy swelling buds appear." When later it was covered with luxuriantly "darker growth," he admitted,

I love to lie beneath thy waving skreen
With limbs by summer's heat and toil opprest;
And when the autumn winds have stript thee bare,
And round thee lies the smooth untrodden snow,
When nought is thine that made thee once so fair,
I love to watch thy shadowy forms below,
And through thy leafless arms to look above
On stars that brighter beam when most we need their love.[15]

More often, however, incidental to the increasing refinement of his art, his "sacrifice of Beauty" took less conspicuous form and had less obvious and less superficial consequences, charging poems with passions which gave them a vitality usually absent from earlier ones.

The emotional effects of three years of self-division and fractional self-hatred, and the attitudes he brought to Harvard at the commencement of the 1837–1838 academic year, can best be understood from an unusual experience he had in August 1837. After a "very pleasant tho' warm" four-hour walk from Salem to Cambridge, he had joined several friends, and early the next morning set out with them on a two-week journey into New Hampshire. During the train ride from Boston to Lowell he was suddenly overcome by terror—terror brought on by the realization of how rapidly he was moving through the countryside. (His account of the incident does not indicate whether this was the first time he had taken the "cars.") The unexpected fear just as suddenly yielded, as soon as it occurred to him that at every moment he stood "amid movements far more worthy of alarm yet with perfect safety": he was, he knew, in the "care" of the God who gave him life. Simultaneously he was struck by a "sense of man's power and gifts," and he "felt how sublime were the workings of that mind" which could transport him on "winged flight with such fearful accuracy." [16]

Through spontaneous insight (or so it seemed) into the moral realities concealed by "facts" and the appearances of things, he recognized the invincibility of the "power and gifts" of man when complemented by God's grace, a combination before which even the resistance of time and space in nature had to give way. In his imagination he no longer was aboard a Boston and Maine train and holiday-bound; he was being borne along by a divine engine and undertaking his life-journey. The rest of his vacation travels, consequently, including the inevitable climb to the summit of "The Grand Monadnock" and the leisurely tour through the White Mountains, were anticlimactic. "As we look even on the most magnificent objects of sense," he wrote in another context, "they seem to have lost some of their grandeur from the state of our mind having become more spiritual." [17] Therefore the epiphany gave him much to think about after his return to Salem on August eighteenth. He said that during the trip he had "pass[ed] on for a while as without time." [18] He not only enjoyed the sensation but was spiritually purged by it, and was encouraged to continue an unrelenting attack upon his real but nameless "enemy." Harvard's ceremonial Unitarianism could never have promised or accomplished so much for him, and so quickly.

The prospect of successful self-conquest also encouraged a new undertaking. For many years, ever since his visit at the age of nine to Helsingor while voyaging with his father, he had fostered more than impersonal curiosity about the man Shakespeare and the hero Hamlet. He had not forgotten that shortly before the death of Captain Very he had actually walked the parapet on which Hamlet was said to have seen the ghost of his father. The unusual circumstances associated with his introduction to Shakespeare had impressed the boy. When he was old enough to gain some insight into himself, they made him vaguely aware that in several ways his own life was related to that of Hamlet. He eventually came to believe that his own emotional predicament (including reconciliation with a beloved father and disentanglement of ambivalent feelings toward a disloyal mother) might be illuminated through Shakespeare.

While working in the Salem auction room following Captain Very's death, he had often thought about Shakespeare and Hamlet. These thoughts were further stimulated by discussions with his early teachers, J. Fox Worcester and Henry K. Oliver, and later with Professor Channing. Moreover, in recent years he had frequently reread the plays, especially his cherished *Hamlet,* and in heightened language he had often spoken to freshman students about Shakespeare. He had familiarized himself too with contemporary criticism, especially that of the new German school, through his reading of the Schlegels, Mme. de Staël, Goethe, Coleridge, and Carlyle. By 1837, therefore, when he was twenty-four years old, his unusually intimate preoccupation with Shakespeare had lasted some fifteen years.

Whatever its psychological and emotional basis, this interest until 1837 lacked any avowed purpose. He had made only passing mention of Shakespeare and Hamlet in his self-revealing undergraduate essays. However, in September 1837, at a time when personal tensions seemed to be nearing a climax, his extended concern with Shakespeare and Hamlet was growing more incisive, and was occupying his thoughts more conspicuously. The remarkable confidence accompanying anticipations of a favorable outcome to his moral struggles led him to believe he could explain the sources of Shakespeare's genius and penetrate the mysteries of Hamlet's troubled spirit. In fact, he was rapidly moving toward the conclusion that by his own life he had consummated a "perfect [spiritual] union and relationship" with Shakespeare. This sacramental penetration into his works would enable him to "really see the same heaven and the same earth" Shakespeare had seen.[19]

Once this extravagant transaction was completed he would be able to speak authoritatively of Shakespeare's motives and intentions, and expose the dynamics of his mind and art merely by looking within himself. Thereby he thought he would be able to discover what was at the heart of Hamlet's mystery. Actually, without realizing it, Very was planning a brilliant tour de force. He would impute to Shakespeare many of his own ideas, ideas he had already worked out in preliminary form in earlier essays and in unrecorded probings of his own mind and personality. This imputation would enable him to discover that Hamlet had shared many of his own feelings and thoughts.

Accordingly, upon his return to Cambridge after the self-illuminating trip to the White Mountains, his most urgent concern was not with Greek classes, or with the Divinity School, or even with his extramural studies in the modern German mode. Instead, on September fourth, coincident with his plan for exorcizing his demonic self, he withdrew from the College library William Hazlitt's *Characters of Shakespeare's Plays* and William Richardson's *Essays on Shakespeare;* on September seventh, an edition of *Hamlet;* on September seventeenth Nathan Drake's convenient anthology of modern Shakespeare criticism and Lamb's *Shakespeare;* and in succeeding months he read an *Essay on Falstaff* by Morgamor, an unidentified book *Concerning Shakespeare,* and a volume from Edmund Malone's edition of Shakespeare's *Works.*[20] These were all indications of the new tactic by which he planned to overwhelm the powerful forces working for the destruction of his God-serving instincts. His researches were compulsive, more symptomatic than substantial, and thus had little bearing on his attitude toward his subject. He was nearing the point of communion with Shakespeare when he need only recall his own inward experiences and relate them to the plays in order to account for the genius of the great dramatist.

Before he could complete his studies of Shakespeare, his most recent spiritual adventures and the confidence they brought left their marks on his poetry. Some nine months after his imagination had transformed the harsh cynicism of Lydia Very into the fragile virtues of a fantasy-mother who could be loved without guilt and shame, he composed a companion-piece to "My Mother's Voice," entitled "The Voice of God." In this poem, written in November 1837, Very directly confronted his recollections of childhood, and more accurately depicted the tone and beliefs prevailing in his Salem home. In his "infancy," he wrote, he had been taught a sardonic doctrine, one which masked total disbelief by contemptuous references to Deity. The "Voice of God," he was told in derision, was an "angry voice," sounding only when thunder's terrifying crash could be heard. The callous explanation, involving a man-hating Power which was "Throned Monarch o'er a guilty world" and exercised authority by hurling "bolts of ruin," had saddened and frightened him. But much later, once he read "words of love" and heard utterances from the "sweet lips of nature," he learned a "holier creed" than the mocking one he was taught as a child. What he had been directed to avoid and fear was actually "my Father's voice," which filled the "wide-spread earth" as well as "heaven." As a man intellectually free of former errors—but, at the time he wrote the poem, not realizing how much he still was emotionally tied to the past—he now knows that

> In all that stirs the human breast,
> That wakes to mirth or draws the tear,
> In passion's storm or soul's calm rest
> Alike the voice of God I hear.

Only for those who remain "heedless" of God's true Voice and Will does He sound in "thunder's pealing wrath,"

> Winging the wanderer's feet with fear
> To fly destruction's flaming path.

However, since by choice he at least is neither "heedless" nor a "wanderer" from true belief, "God dwells no more afar from me." His "Father" has an existence verifiable by perceptions which are not restricted to the findings of physical senses or to the superficial sort of rationality dependent upon them.[21]

The qualities Very missed in his mother, Christian faith and prescience, mildness, self-composure, and a hopeful, trusting spirit, unexpectedly appeared at the end of 1837, embodied in a poem about an anemone. Called "The Wind-Flower," it was his first sonnet to fuse characteristics found later in his most success-ful poems. Deceptively simple in conception and movement, it patently was an act of sincerity, but one which avoided shallow prattle as well as disconcerting confessions of a more intimate sort. Unabashedly moral and pious without becoming tedious, it employed flat and somewhat familiar language, kept from seem-ing prosy or trite by cultivated archaisms and sudden turns of delicate phrase and feeling. It was composed seemingly without the intrusion of deliberative thinking or conscious prosodic exper-iments and devices. What made this cluster of qualities and characteristics all the more significant is that they were joined in the first of Very's poems in which Jesus appeared. The presence of the Son in "The Wind-Flower," even if on the poem's pe-riphery, foreshadowed an important direction many of his sonnets would take within a year.

> Thou lookest up with meek confiding eye
> Upon the clouded smile of April's face,
> Unharmed though Winter stands uncertain by
> Eyeing with jealous glance each opening grace.
> Thou trustest wisely! in thy faith arrayed
> More glorious thou than Israel's wisest King;
> Such faith was his whom men to death betrayed
> As thine who hearest the timid voice of Spring
> While other flowers still hide them from her call
> Along the river's brink and meadow bare;
> Thee will I seek beside the stony wall,
> And in thy trust with childlike heart would share,

O'erjoyed that in thy early leaves I find
A lesson taught by him who loved all human kind.[22]

The "lesson," simple as it was, was nevertheless one Lydia Very refused to learn, or was having difficulty learning. In spite of her son's inspired efforts to instruct her, she persisted in her peculiar ways and heterodox opinions. Her aggressiveness, her vehement loves and hates, her disregard for the normal conventions of society, her conviction that a vicious Providence had singled out her family and herself for undeserved misfortunes, her "coarse materialism," and her long-standing "war with the world for Atheism's sake," was an impressive array of perversities. They seemed immune to all the spontaneous arguments, emotional pleas and urgent prayers, and threats of impending spiritual doom her agonized son could muster.

At a time when her hardheartedness seemed unbearable, and Very's turbulent mind sought relief in contemplating the progress of his "sacrifice of Beauty," the result was a sonnet. Printed in the Salem *Observer* one week after "The Wind-Flower" and entitled simply "Beauty," it represented a symbolic encounter with the succubus he was trying to remove from consciousness. Startling even on its literal level, the experience was further heightened by what purported to be a total surrender of intellect, apparently a reference to the effect (whether actual or imaginary is not clear) of repressing rationality in the interest of God-given reason. Even if an invention, the pretense of will-lessness was enough to enhance his poetic awareness. At the age of twenty-four, after five years of study, writing, and struggle with discordant feelings, such maturity as he was to know as a poet was upon him. The emotional, intellectual, and artistic uncertainties of his earlier life and poetry had finally been overcome by an energy and patience scarcely discernible from genius.

In "Beauty" experience was engaged and committed to poetry with assurance, sensitivity, and skill. He did not make explicit the natural characteristics of the beauty he was describing, but dealt with it in an allusive way. Only his responses are depicted. He is himself more fully realized than his supposed subject. Who or what initiated the series of images comprising the poem is unspecified, although the impression deliberately left is that he is celebrating his love for a woman, one who either had died or else was no longer available to him. The poem's point of departure may not have been a particular woman at all, but women in general or the idea of woman (both of which he had renounced in accordance with his "sacrifice of Beauty")—which of course would include the physical presence of Lydia Very.

The poem's form is that of the English sonnet, except that the thematic division into octave and sestet was borrowed from the Italian. This was the modification (without the concluding Alexandrine) he had used so successfully in "To the Canary Bird." In "Beauty," however, it sustained the release of frustrations which were oppressing him.

> I gazed upon thy face,—and beating life
> Once stilled its sleepless pulses in my breast,
> And every thought whose being was a strife
> Each in its silent chamber sank to rest;
> I was not, save it were a thought of thee,
> The world was but a spot where thou hadst trod,
> From every star thy glance seemed fixed on me,
> Almost I loved thee better than my God.
> And still I gaze—but 'tis a holier thought
> Than that in which my spirit lived before,
> Each star a purer ray of love has caught,
> Earth wears a lovelier robe than then it wore,
> And every lamp that burns around thy shrine
> Is fed with fire whose fountain is Divine.[23]

While Very had given himself totally to Beauty—once physically, then spiritually—his relinquishment of his sensible intellect modified all subsequent emotions and sensations involving the original experience. The impact of Beauty was so overwhelming that, so far as the poem is concerned, the poet subsequently had no real existence, his life no real meaning, except what was allowed him by his encounter with Beauty. She had gained so terrifying a hold upon him that she threatened to displace his fundamental pieties: "Almost I loved thee better than my God." From this self-immolation evolved a heterodoxical adoration, a love more sacred than profane, more appropriate to worship of Mary than to any worldly feminine or maternal principle:

> And every lamp that burns around thy shrine
> Is fed with fire whose fountain is divine.

Thoughts had become lamps, strife had become flame, and the silent chamber of the heart a reliquary.

Most of the important themes and ideas discovered during Very's extra-Harvard studies from 1833 to 1836 converged in this sonnet. From Mackintosh and Butler derives the moral principle underlying reflection; from Monboddo, the anti-sensationalist idea of the mind freed from physical dependence; from Paley, the realtion of nature (here prefigured as Beauty) to God; from Channing, the moral greatness made possible by sacrifice, and fulfilled by dedication and love of God; from Byron, spiritual redemption achieved in the present through an intense awareness of natural beauty; from Coleridge, the effect of a transforming imagination free to work upon reality in order to evoke a sense of reality in others; from Lieber, the spiritual efficacy of natural phenomena; from Wordsworth, the lasting peace brought by moral sentiments; and from Emerson, the use of outward existence for an inward confrontation between God and oneself.

But the sonnet is more than a recapitulation of Very's apprenticeship. It is more than a symbol of his achieving maturity. It is a poem valuable in itself, one marked by the excitement which accompanies swift self-realization. In it experience was finally engaged and committed in a form which allowed Very to speak with conviction and skill. Once the profundity of the emotions giving rise to the poem is acknowledged, it follows that in form and content "Beauty" looks forward to most of the poems upon which Very's reputation as a poet is to be based. With "Beauty" his quest for poetry was finally concluded, opening up for him a two-year period of remarkable creativity, whose impetus sustained him as a poet for several additional years, until the beginning of extended intellectual and emotional decline in 1841.

The poems of 1837 support his contention that the character and art of the artist are inseparably fused. As he himself gained confidence in his ability to overcome the threats to his spiritual well-being, and to overcome them soon, his poems and sonnets were finding the form and sense which would carry them close to greatness. His life and his work replenished each other, bringing both to what shortly would become memorable levels of intensity and drama. During 1838 and 1839 his activities as a man and a poet earned for him a distinctive place in the literary and cultural world of New England, where for a time he contributed to its intellectual and emotional excitements. Although he intended only to prepare for the salvation of his soul preliminary to effecting the salvation of his mother's, without realizing it he was accomplishing something more, perhaps something more important. He was equipping himself for participation as an equal in a brilliant circle of men and women who were trying in their various ways to save American society from itself.

# *Befriended*

## 1837–1838

S u s a n  B u r l e y  was Salem's most prominent bluestocking.
An ageless spinster and indefatigable leader of the town's fashion-
ably intellectual society, she was completely devoted to Salem's
cultural life. Reputed to be its "cleverest hostess," she had the
knack of discovering talent even among the town's most solitary
men and women, and introducing them to the circle of more
gregarious friends who regularly attended her Saturday evening
receptions. Around the quaintly carved fireplace in her drawing
room gathered individuals who enjoyed books and informed talk.
At informal "readings" conducted in her home, this "highly
educated woman" who corresponded with Emerson often entertained her friends with "free" translations from the German. A
kindly woman too, her "wise counsel" and "clear insight" were
frequently at the disposal of intimates. Whatever sympathy,
encouragement, and patronage they needed, she gladly
dispensed.[1]

It would have been impossible for Jones Very to escape notice
by this "wonderfully wise lady" and her circle of friends, even

had he wished to. His distinguished record as an undergraduate, his reputation as a serious but atypical Divinity School student, his success as Harvard's Tutor in Greek, his local renown as a poet with more than thirty poems printed in the Salem *Observer* since 1833, and the enthusiastic reports brought back by young men of the town enrolled at Harvard could not long be ignored by Miss Burley. Very was giving Salem reason to be proud, and this was sufficient grounds for her interest in him. Moreover, he now desired such favor and company as she afforded. The prospect of complete self-conquest led him to seek additional opportunities for exercising newly won confidence in himself. His expanding emotional and intellectual capabilities made an enlarged field of activity essential for his further development as a man and a poet. A sense of some special mission, still undefined, was unfolding. He knew he needed a public platform or an equivalent by which to make personal contact with an audience larger than that provided by Harvard freshman classes and the student following he had already cultivated.

The only obstacle to his admission into the genteel world guarded by Miss Burley had been Lydia Very's willful rejection of the Christian community. Her eccentricities and godlessness were not forgotten or forgiven by the good people of Salem. However, when her son, contrary to her widely known beliefs and disbeliefs, joined Salem's North Church in 1836, he seemed to be publicly repudiating the sins of a notorious mother, and he thereby overcame whatever moral and social objections remained to his inclusion in the polite world of Miss Burley. He welcomed her advances and accepted her invitation to join her friends in evenings devoted to literate talk. Under her auspices arrangements were concluded with the Board of Managers of the Salem Lyceum for Very to participate as eighth speaker in the 1837–1838 lecture series.[2]

One of Susan Burley's closest friends had recently returned to Salem after an absence of several years. Elizabeth Palmer

Peabody had been away in Boston where she assisted Bronson Alcott with his Temple School experiment in educating young children. When she learned that a Salem neighbor whom she had never met was scheduled to lecture on epic poetry during the last week of December, her curiosity was aroused—as much by Miss Burley's account of the lecturer as by his subject.[3] However, she was not (she thought) moved by the possibility of uncovering another candidate for her gallery of promising young men. She was still too much involved emotionally with the consequences of Nathaniel Hawthorne's first visit to the Peabody home six weeks earlier. Nevertheless she looked forward to the evening of December 27, 1837.

Accompanied by her father, Elizabeth Peabody arrived early at the boxlike classical building which was the Lyceum Hall. She saw the speaker standing alone on the platform, awkwardly staring ahead into the rows of as yet unfilled seats. He presented a tall, lean figure. His high forehead was partly concealed by long, straight hair combed forward and to the side. His eyes were dark and glistening; his mouth small, with thin, tightly pressed lips. High cheekbones and a square, firm chin were covered by taut, sallow flesh, making his face seem pinched and mask-like. His appearance was striking rather than handsome, severe rather than friendly. Above him, making a sharp contrast, spread a graceful mural depicting Apollo ushering in the morn. Elizabeth Peabody took a front seat and stared at Very's gaunt, expressionless face. She was puzzled. Even before he began to speak she became increasingly aware of the distance separating him from the semi-circular tier of auditors. He was a lonely person, she was sure, and he seemed uncomfortable amid his isolation.

After listening for more than an hour to the frail, raspy voice speak with surprising authority about Homer, Virgil, Dante, Milton, and Coleridge, she was not quite certain of her original resolve not to become entangled once again with a man in whom she detected some rare genius. At moments, as he spoke with

deep feeling about matters which apparently were most important to him, she thought she noticed a sweet but restrained smile
upon his face. His was a strange performance, combining
nervousness with confidence. She realized that the quality of his
voice betrayed his conviction that what he was saying was true;
yet she was aware of some intense emotional commitment which
went beyond the apparent themes of his lecture. In the manner as
well as in the content of his talk, she thought she detected a man
of sensitive intellect and feeling. Therefore, whatever her original
reservations before entering the Hall, a chronic, well-intentioned
impulse to ease the discomfort of others (real, or only imagined)
stirred her. She was a woman whose capacity for love, not merely
for kindness, was unlimited.

When the lecture was finished Very "stood for a moment—
uncertain, shy, and embarrassed." Elizabeth suddenly rose from
her seat and before she realized what she was saying, she had
asked him to go home with her. He grasped her outstretched
hand "like a drowning man a straw," and gratefully accepted the
invitation. As she walked home with him she expressed her
"delight" in the lecture and her desire "to hear his thought on all
the current subjects of the day, which were mainly the transcendental topics." She was pleased but not surprised to find "he was
an enthusiastic listener to Mr. Emerson," and he told her "he was
writing upon Shakespeare, who had, he thought, betrayed his
individual spiritual experience in Hamlet." From the beginning
Elizabeth was struck by the intensity of his conversation, especially later that evening when he explained his theory that Shakespeare's genius was imperfect because it was incomplete. *Hamlet,*
he told her, in spite of its abundant energy,

was the utterance of a man who had looked through all human
knowledge yet without being sure of the divine knowledge which
complements it—in order to give the mind peace—and the highest
power. He was the consciousness of Nature but not the full consciousness of *man, . . .* He was possessed by the Universe—perfectly—but

did not possess it. This was his difference from Christ. To the perfect impartiality of Shakespeare to whom all things were equally interesting because they existed, and who painted the fool and the villain with equal interest because they existed, *Christ* adds love of a morally discriminating yet spiritually redemptive character.[4]

Of devout but independent temperament—sufficiently independent to juxtapose Shakespeare and Christ—still Very did not impress Elizabeth Peabody that evening as being either "excited" or "mystical." Rather he seemed to be saying, in startling fashion she admitted, that "every Christian was bound to have, or *could* have, if he were sincere, this impartial appreciation of his fellow creatures." Both Shakespeare and Jesus were necessary for man's fulfillment and redemption. Neither genius alone, nor virtue alone, represent man's highest possibilities. The sensitivities of the poet and the saint must be reconciled: love of what *is* must be coupled with love of what *is good* if man is ever to overcome his sinfulness.

As soon as Very left the Peabody house Elizabeth wrote to Emerson about her unexpectedly refreshing experience. She "begged him to send for Mr. Very at once and make his personal acquaintance and have him lecture." The introduction of rare strangers to each other was her most extravagant indulgence, certainly her emotional fulfillment, and almost her career. At her recommendation Emerson proceeded with the necessary arrangements.[5]

The scope if not the direction of Very's life was affected by the consequences of his Salem lecture. Whenever time could be spared from Harvard duties he returned to Salem's Charter Street for visits with Elizabeth. Both wished to continue their discussion of the "transcendental topics." Very regularly told her of his progress with the "Shakespeare Essay" he had begun, and she in turn told him about friends she thought might interest him, William Ellery Channing (whose secretary she had been), Bronson Alcott, and of course Emerson.[6]

Since Very was not the only frequent caller at the Peabody house, it was inevitable that sooner or later he would meet Nathaniel Hawthorne. A day or two after Very's Lyceum appearance, Elizabeth brought together her two "new treasures." They took an immediate but tentatively reserved liking to each other. On the evening of January 3, 1838 the pair called at the Peabody house to escort Elizabeth to the Lyceum lecture. Sarah Freeman Clarke, who was then a houseguest at Charter Street, remembered many years later that Hawthorne, "shrouded in a cloak, Byronic and very handsome, looked gloomy, or perhaps only shy." Very's presence was overshadowed by that of his companion, but Sarah Clarke—briefed earlier by Elizabeth—already knew that he had written "remarkably spiritual" poems which "savored of Swedenborg." [7]

On Hawthorne's part, as might be expected, the friendship never reached intimacy. Very however was looking to him for more than a casual acquaintance. Although he once told Sophia Peabody how much he delighted in the *Twice-Told Tales,* it was not as author that he sought out Hawthorne.[8] He wanted to penetrate Hawthorne's polite exterior and touch the depths of his heart. In a moment of exasperation with Very's persistence, Hawthorne complained that Very "wants a brother," and a brother Hawthorne was to no man—as Herman Melville later learned to his sorrow. They met frequently, however, not only in the Peabody parlor but also in the more fashionable drawing rooms of Miss Burley and Mrs. Caleb Foote. Very also called at Hawthorne's home. Since he came without formal invitation, he scarcely endeared himself to the members of that privacy-loving household.[9]

While Hawthorne for the most part was treating Very with gentlemanly indulgence, his future wife was much more responsive and did not conceal her enthusiasm. Sophia Peabody became interested in Very as soon as he began to call upon her older sister. Since she had been unable to attend the "Epic Poetry" lecture because of her uncertain health, she waited expectantly for the May issue of the *Christian Examiner* which printed it.[10] An impressionable, pampered semi-invalid of artistic temperament and partial to the gossamer, dreamy side of Transcendentalism, Sophia Peabody soon was referring to Very as "our High Priest of Nature." [11]

But of all the members of the Burley-Peabody-Hawthorne circle, it was with Elizabeth Peabody herself that Very was closest. Once, during their frequent conversations about the "transcendental topics," he indicated interest in Emerson's remarks on "Great Men" and told her that he was already familiar with some of his lectures on biography. She promised to obtain copies from Emerson himself.[12] But she was uneasy. As she came to know Very better and learned the details of his "family history," of his early voyages with Captain Very, his "rapid fitting for college and remarkable career there," and that he was "in the habit of preaching" to his Greek classes,[13] she began to worry about his forthcoming meeting with Emerson. She knew from her own experience that Emerson was restrained and formal even with his closest friends. Friendship, for him, had an intellectual rather than personal basis. He was, he himself admitted, "cold at the surface" where persons touch, but tender at the core where ideas were generated.[14] Consequently she anticipated difficulties. Strangers, even "rare" ones, did not always endure Emersonian hospitality without some discomfort, particularly if they preached to him.

So eagerly did Very want close personal attachments that he tended to be insistent, even dogmatic in his talk, and therefore was a difficult companion. Completely open and artless in conversation, Very possessed a sincerity which led him to talk about himself and his work in most emphatic, seemingly grandiose terms. His sincerity, therefore, could be as exasperating as Emerson's aloofness. Very expected immediate, overt responses, unmistakable signs that what he was and what he was saying and doing were more than politely tolerated. Because his hortatory tone seemed to invite the charge that he had an exaggerated sense of his own importance, Elizabeth Peabody feared his confident egotism—even though not a self-distorting pose—might alienate Emerson before any intellectual basis for friendship could be disclosed.

Three months after his appearance at the Salem Lyceum, on April 4, 1838, Very descended upon Concord and delivered his Epic Poetry lecture at the Concord Lyceum.[15] On this occasion he met Emerson and took dinner with his family. (This was the usual reception for lecturers at Concord since Emerson was embarrassed by the small fee allowed by the town, ten dollars.) [16] Before and after the lecture they had leisure for talk. And, judging from Emerson's comments afterward, they spoke on Very's own terms: that is, about dramatic and epic poetry, about Elizabethans and Greeks, about Christian and pagan poetry, about the differences between romantic and classic modes, and of course about Shakespeare and Jesus. Very doubtless also told his host what he had already told Elizabeth Peabody—of his plans for discussing Shakespeare. He acknowledged "how difficult it was, by a moral and spiritual effort, to see with the impartiality of Shakespeare.—But Shakespeare's insight . . . was *natural,* not spiritual—." Shakespeare "did not realize personally that he saw with Him who sends his rain on just and unjust." The imperfections of Shakespaerean drama, Very said, were due to reliance upon "natural insight." Moreover, Very explained to Emerson that he was himself trying to acquire what Shakespeare lacked, the relationship with God which he called "Identification with Christ." He confessed that he was seeking to perform a "spiritual act" of his own, one which would allow him "to see what was in man," not merely as Shakespeare had done, but as Christ had done. And armed with this Christ-ian vision, which was a consequence of being "hidden in Christ," he would see the reality which was Shakespeare shining through the plays. Thereby the qualities of his genius and of its relationship with Hamlet would be revealed—in much the same way as God had been revealed to the ancient prophets.[17]

If Very's notebook entries at this time are any indication, Very must have told Emerson much more besides. He wrote:

We are too fond of directing that which we should only lend our hand to forward. . . . To abstain from one expense that our selfishness may flow broader and deeper in some other channel is a mark of no virtue. . . . Human actions are but sounds of different pitches, the strong and the weak heard at equal distance each concur[ring] in the same sublime harmony. . . . God is without form and length of days—A Spirit whose only manifestation is all form. . . . We too often apply to the *next* world for a remedy which was intended to be found in *this*. . . . We have but just begun to learn the sublime doctrines of our religion. . . . The passion for that which is extraordinary—both in men and events . . . is derived from the small degree to which the will is submitted to the soul's true impulses.[18]

Emerson understood enough of what Very told him to know he wanted "so remarkable an acquaintance" to return to Concord soon.[19] He was delighted at having received "true and high satisfaction" from both lecture and conversation. Near the end of their first meeting Emerson inscribed the copy of *Nature* which Very had purchased eighteen months earlier and had carried to Concord. "Har[mony] Of Man With Nature Must Be Reconciled With God" accurately summarized the import of their conversation, indicating the area of their agreement as it appeared to Emerson.[20]

The next morning he wrote to thank Elizabeth Peabody for her "sagacity" in detecting "such wise men as Mr. Very." His appreciation was not perfunctory. He "heartily" congratulated himself for "being as it were anew in such company." [21] Very had affected him in a strange way. How, precisely, he was not sure, but he felt radically different from having spent time with the energetic young man. Emerson's puzzlement may have been due to the mixture of the familiar and the strange in Very's distinctive ideas. Perhaps he was reluctant to admit to himself that he had glimpsed something of the *daimon* of the "Great Man" in Very. Perhaps he heard only echoes of his own thoughts transformed by a personality quite unlike his own. There was something vital and exciting about Very which made Emerson feel emotionally charged by his experience. To the gratification of Very's expectations and the relief of Elizabeth Peabody's fears, he made clear that he was looking forward to their future encounters.

Emerson had not long to wait before meeting him again. Very turned up unexpectedly at Concord a few days later with several Harvard friends and Professor Felton. Emerson judged the occasion notable enough to invite Henry Thoreau, Rockwood Hoar, and the local minister, Barzillai Frost, to join his unexpected guests.[22] While so large a company may have dulled the edge of Very's gift for unsettling use of the language of piety, Emerson once again was intrigued by what he said. He considered it "a curious commentary on society that the expression of a devout sentiment by any young man who lives in society strikes me with surprise and has all the air and effect of genius; as when Jones Very spoke of 'sin' and of 'love,' and so on."[23] His second visit, coming just three months before Emerson was to deliver his Address at the Divinity School, cheered Emerson as much as his first. That he had begun to "conceive hopes" for America at this time (less than two weeks after he had agreed to speak to the graduating class), was in part, Emerson admitted, due to the dramatic impact Very twice had made upon him.[24] To hear a Harvard divinity student sounding so unlike a student of Harvard divinity was reassuring. It was a hopeful sign, finding the moral sentiments of this enthusiastic nonconformist thriving in that center of higher conformity. Very's ability to live in "society" without being infected by what was worst and most characteristic of that "society" confirmed Emerson's decision to further stimulate the culture of such uncommon growths. Very thus unintentionally encouraged the rigorous attack upon effete Christianity Emerson was planning.

The search for spiritual vision which Very had discussed with him in connection with Shakespeare brought with it moral insight capable of penetrating the mysterious heart of things, and was not unlike the perpetual revelation central to the remarks Emerson finally delivered at Cambridge on July fifteenth. Although Emerson unwittingly had been at work on that Address for at least six years, ever since his resignation from Boston's Second Church in 1832, the sudden but welcome intrusion of Jones Very into his life at this juncture, not once but twice, spurred him to make the most of the opportunity awaiting him at the Divinity School. He could not fail to notice the way Very seemed to deliberately reject the Christian *mythus* fostered by historical Christianity: Very was seeking divine revelation and redemption within himself. Moreover, his intention to apply the inward resources of faith (by identifying himself with Christ and concealing himself in Christ) to an act of literary analysis and criticism, seemed to Emerson a legitimate extension of the spiritual independence he would urge in his Address. As Very explained it, and as Emerson understood it, the study of Shakespeare now in preparation was an act of the spirit rather than of the sense-preoccupied and rationalizing mind; thus he would be able to draw upon the energies of God available within him, in a manner as miraculous and natural as the acts of the historical Jesus. The timely presence of Jones Very in Concord in April 1838, consequently, provided further evidence for the rightness of what Emerson was intending to tell the young men entering the active Christian ministry.

These two visits to Concord were also important for Very—actually more important for him than for Emerson. Not only did they mark the beginning of a complex friendship which shortly came to have special significance for him, but the beginning too of an ambiguous association with the so-called Transcendentalists, that group of theological, social, and literary radicals who comprised the most conspicuous group of intellectuals in America.

Following publication the first week in May of "Epic Poetry" in the *Christian Examiner,* Emerson introduced Very to members of the Transcendental Club. In the middle of May Very attended his first meeting of this informal group, at the Medford home of Caleb Stetson. There he met Frederic Henry Hedge, George Ripley, Bronson Alcott, Theodore Parker, John Sullivan Dwight, and Cyrus Bartol. Since all had read or heard of Very's essay-lecture by then, there may have been preliminary discussion of his distinctions between epic and dramatic forms and of classic and romantic attitudes; but the meeting itself was devoted to other matters. The men discussed, in the conversational manner customary, the "question of Mysticism," and Very contributed his share of "wit and talent." While no detailed account has been preserved, it is known that remarks were made about the relationship between mysticism and Christianity. Since at least indirectly much that Very had been telling both Elizabeth Peabody and Emerson of his attempt to submerge himself in the spirit of Christ for his Shakespeare investigations was relevant to the discussion, it is likely he was an active participant.[25]

A timely notebook entry made sometime in May indicated the Pauline-Augustinian direction of his religious commitments, and suggests the position he adopted for the purposes of the discussion and the impact he must have made on the other participants:

As physical activity diminishes and mental activity increases, language ceases to address the senses for we no longer follow objects with the body but with the mind, and our terms are drawn from feeling or reflection and not from sensation or perception. . . . Were we true to our spiritual progress we should find that life was not the tame and unromantic scene it is too often felt to be, that there were battles still as severe in our daily path as any fought hand to hand, a hunger and thirst of the soul as real to endure as ever the body felt

and desert as wide and desolate to pass. But these are presented to the
soul which, sunk in the flesh, heeds them not as realities, and they
pass away and are forgotten while we throw ourselves back upon the
physical life . . . content with this life merely and with the selfish
pleasure of being free of all toil and endurance. This is the state of
mind from which we should continually pray to be aroused that our
bodies may be kept in subjection so that we may live purely as
spiritual beings.[26]

As the conversation spun out in Stetson's parlor, to himself if not
to those assembled Very recounted his own struggles with his
wayward "self," and his desire for more-than-natural insight into
human and non-human nature. During his undergraduate days
he had undergone a painful attempt to "justify" his soul, and had
subsequently undergone a *change of heart* which left him with
the conviction that "God is all," and therefore he "ought to have
no will" of his own. But what happiness he then found was
temporary, giving way to a sense of his own inadequacy, which
in turn led him into conflict with his still refractory nature.
However, he came to realize that the power of his inward
"enemy," his own selfish will, indeed was fading. Therefore he
was hopeful of the outcome and happy in the confidence that
through him God's will would someday be done.

This was his status, even as the meeting came to a close. Seven
months later, in spite of the group's discussion, Very insisted that
he "had no expectation" at that time of undergoing "any other
change" in his spiritual condition. Somewhat surprisingly for a
reader of Lady Stanhope and the *History of Enthusiasm*, he
added that he had "never . . . heard of any other." [27]

During the next two months Very continued to show the
effects of the attention paid him by Elizabeth Peabody. In June
1838 his was the first name on the subscription list circulated by
Charles Stearns Wheeler for the American edition of Carlyle's
*Critical and Miscellaneous Essays,* brought out under the auspices
of Emerson.[28] By July he had already gained the reputation for

being "one of those self-sustained individuals . . . remarkable for always speaking the truth and for believing in an Inward Voice." [29] At Professor Channing's house he had a long discussion with the elder Richard Henry Dana, famous for his lectures on Shakespeare. Dana thought Very "talked well and connectedly." He was especially impressed with his "remarkable mental intensity." Very seemed to him to be "all Love—God was a sort of atmosphere of Love which transfused itself through him and over all things." [30] By this time too it was generally known that he was one of those "fine young men who engaged in high debate" with Emerson.[31] His heterodox piety, his perceptiveness and talent for confident judgment, his candor and earnestness, all had been impressive, and were welcomed and encouraged by those of the Transcendental persuasion.

During this period near the end of his second year of Harvard teaching (June 1838), when his "enemy" was gradually yielding and he "went on rejoicing to the close," he felt as if he were going about all his engagements "without any interest in them" that was actually his own. This non-reflective performance of duty, born of love and self-denial, made him "very happy." He had "so long persevered in this course" that it "wrought out" for him "much peace and content." He was finding happiness through "simply trying to do and think good"—in accordance with his soul's "true impulses." He had, he believed, "nothing more to give up" which was distinctively his own. He had "given all" that was in his power to give, although he would not know this until several additional months passed. He "supposed that this state was to be made permanent by all the future relations of a life . . . not yet experienced." [32]

Family circumstances which had once made him almost desperate were being transformed in the process, the changes occurring within himself. He was relieving the guilt centering around his father's death and his anxiety about his mother's life by looking beyond the facts of pain to the truths which stretched out from them. In impersonal terms which were relevant to others besides himself, he described what was involved:

Why these separations of father from son, brother and sister, friend from friend, with which space and time are filled? Why loss upon loss, disease upon disease, decay upon decay? Was it merely that we might sigh for their loss or that a Love might be thence born embracing life, death, decay, in its arms? That we might be born again widening our love from that of an earthly parent to that of a spiritual one who is without form, whose love cannot but be universal for it is that of a Spirit. . . . There is ever a deeper question than how to cure our grief or trouble—it is why are we disturbed or sorrow at all? Why is it that Time and Space and Death have this dominion over us? Is it not that we are living with our friends in the flesh and not in the spirit? . . . It is in spirit alone we live, . . . with a life deeper than death.—It is the earthly buildings we cherish that causes our grief.[33]

Therefore, within a half year of his meeting with Elizabeth Peabody at the Salem Lyceum, Very was showing signs of having established himself on a new basis, and of having made contact with that intellectual and emotional world whose capital was neither Salem nor Cambridge. The life "not yet experienced" seemed hopeful and carefree. Beginning with his "sacrifice of Beauty" in 1835, he had managed to cut himself off from all the "earthly buildings" (including his mother's) that might cause him grief. He responded to his changed circumstances during the spring and summer of 1838 by writing six of his most beautiful sonnets.

These poems, written between April and August, all derive from the same experience, however much their apparent subjects and attitudes seem to differ. Each disclosed a constant state of mind, and was not intended primarily to celebrate the means by which that disclosure was made to the reader. Very's main concern was the experiencing self, not what is experienced. The ever-present "I" of the sonnets is the most important element.

The poems are essentially psychological, concerned with that level of experience to which Very referred when in his *Christian Examiner* version of "Epic Poetry" he spoke of the "mental struggles" preceding action which cause "outward actions" to lose their "grandeur." [34] These, then, are poems written from the advantage of the inward struggle seemingly concluded.

Only incidentally, and in a special sense, are they also love poems. The literal beauty of Nature is apparent throughout the period of conflict but dissolves as the conflict (with its accompanying sorrow and grief) passes. Time is the principle governing the world of that beauty, and is a destructive principle. But through the disease and decay of the material order—ministered to by Time, that "far-reaching idea"—comes an awareness of a moral order, where virtue succeeds beauty as the supreme quality. Love of what *is,* consequently, exists simultaneously with love of what *is good*—when natural forms are loved as embodiments of God's will.

Everything in the natural world, Very was convinced at the time he wrote these six sonnets, participates in the adumbration of God's existence. Just as the "I" continually shines through the sonnets, so the indwelling God continually shines through the natural landscape in which "I" moves. However, in several instances the insight possessed by Jones Very when he wrote the poems was deliberately withheld from "I." This "I" therefore is fictive, an "invention," not an autobiographical projection.

The love projected in "Thy Beauty Fades" is an organic growth. This bloom, which sprouts from the stalk of beauty, is a love unstable as the beauty bearing it. Both are subject to Time. The Lord of Impermanence is an inexorable god who brings forth life from death, only to breed death from life. The rain and sun are his agents, making growth possible, but thereby leading to disintegration. Cyclical decay then is Time's inflexible law, and the beauty and love regulated by it are not only futile but dangerous: the ugliness of decay is the disguised fact of beauty.

Ultimately the love for Nature's beauty is painful, for the lover's hopes are continually frustrated by the rhythm of Time. The marriage with beauty is futile, even if it could be consummated, because it cannot extricate her from Time's destructive grasp.

> Thy beauty fades and with it too my love,
> For 'twas the self-same stalk that bore its flower;
> Soft fell the rain, and breaking from above
> The sun looked out upon our nuptial hour;
> And I had thought forever by thy side
> With bursting buds of hope in youth to dwell,
> But one by one Time strewed thy petals wide,
> And every hope's wan look a grief can tell:
> For I had thoughtless lived beneath his sway,
> Who like a tyrant dealeth with us all,
> Crowning each rose, though rooted on decay,
> With charms that shall the spirit's love enthral,
> And for a season turn the soul's pure eyes
> From virtue's changeless bloom that time and death defies.[35]

Transient beauty, therefore, is the enemy of the soul, distracting it from its proper love, virtue. The *good* is the spiritual equivalent of the *beautiful* and is immune to the deadly claims of Time. Although renounced ("sacrificed," Very would have said in his expanded language of piety), the joys of natural love are not renounced with bitterness. The fading of beauty is a natural act, but also one of spiritual liberation for the lover, for it makes possible his permanent and fertile union with virtue. Gaiety therefore imbues the poem, justified by the implied vision of the sweeter but unspecified joys of virtue's bloom, that spiritual blossom which too is love, but less fragile and exempt from Time.

While the second poem, "The Columbine," begins at the point where the first leaves off, a shift in attitude has taken place. Although the limitations and dangers of the love of natural beauty were intellectually comprehended in "Thy Beauty Fades," the sacrifice of beauty has become only verbal through lack of

will to effect renunciation. The anticipated joys of the nuptial
hour are irresistible, even given knowledge they are "rooted on
decay":

> Still, still my eye will gaze long fixed on thee,
> Till I forget that I am called a man,
> And at thy side fast-rooted seem to be,
> And the breeze comes my cheek with thine to fan.
> Upon this craggy hill our life shall pass,
> A life of summer days and summer joys,
> Nodding our honey-bells mid pliant grass
> In which the bee half hid his time employs;
> And here we'll drink with thirsty pores the rain,
> And turn dew-sprinkled to the rising sun,
> And look when in the flaming west again
> His orb across the heaven its path has run;
> Here, left in darkness on the rocky steep,
> My weary eyes shall close like folding flowers in sleep.[36]

When read in conjunction with "Thy Beauty Fades," it is evident
that this poem depicts spiritual death, the loss of all sense of
distinctive humanity. Having been transformed into an amorphous natural fact by the failure of his human will, the lover is
not substantially different from any other natural fact. No feeling
of guilt and no awareness that the soul has been betrayed inform
the poem because the existence of the soul has been denied. The
summer rain and sun which had presided at the wedding of
beauty in the first poem reappear, but the "I" of the poem is now
*natural* man subject to Time, and his beloved now is the seduc-
tive columbine, not some formless abstraction. Her lover responds
automatically and naturally while lying beside her, finally losing
consciousness in sleep as darkness succeeds light. The wedding
night has been vicariously and innocently celebrated, all passion
spent, and the wide-open, gazing eyes of the opening line are
closing as the sonnet ends.

The third of the poems written shortly after Very's two meetings with Emerson is called simply "Nature." It explains and resolves the contradictory attitudes implicit in "Thy Beauty Fades" and "The Columbine." Here not beauty is loved, nor the beautiful columbine, but these and more: what *is* is loved, and what *is* finally is discovered by the open-eyed, gazing lover transported by the river of Time to be the mirrored locus of God. (In April Very had said that God was "A Spirit whose only manifestation is all form.") [37] The sky, which embraces all of Nature, when reflected in the ocean is seen no longer as the sky, but as heaven—as a spiritual rather than natural fact. As Very had predicted in the marginalia in his copy of *Nature,* "looking steadfastly at Nature or a scene in it" (p. 64), does indeed open up startling visions of God.

> Nature! my love for thee is deeper far
> Than strength of words though spirit-born can tell;
> For while I gaze they seem my soul to bar,
> That in thy widening streams would onward swell
> Bearing thy mirrored beauty on its breast,—
> Now, through thy lonely haunts unseen to glide,
> A motion that scarce knows itself from rest,
> With pictured flowers and branches on its tide;
> Then, by the noisy city's frowning wall,
> Whose armed heights within its waters gleam,
> To rush with answering voice to ocean's call,
> And mingle with the deep its swollen stream,
> Whose boundless bosom's calm alone can hold,
> That heaven of glory in thy skies unrolled. [38]

The river of Time—the force which animates Nature by its recurring rise and fall and expansion as it flows into the sea—now carries the lover's swelling soul, oppressed even by "spirit-born" words of renunciation. From "lonely haunts unseen," where flowers and trees are "pictured," down past the harsh reflection of the towering city of men, the lover's soul is swept along toward the glorious city of God.

The flow of Time through Nature had become the access to God, the current by which heaven finally was glimpsed. This explains why the "far deeper love" in the opening line is recalled near the end of the poem when the ocean's "deep," with the immense capacity for "calm" of its "boundless bosom," is reached. The soul no longer is barred, no longer obstructed by words as it formerly had been. The lover is at last on the verge of *realizing* the vision of God. (In a June notebook entry Very wrote: "Thou God seest me—hard to realize.") [39] This vision, the ultimate experience, occurs through Time-in-Nature. It is possible because all of Nature is the mirrored beauty of God, and all of Nature— even the ominous city of commerce, when reflected in the river—is loved.

A different transfiguration informs the fourth sonnet written during the spirng and summer of 1838. "The Song" begins at the same point as "Nature," with a complaint about the inadequacy of words. But the lover is not now confronting the all-inclusive Nature. He is overwhelmed by "crooked streams and fields" he sees before him. Significantly, they seem to originate from himself, as if he were the center of the natural world from which all phenomena derived. Not his soul but his words passively yield to this impulse, and they carry him down the river of Time once again. However, the river's flow is now reversed: he is carried away from the prospective vision of God, and to a vision of his own youth.

> When I would sing of crooked streams and fields,
> On, on from me they stretch too far and wide,
> And at their look my song all powerless yields,
> And down the river bears me with its tide;
> Amid the fields I am a child again,
> The spot that then I loved I love the more,
> My fingers drop the strangely-scrawling pen,
> And I remember nought but nature's lore;
> I plunge me in the river's cooling wave,

Or on the embroidered bank admiring lean,
Now some endangered insect life to save,
Now watch the pictured flowers and grasses green;
Forever playing where a boy I played,
By hill and grove, by field and stream delayed.[40]

The effect of his journey in Time is that, temporarily, his love once more became the instinctive love of the child, the love of what *is* without regard for what *is good*. His sense of the value of his own physical existence returns to him as he goes back in memory to the epical stage of his own development, when outward, unreflective action predominated, and he existed in the natural world of self-centered innocence where being is all. The child, like the columbine's lover, exists only as a natural fact. The poet, by dropping his "strangely-scrawling pen" and reliving his youth, actually recovers something of his lost innocence. The reverse journey in the river of Time therefore also serves a redemptive function.

The backward journey in "The Song" was initiated by the "look" of the "crooked streams and fields." This ability of Nature to look back at the gazer-lover supplied the conceit upon which the fifth sonnet is based. Very developed it in "To the Pure All Things Are Pure" to illustrate the inscription in his copy of *Nature*. Emerson had written: "Har[mony] of Man With Nature Must Be Reconciled With God." As indicated by the revised title assigned the sonnet by Very sometime after 1839, "Man in Harmony with Nature" is the specific theme. The harmony is dramatized by flowers seeing the lover, birds listening to his voice, and the brook leaping in joy at his approach. Indeed, all of Nature acknowledges his existence (just as God did, although it was difficult to *realize* that), responding to his unqualified acceptance of whatever *is*. The lover of Nature now has become beloved by Nature as well. However, what had been intended at first only as a conceit is transformed by the middle of the sonnet into a spiritual fact.

The flowers I pass have eyes that look at me,
The birds have ears that hear my spirit's voice,
And I am glad the leaping brook to see,
Because it does at my light step rejoice.
Come, brothers, all who tread the grassy hill,
Or wander thoughtless o'er the blooming fields,
Come, learn the sweet obedience of the will;
Then every sight and sound new pleasure yields.
Nature shall seem another house of thine,
When he who formed thee, bids it live and play,
And in thy rambles e'en the creeping vine
Shall keep with thee a jocund holiday,
And every plant, and bird, and insect, be
Thine own companion born for harmony.[41]

The poem presents the mature and knowing counterpart to the youthful dalliance depicted in "The Song." The innocent thoughtlessness which had made the earlier experience possible is here replaced by a deliberate mental act which must be learned, the "sweet obedience of the will." The resulting fantasia of companionship is therefore wrought by self-conquest. Successful conclusion of the inward "struggle of the will to control the springs of action" makes man's "Harmony with Nature" a reality. Once the identity of whatever *is* with what *is good* is recognized, once the moral basis of all existence is learned, man-forming God intervenes to make Nature appear to be "another house." This additional dwelling place for man's spirit serves the same function as his natural body. But since it is by God's will that Nature may "live and play," Nature is the medium through which man comes in contact with God's will and submits to it. Man thereby is "Reconciled With God." The only will man then can know is the will of God. All of man's actions subsequently are *good* because God wills them all, and man effortlessly carries them out. Instead of "directing" them in an assertive way, he "forwards" them by following the "true impulses" of his soul, and by gladly "lending his hand." No non-divine will therefore exists in the mind of the man reconciled with God, and such a man is man perfected.

The exaltation which is the donnée of "To the Pure All Things Are Pure" was not maintained in the last of the six sonnets written in the months immediately following Very's visits to Concord. "The Stranger's Gift" nevertheless complements that poem by showing the pain accompanying the "new pleasures" of harmony. The sonnet is retrospective, looking back to the time between childhood and maturity when the lover, still estranged from that Power bidding Nature "live and play," was among the company of those who "thoughtless" wander over the hills and fields of life.

> I found far culled from fragrant field and grove
> Each flower that makes our Spring a welcome guest,
> In one sweet bond of brotherhood inwove
> An osier band their leafy stalks compressed;
> A stranger's hand had made their bloom my own,
> And fresh their fragrance rested on the air;
> His gift was mine—but he who gave unknown,
> And my heart sorrowed though the flowers were fair:
> Now oft I grieve to meet them on the lawn,
> Scattered along the path I love to go,
> By One who on their petals paints the dawn,
> And gilt with sunset splendors bids them glow,
> For I ne'er asked 'who steeps them in perfume?'
> Nor anxious sought His love who crowns them all with bloom.[42]

The tangled mat of lovely spring flowers had originally saddened him because they seemed without meaning. He did not at the time suspect their significance: through them he might see spiritual facts represented. Saddened by his former ignorance of the complex relationship between himself, God, and Nature, he now suffers guilty anguish at his failure to have sooner recognized the need for knowledge of the unknown God, and for the love He freely expresses in natural phenomena.

The six sonnets seem vaguely "Emersonian." The ideas implied in them resemble some of Emerson's characteristic ideas, especially those prompting the marginalia in Very's copy of *Nature*. As Emerson presented it, Nature is both a material and spiritual reality, and has a transformative effect upon the man who recognizes and relies upon the oneness of himself and Nature. Moreover, Nature is seen as a dynamic process, and where man comes into contact with it, both are affected by its activity. Man learns, for the experience is instructive. But because the experience is also constructive, his *nature* and its *nature* are changed from a random multiplicity of perceptions and phenomena into an organized system, an organic unity in which is recognized the same divine principle animating both.

Very's refinements of such general ideas are his own. Unlike Emerson, he saw the divine principle working from a position opposite man's consciousness. Nature initially acts as a barrier separating man's will from God's as they confront each other. Therefore, only when man approaches and uses Nature properly, by obliterating his own distinctive personality and its associated will, is he able to bridge the distance between himself and God. Thus, by a purging of self in which Nature is instrumental, he actually converges with God, experiencing the same divine energy in himself which activates Nature and gives it spiritual significance. Nature has a redemptive effect, and man subsequently is no longer natural man, but Christ. Upon completion of "identification with Christ," God resides totally in the new-born Christ-ian man.

For Emerson, then, the resemblance between man and God is natural and instinctive; for Very, the identity (rather than resemblance) must be cultivated and induced by self-conscious desire. This desire, or "love," comes with knowledge of the spiritual possibilities of material Nature. The extended interval between mere knowledge and actual transfiguration—when God is still a "stranger"—is painful because redemption is yet an unfulfilled promise. Very "often" explained to Emerson that this intermediate stage occurred when the "soul" still is in its "travail." [43] But following the preparative torment a life of "revelation" awaits, in which God, embodied in man, will once again walk the earth. Only for such a regenerate man is self-reliance God-reliance.

The second visit to Concord, during which Very had spoken about "sin" as well as about "love," had made such qualifications clear to Emerson. Although he took Very as seriously as Very took himself, with playful inversion he simply told Mary Moody Emerson—his strong-minded, idiosyncratic, militantly Calvinist aunt—that Very "does not agree to my dogmatism." Emerson thought Very would "interest" her, as much as (for different reasons) Very interested him. He went on in his letter of September 1, 1838 to explain that Very "studies Shakespeare now and will presently finish and probably publish an Essay on S. and from a point of view quite novel and religious." [44]

## X

# The Rhetoric of Grace

SEVEN WEEKS after Emerson's assault upon the professions of the Divinity School faculty in his Address to their July 1838 graduates, Cambridge officials were still in disagreeable humor. Compounding their bitterness and discomfort was the conviction that Emerson was guilty of unpardonable acts of treachery and ingratitude as well as of discourtesy.[1] His Address had struck them as being a mixture of rudeness, folly, and atheism.[2] Instead of offering the "customary discourse"—which would have aimed at inspiring all without offending any—this prominent alumnus (they collectively felt) had used Harvard's Divinity Hall pulpit for an indictment of their own orthodoxy, accusing it of fostering static, formalized Christianity. In addition to the six graduating candidates for the ministry, more than a hundred invited guests (including many leading Unitarian ministers), heard him call for a "new Teacher," one who would be able to view the world as the "mirror of the soul." Emerson's alarming words were still reverberating and still causing uneasiness at Harvard in September 1838 as Jones Very began his third year of instructing freshmen.

Emerson's Address had been a declaration of independence for "man teaching," based on a conception of Jesus as the representative Man Teaching, who specifically taught the human potential for moral greatness through self-reliance. Jesus, Emerson said, was true to the "eternal revelation" in his heart. Since Jesus had truly understood that the moral law is found in man's own nature, and that the moral principle indwelling in man *is* God, he had further understood life to be a continuing revelation, the world a perpetual miracle, not only for himself but for everyone recognizing that "God incarnates himself in man." Stirred to hyperbolic rhetoric by the magnitude of this disclosure, Jesus proclaimed himself divine. He said God acted and spoke through him; moreover, wherever he is God is. Emerson explained the verbal ambiguity to a startled audience: Jesus meant that by virtue of the "divine and deifying" moral sentiment present in all men, a man was God to the extent he was "at heart just."

According to Emerson, subsequent generations had distorted Jesus' meaning by considering him exceptional, interpreting his figurative language literally, and organizing churches which exaggerated the uniqueness of his person at the expense of the merit and potential of all other men. Although Jesus was inspired and prophetic, he held no monopoly on inspiration and prophecy. These were the natural but forgotten attributes of man teaching, Emerson told the graduates. Each of them was a "newborn bard of the Holy Ghost," with a moral duty to himself and society to cast off all "conformity" to the traditions of "historical Christianity," and to teach as Jesus had done. Indeed, the "age of inspiration" was not past: the "gleams" even now flashing across the mind of every man loyal to his own moral intuitions are not his own but God's. Life is still a continuing revelation, and the world still a perpetual miracle—to all men sharing the convictions of Jesus.

Because of the "universal decay" of faith caused by the Cult and Myth of Christ, which in turn had been perpetrated by "historical

Christianity," the need for "new revelation" never was greater. Each of the graduates had to stand his individual ground against the formalists who were mistakenly dedicated to institutionalizing Jesus. Required now more than ever before was moral teaching based upon the present status of the soul, instead of recollected distortions of the past. Each had the responsibility to acquaint men with Deity, as manifested in his own self and in their own.[3]

Although the Address had been delivered on July fifteenth, the "storm in our washbowl" (as Emerson called it) [4] was still blowing briskly when Very resumed teaching in September. On August twenty-seventh the unofficial spokesman for Harvard orthodoxy had publicly replied. Religion "had been insulted" by Emerson, an embittered Andrews Norton wrote in the Boston *Daily Advertiser*. Norton was so infuriated by the "restless craving for notoriety and excitement" which keeps "our community in a perpetual stir" that he used his article to denounce all men obsessed with "missions," all who "announce themselves as the prophets and priests of a new future" and discern "transcendental truths by immediate vision." Such individuals, Norton said, suspend reason and reject all "modesty." In imitation of Carlyle they confuse their "over-excited and *convulsionary* style" of speaking with eloquence, and "shamefully" abuse the traditional language of religion in an attempt to disguise their atheism.[5]

Seemingly unperturbed by the commotion generated by his friend's Address, Very went about his work of calling the attention of freshmen to the beauties and mysteries of Greek—in his own distinctive manner, however. One of his new students was the impressionable sixteen-year-old Samuel Johnson, Jr., the pious son of a prominent Salem physician. A remarkably perceptive and conscientious young man, he graduated second in his class four years later, spent a year in Europe (accompanied by Jones Very's brother), returned to Harvard, became a leading liberal minister, and finally gained distinction as one of America's finest orientalists. But on September 6, 1838 he was still a dutiful son describing his first week of college to an anxious father. Contrary to expectations he found his instructors "remarkably agreeable." He was particularly impressed by the digressions of the Greek tutor: "Mr. Very's conversation in the recitation room turns wholly on religious and moral subjects, and he seems to labour hard for the good of his class." That some classmates were "rather impatient" with this extraordinary concern for the state of their souls puzzled him. But by the second week it was clear that whatever others thought of Jones Very, he was his favorite instructor, found attractive as much for his high moral tone as for his insistence upon high academic standards.[6]

To reassure his father of his own good sense and application to duty, young Johnson summarized certain "excellent instructions" given by Very which he had "attended carefully to." Jones Very

bases all these instructions on the submission of our will to that of God: to adapt everything to that: to act, to speak, to move only as it is conformable to his will: then, when we have arrived at the degree of excellence, we shall see God; we shall be able to form ideas of him suitable to his nature and attributes; one glance into the works of Creation will afford us more instruction than a life of intense study of Greek and Latin, of arts and sciences: We are not to consider our bodies as our own, Mr. Very tells us, but as given us by God to be subservient to our souls; that is to say, to the influence of the spirit of God in us; and this is manifested in the conscience, which is His voice speaking to us, when we are doing our own will: he knocks, and too often is refused admittance—: "he comes unto his own, and his own receives him not": Now this is to be revolutionized. Whatever we are called upon to do, we must consider if it is God or our own evil desires which call on us to act thus: Conscience will tell us in a moment: and we must act accordingly: then God will take up his abode in us, and we shall feel his presence, which we cannot immediately do in our present state: Study is not to be a mechanical performance, but a duty imposed on us by the will of God, to render us better and happier: thus we must always consider it, without regards to marks of merit or demerit.[7]

Quite confident of parental approval for Very's remarkable proposals for self-reform, Johnson promised to "adapt" himself to them "as far as possible."

Much of this, in spite of indirect transmission and Johnson's disjointed presentation, is familiar. Unspecified "evil desires," the moral incompatibility of human will and God's will, and the need for electing one rather than the other, recall the tone as well as the substance of earlier assertions by Very. Instead of a loose paraphrase Johnson closely reconstructed for his father a portion of what Very had actually told the class.

But Very's discourse is also familiar in another connection. It sounds surprisingly like a recast of Emerson's Address. While Very colored the "instructions" with his own non-Emersonian diction and qualifications, and interpreted and applied Emerson's remarks in a more literal and specific way than Emerson intended, the relationship is clear. This was Very's less formal equivalent of the declaration of independence for man teaching, delivered to freshman students instead of Divinity School graduates.

That it was undertaken as a deliberate imitation of Emerson's statement or as an artful demonstration of what a man might do were he to act in accordance with Emerson's recommendations, is unlikely. Nevertheless Very's remarks were based on the present status of his own soul, as Emerson had urged. Moreover, they were not grounded in the impersonal traditions of Harvard classrooms, but upon Very's own introspections and experience of life. In 1838 he had felt, he said, a "gradual increase of joy"—the result, he was certain, of having made his life "more and more regularly a sacrifice in all things."[8] He was compelled to speak accordingly. In effect if not design, what Very told his students was an analogue of Emerson's talk to the Divinity Hall audience, allowing for the different individuality and circumstances of the two men. In addition, Very sounded suspiciously like the "Teacher" Emerson said he awaited. His allusion to Emerson's claim that wherever comes a true man like Jesus, "there comes revolution" further related the "instructions" to the Address. In an unexpected way then, Emerson's words indeed were still re-echoing within the halls of Harvard early in September. The voice however was Jones Very's, and the shifts in emphasis his responsibility alone.

Although Very was unsparing of his time and energy in an effort to instill the "due appreciation of religious subjects" in his students, not all freshmen responded with Johnson's eagerness. The impatience of some gave way to cruel rumors. According to Johnson, Very had

gained the fame of being cracked (or crazy, if you are not acquainted with Harvard technicalities) among a set of thoughtless and ignorant young fellows, who make him a butt for their ridicule behind his back: I have been asked two or three times by young gentlemen from Salem, if Jones was not in a fair way to—but I will not use the expression, it is too ridiculous and offensive.[9]

Continuing loyalty to his teacher, in spite of the murmurs of classmates, was the measure of the self-reliance Johnson was learning. He was "much gratified" by Very's classroom discourses. From the beginning he had however recognized that Very's "language and terms" were

very peculiar, and many of the ideas he expressed were far different from any which were ever before presented to my mind: he carried his reasoning farther and deeper into the subjects on which he spoke, than that extent to which I have been accustomed to hear them urged: But observing in the general current of this stream of thought . . . nothing indeed which clashed openly with my previous ideas on the subject, I received the whole or the greater part as true religious instruction.[10]

Even more astonishing than the presence at Harvard of an Emersonian "man teaching"—as yet undetected by college authorities, even though Very attended the regularly scheduled meeting of Harvard faculty on September tenth—[11] was a psychological experience Very had a few days after the discourse reported by Johnson. According to Very's own account several months later, it was qualitatively different from the "gradual increase in joy" he had already felt for some time.

. . . I felt within me a new will, something which came some time in the week but I could not tell what day exactly. It seemed like my old will only it was to do good—it was not a feeling of my own but a sensible will that was not my own. Accompanying this was another feeling as it were, a consciousness which seemed to say—"That which creates you creates also that which you see or him to whom you speak," as it might be. These two consciousnesses, as I may call them, continued with me . . . and went as they came impercept[i]bly.[12]

A day or two after its onset the new and mercurial status of his soul had an outward manifestation so sublime that official Harvard could not long tolerate it. On Thursday September thirteenth Very realized he actually had completed the "identification with Christ" discussed with Elizabeth Peabody and Emerson earlier in 1838. It was an even more radical version of the "state" recently urged upon young Greek scholars.

Spurred by Emerson's Address and the gradual resolution of his own private dissatisfactions, he finally felt God's presence animating and abiding in him. He had taken Emerson at his word: he was now a "newborn bard of the Holy Ghost," having realized in himself—if only on a temporary basis since the impersonal consciousnesses came and went—the same incarnation of God that led Jesus to proclaim himself divine. But just as the Christian formalists whom Emerson reproached had understood Jesus' metaphorical declarations literally, so Very literally accepted Emerson's figurative explanation of the universal impli-

cations of Jesus' claim. Whenever visited by the two "consciousnesses" not his own, he was (Very said) "moved entirely by the
spirit within to declare to all that the coming of Christ was at
hand." [13] At first confused by this declaration, the Harvard tradi-
tionalists would be horrified once they grasped its significance. In
effect Very was promulgating a new Cult and Myth of Christ,
finding biblical sanction for Emerson's conception of Jesus and
attempting to give it a rigid form—which Emerson of course had
never intended.

While the "spirit" was in him Very was "moved" to undertake
a significant mission, his first invasion of an important stronghold
of Unitarian orthodoxy outside the classroom. On the evening of
the thirteenth he called upon Henry Ware, Jr. By this time Very
probably knew that the Professor of Pulpit Eloquence and
Pastoral Care (and sponsor of the group desiring "religious
improvement" which Very had joined in 1834), was working on
the first official reply to Emerson's Address. His sermon, entitled
"The Personality of the Deity," was scheduled for delivery at the
Divinity Hall Chapel in ten days.

When Very entered Ware's study unannounced, he ignored the
several students who were chatting with the Professor. His business was with Ware. George Moore, a divinity student, witnessed
the interview. His account recaptures something of the evening's
excitement:

After speaking of many passages of scripture and giving his interpretation of them, Mr. Ware objected to some of his interpretations. Mr.
V then asked him for the New Test[ament] saying he had had a
revelation of the XXIVth chapter of Matthew and would like to
explain it. He went on thro' it, giving a sort of spiritual
interp[r]etation throughout. To Mr. Ware's objections, he said he
was willing to yield, but the spirit would not let him—that this
revelation had been made to him, and that what he said was eternal
truth—that he had fully given up his own will, and now only did the

will of the Father—that it was the father who was speaking thro'
him. He thinks himself divinely inspired, and says that Christ's
second coming is in him.

While Emerson, without actually naming Ware, had by implica-
tion accused him with others of having perpetuated the intellectual error embodied in "historical Christianity," Very went
further. Since Ware "opposed some of his views," Very could
now specifically charge him with willful disobedience of God.
Affecting "great solemnity," he said to Ware: "I had thought you
did the will of the Father, and that I should receive some sympathy from you—but I now find that you are doing your own will,
and not the will of your father." [14]

Moore's account of the incident failed to mention that when
Ware refused to acknowledge the divine authority by which he
spoke, Very may have been frustrated enough to cry.[15] Tears may
also have been shed at the failure of his inspired testimony, with
the confirmation of the Bible, to convince Ware of the essential
rightness of Emerson's view *when properly interpreted*. But
Moore did mention that he later learned Very had been explaining this chapter of Matthew in the same way to a "great many"
persons, and his conduct in other respects recently had been
"singular." Even were he to disregard the rumors, from his own
observations at Ware's house Moore could only conclude that
Very was insane. As for Ware, a cautious man and long a friend
of Very, he "did not know" at this time "what to make of him." [16]

Since Samuel Johnson, Jr. was not an upperclassman or graduate
student, Very's most resolute partisan at Harvard was not present
for his confrontation with Ware, and therefore had no reason to
revise his admiration for him. The next morning, before going to
Greek class, and still not knowing what had taken place in
Ware's study, Johnson wrote home once again. With typical
enthusiasm he demonstrated his defiance of the thoughtless

campus gossips who were ridiculing his instructor. He told his father:

I consider no man in [the] College Faculty more sensible than Mr. Very, whose greatest fault is that he is too frank and open for much communication with the deceitful world. I will say no more here on his point, leaving to some time when I can truly tell you, that his teachings have brought me to some degree of advancement in this state of mind.[17]

Later in the day Johnson arrived at class and regretted his letter had already been posted. He was shocked when Very

used language so wild, and broached ideas so startling, that the truth could no longer be undiscovered: . . . his whole conduct was such as to indicate absence of reason: while the accounts given . . . by members of the other [freshman] divisions were yet more astonishing; it seemed that he had declared to them that he was infallible: that he was a man of heaven, and superior to all the world around him: I dare not mention other of the startling facts . . .[18]

What Johnson couldn't bring himself to relate was that Very—apparently disappointed in the results of his declaration of the "second coming"—had adopted an even more apocalyptic refrain. He cried out to one of his sections, in resounding tones so unlike his usual voice, "Flee to the mountains, for the end of all things is at hand."[19] With reminiscences of the Olivet discourse (Matt. 24:16), the "revolution" predicted by Emerson had been transformed by Very's swelling imagination and preference for dramatic exaggeration into a cataclysm of cosmic proportion.

Several hours later Very again encountered the "deceitful world." He delivered an unscheduled address to the startled members of the Divinity School debating club, expressing views similar to those announced to Dr. Ware and the Freshman Class. He told them they were all merely men, doing their own wills, while he was carrying out the will of God: "he was no longer a man, but the Holy Spirit was speaking in him, and . . . what he said was eternal truth." George Moore was again present, but was now less certain that madness was the only explanation for Very's behavior.

He appears to do very much as Geo[rge] Fox [the Quaker] is represented to have done, and to have very similar views. It is almost fearful to look upon him, and see his deep earnestness, exhibited in his face, and to hear the tremulous tones of voice as he utters himself —and at the same time to think that he is fully possessed with this great idea that the Spirit is revealing itself in him. I hardly know what to think of the man.[20]

If George Moore was perplexed and Samuel Johnson severely shaken by such events, at least one man at Harvard was infuriated. On the evening of the fourteenth, shortly after Very's performance at the debating club, the President of Harvard, Josiah Quincy, called upon Charles Stearns Wheeler at his dormitory room and hurriedly told him that Very had suffered a "nervous collapse." Without giving additional details, he asked him to relieve Very as Greek Tutor. Wheeler agreed. The next morning President Quincy informed the Freshman Class that "in consequence of the sudden illness of Mr. Very," Wheeler had agreed to assume the duties of Tutor. Since his memory of the disturbances associated with the "Dunkin Rebellion" of 1834 was still vivid, Quincy was cautious but firm. He told the freshmen that Wheeler was replacing Very "temporarily," and that he should be "respected accordingly." [21] The President, after all, did not know the extent to which Very had won the favor of students and had infected them with his dangerous principles.

Wheeler thought Very's return to Salem was the "sad end of his ambitions to move the world." [22] When George Moore learned that Very had left Harvard, he expressed the hope that his friend would soon return to his "very useful labors" at the College.[23] Young Sam Johnson, apparently too shocked to write a retraction to his adulatory letter of the previous morning, seems to have tried to comfort himself with silence. And Dr. Ware must have now been even more convinced of the evils of Emerson's recent discourse as he returned to his work-in-progress.

A reasoned counterpart to Norton's newspaper invective, Ware's sermon was directed against the "doctrine of the Divine Impersonality." By this Ware meant the idea that God exists only as an indistinct influence having no stable existence as a differentiated Being, and therefore is without personal attributes except as God might take form in man. This doctrine, Ware said, treats all high and pure human thought as if derived from God, having a divine authority which resides in its own "evident truth." All men of high and pure thought consequently, not Jesus alone, become revealers of divine truth.

Such a view, said Ware, not only deprives the Gospel of its "special divinity and authority," but is a "virtual denial of God." It "overthrow[s] worship and devotion," does injury to human happiness, relieves men of responsibilty for their actions, and "excludes the possibility of a revelation in any proper sense of the word." Contrary to the "doctrine of the Divine Impersonality," Ware explained, the laws and principles active in the world actually derive from a unique Being, separate from all other beings, and this Being is God, not man. Although no great numbers, comparatively speaking, "can be misled by the ingenuity of an imaginative mind" entertaining this false doctrine, he felt this did not justify its toleration. To the extent that it denies the Person of God, it alienates men from God and therefore must be resisted.[24]

Not only Emerson's Address but the behavior of Jones Very, seemingly inspired by it, must have been in Ware's mind as he wrote his sermon. For Emerson to claim that God was in all men did they but realize it was relatively innocent compared with Very's insistence he was Christ. However, Very's irresponsible conduct, touching even the young men studying at Cambridge, was seen by Ware to be the consequence of the "doctrine of the

Divine Impersonality." Very was an example of a man who not only entertained Emerson's "speculative rejection" of God, but was implementing it at the expense of his sanity. Moreover, his actions seemed to justify Norton's condemnation of the disruptive enthusiasm allegedly encouraged by men like Emerson. Norton's article had warned against the dangers of messianic obsession, irrationality and immoderation, the grotesquely inflated rhetoric profaning the language of religion, and the parody of Christianity which was only an excuse for atheism. His words seemed prophetic in the light of Very's spiritual adventures.

Twenty-three-year-old Washington Very, now a Harvard freshman after spending a number of years as a Salem schoolmaster, was summoned to take his brother home on September fifteenth. Before leaving Cambridge on that Saturday afternoon, Jones Very tried to obey the only two commands of the Spirit then outstanding. Although he was permitted to recover some papers left a few days earlier with Edward Tyrrel Channing, the Professor of Rhetoric, his desire to stop at Concord to speak with Emerson and deliver in person his newly completed manuscript was not respected.[25] Before he departed for Salem his brother did however allow him to send Emerson the long-promised essay on Shakespeare and an explanatory letter.

The letter raised more questions than it answered. In it he denied ultimate responsibility for the essay, explaining that instead of being the product of his own volition it related what the divine voice had told him about Shakespeare. His responsibility was limited to whatever distortions were introduced by his own consciousness during the actual writing. After he completed the essay the baffling interference of self, which prevented the document from being a wholly authentic revelation, had disappeared—at least long enough for him to deliver the unmuffled words of the Holy Spirit, first to students and faculty, and now to Emerson.

*Cambridge Sept—1838*

My Brother

I am glad at last to be able to transmit what has been told me of Shakespeare—tis the faint echo of that which speaks to you now. That was the utterance of the soul still in its travail but the hour is past of which I have often spoken to you and you hear not mine own words but the teachings of the Holy Spirit. Rejoice with me my brother and give thanks with me to the Father and our Lord Jesus Christ who have now taken me to themselves and will not let me go any more from them. I feel that the day *now* is when "the tabernackle of God is with men, and he will dwell with them, and they shall be his people." The gathering time has come and the harvest is now reaping from the wide plains of earth. Here, even here the will of the Father begins to be done as in heaven. My friend I tell you these things as they are told me and hope soon for a day or two of leisure perhaps in two or three weeks when I may speak with you face to face as I now write. . . .[26]

What impairs Very's acknowledgment of the common source of both essay and letter is that this account was not written while the Spirit was active. Rather, since he was able to distinguish between himself and "the Father and our Lord Jesus Christ," he was writing from recollection of the presence of the two volatile consciousnesses. Nevertheless, whether recalling the substance of the newly received "teachings" or quoting the Spirit directly, he could still manage to speak by his own lesser authority. But even then he spoke in tones so saturated with recent experiences of glorification that he seemed himself uncertain where his own words left off and those of the Spirit began. It was as if past and present had become one, and in turn had mingled with his anticipations of an endless bliss to come. Accordingly he affected a uniform diction which was more appropriate to the King James Version than to a brief note by the son of a Salem shipmaster. So rigorously was this vocabulary used that at the end of the letter a polite wish to be remembered to Emerson's family is almost cryptic: "Tell Mrs. Emerson that I have the love for her where-with the Father has loved me and kiss your son for me as my mail in hope to an unborn brother of the kingdom." Very's illumination thus transformed even the simplest sentiments into expressions of what he felt were momentous truths.

Emerson's initial reaction to the letter, and especially to its claim that man is the sanctuary in which God literally takes up residence, is not known. Although a familiar conception, indeed fundamental to his Divinity School Address, it must have seemed strange to Emerson that Very's restatement deliberately inter-wove Mosaic phrases (Exod. 25:8) with those of the Apostle Paul (II Cor. 6:16). It is likely he reacted in much the same puzzled way George Moore did under similar circumstances, and at first knew hardly what to think of the man or what to make of his message. Until he could study the essay on Shakespeare, Emerson suspended judgment on what he later called "the calamity of poor Very." [27]

# The Genius and the Saint

## SEPTEMBER 1838

IDEAS FIRST revealed in early undergraduate essays and orations were subsequently developed by Very in "Epic Poetry," in conversations with Elizabeth Peabody and Emerson, and in the series of related sonnets he wrote in the summer of 1838. Prior to their dramatic implementation at Harvard during the second week of September, these ideas had been further extended and clarified in "Shakespeare," an omnium-gatherum of his basic attitudes. Formally conceived as early as December 1837 when he had discussed his intentions with Elizabeth Peabody following his Salem Lyceum lecture, "Shakespeare" was completed during the first week in September 1838, left with Professor Channing, and then urgently dispatched to Emerson. This essay, whose roots go back to his childhood voyage to Denmark with his father, is a crucial document. To the extent that it explains and justifies his strange behavior at Cambridge it is both a spiritual autobiography and a blueprint for action. It is his most ambitious disclosure of principles, and of all his statements the longest and most difficult to unravel.

The essay is a monument to Very's radical egotism. It not only purports to account for Shakespeare's greatness and limitations but also for the failure of all readers and critics—except Very himself—to understand the man Shakespeare and the significance of his work. To accomplish this self-glorifying feat Very delivered a general explanation of human genius applicable to the philosopher, the man of action, and the poet. Because he was particularly interested in the last, the essay embodies ideas on poets and poetry—ideas which of course are relevant to his own poetic purposes and accomplishments. The essay however is not primarily devoted to literary matters. In it Very contrasted the man of genius (exemplified by Shakespeare) with the man of virtue (clearly Very himself, but figured as Christ), and concluded that the saintly man represented the highest development of human potentialities—especially when the saintly man was, like himself, also a poet. These circumstances allowed him to adopt a moralistic position from which he issued a general indictment of the contemporary American personality and society. Accompanying this critique were directions for individual and (to a lesser extent) social reform based upon man's reconciliation with God, a reconciliation patterned after Very's own aspiration and experience.

What makes "Shakespeare" both impressive and difficult is that even though Very's multiple intentions were closely bound to each other and the interrelated themes all derived an emotional consistency from his consideration of Shakespeare, the essay lacks conventional structure and development. Its structural principle is harmonic rather than logical: the various thematic lines, personal and impersonal, are strung out simultaneously, and consequently mix and cross in non-consecutive fashion. The essay seems an act of orchestrated spontaneity which at times almost lapses into incomprehensibility in spite of the recurrence of phrase and idea. But since Shakespeare provided the nominal center from which everything else in the essay radiated, Very returned to him for each of his non-sequential excursions.

Notwithstanding the discontinuities and iterations, to which he seemed to allude in the accompanying letter to Emerson, he felt the essay was successful. By way of explanation for its rhythmic orientation, Very once told Emerson that if he could first "move Shakespeare" he could then "move the world." With solemn voice and fervid appearance belying the irony of a pun, he added: "I begin to see him shake already."[1] The shock waves from his efforts to relocate Shakespeare were the various thematic pulses by which he sought to transport the world. Charles Stearns Wheeler's opinion to the contrary, the forced departure from Cambridge was not the "sad end of his ambitions to move the world." Since Very's self-assurance derived from his unique relationship with God, it could scarcely be undermined by the minuscular powers of Harvard. But to be sure Emerson understood this, Very tried to see him on his way to Salem.

Had Washington Very allowed his brother to stop at Concord, Emerson would have learned then (and not six weeks later) why the Shakespeare "problem" was so important, and why its solution could transform the world. What had aroused Very "was the fact that all young men say, Shakespeare was no saint,—yet see what genius!"[2] It was to explain the connection between virtue and genius, using Shakespeare as the modular great but unsaintly man, justly admired but for the wrong reasons, that he had undertaken the essay. "To the preëxistent Shakespeare Wisdom was offered," he told Elizabeth Peabody, "but he refused it and *fell* into genius."[3] That "Genius" is a decadent or deficient variety of "Wisdom," that it represents a partial realization rather than consummation of human possibilities, is central not only to the essay but also to the new basis for Very's own life. He therefore wished to explain to Emerson that unlike Shakespeare he had not declined when the gift of Wisdom was offered. Instead of the "universality of Shakespeare" he had elected for himself the universality of Christ and had thereby become an avowed instrument of Revelation.

Very's incipient self-hatred and compulsive need to be identified with some self other than his own is the starting point of the essay.[4] Dissatisfied with the possibility of being only a "companion" of Shakespeare's "earthly presence," he believed he had achieved a "perfect [spiritual] union and relationship" with him by retaining nothing that was distinctively his own. This complete identification was possible because Very was confident he had already laid aside everything in his character which was "provincial and selfish," "false and artificial." He was thus convinced of his ability to understand and love Shakespeare as the "unconscious work of God" rather than as a manifestation of man. With this as a beginning Very undertook to describe "Shakespeare's self," a self now coincident with his own. (Pp. 39–41.)

Since Very was describing (or thought he was describing) the "iron framework" and "great law" of Shakespeare's being, he viewed him not as a poet or dramatist so much as a psychological phenomenon, and his plays only as they permitted speculation about the activity of Shakespeare's mind. He was interested in representing the elusive dynamics within Shakespeare which generated the plays. What concerned him then were the "veins of a primitive formation" present in his "massy mind." (Pp. 41–42.) In effect Very was attempting to see Shakespeare with the perfect knowledge available to God, and was satisfied that he could do so because the subjective fabric of Shakespeare and the objective resources of God now seemed conveniently available to him. From a position apparently within Shakespeare's own mind Very proceeded to describe in psychological terms a protean personality.

He developed the thesis that Shakespeare was more often "possessed by" his genius than in possession of it. That is, Shakespeare's mind functioned spontaneously, without deliberate control. Its actions were not willed but reflexive and automatic. (P. 81.) Moreover, since they were "natural movements," and were so because in harmony with Nature, the form taken by his personality and his life was like Nature's, "various and all-embracing." (Pp. 60, 40.) External objects and scenes were absorbed by Shakespeare until he was no longer aware of himself but lived and breathed in other beings and possessed no life distinctively his own.

Like the ocean his mind could fill with murmuring waves the strangely indented coast of human experience from the widest bay to the smallest creek; then ebbing, retire within itself, as if form was but a mode of its limitless and independent being. [P. 48.]

This activity of mind, finding within itself "an answering expression" to all existences outside itself, was accompanied by a "sense of life" so strong and teeming it overflowed its limits. (Pp. 50, 55.) Hence the "universality" of Shakespeare: it consisted of his "power" to adapt himself to his characters and their circumstances so completely that nothing of himself is seen in them; yet every character he respresented was his own.

This paradoxical situation followed from the natural law of existence by which what is individual is but an aspect of what is universal. (Pp. 57–58.) His plays present characters which are "necessary growths or offshoots" of his own multiple personality, and they exist as "facts," as "real events," which cannot be altered or improved any more than can "the branch of a tree, or the visible realities themselves." (Pp. 61–62.) Yet Shakespeare was an imperfect poet. His mind was

a pure and spotless mirror in which to reflect nature; but it was the purity and spotlessness of innocence, and not of virtue. Had that love of action which was so peculiarly the motive of Shakespeare's mind been followed also as a duty, it would have added a strength to his characters which we do not feel them now possess. They are, it is true, natural, but they are no more than nature. . . . Had Shakespeare felt [a revelation of higher motives], his characters would have been more consciously natural. For the erring, he would have made us feel a deeper pity; for the wicked a stronger aversion; for the virtuous, a more enduring love. [Pp. 77–78.]

Unfortunately Shakespeare did not realize that the "angel visitants" filling his active mind were sent him by a God who intended that he do something more than merely "admire and number" them. (P. 81.)

Since he acted instinctively, like Nature he acted from motives neither good nor bad. His love of existence, of whatever *is,* was not complemented by love of what *is good.* His art therefore was completely descriptive: he represented "man as he is," in all his weakness and sinfulness, "unable of himself to find the way, the truth, and the life." (P. 45.) Shakespeare's vision, however accurate, was necessarily amoral. (P. 67.) He lacked the conscious ability to make moral judgments, to discriminate between goodness and evil. Instead he treated both alike—with a uniform love, a love however which was justified and admirable because both goodness and evil do exist. His, then, was a "playful and childlike spirit," essentially innocent, and one which was moved by impulse rather than principle. (P. 64.)

Since Shakespeare's mind operated independently of any human will, its operations, while "natural," were "as unconsciously so as a field or stream." (P. 80.) His work was the product of the "same great vital energy of nature" which animates plants and trees. (P. 43.) Therefore God—not Shakespeare—should be revered for the works of Shakespeare's life: in them are to be seen the "ordinary power of Deity acting in mind," just as elsewhere in the natural world it purposefully molds the "forms of matter." (P. 78.)

While Shakespeare's mind functioned in "obedience to the will of God," that obedience was "unconscious." Like Nature—but unlike God, and Jones Very—Shakespeare was unaware of the extent to which he was the passive vehicle of God's will. Because of his inability to take God's presence into account, he was totally committed to his overwhelming sense of life, with the result that he was obsessed by fears that death would end his copious existence. (P. 46.) His troubled attitude toward death (to be further documented in Very's essay on *Hamlet*), was sufficient confirmation of Shakespeare's fundamental fault as a poet. Although possessing the "power of a poet" he could not draw upon the "superadded light of Revelation." (Pp. 76–77.)

Although this is the essence of Very's comprehension of Shakespeare's "strange individuality," the essay involved much more than finding an "excuse" for what "seemed impure in his writings." (P. 41.) Since Shakespeare was the exemplary man of genius, matters which clarified and went beyond the immediate problem of his character filled the essay. By considering Shakespeare symptomatic of something more far-reaching, Very developed a theory of genius for which Shakespeare was only the primary illustration.

When he referred to Shakespeare's "playful and childlike spirit" (p. 64), he was alluding to an essential quality of the man of genius. The child occupies a special position in Very's psychotheological schema. Characteristic of the child is complete un-selfconsciousness, a "sense of existence" marked by instinctive love and joyous sympathy with the variety of life. The child indiscriminately feels the "connecting link" between himself and all things. He is entirely at one with the world in which he exists. (Pp. 47–48.) Through an "inborn force"—a force identical with that animating Nature—the child's mind is in harmony with Nature, and "universality" attends its actions. Childhood therefore is the archetypal condition of innocence, the Edenic condition which makes the child as much the "lord of creation" as Adam. (Pp. 55–58.) Since children act in response to the same force animating the natural world, they are no more moral agents than are birds or flowers or trees, and their actions consequently are involuntary, instinctive, and spontaneous. The child unconsciously responds to the Divine Will everywhere operative in Nature. The child, like Nature, just *is* and automatically loves whatever else *is*. The man of genius, with his undifferentiated love of activity and existence, is thus a *child-man,* retaining his prelapsarian heritage through unwitting obedience to the Divine Will. (P. 68.)

But it is only the exceptional man like Shakespeare who can preserve his youthful sensibilities when exposed to the false teachings of an unnatural world which values only the acquisition and retention of material goods, and desires only the transient pleasures they bring. In becoming a man the child who lacks "genius" is "schooled by the selfishness of sin" (p. 57), and learns from the "corrupt world" to sacrifice his "being" before the "idol of [his] desires." Forfeiting his harmony with nature, the natural child has thus become unnatural man, disobedient to the natural law of existence and indifferent to the condition of his soul. (P. 48.) He alienates himself from God by cultivating a distinctively human but unnatural faculty, his own private will. He now acts consciously and deliberately to set himself against the will of God, and thereby loses his status as a natural being. He sins "in the light of nature and revelation." (P. 78.) By becoming "enchained" to his own will he forfeits his natural freedom and falls from the "primaeval state of innocence." (P. 60.)

While sin is the ordinary state of man, it is neither an inevitable nor a natural condition. The alternative to sinfulness, human greatness, is a real if difficult possibility. It is possible only through genius or virtue, for these alone can sustain the natural, unfallen condition in men. Both genius and saint constitute exceptions to the child's unnatural development into man at the expense of innocence. They are exempt from sin because in different ways they achieve maturity without sacrificing their natural "harmony." Their greatness comes from "obedience." This may or may not be conscious: it is unconscious for the genius, conscious for the virtuous man. But whether or not conscious, it is a rare condition: the mass of men lead disobedient, unnatural, and sinful lives. (P. 79.)

Both forms of greatness require subordination of the human will to that of God since it is responsiveness to the Divine Will which distinguishes what is natural from what is not. Because his obedience is unconscious, the man of genius is subject to no law except the natural law of his being. While his will effortlessly coincides with the Divine Will, it does not deliberately conform to it. (P. 76.) Only in this non-conforming sense is he a free agent. He is a eudaemonic man, whose strength is derived from his own native impulses, his dominant impulse being to equate his individuality with universality, to love whatever *is*. Since his mind operates as part of the natural order, but by no exertion of his own will, he is the *child-man* innocently doing whatever he is impelled to do, whether his greatness is that of "the poet, the philosopher, or the warrior." (P. 52.)

Because the obedience of the virtuous man is conscious, his greatness is superior to that of genius. He possesses "Wisdom." His will is not, like that of genius, "borne down and drawn along by the mind's own original impulse"; while able to resist, his will instead "yields flexibly" and voluntarily to all the "natural movements" of his mind. (Pp. 41–42.) He makes his will conform to the Divine Will, forcing it to overcome the unnatural reluctance it has acquired by exposure to the "corrupt world." (P. 79.) Consequently he is more a free agent than the man of genius. His higher freedom has been won "by an exertion of the will" in the presence of unnatural desires and selfish objectives; whereas love of what *is* provides genius with immunity, and thus its integrity is not threatened by the corrupt world. Since the virtuous man intentionally seeks to obey the will of God as an alternative to sinfulness, and since his deliberate actions are consciously motivated by duty and love, he is moral rather than innocent, and righteous rather than sinful. (P. 45.) Through the perfect "service" made possible by painful self-discipline, he obtains his "perfect freedom." (P. 81.)

Basic to Very's consideration of Shakespeare and to the broad implications of his analysis are two terms which, as Emerson noted soon after meeting him, were mannered elements in his vocabulary and emblems of his special intelligence—"love" and "sin." [5] Around both terms clustered a number of related meanings. Love, applied to the man of virtue, is a "relationship" and "communion" with God, the voluntary distribution of His "general gifts," the "free-following of Christ," and the activity of mind "connected with the sense of eternal life." (P. 45.) Applied to the man of genius, whose mind operates without awareness of its dependence upon God, love is a "yearning" of the human spirit for "being" or "universality," and an unceasing delight in Nature's "diversity," and sympathy with whatever *is*. (Pp. 51–52.) Relating "love" to the circumstances of both genius and goodness is self-forgetfulness, the denial of self, and the loss of one's sense of separateness. (P. 56.)

The negation of love is sin—the willful substitution of "selfishness for love." (P. 61.) Sin is then relevant to neither child, nor genius, nor saint. It is insistence upon self at the expense of universality, the "provincial and selfish" narrowing-down of a man's views to his "own selfish ends." (P. 40.) It is man's "torpid inanimation" in the presence of "objects of sense" (p. 45), and the opposition of the self to "the will of God being done." (P. 72.) It is action at variance with the inward world of genius and goodness. (P. 53.)

The "self" which love denies and which sin affirms is not the natural self preserved by the innocent child in equilibrium with universality.

Could we but feel aright, we should see . . . that did we love in ourselves what was truly worthy of our love, there would be no object throughout the wide circle of being whose lot and happiness would not be our own. It is thus by becoming most universal we at the same time become most individual; for they are not opposed to each other, but different faces of the same thing. But selfishness is the farthest removed of all things from the universality of genius or of goodness. For, as the superiority to the objects of sense which the soul naturally has, which, when lost, love would restore, diminishes, these senseless objects in their turn become masters; we are the servants of sin, bowing to an idol that our own hands have set up, and sweating beneath the burthens of a despot strong in our own transferred power. [Pp. 53–54.]

Love denies and sin affirms the unnatural self, all that is "false and artificial" in a man's character, introduced there by the "corrupt world" maintained by men already committed to ancient evils. This was the world Very was trying to "move" by "moving" Shakespeare.

Unlike the greatness of genius which is independent of the human will, the greatness of virtue is attainable by every man, however extensive his sinfulness. Required is an exercise of will in accordance with love and duty. Only this painful effort can overthrow the unnatural self and reassert the rightful claims of the natural self in a world long-governed by false values.

Like the ancients we too find a deity in each of the objects we pursue;—we follow wealth till we worship Mammon; love, till we see a Venus; are ambitious, till our hands are stained with the bloody rites of Mars. While in the physical world we are waging by our railroads and engines a war of utter extermination against time and space, we forget that it is these very things, as motives, that urge us on. . . . While in the physical world we are driving to annihilation space and time, it is for the very sake of the things of time and sense that we do it. . . . Our words confess that all things are God's while our hands are busy in fencing off some corner of the wide universe from which to exclude our brother man. [P. 54.]

This self-assertive "strength" of sinful man, whatever its momentary effectiveness in his corrupt world, is illusory. It is "worse than weakness" for it jeopardizes eternal life. Genius demonstrates and revelation teaches that true strength derives only from the strength of God: without the active participation of God man can do "no positive act." (P. 82.) The "false pride" sinful man takes in his "seeming strength" derives from willfulness. (P. 57.) Since man's mind is so constituted by nature that it is not his own, he sins whenever he acts as if it were. He must therefore learn from genius and revelation that his "highest glory" consists of "conscious submission" to the Divine Will. (P. 42.)

To accomplish this, sinful man must return to innocence: "by being born again, by becoming again through obedience as little children." (P. 61.) Had man's nature (as distinct from the nature of the child), not been so weak and poor, so liable to debase itself through selfishness, a "revelation of higher motives" would not have been necessary.

To become natural, to find again that Paradise which he has lost, man must be born again; he must learn that the true exercise of his own will is only in listening to that voice, which is ever walking in the garden, but of which he is afraid and hides himself. [Pp. 78–79.]

By following conscience man shall learn to love whatever *is good*. Were man to realize this and undertake the heroic struggle to overcome his selfishness, love would restore his lost superiority to "objects of sense," and the human will would once again "assent to the Divine." (Pp. 54–55.)

Responsibility for indicating to sinful man the "dark paths of destruction" he treads (p. 81), and for effecting his renunciation of an unnatural self, is voluntarily assumed by the great poet who is also a man of virtue. Moved by love and duty, such a poet is the "perfect poet" because of the redemptive power of his poetry. His mind not only "harmonizes" with Nature by relying on its "inborn and free-working energies," but in addition it can provide the "spiritual interpretation" for Nature's "silent and sublime growth." (Pp. 53–54.) For the perfect poet, the making of poetry is a sacramental act.

All great poetry (even the non-sacramental poetry of genius) is produced by "humble obedience," conscious or not, to the "Holy Spirit," and is "the word of God uttered through the soul." (P. 71.) Such poetry is an organic development which unfolds according to principles over which the poet exercises no control. Under the "transforming power" of his mind "all is plastic" and "words partake . . . of motion, form and speech." Like "atoms on the magnetic plate," words take shape by feeling "instinct with order and design." They exist as a divine necessity. (Pp. 44–45.)

But for perfect utterance, to be inspired by God and therefore speak spontaneously and completely His actual words, the poet's "war of self" must cease. He must consciously seek to do the Father's will. Once "striving" has ended and inward "peace" been gained, everything belonging to God is made available. Everything, including the unlimited resources of God's intelligence, is now his own, and perfect poetry (including such prose equivalents as Very's own essay on Shakespeare), for the first time becomes possible. Then from the "deep bosom" of his "spiritual love" will sound a "full and perfect voice" for the poet's use, a voice suited to "all the utterances of joy and grief." If the "perfect poet" will thus knowingly allow divine wisdom to guide his poetic skills, he will "live forever" as a "teacher." His teachings are the words he hears from the Father and transmits unaltered through poetry. (Pp. 73–74.)

These teachings constitute the "Wisdom" the "preëxistent" Shakespeare declined and which Very accepted. Unlike his subject, Very considered himself equipped with a moral insight enabling him to expose the workings of mind and the provenance of genius and virtue. This long-sought but newly acquired vatic gift he employed in engagements with Cambridge students and friends during September 1838. Since its operation, befitting a "teacher," was as much proscriptive as diagnostic, "Shakespeare" contains much higher criticism of a special sort: the essay at times is a Poetics of Revelation.

Being totally committed to expressing received truth, the perfect poet cannot by the "handiwork" of his mind impose a "prescribed pattern of goodness" upon his representations in poetry. The possession of the suprahuman "voice" gives no warrant to be "more moral than Providence." The poet's function is not to "quicken" with his own discretionary life the "dry bones of moral death" surrounding him. As a "teacher" he can only "describe the height and depth" of "thoughts and passions" as they are and "interpret their [hidden] meaning." (Shakespeare had the "Genius" to do the former but lacked the "Wisdom" to do the latter.) Nature must be portrayed accurately, from a feeling of love and a sense of duty rather than from impulse. Similarly human character: the poet must illuminate the "dark and labyrinthine caverns of sin" so others can extract from their own "lowest depths" the "treasures of wisdom" concealed there. If instead the poet is inferior to his vocation and depicts "what *ought to be*," his teaching is false and ineffectual; it is then merely the handiwork of his own mind. But if "what *is*" is seen and understood "with a spirit more nearly allied to Him who sees all things as they are," then poetry will exhibit God's presence and be as efficacious. (Pp. 74–75.)

The only proper subject for the "perfect poet" then is "what *is*"—the "ever new, ever changing aspect of nature and of man." But by means of the "perfect and entire action" of the poet's mind, truth and time are seen "blended in the life as primary colors in the common light of day." "Truth" is the stable aspect of Nature, its universal, spiritual meaning, while "time" is its ever-changing, particular aspect; "truth" is the interpretation of "time," while "time" is the description of "truth." Poetry of genius (like that of Shakespeare) responds to God's will only at the level of time, whereas perfect poetry (spoken with the full and conscious voice of God) operates at the level of truth as well as time. (P. 61.)

Accordingly, the "power of the poet" to represent "what *is*"—the universal in the particular—is augmented to the extent his will "conforms to that of his Maker." Although artificial standards of virtue and vice cannot be substituted for the living realities of truth-in-time, what *is good* must be distinguished from what *is*. But virtue need not be "brightened" nor vice "darkened" by the poet's independent judgment. To his "spiritual eye"—capable of perfect rather than merely natural vision—the virtuous are "angels of light." As for the wicked, while the sun of "Divine Favor" sets behind them, their "lengthening shadows" do "blacken and dilate into more gigantic and awful proportions." With the passing of "time" only "truth" remains. The perfect poet need only represent this more-than-natural drama enacted before him. Perfect poetry consequently is "Revelation," conducted by the poet in such a way that what he reveals is "conscious nature." Through his efforts Nature itself gains his distinctive quality of "consciousness," which in turn raises Nature's formerly automatic "obedience" to the higher, more spiritual level of truth-in-time. (Pp. 75–76.)

The prototype for Very's perfect poet was not some idealized man of letters but the Perfect Man of Perfect Virtue "who came not to do his own will." At the Father's bidding, He urged men to "become as little children" in order to gain that "state of mind" known as "eternal life." (Pp. 47, 49.) Had Shakespeare or any other great man similarly acted in conscious submission to the will of God, he would have been indistinguishable from Jesus. (P. 81.) Since a man can "impart" only what he himself is (p. 68), "true virtue" would become for the perfect poet "conscious genius." (P. 55.) Love would then cause genius—that "erring, though innocent child"—to follow the "maternal guidance" of virtue. (P. 73.)

In addition to Shakespeare and the consummate maker of poems who served as Very's conceptual standard, the essay discusses three other poets. Milton and Wordsworth, according to Very's analysis, were neither men of genius like Shakespeare (and Homer), nor of accomplished virtue and perfect obedience like Jesus; rather, they were poets of an intermediate spiritual condition in whose poetry he recognized signs of "the war of self" still in progress. Since they had not yet won that "peace" which makes "all that God hath" their own, they themselves were the virtual heroes of their poems. Each spoke in his own voice and revealed a "single-sided individuality," whether in *Paradise Lost,* "Ode to Duty," or the *Immortality Ode.* Very therefore understood such poems as symbolic and psychological depictions of the inability of both poets to "escape the consciousness of themselves" while struggling to become "perfect" men. Theirs was poetry of spiritual conflict and crisis. While they deliberately tried to go beyond the unconscious grandeur of Shakespeare, they fell short of the ultimate possibilities of poets. In neither was the "perfect poet" realized. (Pp. 72–73.)

By contrast, Byron consciously repudiated perfect poetry. Byron was the perfect anti-poet, who sought to "restrain virtue" (p. 67) by imparting something of his diabolical self to all he described:

he would not and could not, like Shakespeare, put before us a virtuous man with the same pleasure as he does a vicious one; he has not, like him, held a pure and untarnished mirror up to Nature, but reflected her back upon us from his own discolored and passion-stained bosom.

Delighting in what is not good, Byron celebrated his unnatural self in the outcasts and criminals who populate his poems. With him poetry of the perverse and morally grotesque, so different from the "playful and childlike spirit" Shakespeare brought to "vicious character," and from the moral heroism implicit in the work of Milton and Wordsworth, reaches its optimum development. (Pp. 64–65.)

[ 211 ]

Had Byron—or had Shakespeare, Milton, or Wordsworth—possessed the Wisdom transmuted from genius by the intentional destruction of what was unnatural within, they would have willingly disseminated it in poetry as an instrumentality of God, thereby restoring to Revelation its original role as a continuing influence upon the lives of men. In effect the poet functioning as "teacher" in this evangelic sense would embody the Second Coming. Provided he were motivated by no selfish will, it would be appropriate to his character and function were he even to utter so apocalyptic a cry as "Flee to the Mountains, for the end of all things is at hand." It would be appropriate too were he to complain that God was being denied whenever his words were opposed and the authority of his teachings questioned.

The essay extolled human action in which God's will alone was decisive, action which sent heaven's lightning to "flash in warning across the dark path of destruction" trod by the mass of men. (Pp. 80–81.) September 1838 saw lightning flash frequently in order to purify "the moral atmosphere" at Harvard. In confrontations with the Freshman Class, Dr. Ware, and the members of the Divinity School debating club, and with whomever else would listen, Very acted out and urged upon others the principles of greatness he attributed in the essay to the man of virtue. He tried to "move" the College in much the same way he was trying to "move" Shakespeare. His effort to regenerate at least a portion of the "corrupt world" by revealing "Wisdom" through personal appeals and writings, committed him to a "teaching" career of which the Harvard Board of Overseers would scarcely approve. His persistence in distinguishing what *is* good from what *is* at Harvard came from the moral superiority he gained through his relationship with the Father. No longer only Greek Tutor and divinity student, he now was performing the work of the Son as Teacher, and as Paracletic Man he was bringing the comfort of the Holy Spirit to Cambridge, without being invited to do so. Having glimpsed the form of God shining through the natural landscape—as he hoped he might when he used the margins of Emerson's *Nature* to relate the Book of Revelation to his own circumstances in 1836—he could no longer remain silent. Biblical accents, consistent with his new authority and in the form of quotation and paraphrase from the New Testament, enlivened not only the essay on Shakespeare but also his Cambridge discourses.[6] Accordingly he was required by college officials to retire to Salem for an unspecified period.

While ostensibly his sudden departure was due to serious impairment of his health by overwork, campus gossips less politely whispered that Very had gone completely mad. But whatever the actual condition of his health, his continued presence at Harvard could no longer be tolerated. He had become an embarrassment if not an overt threat to institutional decorum. His strange manner and doctrines followed soon after (and seemed to resemble) the Address delivered by Emerson, and it was generally acknowledged that Very had some sort of connection with Emerson, perhaps that of a disciple.

From Very's point of view, however, the illness causing his return to Salem was not so much his own as Harvard's. Symptoms of the almost universal malaise afflicting the human spirit —moral disease, decayed values, artificial manners, insensitivity, defective sympathies, mechanical routine, and indifferent teachers offering enervating instruction—pervaded Cambridge and were developing "unnatural" young men. He therefore tried to effect a cure by demonstrating energetically and dramatically that God was a dynamic force in the world; that human greatness drew upon His resources; that the great man was called to educate others; that prophecy was still a legitimate mode of truth; that all men might attain the status of Jesus could they but bring themselves to renounce whatever alienated them from God; that all men were personally responsible for the impoverished state of spiritual affairs everywhere evident; that the superiority of the saint to the genius was absolute; and that love and duty can overcome the human inclination to sin by resisting selfishness and by repressing the desire (acquired during the passage from childhood), for material prosperity and physical pleasures. While few of these articles of belief were necessarily offensive even to men of conservative temper, the intensity with which Very attempted literally to exhibit and implement them led him to actions which alarmed the practical-minded and complacent members of the academic community. His departure on Saturday September fifteenth may have relieved tensions at Harvard somewhat, but because he was not at all discouraged by the less than warm reception this "Wisdom" had so far found, his arrival at Salem later that day soon gave others cause for anxiety.

# Crisis-Comedy in Salem

## SEPTEMBER 1838

EARLY ON SUNDAY MORNING, September 16, 1838, less than twenty-four hours after his reluctant return to Salem, Jones Very left his home. He made a number of calls at houses in the vicinity where he had always found welcome before, informing friends and neighbors what Harvard had already learned, that the "coming of Christ was at hand." [1] Several hours later, after leaving behind a trail of astonished townspeople, he walked briskly along Charter Street, some distance from his home. Hurrying past the Old Burial Ground at about ten o'clock on this remarkable day, he leaped the two stone steps before the shallow porch of house number 53, as he had often done whenever he was in Salem during the last nine months. He impatiently knocked. His face was flushed with excitement. His eyes were "very brilliant and twinkling." [2]

When Elizabeth Peabody came to the door and recognized her unexpected caller, she sensed at once "something unusual—and dangerous in the air." Without hesitating she invited her breathless friend in, even though it was an unusual hour for her to receive visitors. She hadn't seen him for almost a month, and was anxious to learn of his latest progress with students and how far he had carried his own studies and writing. At this time she knew nothing of his odd behavior at Cambridge, nor that he had been sent home because of it.

As soon as they were within the parlor he stood uncomfortably close to her. He did not even offer a familiar greeting. She was puzzled at first and then slightly embarrassed. As the seconds passed it suddenly occurred to her that for the first time they were alone together in the lower story of the house. Her uneasiness was scarcely relieved when, still without having said a word of explanation, he affectionately placed his hand on her head. The prolonged silence was proving no less painful to her than her fear of what he might do next. At last he spoke. In a strange deep voice he said: "I come to baptize you with the Holy Ghost and with fire."

To her further amazement and before she could protest or call out to others in the house, he began to recite from memory passages from the Olivet discourse in the twenty-fourth chapter of Matthew:

. . . There shall not be left here one stone upon another, that shall not be thrown down. . . . When *shall be* the sign of thy coming, and of the end of the world? . . . Take heed that no man deceive you. For many shall come in my name, saying I am Christ; and shall deceive many. . . . All *these things* must come to pass, . . . and there shall be famines, and pestilences, and earthquakes in divers places. . . . But he that shall endure unto the end, the same shall be saved. And this gospel of the kingdom shall be preached in all the world . . . and then shall the end come. When ye therefore shall see the abomination of desolation . . . stand in the holy place, . . . Then let them which be in Judaea flee into the mountains: . . . For as the lightning cometh out of the east, and shineth even unto the west; so shall also the coming of the Son of man be. For wheresoever the carcase is, there will the eagles be gathered together. . . . Watch therefore: for ye know not what hour your Lord doth come. . . .

Without pausing to indicate the end of the recitation, he began to interpret the text. While the words of Jesus were still sounding in the room, he was speaking for himself—but in the diction of the King James Version.

Elizabeth did not immediately detect the shift, so consistent was his tone. She continued to stare in amazement, her face still held close to his by the tender touch of his extended hand. His comments—once she recognized them as his—she thought "rather fanciful—but not absurd." His words, to her surprise, actually "thrilled" her. He was "so gentle and happy" while delivering his message. Yet she "trembled to the center" as she stood under his hand without resisting. Then he prayed. He prayed that she might have "his witness of the Holy Ghost." Although still dazed by it all, she instinctively knew she must be "perfectly quiet" and must not protest or otherwise interfere lest she "antagonize" him. The prayer brought the ceremony to a close—but not the visit or the "instructions."

"When he had done," she recalled sometime later,

I sat down, and he, at a little distance, did the same—and there was a dead silence. Soon he said, with a slightly uneasy missionary air, "How do you feel?" I replied gently—"I feel no change."—"But you will'—said he, hurriedly, "I am the Second Coming—give me a Bible." There was one in the room to which I pointed. He went to the table where it was and turned to Christ's prophecy of the Second Coming—and read it, ending with the words "This day is this fulfilled in your caress." I was silent but respectful, even tenderly so.

Very thereupon began to speak with her in the most matter-of-fact way, just as he had done on numerous occasions, without once mentioning what had just taken place between them. He told her he had completed the essay on Shakespeare and that he wanted her to have it since it was written especially for her, but he had sent it first to Emerson whom he intended to visit soon and tell of his "discovery." Having said this, and before she could question him about what he had done to her minutes before, he abruptly excused himself and left, not even waiting for her to get up from her seat to see him to the door.

Still shaking with excitement and stunned by what had happened—but relieved that it was nothing worse than the consummation of a spiritual marriage—she tried to account for Very's behavior as impersonally as possible.

It was probably induced by intense application. He was superintending the Greek class—out of which he has got a vast deal of studying—and he has the idea of a great moral responsibility—which arose I suppose from his success in awakening the sentiment of duty in others. Besides, he has been for a year or more in his divinity studies, and writing besides.—I have feared insanity before—I thought (at the time) that the visit to Groton showed it.[3]—These impulses from above—I think—are never sound minded. The insanity of Quakers—(which is very frequent under my observation) always grows out of it—or rather begins in it. . . . I thought this was perhaps a passing frenzy caused by overtaxing his brain in the attempt to look from the standpoint of Absolute Spirit.

But she knew that Very's actions could not be explained away so easily. So long as he was in this unsettled state of mind mischief by him and to him was inevitable. Such gestures of love as he made, even to so sympathetic a friend as herself, did not bode well for his earthly future—whatever they might promise for spiritual salvation. There were many in Salem who would not long tolerate such sacrilegious conduct in their city of peace.

As soon as her composure returned she was moved as much by curiosity as by honest concern for his safety. She hurried from the house to call upon her friend Mrs. Caleb Foote, from whom she hoped to gain answers to at least some of the questions she was unable to ask Very. She quickly learned from her that what she feared most had already occurred. Before coming to Charter Street he had gone to see several ministers in the town. Why? To baptize them—and with disastrous results. John Brazer, minister of the Unitarian North Church (which Very had joined in 1836), was the first to be blessed. He

was ninny enough to ask this poor crazy youth for the *miracles* that tested his mission. Very said "this revelation would not have miracles." "Then," said Mr. B, "I must say to you—you are laboring under hallucination! &c.". . .

Two [ministers] had resisted him. [Lucius] Bolles—the Baptist minister,—had actually put him bodily out of the house, and Mr. [Charles Wentworth] Upham, who at that time was a good deal excited against the transcendentalists, calling Mr. Emerson an Atheist—and declaring that it was wrong to listen to him,—had told Mr. Very that he should see that he be sent to the Insane Asylum.

Upon hearing the details from Mrs. Foote, Elizabeth was terrified. She ran to the home of the Rev. Mr. Upham. This influential citizen—a classmate of Emerson, close friend of Andrews Norton, Minister of Salem's fashionable First Church, and later the man responsible for Hawthorne's removal from the customhouse—was indeed outraged by Very's presumption. He repeated to her his threat to have him confined, forcibly if necessary. She discussed Very with him for a long time, trying to dissuade him from resorting to violence. Nothing she said could calm him. Ever since Emerson's publication of *Nature* in 1836 he had spoken out strongly against Transcendentalism, considering it "absolutely and not remotely, of infidel tendency and import."[4] Since he knew that Elizabeth Peabody, like Jones Very, was friendly with Emerson, he was not the least impressed by her pleas for moderation.

Alarmed by the vehemence of the good minister's language, she hurried to warn Very's mother of the danger which threatened. Although she had never met Lydia Very before, she had long known the gossip about her. Under the circumstances it would have been natural for Elizabeth to slow her pace as she approached the house at 154 Federal Street. With its crabbed austerity and its squat solidity pushing out to the edge of the public walk and almost threatening to crush all passers-by, it seemed to reflect the temperament of its notorious owner. To gain time and prepare her nerves for what promised to be a painful interview, she may have paused to study the house before knocking.

Had she done so, she would have seen a boxlike frame structure with weathered siding, built in the graceless style popular at the end of the eighteenth century in Salem. Its front almost completely concealed from view a narrow tract of terraced garden which sloped down to the bank of the North River several hundred feet beyond. A single low stone step offered entry to the house. The narrow doorway, situated casually among three ground-floor windows, gave the house an uncongenial, asymmetrical appearance. Its shallow doorhead, with supporting pilasters but no carved ornament, was a poor substitute for the porches of more formal "Federalist" homes. Above, four shuttered windows on the second floor failed to restore balance as they rose to the leading edge of the gambrel roof. Three dormers jutted through the lower roof-slope, making a foreshortened third story. At top stood a massive brick chimney, designed for the comfort of the occupants but incompatible with the pinched face of the house. The total effect of severity and awkwardness was softened somewhat by towering maples set in close to flank either side of the house; but they were separated from the street by meager stretches of high board fence which restored the harshness. By no means an inviting house—it even stood on a site within easy walking distance of Gallows Hill—it nevertheless was not the sort likely to discourage an aroused Elizabeth Peabody from attempting to gain entry.

She was met at the door by the mistress herself. Before she

could explain her errand, she found Lydia Very already alerted to the perils threatening her son. She had begun to protect him by suspecting the motives for even this well-intentioned visit, as Elizabeth's account of the meeting makes clear.

She did not receive me graciously at first—but I persevered till she recognized that I was opposed to all violent methods—and had the greatest reverence for her son. She told me she was sure he was not insane, but more sane than others, that he was an *angel* whom God inspired, and a *proof* that there *was* a God above us, who was Infinite Love. . . . She had heard about my interview with Mr. Upham I found [15] and declared that Mr. Very should *not* be carried to the Insane Hospital. She said if there was anything in him that seemed insane it was caused by the brutal manner in which he had been treated. I left the house about twelve o'clock and understood from her that he was resting in his chamber.

Elizabeth Peabody returned home still troubled but confident that she had done all she possibly could.

Reflecting upon the day's events she found the interview with the mother almost as disconcerting as the behavior of her son. She recalled what she knew about Lydia Very:

She was a person of great energy—was said to have more than doubts of another world and of the existence of God—having had a severe experience of life, and being at odds with the existing state of Society—a disciple of Fanny Wright. . . . I was so struck with what she said [about her son and God], that it seemed to me that to produce such a result in her mind [i.e. her acceptance of God after a lifetime of atheism] was reason sufficient for Providence giving her the Word in [her] son.

While Elizabeth now suspected some connection between Very's aberration and his mother's sudden renunciation of atheistic materialism, she lacked full insight into their motivations.

Much of Very's peculiarity of mind had been brought on by his guilt-prompted conviction that he alone must save his mother from the curse of her disbelief. After being himself reborn, thereby removing the taint from his unsanctified natural birth, he could then begin to redeem her by strength of his own will and imagination. A consecrated union with the Father, for which there was no parallel in her irregular "marriage" to Captain Very, awaited her regeneration. By exploiting her passionate feelings for him, her son undertook to make her aware of God through the physical senses she believed she could trust. To her intellectual and emotional satisfaction he demonstrated the reality of God by the simple device of locating God within himself. Her love for him then became love for God, and was transformed into convincing evidence that God exists, proof that God was close to her, and that God returns her love. Since God embodied Himself in her beloved Jones Very, she could no longer refuse to acknowledge His power. By suppressing his own individual personality, by obliterating all traces of his unnatural will, Jones Very—*qua* the Son—was sacrificing Himself in order to redeem the fallen. Literally then, as Very was in effect proclaiming in a more impersonal style to whomever would listen, the "coming of Christ was at hand." The sinful woman had already redeemed herself, and was brought into God's presence by accepting Him. If one of the reprobate could be regenerated in this way, then others could—or so Very now seemed to believe.

Even without the completion of her analysis of the relationship between the mother and the son, it had been an exhausting day for Elizabeth Peabody. She was feeling "wretched," pained by the thought that "such a beautiful light" as Jones Very possessed "had gone down in darkness." Although she already had quite enough to think about and puzzle over, the excitements of September sixteenth were not yet passed. According to her record of the events, Very's work for the day was not complete until much later.

*That evening* he again appeared at my door. He came in very quietly and said, "I misunderstood the Holy Ghost—the time is not yet for the baptism of fire. Nothing can be done with violence in the Second

Coming—in the baptism of John—I only am in the Son—and I must speak as the Son."

With these words (or to this effect), he unfolded a monstrous folio sheet of paper, on which were four double columns of Sonnets—which he said the Spirit had enabled him to write, and these he left with me to read as the utterances of the Holy Ghost.

There is little reason to believe that Elizabeth Peabody rested easily after she retired for the night.

If she dreamed that Upham managed to force entry into that ugly house on Federal Street, abducted Very in spite of his mother's screaming protests, and carried him off in the darkness to Charlestown's McLean Hospital—she would have wakened the next morning to learn that her nightmare was a reality. When Very left Salem, she subsequently told Emerson,

his greatest grief seemed to be that he was so persecuted he could not give *you* his revelation. He was promised that you should be informed he was [at the hospital]. He also wanted to enlighten Mr. [Convers] Francis. He used Christ's words all the time and in the whimsical manner an insane person might.

Later that day, after she learned the grim details, she was so upset she couldn't discuss her recent adventures. In an informal note to Elizabeth Hathorne she merely inquired whether her family had heard that "poor Very has gone *insane*." [6]

As far as Lydia Very was concerned, the relevant issue was not whether others considered her son sane or insane, but whether his actions on the sixteenth of September were peaceable. She insisted to all who approached her, including Upham, that he physically endangered no one, not even himself, and therefore it was wrong to have him confined. She failed however to gauge accurately the sensitivity of the leading citizens of Salem. They were convinced that whatever her son's actions were, his beliefs were not peaceable. They were explosive, tending to obliterate the customary distinction between humanity and divinity. His was an intellectual violence which boldly violated Christian traditions honored by the orthodox of every denomination. This violence which so alienated the feelings of Salem's most righteous citizens took form in ten sensational ideas he entertained about himself, self-dramatizing ideas which reasonable men found insufferable because they invalidated the Christian conception of reasonableness itself.

Although Very did not hesitate to make these ideas explicit to the Salem ministers he encountered that Sunday, he withheld them from Elizabeth Peabody, restricting his mission to her to dramatic ritual, scriptural reading and commentary, and talk about Shakespeare and Emerson. From her point of view, therefore, he was insane not because of his ideas, but because he deluded himself into believing he had revealed some revolutionizing truth when actually he had no ideas to disclose. However, confining him against his will was no remedy for this delusion. She felt that only sympathy, understanding, and generous feelings might restore his clarity of mind.

According to one contemporary witness who was more analytical than most, the bluntly stated ideas which so aroused Salem—and exorbitant ideas they were—could be systematically stated in this way:

(1) Jones Very can discern truth better than other men;

(2) he has advanced further than other men in gaining knowledge of God;

(3) he is a *perfect* man;

(4) being perfect, he is not subject to the same temptations to sin as other men;

(5) God has taken up residence *within* him;

(6) God within him impels him in such a manner that although he has a human will of his own, his volitions are not his own but coincide with, correspond with, and produce actions consistent with the Divine Will;

(7) even if he were not a perfect man, the divine influence operating

within him would nevertheless prevent the *effect* which temptation to sin might otherwise have upon him;

(8) because of the presence of God within him, he *cannot* sin;

(9) even were he *capable* of sinning, he *will* not sin because God within him would prevent him from sinning; and

(10) the second advent of Christ has taken place in him.

Learning that his mission involved the propagation of such dogmas, the Salem clergy and their devoted parishioners were understandably outraged. Not only did Very believe these self-inflated articles but he tried to persuade others to believe them. He sought converts. He told prospective followers (whomever he approached) that they would attain salvation by earning a special human status identical with his own.

Dr. Samuel Johnson, the prominent Salem physician, had more reason than most of his neighbors to be alarmed by such principles. When he learned that Very had been relieved of his teaching duties, and when he could observe for himself the confusion Very brought with him upon returning home, and which quickly led to his residence in a lunatic asylum, he feared for the sanity of his sixteen-year-old son. For several weeks he had been receiving enthusiastic letters from young Samuel, describing how he had been "improved" by the religious instructions of his Greek Tutor. But he had not told his father those details of Very's classroom behavior which caused his dismissal. The doctor therefore wrote his son a blunt, questioning letter which did not conceal his anxiety. He ordered him to return home as soon as possible for a complete examination.

By the time this saddened young man received his father's letter, he was ready with carefully chosen words to defend himself and explain why he had been "much gratified" by Very's instruction. "This occurrence, of which you speak," he wrote in reply,

is indeed most melancholy, and I am not at all surprised that the contents of my last letter excited your apprehensions for me: . . . I believe there was but one day between the date of that letter and the removal of Mr. V. from College; but on that day the truth was rendered evident to my mind: . . . Had the ideas subsequently broached by him, been before heard by me, my letter would have contained a far different account: not that the general facts which he then offered to us, would strike me in a different light from what they formerly did, but that, coming from the lips of one in his state of mind, they were not proper topics on which to reason in his method. Therefore I should have let them pass, without more notice in my letter, than I should have bestowed on them had they casually presened themselves to my mind. The general facts, though not the insane ideas which he wove into them, still strike me with as much force as ever: such as the object of study being to fit ourselves more completely to do God's will in benefiting mankind and ourselves. I will explain farther, if possible, when I arrive: but be assured, dear Father, if this dangerous situation in which our class have been placed, in regard to a proper understanding of religious truth, has indeed in some little measure, been injurious, its bad consequences have now passed off, and been averted, and we are rendered by experience more cautious and less credulous.[7]

Although this sensitive youth had proven himself highly susceptible to Veryism, there was little likelihood his "more cautious and less credulous" elders would be infected.

For Salem Unitarians especially, Very's beliefs more than his overt actions were the irritant. While blessings and prayers could be delivered with appropriate decorum even in drawing rooms, his dogmas—which acts of blessing and prayer merely implemented—offended the dignity of even the more liberal townspeople. That his personal creed was still recognizably Unitarianistic was an incredible embarrassment. Doctrinal acceptance of the essential goodness of men in general, or of man in the abstract, was comforting; but for a particular man, their own neighbor, to declare himself to be *the* good man was a terrifying presumption. Institutional Unitarianism in Salem if not elsewhere would surely be threatened did the aberrant theology of this Harvard-trained enthusiast become widely known. Unitarianism would be directly discredited by the self-glorifying tenets of the Veryist heresy. It would be discredited too by the spokesmen for an aroused Calvinism, who would certainly accuse the Salem Unitarians of fostering this final degradation of traditional Christianity.

Very allowed his enemies no alternative to having him placed in an institution for the insane. He was not a prudent man. He rejected that practical wisdom which recommends complete silence when argument must—but cannot—be tempered. Since his shocking ideas were not merely entertained privately but were publicly and proudly announced, he had to be dealt with at once. Further scandal could be avoided only by providing him with an audience immune to his corrupting influence. Such an audience was conveniently available at the McLean Hospital in nearby Charlestown.

Salem had estimated Very perfectly. When interviewed by Dr. Bell, the attending physician, he refused to be cautious. He spoke candidly of his mission since he was a compulsive talker on this subject. Even within the walls of a madhouse he remained faithful to the "impulses" of his "soul." Dr. Bell, once he heard the *truth* as Very understood it, had little choice but to admit him as a patient.

While confining Very was temporarily effective, something more had to be done to preserve the honor of Salem Unitarianism. Upham, Brazer, and other leaders of the offended party attempted to anticipate the Calvinist charges and shift blame away from themselves. They charged Emerson with engendering Very's insanity: he, they claimed, was responsible for Very's parody of their basic tenets. Judging from a letter George B. Loring wrote to James Russell Lowell just two days after Very's admission to the hospital, their plan was succeeding. He told his friend:

I learnt in Salem that Jones Very has become insane—and imagines he is another Christ divinely commissioned. Now I can easily conceive of all this; but then that he should be thus blown up by Emerson, as one and it, is too strange. Perhaps between them they have put the standard of perfection found in Christ so low that one if not both think they have reached it or think he has reached it. The latter is preferable— [8]

The effectivenesss of the campaign to link Very's insanity to Emerson may also be gathered from a letter the senior Richard Henry Dana wrote about Very to William Cullen Bryant almost two years later:

He is quite intimate with Emerson and the other Spiritualists, or Supernaturalists, or whatever they are called, or may be pleased to call themselves; and his insanity has taken shape accordingly. I am told that some of them are absurd enough to say that he is not insane—but that the world does not understand him. Would their insanity were no worse than his; but "madness is in their hearts." [9]

If then in September 1838 Very was already a liability to the Salem Unitarians, he was likely to become one to some of his friends as well.

Apparently the first to realize this was Charles Stearns Wheeler of the Divinity School, and Very's replacement as Tutor. He was angered when he heard that Upham was circulating the report that Very's insanity was brought on by listening to Emerson.

This is very untrue. Very does not believe even as Emerson does. Very bases all his insane notion of Christ's second coming in him upon the authority of the Bible. Emerson's faith allows no authority, . . . to any man or book. Emerson can rise above and explain the enthusiasm of the Quakers and the raptures of the Swedenborgian, and the new-birth of the Calvinist. Very's insanity seems closely allied to these. [10]

Meanwhile, Emerson seemed oblivious to what was happening, although he heard of Very's misfortune "very like in an insulting way." Nevertheless, while "Satan seem[ed] to be let loose" upon him and "all the people who have hold of the press" seemed to have gone "rabid," Emerson remained calm.[11] On the twentieth of September he wrote to William Henry Furness:

There is a young man at Cambridge, a tutor, Jones Very, who has written a noble paper on Shakespeare, which I have just been reading. Yet I am distressed to hear that he is feared to be insane. His critique certainly is not.[12]

He was acting as if he had forgotten the tempest he brewed with his July Address to the Divinity School graduates, and as if the local affairs of Salem could have no bearing upon those of Concord or Cambridge or Boston. Emerson of course knew otherwise. But Elizabeth Peabody, for one, underestimated his loyalty to Very and his capacity for stoic heroism in his own behalf. She wrote to Emerson exactly one week after Very's removal to Charlstown, and one day after Henry Ware delivered his sermon on "The Personality of the Deity." She delayed her letter until she could unravel the implications and follow the consequences of the affair.[13]

Since he had already been advised of the facts, she described only briefly the "Revelation" delivered to her on the "very day poor Very was carried to the Insane Hospital." She wrote for other reasons. First, she wanted it clearly understood that she completely rejected Very's "mission," and did so because he had "no Idea to Communicate." From her own experience with him she knew it amounted merely to an impressive ceremony. In her opinion Very was unquestionably insane. His insanity however consisted only in believing that the ritual was something more, in "thinking he had communicated something very important." She attributed his condition to overwork, and feared the worst. Her hope to learn his distemper was brain fever—"which would prove his insanity but a temporary delusion"—had not been realized. Reluctantly she concluded he was suffering from "water on the brain," and therefore his recovery was impossible.

That being the sad prospect according to Elizabeth Peabody,

two matters remained to be settled. She wanted Emerson to understand that Very had written the Shakespeare essay expressly for her, and therefore it should be delivered to her when he finished studying it: "If you should ask why I have written this letter—perhaps you would not [want me to] answer the question—it is to say that the manuscript of Very's *belongs to me.*" But more important than this, she wanted to be certain Emerson realized the vulnerability of his own position. He had been publicly implicated in the affair by Very himself as he was being forcibly led away to Charlestown. And others, in addition to Upham and Brazer, were guilty of "old womanly talk" which identified him as the cause of Very's derangement.

They evidently impute to [Very's] transcendental ideas—this misfortune—considering that his notions grow straight out of the idea that the evidence of Revelation is a more inward one than *miracles.* . . . But the thought which has pressed itself on my mind most is—how some people have taken it all—as nothing but *transcendentalism*—which shows how very entirely they do not apprehend *the ground* of a *real belief* in *Inspiration.* What a frightful shallowness of thought in the community that sees no difference between the evidence of the most manifest insanity and the Ideas of Reason!

She was quick to suggest measures which might absolve Transcendentalism and its partisans. Someone should publicly deny Emerson's responsibility for what had happened to Very, and preferably Emerson himself should do it.

I wonder whether something might not be written by a believer in the doctrine of Spirituality which would show the difference between trusting the soul and giving up one's mind to these *individual illuminations.* . . . I wish you would give us a course of lectures on the *Art of thinking.* If you would not—I think I shall try to stimulate H[enry] Hedge to do it. Nothing do we need so much. You might append it to your Goethe lectures on the art of Studying—indeed it is an identical subject.

This proposal—so characteristic of her capacity to irritate friends whenever she tried to help them with unsolicited advice—failed to move Emerson. Instead he preferred to await further developments. He told Margaret Fuller of his excitement over the Shakespeare essay.

Ha[ve] you heard of the calamity of poor Very, the tutor at Cambridge? He is at the Charlestown Asylum and his case tho't a very unpromising one. . . . I received from him his Dissertation on Shakespeare. The letter accompanying it betrayed the state of his mind; but the essay is a noble production: not consecutive, filled with one thought; but that is so deep and true and illustrated so happily and even grandly, that I account it an addition to our really scanty stock of adequate criticism on Shakespear. Such a mind cannot be lost.[14]

As an authority on Jones Very, Emerson obviously had greater confidence in his own judgment—even when it was based on indirect evidence—than he had in either that of Elizabeth Peabody or Upham and Brazer, each of whom relied on actual observation and the resultant "facts." Emerson had standards different from theirs for measuring the extent of a man's right mindedness. He apparently agreed with Very who had said in "Shakespeare" that a man can communicate only what he himself is.[15] Whatever Very *was,* according to Emerson's appraisal, was worth preserving, regardless of the expense to Very or to himself.

# XIII

## *From Bedlam to Concord*

### SEPTEMBER–OCTOBER 1838

VERY SPENT one month at the hospital. When he arrived he appeared to Dr. Bell to be in "comfortable health." The only indication of possible disorder was his insistence that he was under direct inspiration from God who had given him a mission, and that the eternal well-being of his soul depended on its success. To convince all who were skeptical he would refer to passages from the Bible. It was evident from the dog-eared copy he brought with him, crammed full of notes and papers in what seemed wild disorder, that he had reflected long and intensely upon the subject of religion. In all other respects he appeared healthy. No signs of physical exhaustion or of having overtaxed his energies were present.

Instead of taking advantage of the opportunity for rest his detention afforded, he was continuously active, taking long walks and rides through the hospital grounds and into the nearby countryside. Whenever he was not permitted his customary exercise he felt "rather discontented." Except for this natural uneasiness with enforced leisure, he was cheerful at all times. There was no reason for him to be unhappy even in the asylum: wherever he was and whatever he did, he knew he always had the Father with him. Much of his time was spent in studying and writing about Hamlet—like himself a son whose invisible, ever-present father had imposed upon him a special mission.

With only one exception an impartial observer could detect, Very's feelings and views upon the particular subject of his obsession remained unchanged during his confinement. After the first week he "professed" to have given up his "duty" to actively "promulgate" his views. He supposed it was a too diligent dissemination of his ideas that had offended the people of Cambridge and Salem, and had caused him to be brought to the asylum "contrary to [his] will." He subsequently wrote several letters to college officials, informing them of this "change" and requesting reinstatement as Tutor. He expected his request would be granted. But disappointed to find himself still at McLean's two weeks later, he began to converse with fellow patients in order to help them achieve the "peace" he had found. The fourth and last week of his confinement he spent in reciting from the Bible, in studying *Hamlet,* and in writing. It was then he realized he soon would be discharged from the hospital. "Under the influences of the spirit," he felt that his "usual manner" had "retur[n]ed in all things"—except that he now obeyed the spirit as his "natural impulse." No longer could he distinguish between his "old will" and a "sensible will" that was not his own. These "changes" he "passed through" at the asylum, he thought, were "such as every-one born of God must experience." They are "within," and they "lead on from glory to glory." [1]

Dr. Bell could only conclude that from a medical point of view there had been no significant improvement in his condition, and that under the circumstances nothing more could be done for him at McLean's. He was in good physical health; he was not violent; he was not depressed; his attitudes were constructive; he was anxious to have his freedom of movement restored; and he was looking forward to resuming his place as a responsible member of society. Moreover, his mother had been petitioning for his release. Therefore on October 17, 1838, exactly one month after his arrival, Jones Very left the hospital. As he was preparing to leave, "the patients severally thanked him" for having been "of great service to them." [2]

Once it became generally known in Salem that Very had returned, some of the townspeople assumed that the curative skills of Dr. Bell must have saved him "from the delusion of being a prophet extraordinary." According to these local gossips, his "digestive system" had been "entirely out of order" and was now much improved. Other townspeople, however—including Elizabeth Peabody—had misgivings when they realized he was now free "to do as he pleased—and go where he pleased." They thought he was "as crazy as ever." [3]

On the third day after his return to Salem he called once again upon Elizabeth Peabody, spending an hour with her.[4] In a curious way he apologized for his strange behavior during his last visit, the occasion of her spiritual baptism. He said that on that day "he was intoxicated with the Holy Ghost," but that now he was "sobered." In temperate fashion he rapidly reviewed the tenets of Veryism which he had not explained to her in detail before. He told her of his being directly inspired by God, of his being the instrument by which God communicated with men less perfect than he, and of being the means by which sinful men might be purged of their sins. She listened attentively to all he said, without interrupting him or showing any impatience. When he had finished his explanations she told him that the "truth he utters . . . is no revelation" to her. She said that "on a general principle" she did not "expect *personal* prophets—or regard God as dealing *personally*" with men. Very agreed, but the next moment insisted he was an exception to the "general principle." Suppressing her annoyance, she calmly told him "he should take medicine and obey his friends—because if it is truth he utters—

medicine will not purge it away—and that Jesus always acted on the 'proximate motive,' etc."

Then they spoke of the Rev. Mr. Brazer. Very said he had already seen him. Brazer had come to his home, and spoke to him once again "about working miracles to prove his mission or yielding the point he is insane." Elizabeth could not control herself. She called Brazer a "doubly distilled old woman." Brazer, said Very, had in addition told him that Emerson was to blame for his troubles, that Emerson was "universally acknowledged" to be an atheist, that everyone was denouncing him, and that "measures" were being taken to prevent Emerson "from having any more audience to corrupt." He urged Very not to have anything more to do with him. Elizabeth then said that Brazer's every word was malicious nonsense and utter philistinism. Very, however, had reached a somewhat different conclusion. He told her that Brazer was part of a conspiracy against Emerson and himself, and that they both were being persecuted. He then spoke to her about his intention to visit Emerson in a few days in order to deliver his "revelation" to him. Since he thought Emerson "quite *prepared*" to receive it, "but not yet arrived at the Father's mansion," he was going to Concord expecting "full sympathy" from him. He would have gone sooner had he not needed several days to finish his essay on *Hamlet*. While at McLean Hospital he had managed to get most of it done. Now he wanted to take this companion-piece to "Shakespeare" with him when he went to Concord.

After Very left, Elizabeth wrote to Emerson to give him *"the data."* She described Very's visit and conversation, and warned him what to expect when Very arrived. She still thought him "manifestly insane," but not beyond help. She felt that the forthcoming interview between them "may possibly be of some advantage" to both. Then she offered Emerson advice on how to act, based upon her own experience.

He is much more amenable to me than to anybody else—and I think it is because I treat him simply—I let him say his say . . . and he does say much not inconsistent with truth—except perhaps in its exaggeration. . . . I give him no false sympathy. . . . He is very harmless—and when gently dealt with will allow the other party to say his say—and I think you may assume an *authority* which I cannot. You could at least try that experiment once. But I would not—if I were you—stretch your charity so far as to invite him to stay in the house—or if he comes late and you have to—in charity—limit your invitation; else you may not easily get rid of him.

I will not apologize for the liberty I take in making this suggestion for I am sure your kindness will agree with me—that it is worthwhile for you to take advantage of the association of Ideas—which you have in your favour in his mind—to govern it a little. You are the only individual who has the slightest chance of doing him this service.[5]

In a day or two the essay on *Hamlet*—planned sometime before "Shakespeare" was finished, and mainly written while Very was in Dr. Bell's care at Charlestown—was completed. Although much shorter, less intricate in form, simpler in content, more consistently focused, and better balanced in tone than "Shakespeare," "Hamlet" was an integral part of Very's conception of Shakespeare's genius, and derived from the same complex of tensions and ideas. His assumption that readers of "Hamlet" were already familiar with the basic themes and conclusions of the earlier essay confirms the judgment that Dr. Bell's prescriptions caused little if any readjustment in his critical sense. As he did for "Shakespeare," Very subsequently claimed "Hamlet" was "given him" by the Holy Spirit and was "not only the true word, but the best word, that had been spoken on the subject." To question its statements was not merely unreasonable but blasphemy and sacrilege.[6] The only significant difference in attitude between the two essays was that the assertions of the Spirit seemed now more circumscribed and scholarly. However, the essay by no means lacked Very's usual moral and theological bias.

When Very wrote in his first Shakespearean essay that a man

can communicate only what he himself is, he already possessed the informing idea for the second essay.[7] *Hamlet,* he subsequently wrote, was "more vitally connected" than any of Shakespeare's other plays to the "great characteristics" of his mind.[8] Controlling Hamlet's destiny were events occurring not at Elsinore but in Shakespeare himself, events which accounted for his "more than common sympathy" with Hamlet. (P. 95.) For this reason Hamlet's character discloses the "basis of Shakespeare's own being." (P. 88.)

Taken in its entirety, the play demonstrates that Shakespeare was moved "more strongly, perhaps," than any other man by what "To be or not to be" involves. This "mystery," which cloaks human existence, is inscribed upon the play's every scene. (Pp. 100–1.) It is as much an expression of Shakespeare's fundamental dilemma as it is of Hamlet's, because Shakespeare must have often thought

that to be or not to be forever, was a question which must be settled; . . . Other motives had no hold upon him . . . but the thought of death touched him in his very centre. However strong the sense of continued life such a mind as his may have had, it could never reach that assurance of eternal existence which Christ alone can give, . . . Here lie the materials out of which this remarkable tragedy was built up. From the wrestling of his own soul with the great enemy come that depth and mystery which startle us in Hamlet. [Pp. 85–86.]

If, as Very said in "Shakespeare," a man can communicate only what he himself is, then the essay on Hamlet is a subtle but illuminating guide to what Very *was* in September and October 1838. His observations on Shakespeare and Hamlet are more revealing as autobiography than as literary criticism.

When he was writing the essay he could still recall the recent failure of Dr. Ware and President Quincy, and of the Reverends Brazer and Upham to understand him. The treatment he received from them underscored remarks he made in the essay about the failure of Dr. Johnson, Goldsmith, Goethe, Coleridge, and others to explain the play, because they lacked a "just conception of Hamlet's situation and character." (P. 83.) Similarly, had he been viewed by his Cambridge and Salem contemporaries from his own vantage (identical with that of God, he thought), and had Hamlet been viewed by Shakespeare's commentators "from the position in which Shakespeare must have seen him," none would have been diverted "by the mere show of madness and inaction." They would have looked beyond these and seen the "deeper meaning" he and Hamlet expressed. (P. 92.) Their inability to recognize himself and Shakespeare as counterparts caused the parallel failures.

Hamlet has been called mad, but . . . Shakespeare thought more of his madness than he did of the wisdom of the rest of the play. Like the vision-struck Paul, in the presence of Felix, he spoke what to those around him, whose eyes had not been opened on that light brighter than the sun, seemed madness; but which was, in fact, the words of truth and soberness. Men have felt that though mad, . . . there was something in his language which revealed them to themselves, and to which, though ignorant of its full meaning, every human heart must and does beat responsive. [Pp. 96–97.]

The thoughts of Shakespeare (and also his own, Very believed), "though common . . . as the sunlight and the air, are, like them, mighty hieroglyphics which . . . can never be interpreted until the wisdom of God is shed abroad." Only men who have achieved the "peace" which follows the successful struggle against unnatural selves and which brings divine Wisdom, can properly comprehend Shakespeare, or Hamlet, or Very. (Pp. 103–4.) From Jesus, and from those (including Very himself)

upon whom Christianity has had its true effect, as from before the face of him whom John saw in vision sitting upon "a great white throne," "the earth and the heavens have fled away, and there is found no place for them." [9] Shakespeare was . . . the childlike embodiment of this sense of existence. It found its *natural* expression in the many forms of his characters; in the circumstances of Hamlet, its *peculiar* one. [P. 85.]

Just as "the divine meaning of that eternal life of which Jesus speaks" cannot be understood "until we have experienced that death of our own wills," so too the words of Shakespeare. Like the words of "all true men"—in whose company Very placed himself—they "have a meaning whose fullness can only be felt by a spirit in a similar state to his from whose lips they fell." Otherwise "they are but sounds filling the empty chambers of the soul with noisy echoes." (P. 97.)

Actually the character of Hamlet is *"something more than natural"* because in him are dramatized the "great features of Shakespeare's own mind." (P. 84.) Very too considered himself *"something more than natural"*; in himself, as in all "true men," were dramatized the "great features" of the mind of God. If, as Very believed, "Hamlet is rather such a son as Shakespeare would have made, than the Hamlet of the king's own household" (p. 95), then God's Very in similar fashion is completely different from Lydia Very's natural son.

His specific understanding of Hamlet, as disclosed in the essay, is also self-revealing. It embraced a sensitive, imaginative young man whose soul was stripped to the "clear groundwork of being" by the slashes of the "great foreplane of adversity." (P. 85.) Repelled by the "desolation" spreading uncontained around him, he engaged the "mystery of his own being, the root of all mysteries," until it became an "overmastering element" of his thought. (Pp. 87–88.) In his "far-seeing mind" he contended bravely with the "great realities" which stretched beyond his despised present life; but this mental struggle never was concluded. (Pp. 88–89.) He "endured and clung" to his anguish because, in spite of his "prophetic eye," he "doubted" the existence of another life. (Pp. 90–91, 93.) Nevertheless, his own nature, conspiring with circumstance, forced him to deal with two worlds at once, with the world of "objects of sense," and with the "invisible world of

spiritual realities." (P. 94.) As he faced the "grim reality" nurtur-
ing, stimulating, and finally destroying him, he exposed a "wild
tumultuous sea of thoughts" which transfigured "the idea of
death and the presence of things invisible": they "stood sensible
to sight and touch before him," while "time and space . . .
dwindled to what they really are, but golden points of an im-
mensity." (P. 96.)

For both Hamlet and Shakespeare the relevant question was
one of being or not-being; but for the numberless sinful and
unnatural men (as it had been for Very himself before his
rebirth), it is not a proper question. It is, mistakenly, considered
by them already settled. For the unregenerate, "to be rich or not
to be rich, to be wise or not to be wise, to be honored or not to be
honored,—these are the questions." Because they "live so continually in this state of mind," they cannot accurately conceive of
Hamlet's character, nor can they "see Shakespeare himself in his
creations." (P. 99.) The failure of Shakespeare's readers is thus a
moral failure, and relates to their failure as men. The critics of
both Shakespeare and Very could not understand that the truest
form of heroic action was mental and inward, even were it never
to lead to any outward deed. (P. 84.) Hamlet was neither
cowardly nor mad, and Jones Very was neither irresponsible nor
maniacal; both lived in worlds regulated by depravities of which
they were themselves free. But since the former's innocence was
natural while the latter's freedom from guilt was purchased by
Christ, in his own "creations"—Very continued to insist—were to
be "seen" not his own self but God's. And the uncertainties which
tormented Hamlet's fertile mind were replaced in his by impatience with the slow passage to eternity and the full realization of
God's kingdom.

As soon as this essay was completed, Very was ready to travel
from Salem in search of disciples. On Wednesday October twenty-fourth, one week after Dr. Bell had discharged him, Elizabeth
Peabody's "somewhat too angelic" young man who *"loves* dark-

ness better than light," set out for that part of "this world of sin and woe" mischievously named Concord.[10] He expected to find there the receptive audience so far denied him. Except for his mother (who now believed all he told her and who was willing to accept God on his terms), only Elizabeth Peabody had so far treated him with anything resembling the sympathy he sought. But she, in spite of her kindnesses, refused to believe. Thus, carrying his essay on *Hamlet,* Jones Very arrived at the home of Ralph Waldo Emerson for a five-day visit.

At Concord Very was not at his most agitated. The "extravagance and wildness of manner and language" which had so unnerved Cambridge and Salem in September had almost entirely disappeared by this time.[11] Still, even a relatively quiescent Jones Very was not a particularly easy guest to house, as Elizabeth Peabody had warned. His self-confidence alone would make him difficult. However, had he shown himself completely tractable and far less idiosyncratic than reports and rumor promised, his host would have been disappointed. But as it happened, the visit was profitable and successful from Emerson's viewpoint, though not from Very's. Emerson was not trying to gain a convert. He wanted the opportunity to observe, converse, question, and speculate on Very's "peculiar state of mind" and on the role he might play in the world.[12] Moreover, he would not, like the more cautiously protective Elizabeth Peabody, advise him to take his medicine and listen to the counsel of friends.

Although originally prompted by curiosity and the desire to explore Very's state of mind, Emerson found that more than these were satisfied by having him for a companion. Very's ideas and criticisms of the present disposition of man and society were illuminating in themselves. According to Emerson, Very was a "monotone," a man capable of intensive, concentrated vision. Whatever he looked at he saw truly, although his eye embraced only a small part of what was there to be seen. Emerson knew that just such a man as this, through his narrowly precise view, could make others "wise to the extent of his own uttermost receivings." Therefore, even at the expense of having his more wary friends and neighbors believe he entertained a "savage society" or kept a "menagerie of monsters" in his home, Jones Very must be welcomed. Emerson could risk ridicule and denunciation because he knew that even the "partial action of [Very's] mind in one direction is a telescope for the objects on which it is pointed."

At first Emerson was puzzled by Very's peculiarly metaphorical and idiomatic vocabulary, a style more scriptural than Yankee. But once he understood it, Emerson was "very happy." Not even a "certain violence of thought and speech," a constantly accusing attitude and a persistently argumentative manner—which Emerson thought discrediting and unworthy of his remarks—could lessen his enthusiasm for Very. Since much of what he said about the present condition of society, of the church, and of the college was "perfectly just," Very struck a balance between oddity and good sense which Emerson could not resist. Consequently he judged the violence merely "superficial." [13]

He especially liked the shameless egotism that led Very to make statements so profound that they seemed to border on the absurd, as when he confessed "he felt it an honor to wash his face" because it was the "temple of the spirit." [14] And to his credit, there was nothing sentimental or affected about him. During a walk through Walden Woods, Very said he was so overwhelmed by the beauty of autumn there he almost forgot "that the world was des[e]rt and empty, all the people wicked." [15] Emerson heard in this the ring of truth. And Very spoke often about his study of Shakespeare, explaining he was led to it by the desire to solve the paradox of Shakespeare's being a "genius" yet "no saint." [16]

They spoke about many things during the five days, but by mutual preference they spoke mainly about Jones Very. Although scarcely any details of these conversations have been preserved, Emerson certainly heard from him what others were hearing at this time. Since both men understood this was the purpose of the visit, Very must have related what had happened to him since their last meeting in May 1838 when the Transcendental Club discussed the "question of Mysticism." [17]

He told him [18] that his earlier *change of heart,* "commonly called the new birth," was only a prelude; it was nothing more than his hearing the "voice of John" in the "wilderness" of his heart; it was merely a preparation for a greater change to come; and it was merely a decision to refrain from doing wrong. He explained his kinship with John the Baptist whose cry, "prepare ye the way," he was emulating; he explained the difference between John's baptism with water and the baptism by the one mightier than John who "cometh after" and baptizes "with the Holy Ghost and with fire"; he explained John's saying that Jesus "must increase, but I must decrease"; and he explained that the tree "which bringeth not forth good fruit"—and which must be "hewn down, and cast into the fire"—was the tree of self. [19]

Very spoke too of the "new will" which came upon him at Harvard about six weeks before, and which even there in Concord at the moment of his speaking with Emerson, was compelling him to initiate good. This transformation, Very explained, was what John referred to as the baptism of the Holy Ghost. Through it there came upon him (while he was still in Cambridge) a continuing sensation—a feeling which seemed divorced from his own consciousness—that a single power was operating in the world, animating not only Jones Very but everything and everybody with whom he came in contact. He tried to make Emerson understand that it was this spirit of God within him which had directed him to declare the Second Coming of Christ to be at hand. He told Emerson why that wasn't the declaration of a madman: Christ is in every man, not only in Jones Very, and needs only to be set free in them, as He had already been set free in himself. The Second Advent consists of this freeing of Christ. Therefore the Second Advent could be brought about even in Emerson—provided he agree to follow the directions of John the Baptist as he (Very) interpreted them. He also informed Emerson that while he was at McLean Hospital he had begun to obey the "spirit" as his "natural impulse." No longer was Christ a power separate from himself.

He spoke to Emerson in this manner:

The purification I experienced in obeying [John], in cutting down the corrupt tree and preparing the way for the one who came after was that of his baptism of water. He, as he said, must *decrease,* he was of the earth; He whom I now know must *increase,* He is from above. I have been in the heart of the earth obedient to John three days and three nights and am risen in Christ as a witness unto you and all, that he comes not by water only but by blood. This blood I daily shed in my sufferings such as he who is born of the Father must suffer; for thereby he is a spirit and to him Christ speaks. . . . As he is imprisoned in you, believe that this is the Christ that is to come and that you are to expect no other. Behold the blind see, the dumb speak, the dead are raised. Believe and go on rejoicing in John's *decrease* and you shall find him who comes after . . .[20]

Emerson's uneasiness over Very's vocabulary can readily be understood from this statement of his revelation and mission. It was such a Johannine deluge of words that had led Elizabeth Peabody and other Salem witnesses to think Very used biblical language "in the whimsical manner an insane person might."[21] Emerson, however, in time came to enjoy "the poetic and original way" Very quoted Scripture.[22]

Since it was a recent idea, Very as well must have told Emerson of his conviction that "there is no such thing as physical evil"; evil consists of the willfulness which brings forth disobedience, and therefore could not possibly be physical; it was a defect of attitude and not of event. In this connection he would have spoken also of the "impiety of detaching Thought from the Will" (the idea Bronson Alcott called "Very's doctrine")—by which he meant that the "God within" must never be questioned; that

His commandments must always be executed without regard to circumstance or consequence; that all His promptings must result in deeds; and that the good intention is inseparable from the good action.[23]

The conversation at Emerson's house was not one-sided, however. Confidences were exchanged during the visit. The confessional mood proved contagious, and Emerson revealed within himself not Very's God but his own demon.

I told Jones Very that I had never suffered, that I could scarce bring myself to feel a concern for the safety and life of my nearest friends that would satisfy them; that I saw clearly that if my wife, my child, my mother, should be taken from me, I should remain whole, with the same capacity of cheap enjoyment from all things. I should not grieve enough, although I love them.[24]

That such an admission was made at all would seem to indicate that Emerson was more than an impersonal investigator of Very's psyche. To some significant extent, but not completely enough to satisfy Very, Emerson's constitutional resistance to Veryism was giving way. It could not have been easy for a man so outwardly restrained as Emerson to bring himself to disclose such private thoughts to a man ten years his junior, with whom he had never before been intimate.

On Sunday the twenty-eighth, the fifth day of his visit, the tension gradually mounting in the Emerson household finally was let loose. Very announced to Emerson—no doubt at some appropriately dramatic moment in the talk—that for him this day was a "day of hate." Emerson graphically described his guest's mood on this particular dismal day:

He discerns the bad element in every person whom he meets, which repels him: he even shrinks a little to give the hand,—the sign of receiving. The institutions, the cities which men have built the world over, look to him like a huge blot of ink. . . . And he is very sensible of *interference* in thought and act. A very accurate discernment of spirits belongs to his state, and he detects at once the presence of an alien element, though he cannot tell whence, how, or whereto it is.[25]

In keeping with this black temper he disagreed with some innocent but surely pious and well-intentioned sentiment spoken by Mrs. Emerson, who was trying hard to accomodate herself to the demands of her husband's friend. Invoking the "Very doctrine," he mechanically snapped his objection: "Your thought speaks there, and not your life." She had made the error of speaking better than she actually was, and was therefore guilty of the "impiety of detaching Thought from the Will." [26]

Lidian Emerson was not the only one to be accused by Very that otherwise pleasant October day. Emerson himself was not spared. "He thinks me covetous in my hold of truth," Emerson observed, and

of seeking truth separate, and of receiving or taking it, instead of merely obeying. The Will is to him all, as to me (after my own showing) Truth. He is sensible in me of a little colder air than that he breathes. He says, "You do not disobey because you do the wrong act; but you do the wrong act because you disobey; and you do not obey because you do the good action, but you do the good action because you first obey." [27]

Whenever Emerson tried to justify himself, Very would listen patiently but stand his ground, refusing to argue, and insisting "It is the necessity of the spirit to speak with authority." With the invocation of this corollary to the "Very doctrine," discussion had reached an impasse. Sometime after this incident Very admitted that he had "tried" to tell Emerson that he was "also right," but Very was informed by the "spirit" within him that on the contrary, Emerson was "not right" at all. It was as if, Very continued, "I should say, It is not morning; but the morning says, It is the morning." By way of further clarification, Very proclaimed to Emerson: "Use what language you will, . . . you can never say anything but what you are." Emerson was being disobedient, willfully ignoring the God Very knew was struggling for liberty within his friend's heart. He was thinking when he should have been grappling with his private will.[28]

But the climax to Very's "day of hate," at least for Emerson, was still to come. He and his family were delighted when Very, driven to pique by their intransigence, assured them he hated them all.[29] Their cheerful reaction to this disclosure surprised and exasperated him even further. It was not compliments for his frankness that he craved. He wanted only to be believed, and to be accepted for the God residing powerfully within him. With characteristic understatement, Emerson explained to him why they were so pleased by his expression of extreme dislike for them. "Sincerity is the highest compliment you can pay," he told Very. This remark, although offered kindly by Emerson, only inflamed the man who spoke "with authority." [30]

That same evening a meeting of Sunday school teachers was held in Emerson's home, and Emerson had the opportunity of seeing for himself why the Salem ministers had hurried Very off to Charlestown. He recorded the incident, describing how Very brought his "day of hate" to a glorious close.

I ought not to omit recording the astonishment which seized all the company when our brave saint . . . fronted the presiding preacher. The preacher began to tower and dogmatize with many words. Instantly I foresaw that his doom was fixed; and as quick as he ceased speaking, the saint set him right and blew away all his words in an instant,—unhorsed him, I may say, and tumbled him along the ground in utter dismay, like my angel of Heliodorus.[31] Never was discomfiture more complete. In tones of genuine pathos he "bid him wonder at the Love which suffered him to speak there in his chair, of things he knew nothing of; one might expect to see the book taken from his hands and him thrust out of the room,—and yet he was allowed to sit and talk, whilst every word he spoke was a step of departure from the truth, and of this commanded himself to bear witness!" [32]

No wonder then Very "passed with some of the company for insane"; the wonder was, to Very's great credit, that "all were struck with his insight." [33]

Realizing rightly that nothing more could be accomplished by continuing the interviews at this time, Very informed Emerson that he would leave the following morning for Cambridge— intending to convince Harvard authorities that he should resume his duties as Greek Tutor. Fascinating as he was to Emerson, there was little chance of this. Even for Emerson, Very was the kind of man easier to talk and write about than to talk and live with. For self-protection (his own level-headedness had been under attack for nearly a week), as much as out of kindness, Emerson offered to drive his guest as far as Waltham. [34]

By the time Very was anxious to leave Concord, Emerson had realized that his eager, naïve friend was essentially a tragic figure, with whom he could sympathize in silence (and perhaps envy in moments of perversity), but to whom he could say little and for whom he could do less. Very's ingenuousness made him a conspicuous target for the sophisticated and the unwise, as his adventures with the pious men of Salem showed. And Very persisted in acting as if he didn't realize how dangerous his mission was. Curiously enough, Emerson made no attempt to warn him or dissuade him from pursuing his suicidal course. He preferred not to meddle, and was anxious to see precisely what would develop were Very left to his own instincts. He was sanguine enough to note that Very's only defense in visiting others is that "he goes to do them good." [35] As Emerson well knew, of all motives this is the most objectionable to the bene-ficiaries, and the one which affords least protection to the patron.

Very was for Emerson then a tragic figure. He was tragic not because of some distortion of mind, not because of fallacies marring his logic or conclusions, but because of the openness and stubbornness with which he expressed his convictions, and because he required too much from his friends by insisting they accept them. He was indeed, as Emerson said, "our brave saint." His was the heroism of certain defeat. His was the rebirth for martyrdom.

Since he was also a man "to whom life was more than meat, the body [more] than raiment,"[36] Very differed from the reformers, the spiritual exhibitionists, the professional improvers of individuals and societies, and other do-gooders toward whom Emerson was cool.

He lives in the sight of he who made him, made the things he sees.
He would as soon embrace a black Egyptian mummy as Socrates. He would obey, obey. He is not disposed to attack religions and charities, though false. The bruised reed he would not break; the smoking flax he would not quench.[37]

It was not that Very was too passive or a quietist. Rather, strenuous commitment to his mission went beyond individual preferences and served the pleasure of God alone. His dedication was scarcely human; his sense of duty hardly practical.

Unlike Very, who "has nothing to do with time because he obeys,"[38] Emerson knew that Very was demanding too much from disciples for his mission to succeed. He understood that the kind of obedience Very expected from others belonged not to the world of time but to eternity. It failed to take into account the weakness of all but the exceptional human will. Certainly Emerson's own will lacked such single-minded discipline as Very imposed upon his.

Still Emerson was impressed with his quixotic courage, his self-assurance, and his large measure of truth. It was with regret and admiration, some feelings of guilt and possibly some fears, that Emerson allowed Very to depart.

He is gone into the multitude as solitary as Jesus. In dismissing him I seem to have discharged an arrow into the heart of society. Wherever that young enthusiast goes he will astonish and disconcert men by dividing for them the cloud that covers the profound gulf that is in man.[39]

The next day Emerson recalled his obligation to Elizabeth Peabody. Scarcely did he agree with her that Very's friendship would be a personal liability to him. Her fears that Very's position would be confused with Transcendentalism, thereby unduly arousing people against her close friends,[40] was not shared by Emerson. He reported his findings to her:

he is profoundly sane, and as soon as his thoughts subside from their present excited to a more natural state, I think he will make all men sensible of it. If it shall prove that his peculiarities are fixed, it can never alter the value of the truth and illumination he communicates, if you deal with him with perfect sincerity.[41]

Margaret Fuller also was kept informed:

Very has been here himself lately and staid [*sic*] a few days confounding us all with the question—whether he was insane? At first sight and speech, you would certainly pronounce him so. Talk with him a few hours and you will think all insane but he. Monomania or mono*Sania* he is a very remarkable person and though his mind is not in a natural and probably not in a permanent state, he is a treasure of a companion, and I had with him most memorable conversations.[42]

But Emerson's most revealing reaction to Very was reserved for the privacy of his journal, recorded a month after his departure, when the question of his sanity was for a time no longer urgent. The similarity he had earlier recognized between Jesus and Very persisted, but was now placed in a more realistic context.

The great distinction between teachers sacred or literary; between poets like Herbert and poets like [Thomas] Wharton; between philosophers like Coleridge and philosophers like [Sir James] Mackintosh; between talkers like [Sampson] Reed and Very and talkers like [James] Walker and [George] Ripley, is, that one class speaks *ab intra,* and the other class *ab extra.* It is of no use to preach to me *ab extra.* I can do that myself. Jesus preaches always *ab intra,* and so infinitely distinguishes himself from all others. In that is the miracle. That includes the miracle. My soul believes beforehand that it ought so to be. That is what I mean when I say I look for a Teacher, . . .[43]

It is significant that following this visit to Concord, Emerson ignored Very the poet, Very the essayist and critic of Shakespeare, and classed him with the "talkers." A personal relationship had grown up between them and was valued by both. Each, however, appraised the relationship differently.

For Emerson, Very was a preacher or "Teacher" whose communication was integral and immediate, and who generated his communication *from within,* from his own experience, and from his sense of the rightness of his convictions. Thereby he disclosed for others what until then they had not suspected in themselves. For Very, Emerson was a man urgently in need of guidance because he preferred truth to goodness, time to eternity, and thinking to being and doing. His dissociation of Thought and Will was not merely unreasonable but spiritually deadening. And only he, Jones Very, could provide him with the means of redemption.

To his journal Emerson confided what he kept from Very. He did indeed recognize the "authority" with which he spoke, even though he could not give himself up to it. He could only acknowledge; he could neither approve nor disapprove of Very's mission. While both men sought to be self-reliant, Emerson preferred to rely upon his own self—not Very's. Therefore the kind of sympathetic response and acceptance Very yearned for he would not and could not provide. However, with his "accurate discernment of spirits," Very sensed that although Emerson wanted to be no man's disciple, he was willing to learn from all men. Encouraged by this limited access to Emerson's "alien element," he was hopeful of total victory over his recalcitrant self.

After taking leave of Emerson on the morning of October twenty-ninth, the somewhat emboldened young man made his way to Cambridge. He (or more accurately, the "Spirit" within him) wanted to speak with President Quincy and Professor Felton about reinstatement as Greek Tutor, and with Dr. Ware about resuming studies with the Divinity School "middle class." Since his formerly terrifying speech and behavior seemed to have disappeared, college authorities listened politely to his appeals. However they refused to forget that six weeks before he had placed the freshmen in a "dangerous situation" with regard to their "proper understanding of religious truth," and in other ways had thoroughly unnerved the Cambridge community. Although the "bad consequences" of his strange discourses and outbursts of feeling had either been "averted" or had "passed off," his requests were firmly denied.[44] But as a courtesy, in view of his present reasonable tone and chastened manner, he was permitted to spend more than a week as a visitor, freely roaming the Yard, speaking informally with students whenever he wished, and calling at the rooms of old friends. Samuel Johnson, who had been Very's most loyal disciple, regretted not having had the "pleasure" of seeing and talking to him during his temporary return to Cambridge.[45]

Very's disappointment was limited to learning that under no circumstances would he be restored to his former position, and that Charles Stearns Wheeler would receive permanent appointment as Greek Tutor and Instructor in History. To the relief of President Quincy and the Board of Overseers, Very agreed to submit his resignation.[46] But Very was not depressed by his visit to Harvard. He was enheartened by the warm reception given him by some of his former students and the Divinity School scholars. Ten days later Very quietly returned to Salem, uncertain of his plans for the future but still convinced that God had singled him out for some special mission.

# PART THREE: VISIONS AND REVISIONS

"*Swedenborg.* He reminds me again and again of our Jones Very, who had an illumination that enabled him to excel everybody in wit and to see farthest in every company and quite easily to bring the proudest to confusion; and yet he could never get out of his Hebraistic phraseology and mythology, and, when all was over, still remained in the thin porridge or cold tea of Unitarianism."

—*Ralph Waldo Emerson November 5, 1845*
Journal *entry, VII, 136–37.*

# *Friendly Evaluations*

## WINTER 1838–1839

FOR JONES VERY the winter of 1838–1839 was a period of continuing contacts with friends, and of repetitions of his frantic warnings that they were in immediate danger of forfeiting all possibility of reconciliation with God. However, in spite of these familiar attitudes and patterns of conduct, this was also a period of significant change—both for his tactics of redemption and for the responses they elicited from those he was trying to help. His actions still betrayed his excited state of mind, and he continued to worry about the sinfulness evident everywhere around him but of which he was himself miraculously free. Nevertheless it was a creative period for him, and as it developed a satisfying one as well.

At the time of his discharge from McLean Hospital in the middle of October, he was certain he was obeying his new God-given will as if it were his "natural impulse." Otherwise, he said, his "usual manner" had returned, concluding the series of inward changes he had undergone and which he believed "every one born of God must experience." [1] Writing sonnets had been an important part of his "usual manner" for more than a year, and this remained unchanged, except for the consequences of his conviction that he now was writing from "natural impulse." How this affected his poetry may be surmised from the first of his sonnets accepted for publication in the Salem *Observer* after this psychological adjustment. "The New Birth," printed in the October twenty-seventh issue, described the effects of what had happened to him:

> 'Tis a new life—thoughts move not as they did
> With slow uncertain steps across my mind;
> In thronging haste fast pressing on they bid
> The portals open to the viewless wind,
> That comes not save when in the dust is laid
> The crown of pride that gilds each mortal brow,
> And from before man's vision melting fade
> The heavens and earth; their walls are falling now—
> Fast crowding on, each thought asks utterance strong;
> Storm-lifted waves swift rushing to the shore,
> On from the sea they send their shouts along,
> Back through the cave-worn rocks their thunders roar;
> And I, a child of God by Christ made free,
> Start from death's slumbers to Eternity.[2]

With loss of the distinction between heaven and earth, man and God become one; defeats are victories, and pain gives way to joy. The Divine breath flowing without interruption or interference now transmits visions and images of startling vividness, filling the vacuum left by the repression of physical being. Confident of the special sanction to his new and vigorous mental life, Very felt he now could act in a way consistent with his exalted thoughts. The transformation of his nature was complete. All things now were possible, even the difficult mastery of his art.

The tempering of this irresistible but non-rational optimism by the crush of realities and expediences at Concord and Cambridge was not severe. Nor were his expectations and confidence in himself belied. In the middle of November Emerson's cautious attitude toward him changed. The farewell bid Very at the close of the October twenty-fourth to twenty-ninth visit—when Emerson dismissed Very "as solitary as Jesus," discharged as an "arrow" into the "heart of society"—had seemed at the time to mark the end of their relationship, so far as Emerson was concerned. Only Very's personality, his eccentric behavior, and the two Shakespeare essays had prompted Emerson's patience and cordiality. In spite of Very's brilliant moodiness, his irritability and accusations whenever confronted by an audience he considered openly hostile to his astonishing claims for himself, and his sweeping denunciations of "wickedness" in others, the visit proved satisfactory for Emerson. He observed, listened, and learned. He also studied the essays and asked questions about them. But since he still was not certain he understood the "whole import" of the dissertations on Shakespeare even after Very's attempts at clarification, he asked for and received permission to have them copied. Emerson wished to examine them further after Very's departure. He promised to finish with the original manuscripts within ten days and forward them to Very at Harvard.[3] In less than a week Emerson was satisfied he had unraveled the baffling intricacies. His judgment was that they were "pretty great criticism." They deserved to rank with the best writing on Shakespeare and *Hamlet* by Johnson, Lamb, Coleridge, Schlegel, Herder, and Goethe.[4]

Since no one passed through Concord early in November whom Emerson could trust to carry the original manuscripts to Very at Cambridge, he held them until certain Very had returned to Salem. Then he arranged to have Miss Susan Burley, his Salem correspondent, deliver the "pacquet" containing them and an accompanying letter.[5] "I send herewith," he wrote to Very,

your two manuscripts with hearty thanks. I have availed myself of your permission to copy them, and shall endeavor so discreetly to use the copies, as not to prejudice your rights and convenience, if you should choose to read them as lectures. I shall presently read them both again, with attention, in the transcript . . . I am very sorry that the MSS. should have been detained by me beyond the allowed ten days; . . . I trust you have not wanted them.[6]

In spite of Emerson's high opinion of the essays, his continuing interest in them, and his intention to circulate copies among knowledgeable friends like Margaret Fuller,[7] he still thought that five days had quite exhausted the possibilities of personal intercourse between them. He saw no advantage to Very or himself by resuming close connections with him. But Very thought otherwise.

Within a week of returning from his unsuccessful but not discouraging mission to Harvard, Very sent Emerson a newspaper clipping of two of his most recent sonnets, "In Him we live, and move, and have our being" and "Enoch." Immediately Very gained new significance for Emerson. Until then Emerson had never considered him a poet. Either he did not know or was not impressed by the knowledge that in six years Very had written approximately two-hundred poems which he considered worth preserving, and that some forty had already appeared in Salem newspapers. Emerson had not read any of them, and had not indicated any desire to do so. Very was important to him for other reasons. He saw him primarily as a personality, as a conversationalist and moralist, and as a lecturer and writer of essays. But when he read the two poems, he completely revised his conception. He was surprised and delighted. On November eighteenth he wrote to thank Very for sending them.

I love them and read them to all who have ears to hear. Do not, I beg you, let a whisper or sigh of the Muse go unattended to or unrecorded. The sentiment which inspires your poetry is so deep and true, and the expression so simple, that I am sure you will find your audience very large as soon as the verses first take air and get abroad. And a man should be very happy and grateful who is the bringer to his fellowmen of a good so excellent as poetry.[8]

What had so stirred Emerson were these two sonnets, typical of those Very had been writing since September 1838:

Father! I bless thy name that I do live,
And in each motion am made rich with thee,
That when a glance is all that I can give,
It is a kingdom's wealth if I but see;
This stately body cannot move, save I
Will to its nobleness my little bring;
My voice its measured cadence will not try,
Save I with every note consent to sing;
I cannot raise my hands to hurt or bless,
But I with every action must conspire;
To show me there how little I possess,
And yet that little more than I desire;
May each new act my new allegiance prove,
Till in thy perfect love I ever live and move.

I looked to find a man who walked with God,
Like to the Jewish patriarch of old;
Though gladdened millions on his footstool trod,
Yet none with him did such sweet converse hold;
I heard the wind in low complaint go by
That none its melodies like him could hear;
Day unto day spoke wisdom from on high,
Yet none like David turned a willing ear;
God walked alone unhonored through the earth;
For him no heart-built temple open stood,
The soul forgetful of her nobler birth
Had hewn him loftly shrines of stone and wood,
And left unfinished and in ruins still
The only temple he delights to fill.[9]

Emerson's surprise and spirited praise notwithstanding, his letter revealed him as somewhat less than a worshipful reader. It was characteristic of Emerson—especially in his estimates of Very and outward show of feelings for him—to have reservations, to qualify his approval, to hedge his enthusiasm with a patronizing tone. He balanced his admiration, therefore, with advice for improving the second sonnet. He suggested that "Jewish" be replaced because it was "an alibi" and inaccurate. "The country of Enoch I suppose cannot very well be settled though I should think 'Syrian' would not be too great a licence." [10] Very wisely rejected the specific proposal, while accepting the principle behind Emerson's criticism. When the sonnet was reprinted in 1839, the second line read, "Like the translated patriarch of old;—" [11] thereby proving Very the more imaginative and experienced poet, if only on the subject of Enoch and his direct ascent into heaven.

Emerson made three additional suggestions, none of which Very could resist, especially since at one point the phrasing resembled Very's own language of piety:

you must after a little more writing—collect your prose and verse in a volume and make the bookseller give you bread for the same. And let me help you with some of my recent experience in the matter. . . . If you write again in the Observer, send me a copy, if you can.

His obvious desire to reopen communication with Very, and to establish it on different terms, received further confirmation in the same letter. Emerson promised to send him a ticket for his "Human Life" lectures, scheduled to begin in Boston in December. And even more significantly, he extended Very an invitation to come to Concord after the lecture series was completed. He felt a second visit was now indicated, and hoped Very would not refuse. He reminded him that he was remembered "with great affection and hope" in the Emerson household, and that he would be welcomed by others besides himself. [12] Emerson's "dismissal" of Very at the end of the October visit now appeared premature.

Emerson, however, kept his unexpected reappraisal of Very to himself. Very also remained silent about these overtures. Elizabeth Peabody, although a close friend of both men, knew nothing of the new basis for Emerson's interest in Very. Two weeks later she scolded him for his apparent insensitivity to Very's genius:

I mean[t] to have written you a castigation . . . for your obstinate blindness to this real *Poet*. I remember you once said in a sermon that if you found you could not discover the Milton or Plato of your own day you should feel that you probably had no real apprehension of them at all ———— Perhaps "out of your own mouth etc"!! [13]

Emerson's private enthusiasm but public reticence for Very was becoming an embarrassment if even his own words could convict him of not doing enough for so demanding a friend.

Jones Very was naturally encouraged by the kind letter of November eighteenth, but in a way its writer could scarcely have foreseen. Not having shown prior interest in his poems, Emerson did not know at this time what Very was insisting to all who were impressed by them: they were not really his—they were "given him" by the Holy Spirit within him. He regarded his poems as "the Word" of God in fact.[14] Consequently, when the Peabody family told him how much they enjoyed them, he smiled and said that unless they were thought beautiful because they also heard "the Voice" of the Holy Spirit while reading them, "they would be of no avail." He himself valued the sonnets precisely because they were not originated by him.[15]

Responding to them the way Very intended was a more complex process than a casual reader was prepared for, as Emerson should have realized. It involved an eschatological and epistemological commitment of the kind Very discussed in his Hamlet essay. There he wrote:

We must not suppose from the impression that words make upon *us* that we necessarily understand what they mean to others. We are but too apt to mistake for knowledge the sounds that give us a mere outside recognition of the states of mind from which they proceeded. It is the spirit that quickens what we hear,—the mere hearing is nothing. . . . Let us not then suppose that, by treasuring up the golden language that has fallen from other tongues of power, we are gaining for ourselves a fast possession; for, unless their spirit is growing up within us to fill their dumb words with the eloquence of life, our piled wealth, like the rich-colored leaves of autumn, will shrink in our hands to the dark and worthless emblems of decay.[16]

Language, according to Very, reflects the inward state of the user, the condition of his soul. ("Use what language you will," Very had told Emerson in October, "you can never say anything but what you are.") [17] Meanings are readily distorted unless the words are understood from the standpoint of the original user. (Very, for example, believed he understood *Hamlet* as Shakespeare had intended because he had completed a "perfect union and relationship" with Shakespeare.) [18] Therefore, when the words are those of the Holy Spirit—as happens whenever the speaker possesses the greatness of "genius" or of "virtue"—comprehension necessitates an acknowledgment of their ultimately divine origins. This acknowledgment is possible only when the reader has a relationship to the Spirit not unlike that of the user, which enables him to detect the supernatural "Voice" giving rise to the words.

Given this avataric conception of his poems and his confidence in Emerson's perceptivity, Very at once construed Emerson's praise as an indication that his mission to him was finally beginning to succeed. He replied to the letter accordingly.

I was pleased to hear that my stay with you was improving [i.e. spiritually beneficial], and that you love that which is spoken by the word. If you love it aright in the spirit of obedience it shall be unto you given to hear and speak of the Father in Christ. . . . Every scribe instructed in the kingdom . . . shall hear the word of the Father and anew interpret for men the old. . . . You seem desirous to hear.[19]

The "Voice," whose words had so impressed Emerson in the two sonnets (or so Very believed), spoke directly to him once again through the agency of Jones Very. This time it spoke in prose, and addressed him as "Good and faithful *servant.*" It commanded him in tones which would be satisfied by nothing less than immediate compliance: "enter thou into the joy of the Lord; that is, be a son and therefore heir."

Much encouraged, Very resumed his campaign for regenerating Emerson, and proceeded to instruct him further.

You must pass out of that world in which you are, naked (that is, willess) as you came in. Then shall you have a *new* will born of the spirit which also when submitted to the Father you shall be one with Him; that is, be prepared to see him as a spirit. . . . You must not even wish where you are, but be happy in absolute nakedness. You brought nothing with you, you have nothing to exchange for it, you cannot buy it with gold or desire but must, having sold *all,* wait, and receive; then shall you hear well.

Appropriate explanations followed:

The believing which the kingdom requires is *being.* This is the true belief in every age for the Father seeketh such to worship Him. This is a hard saying, harder than that Swedenborg and many others can bear. Many are the hearers of John that rejoice awhile in *his* light but go not onward into the perfect day. . . . He who hears can only interpret it aright and before the right interpretation who can stand? It is the two-edged sword—the appointed means of God for the destruction of the adversary. When you shall have bound the strong man within you (that is, your will) then you shall be gifted with this weapon and can plunder the goods of the evil one. But hasten to receive it for the abomination stands already in the holy place.[20]

This energetic appeal for spiritual awakening also contained a less strident, more personal plea. Dropping the mask of divinity, Very spoke for himself. In tones stripped of all ecstasy, he revealed how sadly he bore the isolation which accompanied adherence to convictions repudiated by almost everyone he approached. (Only his mother did not think him "sick"—but according to Elizabeth Peabody, Lydia Very "foolishly" pretended to believe everything her son said.) [21] Therefore he inquired of Emerson:

When shall we learn that the true return is in the same thing that we give? That love calls for mercy and not sacrifice? You and the others can return me this and not let me remain alone without a brother in the kingdom. I hun[ger and] thirst for righteousness and power yet none give me even the cup [of] cold water in the name of a disciple.

Once having relaxed his posture of confidence, he attempted to show Emerson his willingness to overcome this unwanted isolation. He acknowledged Emerson's gestures of friendship and sympathy:

Your delay of the manuscripts was not minded and your care in having them copied, may it be rewarded by that spirit with which they are written. . . . The ticket for your Lectures [I] should be glad to receive as the means of seeing you when in Boston, if there this winter. I go to Cambridge on Wednesday [December 5, 1838] or Monday [December 3, 1838] of next week and shall call on Mr Alcott if permitted and Dr. Channing. If you are in Boston I shall learn probably. Your invitation after your lectures are finished I shall be glad to avail myself of if so my feet are directed.[22]

The qualifications "if permitted" and "if so my feet are directed" reflected Very's own doubts about such efforts to overcome his loneliness. He continued his quest for acceptance on his own terms. He could not, he believed, anticipate the future promptings of the Spirit; he could only prepare for the moment when they were revealed to consciousness and could be obeyed by "natural impulse."

Very's preoccupation with salvation, however, did not prevent him from recognizing—as Emerson had already done—that through his writings, if not personally, he might gain the emotional responses he so hungered for. Through Emerson's encouraging letter about the sonnets he came to understand that people have listened to poetry when they were deaf to dogmatic assertions. Therefore he told Emerson:

I should be glad to have your aid whenever it is so ordered for the junking and disposal of that which is placed in my hands. Whenever as you say the weary ones shall hear they will demand and pay the laborer by his poor pittance of bread.

Reading this, Emerson must have been both amused and exasperated. Very seemed incorrigible. And the letter came to an appropriate close, one which could only have further annoyed Emerson:

Soon may you learn that to obey or disobey the will within is all that we can do, and that of all other things the Father alone has the power. That you and your family may soon live and move, [and] have your beings in Him, is ever the spirit's prayer. Amen.[23]

The deliberate echoing of the title of the sonnet for which Emerson could not suggest any improvement was a subtle gibe. Even in an exalted mood Jones Very was capable of mortal impishness.

Two days after writing to Emerson, Very was still elated and in good humor. He called at Charter Street on December second to find all the sisters at home and Mrs. Caleb Foote their guest.[24] On this Sunday evening he was unusually attentive to Elizabeth Peabody, and largely ignored the others. He spoke to her "like an angel" while trying to "promote the new birth" in her. He smiled as often as he spoke, and Elizabeth thought it was because he recognized that from her point of view all his talk must seem "absurd." From his cheerfulness she concluded he was making "allowance" for her. She in turn felt complimented, found him "very charming," and was touched deeply by his words: "when he explained and explained in answer to my questions and self-analyses—it seemed as if I thought and believed exactly so—though I did not acknowledge it quite—that is—I contended for a less violent and more compromised expression of the same ideas." Much later she still remembered his "most beautiful, considerate, tender smile," which was his silent and only reply when she told him, "Mr Very—I feel as if I *could* take your point of view—but I do not dare to—because if I did I am afraid I should lose my sense and could never recover myself again." [25]

Elizabeth Peabody knew that elsewhere in Salem Very conducted himself quite differently. Whenever he called upon the Burley family, it invariably would become a "dismal day." In exasperation he would make free use of the word "hate," and talk a "good deal more violently" than he would with Elizabeth. It was as if he were "driven into extremes" by the gentle arguments they offered. They said he expressed "deep gloom" and looked "gloomy" whenever he was with them, and would tell them they were "wicked" and that "truth itself is a poison to them." He spoke of the "misery" caused him by "living with people he cannot esteem," and frankly admitted "there has been no good man since the apostles until himself." Susan Burley herself said that Very "always appeared to her extremely *good*—and with great powers of apprehension on *points,*" but she thought he was "naturally excessively *conceited*—putting the most inordinate values on all his own thoughts and not capable of complete views on sound subjects."

While Elizabeth Peabody could account for the difference between his behavior at Miss Burley's and in her own home with the theory that he was "absolutely insane," such an explanation did not satisfy her. The more time she spent with him, the less certain she was that his claims and accusations could be explained away as mental aberrations. It amused her to report to Emerson that although Very did not really frighten Susan Burley, he nevertheless "affect[ed] her dreams at night." Elizabeth was flattered to find that the "extreme tension" of his mind "seemed gradually to subside" whenever he spoke with her.[26]

But during the visit on December second Very had more to tell Elizabeth than how to relieve the subtle anguish of her soul. He told her he was thinking of leaving Massachusetts. He wanted, he said, to go to "the West." There he thought he might be able to preach without prejudice, and might even settle permanently in a church of his own. Elizabeth agreed. Although she encouraged him in his dream of somewhere finding a sympathetic audience for his radical enthusiasm, she did not share his hopeful view of the prospects of remaining away permanently. She merely thought the journey itself might "do him good." It would for a time take him away from the bitterness and suspicion which now surrounded him. In her opinion it might therefore be "useful" were he to come in contact with "such unmystical and yet free and liberally disposed people as the Westerns."

She informed Emerson of Very's new ambition and of its possible benefits. She also repeated something else Very had said that pleased her. Because of Very's practice of attributing each of his desires to the promptings of the God within him instead of to external human agents, she repeated something she didn't realize Emerson already knew and had been thinking about for several weeks. Very, she said excitedly, wanted to publish a collection of his sonnets. "How marvellously they flow from him—impromptu—one or two a day. And don't you think they have great artistical merit? Why should they not be printed—and the Shakespeare's too—and why should he not introduce the whole with an account of his states—a psychological autobiography?" Quite unnecessarily she added: "I wish you would think of this and put him up to it." Transcendental communications could indeed be muddled at times.

Her timing was much improved when she delivered the lecture ticket Emerson had sent for Very. Before leaving her that Sunday evening he told her he would go to Boston for the opening session. Nothing more. Either the Spirit within him had already directed him to accept the invitation, or in his delight over an evening passed with such an agreeable companion he had forgotten to make the inquiry.

On Wednesday December fifth, three days after his pleasant visit with Elizabeth Peabody, Very came to Boston to hear Emerson lecture on "The Doctrine of the Soul," and to attend the informal meeting of the Transcendental Club scheduled to follow at Cyrus Bartol's house. Since word had reached Very, probably by way of Elizabeth, that William Ellery Channing had expressed the desire to speak with him on "religious subjects," [27] he decided to call on the elderly minister before going to the lecture. When he arrived, he found James Freeman Clarke and Wendell Phillips already there. He interrupted their conversation, and Channing "listened attentively" to all Very had to say about his God-sponsored "mission." As Very spoke and answered questions, Channing was "immensely impressed and touched with his gentleness [and] modesty and yet complete sense of his word being the utterance of the Holy Spirit." [28] When he finished explaining his mission, Channing asked him "whether it was in consequence of his invitation or in obedience to the Spirit that he came to Boston that morning." Very replied that he was "directed" to accept Channing's invitation. Then Channing said that he noticed that during their conversation Very had gotten up from his chair, and while continuing to speak, had walked over to the fireplace and placed his arm on the mantel. Channing wanted to know whether Very had done this of his own accord, or "in obedience to the Spirit." Without hesitating, Very replied, "In obedience to the Spirit." [29] Had this exchange been instigated by someone other than the acknowledged saint of Unitarianism, Very might have thought it a rude jest and proclaimed a "day of hate." However, according to Wendell Phillips, Channing's attitude was one of "tender reverence throughout," for which Very was thankful. Actually he had never been treated more warmly. He received so sympathetic a hearing that he concluded that Channing was "nearer to the kingdom of heaven than any body he had yet seen." For three hours Channing listened patiently, in what seemed to Very to be the "most docile manner." [30]

Although Elizabeth Peabody was not present at the interview between them, she subsequently was told about it by Channing. "Yes," her oldest and dearest friend told her,

"he had lost his senses—but only that part of his mind which was connected therewith—there was an iron sequence of thought. Men in general," said [Channing], "have lost or never found this higher mind. *Their* insanity is profound,—*his* is only superficial. To hear him talk was like looking into the purely spiritual world—into truth itself. He had nothing of the self exaggeration. He seemed rather to have attained self annihilation and become an oracle of God."

For her benefit Channing quoted some of his "sayings," which she thought "identical with many parts of his sonnets." Channing considered them "proofs of the 'iron sequence' of his thought." His conclusion was that Very "has not lost his *Reason*. He has only lost his *Senses*." Elizabeth Peabody agreed. To judge Very in terms of physical or mental disease was an oversimplification, and unfair to his peculiar genius.[31]

James Freeman Clarke also listened with increasing amazement to Jones Very that December day, and reached conclusions similar to Channing's. Editor of the transcendentally oriented *Western Messenger,* he had come home to Boston to see old friends after an absence of several years in Louisville, Kentucky. He had not met Very before, but when he heard about him from his sister, he was eager to travel to Salem if necessary in order to speak with him.[32] From reports he had received, and from his own observations in Channing's study, he learned that Very was

a young man of much intelligence and of a remarkably pure character, whose mind had become extremely interested within a few months, upon the subject of religion. He was said to have adopted some peculiar views on this important theme, and to consider himself inspired by God to communicate them. Such pretensions had excited the fears of his friends, and by many he was supposed to be partially deranged. The more intelligent and larger sort of minds, however, who had conversed with him, dissented from this view, and although they might admit a partial derangement of the lower intellectual organs, or perhaps an extravagant pushing of some views to their last results, were disposed to consider his main thoughts deeply important and vital.

After Clarke returned to the West in January 1839, he informed his readers about Jones Very, and thereby further clarified Channing's own reactions. He introduced his observations with a psychological discussion of genius, and of "society's" inevitable failure to respond to it as it deserved. The "charge of Insanity," he wrote,

is almost always brought against any man who endeavors to introduce to the common mind any very original ideas. . . . It is also, however, to be remarked that the intense contemplation of any vast theme is apt to disturb the balance of the lower intellectual faculties. While the Reason, which contemplates absolute truth, is active and strong; the Understanding which arranges and gives coherence to our thoughts, may be weakened and reduced to a state of torpor.

Clarke's subject was remarkably suited to his own religious preferences. The result of this fortunate match was a brilliant defense of Jones Very, and a reasonable statement of his ideas in brief (as understood by a sympathetic listener), placing them in a familiar but inevitably suspect Christian tradition.

With respect to Mr. Very, we have only to say that the intercourse we have ourselves had with him has given no evidence ever of such partial derangement. We have heard him converse about his peculiar views of religious truth, and saw only the workings of a mind absorbed in the loftiest contemplations, and which utterly disregarded all which did not come into that high sphere of thought. . . .

Mr. Very's views in regard to religion, . . . were not different from those heretofore advocated by many pure and earnest religionists. He maintains . . . that all sin consists in self-will, all holiness in an unconditional surrender of our own will to the will of God. He believes that one whose object is not to do his will in anything, but constantly to obey God, is led by Him, and taught by Him in all things. He is a Son of God, as Christ was the Son, because he *always* did the things which pleased his Father. He professes to be himself guided continually by this inward light, and he does not conjecture, speculate or believe, but he *knows* the truth which he delivers. In this confidence however, there is nothing of arrogance, but much modesty of manner.[33]

Clarke's timely presence at Dr. Channing's home on December fifth had evidently made a special trip to Salem unnecessary. In three hours he had learned all. Unfortunately, Very never did have the opportunity to discuss with him the prospects of finding a Western ministry. Although Very had intended to do so, the discussion in Channing's study was conducted on too impersonal and elevated a level to permit the intrusion of such a practical matter, and Clarke returned to Louisville several weeks later. Nothing more was ever heard by Very's friends of his wish to establish himself outside Salem. Although continuing to travel widely *in spirit,* Very never undertook any actual journey to "the West."

Unlike Clarke, Bronson Alcott did not witness Very in action at Channing's house. However, he did see him later in the day during Emerson's "grand and inspiring statement of the primal facts of the soul," and his impressions were compatible with those of Channing and Clarke. At the lecture Alcott recognized "every hopeful, devout person" of his acquaintance, "whether youthful or of matured age." Following the lecture "several gentlemen repaired to Mr. Bartol's and had further talk on the Doctrine of Life." [34] Very was among them, and Alcott heard his "interesting remarks on life—will—love, etc."

He said much that was true, and expressed himself with great beauty. His language is that of an Oriental, and one might almost fancy himself in the presence of St John, whose words he affects. He is a phenomenon quite remarkable in this age of sensualism and idolatry. He is a mystic of the most ideal class; a pietist of the transcendental order. How few there are of sufficient insight into the soul to apprehend the facts of which he speaks, divested of the oriental dialect in which he puts them. He will be deemed insane by nearly every man.[35]

Alcott, like Emerson from the first, and Elizabeth Peabody more recently, saw no discrepancy or incompatibility between the religious intuitions of Veryism and the confident individualism being propounded by the Transcendentalists. His language and patterns of thought may have seemed old-fashioned or foreign to advocates of "the Newness," but the essentials of his life and thinking, his underlying intentions and aspirations were familiar and acceptable. Alcott did not hesitate to call him a "pietist of the transcendental order," nor was he at all embarrassed by the likelihood that the profound truths effortlessly uttered by him in prose and verse would be mistaken for madness by the uninitiated. Indeed, the prospects of this kind of scandal made Very all the more attractive to Alcott. He himself possessed the rare gift of stirring up the complacent and smug-minded, and admired the ability of others to do the same. Instead of dissociating himself from the seeming extravagances of Jones Very, the spiritually adventurous Alcott endorsed his activities, and was himself much moved by his new friend's effectiveness in warning against the most dangerous variety of lethargy, that of the soul. And in his response he clearly was not alone.

XV

# *The Prices of Deification*

## WINTER 1838–1839

For nearly three months Jones Very had been walking the streets of Salem, Cambridge, Boston, and Concord believing that he had completed that "sacrifice of self" which made him "the voice of the Holy Ghost pure and simple." This personal "identification" with the Spirit of God was a *"biding* in Christ," or as he also called it, a "rest." [1] And for nearly three months he had been restlessly goading others to destroy their egos and thereby liberate the God entombed within them. Although he had strained body and mind to convince all who willingly or unwillingly could be made to listen, his success in convincing others that he was a spiritually superior man, who spoke with special authority and by special grace, had so far been disappointing. The qualified encouragements of Emerson, Elizabeth Peabody, Channing, and of a few similar minds, was not—he knew—the total belief needed for their redemption.

He realized that some sort of practical compromise had to be arranged if his mission were to have any chance of succeeding. Occasional expressions of sympathy and qualified admiration for the course he had taken were ineffectual. He wanted disciples, followers dedicated to the truth exactly as he revealed it, but none had come forth to embrace him. Therefore he found it necessary to redefine his "mission" in terms less likely to alienate candidates for immediate redemption and Eternity-on-earth. Their reservations, intellectual as well as emotional, prevented them from achieving what he had already won for himself.

During November and December 1838 his conception of what was required from others for salvation changed noticeably. He gradually came to understand that his insistence upon inward obedience was too vague to be acted upon by them, and his requirement that the unnatural self be despised and then destroyed was too severe to be directly and literally adopted. As far as they were concerned, the commandment to "cut down the tree of self" scarcely offered any comprehensible program for deliverance. Since it seemed to those he approached to resemble manic raving more than the Voice of God, Very sought to correct the misunderstanding without compromising the intentions of the Spirit. He was disturbed by such characteristic reactions as Elizabeth Peabody's feeling that he had "no Idea to communicate," and by her fear that if she did follow Very's directions she might never recover her senses.

Others, he now said during the winter of 1838–1839, might attain the spiritual repose and contentment he had achieved as soon as they made "the final sacrifice," a sacrifice which took "different forms in different individuals." [2] His mission therefore was being simplified. It was growing more specific and individualized in his attempt to make his message more readily understood. As a result, even his own comprehension of what had happened to himself underwent clarification during the final weeks of 1838.

What was required for personal deliverance was the deliberate surrender of whatever meant most to a man. Something of maximum worth which was an integral part of his character, of his emotional life, or of his intellectual outlook, had to be given up. By virtue of being so prized, such a valued trait became sinful for that individual—although in itself and under other circumstances it might be innocent enough. Whatever the dominant characteristic was, this willful controlling factor in a man's personality had to be exorcized. When the last remnant of this individual willfulness was surrendered, the sacrifice would be rewarded by the Holy Spirit. Some subordinate characteristic, one which did not play a decisive part in a man's distinctive personality, could not initiate this special act of spiritual reconciliation.

This sacrificial act represented a symbolic re-enactment of the Father's sacrifice of the beloved Son, and the obedient Son's complete acquiescence. The individual in quest of salvation not only played the dual role of destroyer and victim in this inward ritual, but was himself the stage upon which the symbolic passion was set. So conceived, the sacrificial act itself required an extreme, even agonizing exercise of will, of resolution and punitive self-conquest. Only thus, by destroying what was dominant in a person's character, could the "sin" be suppressed and purgation be accomplished.[8] This psycho-cosmic monodrama was the unitarian gospel Jones Very began to proclaim to his friends during the winter of 1838–1839.

But how was the saving-sin to be identified? How could a man discover the character trait which molded his own special being and thereby imprisoned Christ within him? This disclosure became the purpose of Very's mission and the essence of his "revelation." Very was the only one who knew. He alone—or rather, the Holy Spirit speaking through him—recognized what had to be renounced by men intent on redeeming themselves. Consequently Very would have to intervene personally in order to make the identification. How had Very gained this knowledge? He realized he had himself already performed such a sacrifice, making him privy to God's own wisdom, now enjoyed as his own "natural impulse."

The "bosom Idol" which he had sacrificed in order to perfect his own being was "Beauty." This sacrifice had been undertaken at Harvard when he was twenty-two years old and suffering from "unbridled passions" for women. As love-longing was resisted and then finally ceased altogether, his life became "more and more regularly a *sacrifice* in all things," until he realized he had "nothing more to give up"—he had "given all." At this point the inward changes occurred which led him to be placed under Dr. Bell's care. This successful repression and redirection of his masculine drives won for him the kind of self-mastery which he soon was demanding from others.[4]

His concept of "sacrifice"—its sexual origins obscured—developed into the central feature of his "mission" during the winter of 1838–1839. His own sacrifice of "the love of Beauty" was openly confessed to his intimates in Salem, Concord, and Boston, while he was assigning appropriate sacrifices to others. However, he apparently told them nothing about the specific nature of his own sacrifice, unless the telling took the form of vague remarks on celibacy which spared the more intimate details. Obviously, sometime before meeting Elizabeth Peabody at his Salem lecture in December 1837, he had resumed social intercourse with the ladies. (God apparently had revoked the "law" he had made for himself in 1835, "not to speak or look at women.") [5]

Elizabeth Peabody was told near the end of 1838 that in order to become a *"filial obedien[t]"*—which was, according to Very, "the highest attitude for a finite spirit to attain"—she would first have to sacrifice her "love of truth." Her reaction to this pronouncement indicated that once again she was on the verge of accepting Very's mission.

I think I see and accept what he calls the sacrifices of the love of beauty, love of truth, etc., and as this is the main point, I intend the next time I see him to tell him that I believe I do stand spiritually speaking—where he does. This answer will determine more whether I understand him or not.[6]

She was completely captivated when she learned the spiritual defects of her friends, and thought them all "Angelic sins." He said of Dr. Channing that his "difficulty" was "the love of rectitude." Emerson's "bosom Idol" was "the love of thought." Alcott's was "Spiritual Curiosity." Sophia Peabody's saving sacrifice was "the love of Imagination." [7]

Elizabeth was particularly impressed by Very's insight into the character of her dearest friend. "It expressed Dr. Channing's perhaps *extreme* sense of moral responsibility . . . or *personal* responsibility." [8] Her doubts, however, about the soundness of Very's self-confident manner and staggering egotism persisted.

I am sure he is crazy on one point—thinking that he alone is accessible as a matter of fact to the Spirit. He does not distrust his own *love of obedience*—which is also a crotchet if the other loves are—and his sticking to this notion is as wilful as Dr. C's *love of rectitude*.[9]

When Very revealed his doctrine of sacrifice to Alcott, Alcott of course was also struck by Very's sensitive reading of character, and similarly troubled by it. A vain man and jealous of his capacity for caring for the needs of his soul even at the expense of his family's material welfare, he was somewhat perplexed to learn he was barred from salvation by his "Spiritual Curiosity." In his Journal for the second week of December 1838, he analyzed Very in his own perceptive style for the first time, and completely *Alcottized* Very's original announcement of his unexpected "bosom Idol."

Is he insane? If so, there yet linger glimpses of wisdom in his memory. He is insane with God; diswitted in the contemplation of the holiness of Divinity. He distrusts intellect; he would have living in the concrete, without the interposition of the meddling, analytic head. Curiosity he deems impious. He would have no one stop to account to himself for what he has done, deeming this hiatus of doing, a suicidal act of the profane mind. Intellect, as intellect, he deems the author of all error. Living, not thinking, he regards as the worship meet for the soul. This is mysticism in its highest form.[10]

What had prompted Alcott's exasperated paean was a letter he had just received from Very—a written version of his mission to Alcott, typical of letters he was sending to many of his prospective disciples. "Since my conversation with you, at your house," he wrote,

when I recognized, as I told you, something in you which the Spirit within me did not approve, I was led to get your "Remarks on the Gospels," and I there find that curiosity which I before remarked in your conversation. This I write to you in Spirit, that you should leave all which hinders the Spirit of God from creating you again in his image; for while you retain it you still have some of your own will which we must give up entirely to find rest. . . . You have not yet entirely fulfilled the mission of John, within You. He must entirely decrease before Christ can find the Spirit to baptize you into his kingdom, which is not of that world of your own will, in which you still linger a little. . . . Blessed is he who is not offended or discouraged in coming to me. The way is hard and requires the abandonment of all the will, yet it is sure, and on that very account a rest. . . . May the spiritual John within you be stirred at the voice of him who speaks from Heaven. . . . Many are called by *his* voice, but few are chosen by Christ's. . . . The weary and heavy laden shall find rest.

> Rejoice, ye weary! ye whose spirits mourn!
> There is a rest that shall not be removed;
> Press on and reach within the heavenly bourn,
> By Christ the king of your salvation proved;
> There is a rest! Rejoice, ye silent stars,
> Roll on no more all voiceless on your way;
> Thou Sun! no more dark clouds thy triumph mars,
> Speak thou to every land the coming day;
> It comes! bid every harp and timbrel sound;
> Bring forth the fatted calf; make merry all;
> For this the son was lost, and he is found;

Was dead, and yet has heard his Saviour's call;
And comes within to drink the new made wine,
And as a branch abide forever in the Vine.[11]

You have now the good tidings of great joy, and I hope they are such to you. Be up and doing, for the night is at hand in which no man can work. The Spirit of the Son is at hand and ready to be poured out on every soul, to discover the dark places of sin and build up forever the habitations of the poor. The heralds are sent forth for the marriage feast; may you soon have put on the wedding garment, lest we sit down without you.

If you will read this letter to your class [12] it will be my presence and for their comfort. Remember me to your wife. And if you see Mr. Bartol tell him from me, if you will, that most of my Sonnets have been sent, I believe, to Dr. Channing by Miss Peabody, and I suppose he can see or obtain copies of them in that way. This would be better than for me to send any to him one by one. This is also for your information. Amen.[13]

This remarkable letter, which Alcott painstakingly copied into his Journal without deletions, provides further evidence that during the winter of 1838–1839—when Very was spreading his revised gospel of "sacrifice"—his conception of his own role underwent a drastic revision. His sonnets were an integral part of his strategy, and he now equated his intentions with success. Whether his mission succeeded no longer depended upon its being accepted or rejected. The consequences of his acts were no longer relevant. He "entirely repudiated the role of proselyter." [14]

He had made similar denials to Dr. Bell in the latter part of September, when he was still hopeful of being reinstated at Harvard. However, his subsequent behavior disclosed the deception. But circumstances indeed had changed since then. Now that he more fully comprehended the nature of the resistance he encountered, he was prepared for a tactical retreat. He had no alternative. He now understood that his "whole duty" was limited to uttering the words given him by the Holy Spirit. No longer need he hold himself "responsible for their effect or non-effect upon others." No longer was he burdened by responsibility for their spiritual fates. No longer would rejection be a personal defeat for him. He need only ensure that the "truth" was being circulated as effectively as possible, and Emerson had promised him additional help in providing him with a large audience. Once men were free to refuse salvation without jeopardizing his own, his "days of hate" seemed past.[15]

It was in this relatively carefree mood that he called upon a former classmate, a perfect adversary (he thought) for his new attack upon evil.[16] He had never been friendly with Samuel Gray Ward. In fact, Ward—who had always regarded him as a "laborious drudge" at Harvard—thought Very always had shown himself "quite indifferent" to him. For three years they had sat beside each other with nothing to say to each other beyond what ordinarily was required in the recitation room. Another three years had passed, during which even this tenuous connection was broken.

Once, during his October conversation with Very, Emerson had casually mentioned Ward's name, and Very was moved by this to remedy his former neglect. In January 1839 he made an unannounced appearance in the Boston office of the prospering young lawyer. After exchanging formal courtesies, Very masked the purpose of his visit with deliberate mystification. "I come," he said, "to bid you if you are ready to come to the feast where we are all assembled—and waiting for you." Ward, placed at great disadvantage by his confusion, protested. He said he certainly was not ready. "I hear you," Very replied, "but I take no meaning from what you say. I hear your words, but they convey nothing to me." Again Ward protested.

"How then shall I hear you?" he asked. "How shall I know that what you tell me is right, more than what I tell you—how shall we know whom to believe?"

"Believe all," Very said.

"But some men say what is not true—they deceive themselves."

"No—no one can deceive himself." Very drew his chair closer. He continued to speak in his most matter-of-fact manner, but with a suggestion in his voice that he was about to share a confidence. "I come from the banquet where we are all together. I do not wish to come, for myself. I am happy there—and it pains me to break my repose and come into the world—but I feel that we cannot live for ourselves alone; and so I do come to tell you how sweet the banquet is, and to beg you to come in to it."

Very paused. He noticed a sheet of paper on Ward's desk. "You are writing a letter," he observed. "If you are ready, break it off in the middle and follow me." This was Very's dramatic way of informing Ward he would have to sacrifice what meant most to him—the orderly world of a lawyer's routine.

Of course Ward again refused. He told him abruptly that he was not ready, that he had the letter to finish and he was going to finish it, and that he had his own life to live and he was going to live it. Only when he was ready, he added, would he come.

Very was not at all disturbed by this response. He expected it. "Well," he said, "whenever the time comes you must come—it will be in vain for you to resist—and I have come this morning and laid the axe at your door, and it can never be taken away from there by any one." [17]

The interview drew to a close. Very invited Ward to visit him in Salem. Mischievously he added that he soon was going to have a "new mansion" for himself. Not sure he understood, Ward struck at the bait and asked whether he was referring to his "temporal or spiritual home." Very set his hook with a practised touch. "It was all one," he replied. "There was but one house." Leaving the paradox unexplained, Very cheerfully excused himself and withdrew as unexpectedly as he had come. And one more New Englander was convinced that Jones Very was insane. The "peculiarly sweet, and compassionate" expression on his face, seemingly cast by his sparkling eyes, and his claims to supernal happiness after having "left off thinking," were demonstrably belied (thought Ward) by the "constant nervous twitching" which "checked his words."

Not everyone with whom Very came in contact near the end of 1838 was treated to the solemn frankness which undercut Alcott's sense of his own spiritual worth, or to the whimsical riddles which temporarily interrupted Ward's conduct of more worldly affairs. Nor was everyone Very approached left to wonder about his sanity. Very's resources for implementing his program of redemption were not limited to talk about "marriage feasts" and "wedding garments," and the kinds of responses he elicited were similarly varied.

Although he had never been intimate with Nathaniel Hawthorne, and his cautious advances had never been encouraged by Hawthorne, they encountered one another quite frequently in 1838, not only in the Peabody parlor but also in the more fashionable drawing rooms of Mrs. Caleb Foote and Miss Susan Burley, and occasionally Very saw him at Hawthorne's own home—invariably without invitation or prior warning. To Hawthorne's increasing embarrassment, Very thought of him not as a casual acquaintance but as a kind of spiritual "brother." [18]

Approaching him with the respectful forbearance usually reserved for a few special friends, Very made his supreme gesture of love toward Hawthorne in November. With Elizabeth and Sophia Peabody and Elizabeth Hoar present, he "delivered his mission" to Hawthorne. The "ceremony" followed already familiar patterns, and Elizabeth Peabody did not think it necessary to elaborate on details of procedure when she related the incident to Emerson. Significantly though, Hawthorne was not assigned any special personality trait for his sacrificial offering. Instead, Very explained his "mission" in its unreconstructed form. "It was very curious," Elizabeth wrote to Emerson.

Hawthorne received it in the loveliest manner—with the same abandonment with which it was given—for he has that confidence in truth—which delivers him from all mean fears—and it was curious to see the respect of Very for *him*—and the reverence with which he treated his genius. There is a petulance about Hawthorne generally—when truth is taken out of the forms of nature . . . though the happiest and healthiest physical nature tempers it—so that it only expresses itself on that one occasion. But in this instance he repressed it and talked with him beautifully.[19]

Having at last experienced for himself the special religious bias to Very's conversation and actions, and in its most intensely emotional form, Hawthorne began to view him with other than the mannerly tolerance he had adopted toward him ever since their first meeting in January. He told Elizabeth Peabody that Very

more than realized the conception of entire subjectiveness he had tried to describe in the preacher of "the Story teller." But the intellectual development of Mr. Very was previously so great, that it made his *ecstasy* altogether *sui generis*.[20]

The precise nature of this similarity between Very and one of Hawthorne's fictional characters, and the significance of Hawthorne's new attitude toward him, is clarified through an independent description by Elizabeth of the story-collection Hawthorne projected in 1833 and recalled five years later in connection with Very.

In it [the narrator] describes himself as a gloomy idler who could not make up his mind to get into any profession, and a neighbor of his, as much at a loss as himself for a worldly vocation, who was a religious enthusiast, with an idea that he was sent by God on a mission to call the world to a higher life. These two exceptional Yankees were tabooed by the prosaic community from which they were dissidents; and this brought them into a strange intimacy.[21]

No wonder Hawthorne now looked upon Very with sympathetic attention and would even defend his eccentricity. The coincidence must have been startling to this man said to be "greatly interested" in such "remarkable mental phenomena." [22] A "strange intimacy" indeed had suddenly developed between them. It was almost as if Jones Very were an invention of Hawthorne's own Gothic imagination, a character whom he felt he understood completely, and for whom he was in a sense morally responsible.

On one of several occasions that he indulged in analysis of his "neighbor," Hawthorne told Elizabeth and Sophia that Very was "always vain in his eye—though it always was an innocent vanity." He attributed this self-exaltation to his "want of the sense of the ludicrous." However, he realized that Very's vanity was not like that of ordinary men; it was pardonable because it was "sanctified by his real piety and goodness." And on another occasion when Very's enthusiasm was being discussed in Charter Street, Hawthorne insisted that instead of reverting to normalcy, "he had better remain as he is . . . one organ in the world of the impersonal Spirit—at least so long as he can write such good sonnets." [23]

Such generous opinions did not mean, however, that Hawthorne was comfortable in Very's demanding presence. Very was too conspicuous, too insistent, too conscientious for any kind of enduring personal relationship to be established. On Hawthorne's part, courtesy and tolerance prevented him from taking any action likely to offend Very. He preferred to be inconvenienced whenever no gracious alternative was possible. Just one year after their first meeting, Hawthorne excused himself from a visit with Sophia because he had learned that Very was also expected at the Peabody house that evening. He explained politely that he had something to read which could not be put off to another time because of other engagements.[24] Once he admitted to Mary Peabody (apparently reluctant to confide in Sophia or Elizabeth) that Very's persistent attempts to "convert" him were annoying. He would call upon Hawthorne at home— indeed, "goes there often"—and would interfere with his work. But he was unwilling to tell this to Very, or to risk having someone else tell him. Not knowing what to do in this impossible situation, he sought advice from Mary.[25] Whatever her suggestion, if any, these untimely calls continued for more than another year, at least until the middle of 1840, and probably longer. Hawthorne nevertheless preferred being inconvenienced to hurting Very's feelings. Finally, in July 1840, while still unable to bring himself to speak frankly to Very, he told Sophia of his impatience:

Dearest,—My days have been so busy and my evenings so invaded with visitants, that I have not had a moment's time to talk with you. Scarcely till this morning have I been able to read your letter quietly. Night before last came Mr. Jones Very; and you know he is somewhat unconscionable as to the length of his calls.[26]

Whether Very continued calling upon him as frequently or at all after this is not known. However, in 1842 Hawthorne—perhaps to his own private amusement and relief—referred to him in the *Boston Miscellany* as "a poet whose voice is scarcely heard among us, by reason of its depth." [27] And in 1843, for Lowell's *Pioneer,* he wrote the best of all one-sentence characterizations of Very when he depicted him standing alone "within a circle which no other of mortal race could enter, nor himself escape from." [28]

One reason for Hawthorne's refusal to offend Very was Sophia Peabody's special affection for him. When Very was "troubled," Sophia "comforted him with sympathy." When she thought Very was being misunderstood at Susan Burley's house, she was indignant. When he showed her his sonnets, she showed him her paintings. When he "deeply enjoyed" them, she was so delighted that she told him of her "Ilbrahim," her illustration for Hawthorne's "Gentle Boy"—which she had not yet completed or shown to Hawthorne.[29] When Very was Emerson's houseguest she was uneasy, but she "rejoiced" upon learning that "Mr. Emerson has uttered no heresies" about him. She defended Very, complaining that Emerson thought "because a man [i.e., Very] is born to-day instead of yesterday he cannot move the soul." Emerson's stubborn refusal to accept Very without qualifying his self-generated and self-proving truths, seemed to her to be "quite inconsistent" with his "proclamation" in *Nature* that "the sun shines to-day, also." [30]

Responding to her kindnesses, Very tried in his own way to relieve the pain which almost constantly tormented this semi-invalid. By December 1838 he had sensed the psychological basis of her ailment. Her attitude, he told her, was "below the mark." He disapproved of her "resignation and acceptance of pain," and predicted that "perfect yielding of willfulness would produce freedom from the *sensation of pain itself.*" He insisted she could be like Jesus who, even on the cross, "had no bodily pain." Jesus, he explained, experienced only "mental" pain, and this Very attributed to grief brought on by the sins of others, the sins of those who were "in opposition to his Father's will." [31]

He spent much time in conversation with her, and his attentions were partially rewarded. In connection with the "Angelic sin" he had revealed as the psychological basis for her suffering—the "love of Imagination"—she told Elizabeth in January 1839: "I do not think I am subject to my imagination; I can let an idea go to the grave that I see is false." Of all those in Salem, Concord, Boston, and Cambridge whom he approached with his mission and who listened to his explanations, she alone—excepting Lydia Very—was deeply moved. At tea one afternoon in January 1839 she found his conversation "divine," and the "level rays of celestial light" which beamed from his face she found "lovely to behold." [32] Sophia, according to sister Elizabeth, "receives all" of Very's mission, "except that about *the pain*—and she says she *doubts* about that." She explained her hesitation at accepting this portion of her highly individualized program for redemption by saying she did not feel sure she "surrenders her will" as he was urging her to do. [33] But she tried. "When I am altogether true to the light I have," she told Elizabeth, "I shall be in the heaven where the angelic Very now is."[34] Sophia was almost correct. With her marriage to Hawthorne in 1842, the pain grew less acute and less frequent, and finally disappeared. She had found her earthly paradise—but learned it wasn't Very's lonely, repressive one.

In various ways the people Very approached during the winter of 1838–1839 encouraged him, whether or not they realized it or intended to do so, and whatever the form their reactions took. Very construed all in the most favorable way. The praise and possibilities of friendship Emerson offered, the welcome and sympathies of the Peabody sisters, Channing's benign queries and intense interest, Clarke's effort to see him in psychological and historical perspectives, the resolute but painful acknowledgments of Alcott, Hawthorne's well-intentioned lack of candor, even Ward's self-control when confronted by deliberately unnerving attempts to rouse him from religious apathy—all these served to confirm Very's convictions. The course the Spirit was charting for him may have struck him as difficult, the progress may have seemed excessively slow at times, but Very was satisfied it was as beneficial as it was inevitable and irresistible. His confidence remained unshaken.

## XVI

# Calls to Glory

### WINTER 1838–1839

ALTHOUGH VERY was convinced his saving program was beginning to succeed, the techniques for his "mission" continued to develop, stimulated by the reluctance of some of its beneficiaries and the protests of the rest. The enthusiasms of Emerson, the Peabody sisters, Hawthorne, Alcott, and others for his poetry were instructive. They made him realize more fully during the winter of 1838–1839 that he had available a means of regeneration more powerful than intimate conversation with the unregenerate. This realization caused his strategy to change once more.

First he discontinued visits to those like Salem's Reverend Mr. Brazer who were openly hostile. For this reason, and because Mrs. Very continued to stand guard over his liberty, no longer was there likelihood of any repetition of the September 1838 "abduction," and no longer had Very cause to suspect a conspiracy against Emerson and himself.[1] Then, even acquaintances less antagonistic than Brazer did not see him as frequently. But this did not indicate that he was being any less vigorous in his pursuit of objectives God had revealed to him. Rather, his campaign was gradually entering a new phase. Instead of relying upon the awesome presence and commanding tones which formerly were projected in drawing rooms and parlors, he was depending more than before upon poems and letters. Letters with poems, and poems sent in place of letters now regularly transmitted the prodigious thoughts and feelings which stirred him.

For his attendance at sessions of the "Transcendental Club" he often substituted communications addressed to members, requesting they be read as his contribution to their discussions. And, as he intended, they did stimulate discussions. George Ripley, commenting on a letter read by Alcott, said that "in thoughts and images" it resembled the last letters of George Fox, the Quaker. "The mysticism and pietism," he explained, "were alike common to each." Alcott replied to Ripley's observation by saying that Very's letter was "little more than a repetition" of remarks he had made in person at their last meeting. Moreover, Alcott hoped Very would outgrow his "partiality to the oriental dialect." Archly he added, "A professor of languages, one would think, should incline to a more modern and western speech." Alcott wanted "the facts of the soul translated into a modern dialect." He was anxious for "the English of the matter." What was needed, according to Alcott, was "the gospel of the nineteenth century, published from the soul as it now is, and in the images of this modern world." Nevertheless he was willing to be patient, and was hopeful Very would soon find language and accents better suited to the spiritual needs of the modern age.[2]

To Henry W. Bellows, formerly a college friend and now an influential New York minister, Very wrote that he had recently been publishing what he hears of "the word" in the form of sonnets. He promised to send such reprints from the Salem *Observer* as he "may not be otherwise directed" by the Spirit "to dispose of"— if only Bellows would ask for them.[3] To an unidentified former pupil he wrote to similar effect, promising to send additional "papers" to him and to others "if the pieces in them"—given by the Holy Spirit—were found "acceptable." [4] Emerson and Alcott, therefore, were not the only beneficiaries of Very's shy but salving muse. With increasing frequency the Spirit's "Voice" sounded to Very in the form of sonnets, and the practice of sending them in lieu of letters was becoming customary. But he was careful not to thrust his poems upon those likely to be unappreciative. In January 1839 he wrote to James Freeman Clarke:

Hearing of your want of matter for your Messenger, I was moved to send you [some] sonnets; that they may help those in affliction for Christ's name is ever the prayer of me his disciple, called to be a witness of his sufferings and an expectant of his glory. If you should ask for more as I have them so will they be communicated freely. Amen. [5]

Along with the letter Clarke printed nine sonnets in the March issue, and eighteen more in the April issue, none of which had been previously published.

As a poet Very never lost sight of what he believed to be the justification for his efforts—the way in which his poems were received and their effect upon readers. Usually, but not always, his friends received reprints from the Salem *Observer*. Thoreau was the recipient of at least three such clippings. [6] Two of the six sonnets he copied into his "Miscellaneous Extracts" notebook in November 1838 dramatized the balanced mood of hopeful expectation (sustained in spite of transient disappointments), which characterized Very's personal and poetic outlook since departing the Charlestown hospital.

Even when the angel Love proves elusive in the first of these poems, he is not embittered. Directed by Time, the unsuccessful search leads him back to the city and to the home he had left. According to the fragile allegory (entitled simply "Love"), the loneliness and discomforts he encountered before his return, including the somber fact of mortality itself, all leave him still undiscouraged. The promise of warmth from the sun and from the domestic fireside—both lying just beyond the last lines of the sonnet—seem adequate compensation for his otherwise frustrated efforts.

I asked of Time to tell me where was Love;
He pointed to her foot-steps on the snow,
Where first the angel lighted from above,
And bid me note the way and onward go;
Through populous streets of cities spreading wide,
By lonely cottage rising on the moor,
Where bursts from sundered cliff the struggling tide,
To where it hails the sea with answering roar,
She led me on; o'er mountains' frozen head,
Where mile on mile still stretches on the plain,
Then homeward whither first my feet she led,
I traced her path along the snow again,
But there the sun had melted from the earth
The prints where first she trod, a child of mortal birth.[7]

By finally abandoning the world of Time and quest in favor of that psychic region where the distinctions between divine and not-divine are neither observed nor relevant, the likelihood of encountering Love was increased. "The Son" depicts the mood of hopeful expectation in the Timeless world which remains after the withdrawal from both "populous streets of cities" and from the wintry countryside.

Father, I wait thy word. The sun doth stand
Beneath the mingling line of night and day,
A listening servant, waiting thy command
To roll rejoicing on its silent way;
The tongue of time abides the appointed hour,
Till on our ear its solemn warnings fall;
The heavy cloud withholds the pelting shower,
Then every drop speeds onward at thy call;
The bird reposes on the yielding bough,

With breast unswollen by the tide of song;
So does my spirit wait thy presence now
To pour thy praise in quickening life along,
Chiding with voice divine man's lengthened sleep,
While round the Unuttered Word and Love their vigils keep.[8]

The world Very has envisioned here is a world in which poetry is the primal fact. The present moment of the sonnet is a world on the verge of creation and life, a suspended world in which the poet is God's agent setting all else in motion. It is a world in which *logos* and *agape* are one, and the role of the poet is to be recipient and donor to men of both. The poet's function is mediatory and monitory. He incarnates the Word and illumines the darkness with pre-existent Love.

Alcott for a time was blessed with sonnets every week, and he would paste or copy them into his journal.[9] In December he saved a sheet of newsprint with six sonnets, and the comment in his journal revealed that Very continued to play a disconcerting role even at a distance. He kept Alcott off balance, causing him first to feel awe and then perplexity.

His poetry, like himself, is quite unequal. I see him, at times, and am much impressed by the soul of the man. I reverence it. I feel myself, in the presence of a superiour creature. He upbraids me; he rebukes me. I feel whatsoever of pretence, of show, there may be in me. At other times, he seems wild, mystical, and I rather pity than worship the presence before me. I am the insane now, and now the sane soul. What does this mean? [10]

Although adumbrated by one of the sonnets he thought typical of those Very recently had been writing, the answer to the question eluded Alcott. In "The Spirit Land," a sonnet written within six weeks of Very's return to Salem from McLean Hospital, the doubleness of existence—compounded of visions of God's multiple wonders and disjointed perceptions of the commonplace—is unfolded.

Father! thy wonders do not singly stand,
Not far removed where feet have seldom strayed;
Around us ever lies the enchanted land
In marvels rich to thine own sons displayed;
In finding thee are all things round us found;
In losing thee are all things lost beside;
Ears have we but in vain strange voices sound,
And to our eyes the vision is denied;
We wander in the country far remote,
Mid tombs and ruined piles in death to dwell;
Or on the records of past greatness dote,
And for a buried soul the living sell;
While on our path bewildered falls the night
That ne'er returns us to the fields of light.[11]

To the man reconciled with God, the literal realities (i.e., what constitutes existence for willful individuals), are evil. They filter through a consciousness now aware of an order of being intimately connected with the presence of God. The "son" who here addresses the "Father," however, was living outside both worlds. Unable to accept the deficient literal world, he was not yet able to enter the "fields of light." While aware of the present possibilities of "vision" and still denied them, he was estranged from the world most men find satisfying. Anxious to join the privileged company of the Father's "own sons," he was struggling to leave behind the "tombs and ruined piles," but could not completely climb out of the bewildering "night" enveloping him.

The tone of the sonnets addressed to Thoreau differed significantly from those Very thought Alcott would find "acceptable." Of these, one of Alcott's favorites was "Worship." He felt it best expressed his own indictment of Sunday schools, preaching, the decay of the Church, and the "solemn mockery" which passed for prayer.

There is no worship now—the idol stands
Within the spirit's holy resting place!

Millions before it bend with upraised hands,
And with their gifts God's purer shrine disgrace;
The prophet walks unhonored mid the crowd
That to the idol's temple daily throng;
His voice unheard above their voices loud,
His strength too feeble 'gainst the torrent strong;
But there are bounds that ocean's rage can stay
When wave on wave leaps madly to the shore:
And soon the prophet's word shall men obey,
And hushed to peace the billows cease to roar;
For he who spoke—and warring winds kept peace,
Commands again—and man's wild passions cease.[12]

Alcott commented in his journal:

We are in the midst of a revolution of the thoughts of man. The heart of the simple yearns for release from the thrall of tradition. The advent of truth is near. The prophets are raising their voices, and their words are gaining the ears of the hungry and the naked.[13]

"Worship" is more than Very's attack on contemporary worship in general and upon the Salem ministry in particular. As Alcott recognized when he spoke of the "advent of truth," it is a forecast of the Second Coming. (The opening lines of the sonnet derive specifically from Matt. 24:15.) Moreover, "God's purer shrine" is man himself; but within him now is a false idol instead of a vital soul. The prophet ignored by the false-hearted mass of men is Very himself, and the confident forecast at the conclusion of the sonnet is for the time when the divine source of his inspiration and the miraculous efficacy of his "word" will be demonstrated.

In addition to newspaper clippings Very distributed to friends, long-rolled manuscript sheets of sonnets circulated among interested readers, with Elizabeth Peabody usually overseeing their dissemination.[14] However on at least one occasion Emerson acted as coordinator of this form of publication, forwarding a roll to Margaret Fuller. Very's essays also went "wandering," in the copies Emerson had prepared for his own use in November.[15] At the end of December Emerson delivered the "Shakespeare" to Alcott, who read it "with great delight" and in his own way praised it as highly as Emerson had earlier done, considering it "one of the remarkable things of the day."

It is better than any thing I have seen, aside from "Nature" and the "Growth of the Mind" [by the Swedenborgian druggist, Sampson Reed], of modern origin. I am to have another paper of his on "Hamlet." These with the sonnets, now numbering forty, and more, Emerson now hopes to publish in a volume.[16]

A month later Emerson's copy of "Hamlet" reached Alcott. He studied it closely, and stayed up until after three in the morning copying long passages into his journal.[17]

Delegated activity of this sort did not mean that Very himself was not abroad. Although contacts with friends were less frequent than before, and whenever encountered he seemed less inclined to assume the apostolic tone, he continued to be seen in Salem and Boston. He visited, as was his custom, with the Peabody and Burley families. He saw Hawthorne. And he continued to attend Emerson's lecture series with regularity.

In January the lecture called "The Protest" promised to treat an aspect of "Human Life" which held special interest for him. He hoped his own dissenting voice had contributed something to Emerson's remarks, and this expectation may not have been disappointed. That evening, according to Alcott, Emerson

spoke of the soul inspired by truth, protesting, heroically, against the usurpations of usages, institutions, creeds, and by its nobleness of bearing carrying its point with the world. It was a splendid *Protest* against every lie in life. The large hall in the [Boston Masonic] Temple was filled, and the audience the choicest that could be gathered in N. England, by such a topic.[18]

Alcott was not surprised to see Very there, and was much pleased when he promised to call on him the following day. But Very's presence at once brought to mind his writings, not the man himself with his disturbing "oriental dialect" and puzzling sense of his own special destiny. Very's "genius," for Alcott,

dawns more brightly upon my apprehension as I look on his works. The Essays on Shakespeare, and the Sonnets are remarkable literary productions. Very is a very gifted saint; Emerson, a gifted scholar. Both are men of Genius. The one represents life in the form of Truth or thought: the other in that of good or obedience (duty), and both in images of graceful beauty. I get more from these men than others now extant. . . . Emerson, Very, . . . these are names yet to be known in the springing literature of this period. Very's Essays and Sonnets are soon to be printed.[19]

Occasionally Very also appeared at the formal "Conversations" Alcott moderated in the Boston vicinity. One evening, near the end of January, Very attended a meeting at Lynn when the topic for discussion was "Instinct." In Alcott's judgment, Very addressed "fine statements" to the group. They enumerated "various instances from the corporeal, mental, and spiritual life," illustrating that "on all the great occasions of the soul, the soul acted from instinct." Although each of the participants "had deep insight into the soul," making for an evening of "splendid talk," Alcott was most interested in what Very had to say. He acknowledged that Very spoke with an authority other speakers lacked, yet his reactions mingled regret with admiration.

He is a remarkable phenomenon. He affects me as a spectre. His look, tones, words, are all sepulchral. He is a voice from the tombs. He speaks of having once lived in the world, amidst men and things, but of being now in the spirit; time and space are not save in memory. This idea modifies all his thoughts and expressions; and the thoughts and expressions of others also. It is difficult for those who do not apprehend the state of his soul to converse with him. I find it quite possible by translating mine into his. By so doing, we talk with ease, and understand each other. His speech is Oriental. By putting modern life into eastern images, speech becomes quite possible with him.

He is a psychological phenomenon of rare occurrence. He lives out of his organs. He is dead. Each thought of his soul, when spoken, each act of the body, implies a resurrection of the spiritual life. This somnambulist walks about on the earth, acting and speaking, from the memory of his terrestrial experience, while his soul is in the presence of spiritual realities alone. Matter, space, time, men, things, remain to him merely as memories of a life now extinct. He is out of his senses, in the instincts of the soul. The dark realm of Time, over whose spaces he once trod, and with whose forms he once communicated, through the senses, has passed away; men and things, recal[l] him, for moments, as ghosts and spectres of a life once lived, into the companionship of terrestrial relations, and he stumbles awhile amidst the tombs, and speaks of the life that was, before he arose, and became a supernatural being. He lingers yet a little while on the earth, but hastens to depart, and ascend again into heaven. In him, the resurrection has become a fact, seen with the eyes. . . .

It was the resurrection verified in fact.

I think he will decease soon. He dies by slowly retreating from the senses, yet existing in them by memory, when men or things are obtruded on his thought. Nature to him is as a charnalhouse, and the voices of men, echoes of the dead who haunt its dark chamber.[20]

Accordingly, Very's writings alone seemed to hold promise for his future in this world.

What "living in memory" meant for Very's poetry during the winter of 1838–1839 can be determined from "Time" and "The Spirit," sonnets written in December. Both poems are retrospective, deriving from the period before spiritual transformation although composed months later. The remembered summer of 1838 now is understood from the vantage of the completed spiritual change, not from the limited point of view of yearning which had accompanied it and which had already been recast in "Love." Time no longer is a destructive or deceptive influence: the decay it brings now makes rebirth possible.

In the first of the sonnets, the unuttered secrets of Time concern the passing of death into life; these are natural facts, but they are known only to the consciousness of the prophet-poet. His still unformed words, celebrating the miracle about to occur, will coincide with the resurrection of the world itself, symbolized by the springtime following winter.

> There is no moment but whose flight doth bring
> Bright clouds and fluttering leaves to deck my bower;
> And I within like some sweet bird must sing
> To tell the story of the passing hour;
> For time has secrets that no bird has sung,
> Nor changing leaf with changing season told;
> They wait the utterance of some nobler tongue
> Like that which spoke in prophet tones of old;
> Then day and night, and month and year shall tell
> The tale that speaks but faint from bird and bough;
> In spirit-songs their praise shall upward swell
> Nor longer pass heaven's gate unheard as now,
> But cause e'en angels' ears to catch the strain,
> And send it back to earth in joy again.[21]

In "The Spirit," the effect of the divine Pneuma, within and without him, is anticipated, the poet-prophet suppressing his own respiration so not to interfere with the revivifying breath of God.

> I would not breathe, when blows thy mighty wind
> O'er desolate hill and winter-blasted plain,
> But stand in waiting hope if I may find
> Each flower recalled to newer life again
> That now unsightly hides itself from Thee,
> Amid the leaves or rustling grasses dry,
> With ice-cased rock and snowy-mantled tree
> Ashamed lest Thou its nakedness should spy;
> But Thou shalt breathe and every rattling bough
> Shall gather leaves; each rock with rivers flow;
> And they that hide them from thy presence now
> In new found robes along thy path shall glow,
> And meadows at thy coming fall and rise,
> Their green waves sprinkled with a thousand eyes.[22]

In both sonnets "the life that was" is about to be transformed by the divine spirit into the life that will be—a future no less certain, no less real or possible than the present, and which is its perfection because an organic development impelled by God.

But "living in memory" was largely a circumvention of the present by force of will, and it was with the present itself that most of Very's sonnets now dealt. This aspect of the "realm of Time," said Alcott sadly, seemed "black" to him. Most of his poems then were in moods different from those of "Time" or "The Spirit." They were not poems of fragile subject and delicate feeling, but sonnets full of hatred and implied violence, poems about the "charnalhouse," forceful evocations of the "terrestrial" present which more closely resembled a tomb or prison than a graceful park undergoing seasonal change. These sonnets were concerned with the world of man—with the city as distinguished from the garden—and here the outlook indeed was bleak. These sonnets were Very's direct responses to the spiritual death he confronted daily in Salem, Boston, or Cambridge. They were expressionistic descriptions of humanity: men were recognized as distorted, grotesque, angular figures, whose outward forms were determined by their inward disorders. These were men totally ignorant of their true circumstances, whose disobedient and willful lives were rooted in artifice, pretense, and sin.

"The Dead," one of the earliest of the funereal sonnets, represents a transition from the arboreal world of the garden. While the central image is still drawn from the corresponding but temporary condition of the winter landscape, its symbolic function has undergone a shift. Rebirth is not an inevitable fact of existence in the world of man, as Very well knew from his own rejection by that ugly world.

> I see them,—crowd on crowd they walk the earth,
> Dry, leafless trees to autumn wind laid bare;
> And in their nakedness find cause for mirth,
> And all unclad would winter's rudeness dare;

No sap doth through their clattering branches flow,
Whence springing leaves and blossoms bright appear;
Their hearts the living God have ceased to know,
Who gives the spring time to th' expectant year;
They mimic life, as if from him to steal
His glow of health to paint the livid cheek;
They borrow words for thoughts they cannot feel,
That with a seeming heart their tongue may speak;
And in their show of life more dead they live
Than those that to the earth with many tears they give.[23]

"The Grave Yard" elaborates on the concluding couplet of "The Dead," contrasting physical with spiritual death, and terminal decay with that which leads to subsequent life:

My heart grows sick before the wide-spread death,
That walks and speaks in seeming life around;
And I would love the corse without a breath,
That sleeps forgotten 'neath the cold, cold ground;
For these do tell the story of decay,
The worm and rotten flesh hide not nor lie;
But this, though dying too from day to day,
With a false show doth cheat the longing eye;
And hide the worm that gnaws the core of life,
With painted cheek and smooth deceitful skin;
Covering a grave with sights of darkness rife,
A secret cavern filled with death and sin;
And men walk o'er these graves and know it not,
For in the body's health the soul's forgot.[24]

"The Eagles" presents still another version of man's spiritual death, in terms no less startling since the setting resembles Armageddon, and the occasion is the final battle between the powers of good and evil:

The eagles gather on the place of death
So thick the ground is spotted with their wings,
The air is tainted with the noisome breath

The wind from off the field of slaughter brings;
Alas! no mourners weep them for the slain,
But all unburied lies the naked soul;
The whitening bones of thousands strew the plain,
Yet none can now the pestilence control;
The eagles gathering on the carcass feed,
In every heart behold their half-formed prey;
The battened wills beneath their talons bleed,
Their iron beaks without remorse must slay;
Till by the sun no more the place is seen,
Where they who worshiped idol gods have been.[25]

In these poems there seems to be no hope for diseased humanity.
Only the observer of the scenes, tormented by the death he
witnesses, can look forward to relief from his anguish.

Another series of sonnets, however, depicts the world-prison as
Golgotha—the "skull," a place of torment and burial as well as
martyrdom—and therefore the locale conveys a promise of resurrection. There is then an alternative to the living-death which
shackles men without their knowledge. Calvary, with its suggestion of self-recognition and hope, offers an alternative to self-
mutilation and premature death. Day, after all, succeeds night in
the city as well as in the world-garden, and with it comes the
possibility of spiritual awakening.

The prison-house is full; there is no cell
But hath its prisoner laden with his chains;
And yet they live as though their life was well,
Nor of its burdening sin the soul complains;
Thou dost not see where thou hast lived so long,—
The place is called the skull where thou dost tread.
Why laugh'st thou, then, why sing the sportive song,
As if thou livest, and know'st not thou art dead.
Yes, thou art dead, the morn breaks o'er thee now,—
Where is thy Father, He who gave thee birth?
Thou art a severed limb, a barren bough,
Thou sleepest in deep caverns of the earth.

Awake! thou hast a glorious race to run;
Put on thy strength, thou hast not yet begun.[26]

But intellectual comprehension of spiritual death is not sufficient
to waken man from the sinful life which imprisons his spirit. In
"He Was Acquainted With Grief" (an ambiguous reference to
both Jesus and the poet) pain is the way of redemption. The
suffering of Crucifixion itself must be inwardly experienced
before release from the tomb is possible:

I cannot tell the sorrows that I feel
By the night's darkness, by the prison's gloom;
There is no sight that can the death reveal
The spirit suffers in a living tomb;
There is no sound of grief that mourners raise,
No moaning of the wind, or dirge-like sea,
No hymns, though prophet tones inspire the lays,
That can the spirit's grief awake in thee.
Thou too must suffer as it suffers here
The death in Christ to know the Father's love;
Then in the strains that angels love to hear
Thou too shalt hear the Spirit's song above,
And learn in grief what these can never tell,
A note too deep for earthly voice to swell.[27]

The only instructive and reconstructive suffering, according to
Very, was mental—the form of anguish undergone by Jesus on
the Cross. By contrast, the sensation of bodily pain he thought
symptomatic of the sufferer's defective will, which self-denial and
"obedience" to the will of God would overcome.[28]

The poet of "The Jew" has already undergone this vicarious
experience of Christ-ian grief, having been exposed to the hatred
and treachery of the Salem ministers, among others. Through
their rejection of him he has relived the life of Jesus. In the sonnet
he addresses his tormentors directly:

Thou art more deadly than the Jew of old,
Thou hast his weapons hidden in thy speech;

And though thy hand from me thou dost withhold,
They pierce where sword and spear could never reach.
Thou hast me fenced about with thorny talk,
To pierce my soul with anguish while I hear;
And while amid thy populous streets I walk,
I feel at every step the entering spear;
Go, cleanse thy lying mouth of all its guile
That from the will within thee ever flows;
Go, cleanse the temple thou dost now defile,
Then shall I cease to feel thy heavy blows;
And come and tread with me the path of peace,
And from thy brother's harm forever cease.[29]

At times, consequently, as in "Behold He Is at Hand That Doth Betray Me," the poet can scarcely be distinguished from Jesus:

Why come you out to me with clubs and staves,
That you on every side have fenced me so?
In every act you dig for me deep graves;
In which my feet must walk where'er I go;
You speak and in your words my death I find,
Pierced through with many sorrows to the core;
And none that will the bleeding spirit bind,
But at each touch still freer flows the gore:
But with my stripes your deep-dyed sins are healed,
For I must show my Master's love for you;
The Cov'nant that he made, forever sealed,
By blood is witnessed to be just and true;
And you in turn must bear the stripes I bear,
And in his suffering learn alike to share.[30]

The love and friendship, therefore, sought by the poet who stands apart from the spiritual disorders of the present, has more than mortal significance. The tone of command employed in "Thy Brother's Blood," and the words he utters, deliberately suggest a sanction which goes beyond that of the man Jones Very.

I have no Brother—they who meet me now
Offer a hand with their own will defiled,

And while they wear a smooth unwrinkled brow,
Know not that Truth can never be beguiled;
Go wash the hand that still betrays thy guilt;
Before the spirit's gaze what stain can hide?
Abel's red blood upon the earth is spilt,
And by thy tongue it cannot be denied;
I hear not with the ear—the heart doth tell
Its secret deeds to me untold before;
Go, all its hidden plunder quickly sell,
Then shalt thou cleanse thee from thy brother's gore,
Then will I take thy gift—that bloody stain
Shall not be seen upon thy hand again.[31]

The poems of the winter of 1838–1839, like the letters he so urgently addressed to friends, were written while Very was swept along by overpowering confidence in what he was doing. He believed and said that he was being "moved by the Spirit of Truth which was promised by Christ to his disciples," and this conviction informed his sonnets.[32] After seven years of commitment and practice, poetry had become an instinctive act for him, one which no longer required the disciplined intervention of the analytical mind, and did not need his individual will and effort:

Nor words nor measured sounds have I to find,
But in them both my soul doth ever flow;
They come as viewless as the unseen wind,
And tell thy noiseless steps where'er I go.[33]

Such conviction and confidence enabled him to write more than one-hundred sonnets between November 1838 and March 1839. Automatically, spontaneously, compulsively the words and images came, welling-forth from some uncontrolled and uncontrollable source deep within him which he did not hesitate to identify as the Holy Spirit. His faith in the divine origins of his poems allowed him to tap effectively the possibilities of his own genius, permitting him to draw freely upon the fears, tensions, hopes, and joys which had left their marks upon his being during twenty-six years of life.

What is most remarkable about his performance is not that these poems are uneven in quality (as Alcott recognized), but that so many of them are worth preserving—as Elizabeth Peabody and Emerson as well as Alcott believed. Narrow in range and often repetitive, at times seeming as if the same poem were being written again and again, the poems of this period— even those that are dramatic and bitter rather than lyric and delicate—frequently possess a beauty and eloquence derived from the intensity and integrity of his feelings. These virtues were not denied by his more sensitive contemporaries. On the contrary, to their credit, they encouraged him to continue transmitting the "Word of God" to the world of sinful man.

In February 1839, just one month after the evening spent in "Conversation" at Lynn, Very's appearance and behavior again saddened Alcott. Very rode to Boston with Alcott, and spent the day at his house. He seemed to be suffering physically from the six-month strain of acting as God's agent.

Very seems much less in the spirit than when I last saw him. Life is almost extinct from the organs. He is more spectral than ever. Obviously, he has not long to stay in the body, unless disease, or some physical change, supervenes, to arrest the withdrawal of the soul from the corporeal functions.[34]

While the precise nature of this affliction is clouded by the somber imagery, Alcott's fears are unmistakable. Madness no longer was the danger Very risked. Total surrender to the will of God might require even the abandonment of the human will to live. Very's was literally a self-destructive illumination, and to Alcott at least, his vitality seemed to flicker dangerously. He reported his estimate of Very's condition to Emerson, who in turn told Margaret Fuller. After having "anatomized" him with Alcott, he wrote to her that he feared Very "is dying or becoming hopelessly mad." [35]

On February twentieth Emerson delivered the last lecture in his "Human Life" series. A month later, after the birth of his daughter Ellen, he was free to resume friendships temporarily interrupted, and among others he thought of Very. Recalling the invitation extended him four months before, and after reflecting upon what he had lately heard about him, he decided to arrange for the long-promised visit. Curiosity as well as sympathy, Elizabeth Peabody's urgings that he acknowledge Very's genius for poetry, and perhaps even some private awareness that he was in part responsible for Very's seemingly dreadful state of mind, influenced his decision to write to him.

In all probability Margaret Fuller's estimate of the essays was also a factor. She had recently written Emerson that she found "excellent things" in them, and their "tone" she considered "very noble." Nevertheless she had reservations:

the subject seems rather probed at an inquiring distance than grasped, and yet there is an attempt at mastery. I find I am displeased just in proportion, as the critic attempts to account for things in Shakespeare! . . .

Mr Very is *infinitely* inferior in accuracy of perception to Mr Dana, and has not so much insight, but he soars higher.—I am, however, greatly interested in Mr Very. He seems worthy to be well known.[36]

Emerson thought her estimate of Very's papers "very good—just, under the purely literary view; but the man himself is a rare problem, is or was lately a study worthy of all regard for his inspired and prophetical side." [37] Margaret Fuller's qualified approval therefore helped define the terms of Emerson's current interest in Very.

The tactful letter he finally wrote to Very concealed his anxieties:

I should have renewed my request to you to visit me some weeks ago but for my own ill health and the feeble circumstances of my wife. We are all now in better health and are in expectation of a visit from my brother and his family from New York and also of Miss Fuller from Groton. It seems to me therefore that both you and I will get the most comfort from our conversation if you would come here about the 5th or 6th of April when these friends will probably have left us. We shall then have a good opportunity of settling what is best in regard to an early publication of the Dissertations and sonnets and also, as far as speech can, what is best in life.[38]

To Emerson's dismay, Very replied with a "short and somewhat Judaical note," which intimated that he could not come at once to Concord but would be able to come soon.[39] Its tone and complete disregard for Emerson's wish to entertain him at a convenient time did not bode well. He again discussed Very with Alcott, and again heard Alcott's gloomy predictions. Desiring therefore to forestall what he thought would be a shattering experience were Very to arrive unexpectedly to a house already filled with guests, Emerson sought the help of Elizabeth Peabody. He wrote her of his dilemma:

I always value a visit the more when the time is fixed beforehand. In the peculiar state of Jones Very, this is trebly true. So may I trouble you with a message to him. It was agreed between us, last winter, that he should visit me when my lectures were over. Accordingly, though I heard he was more unwell and unsound, I wrote to him that I should be glad to see him about the 5[th of] April. . . . Now neither would his visit bring any comfort to him or to me, if he should chance to come with other friends whom I expect to see shortly, to whom in his present state of mind he could be no company. If therefore you should know anything of his plans,—I wish you would tell him that he must write me when he can come, and I will endeavour to name a time which will give us opportunity for conversation. From what I have seen and heard of him I fear I am not to hear of any amelioration in his case.[40]

Emerson need not have worried about an untimely visit from Very. The renewed invitation actually had come at an inopportune time, although he could not bring himself to explain this to Emerson in his reply. By the middle of February Very had become increasingly impatient with the slow progress of his "mission," and he apparently began to suspect his own spiritual well-being. His doubts had to be satisfied. The outward signs of his inward irresolution at first were the eerie bearing and aura of mystery which Alcott had observed at the time, but misconstrued. Finally, early in March, disappointed in himself and burdened physically and mentally by his beliefs and aspirations, Very withdrew completely from society. He secluded himself in his room in the house at 154 Federal Street. Cutting himself off from his friends, he spent his time alone—with his introspections and poetry, continuing to record what he believed were the utterances of the Spirit. In spite of this voluntary retirement, he also continued on his own terms to maintain a limited contact with the world which had so far largely denied him. In addition to the poems printed in the *Western Messenger,* twenty-four of his sonnets appeared in the Salem *Observer* between March twenty-third and May twenty-fifth. This then was not a period of inactivity. It was one of intense concentration, whose purpose was to renew his solitary covenant with God and to prepare for his return once again to the world of sinful men.

More than a month had passed since Elizabeth Peabody had last seen him. Upon receiving Emerson's letter, she decided to inquire for him at his house—but first she had to overcome her distaste for the errand. The last time she called there, in December 1838, it was to see Lydia Very. When she left she had promised herself never to visit her again, although Mrs. Very now considered her a friend and had invited her to return whenever she could. But it had been a "painful" experience for Elizabeth to spend even a few minutes with "such a tiger of a woman."

She is almost a maniac from the simple vehemence of passion—She has been long at war with the world for Atheism's sake—and now has adopted the other view—identifying her son with the God in whom she at last believes.—There is something very strange in it all. There is a brother who seems a lovely and rational young man. I wish I could see *him* alone.[41]

Her latter wish was granted. Stirred by Emerson's uneasiness, she overcame her distaste for such a visit and called at 154 Federal Street in May. From Washington Very she learned for the first time that when his brother went into his strange "state" the previous September, he had told his family that he would "come out of it" within a year. After six months had passed, he had decided to wait out the full term in solitude. Consequently, Washington informed her, she could not see him. He would speak to no one.

Washington Very believed his brother would "return to the ways of men in a year" as he promised. Moreover, he told Elizabeth that although he had recently been "somewhat morbidly excited," he has since "benefited" from keeping himself "so quietly at home lately." Elizabeth also learned that while Washington neither shared his brother's "extreme views" nor responded happily to them as did his mother, he still was not certain Jones was "deranged." Therefore he was unwilling to abandon "hope and expectation" that he again will "become like other people." For a time Elizabeth had to be satisfied with this second-hand account of Very's condition. She dutifully reported to Emerson that Jones Very "has kept [to] his chamber for more than two months, being not able, and still less inclined to leave it."[42]

That he was "not able" to participate in the everyday business of life was due to the untenable position he found himself in early in 1839. He despised even those persons, like William Ellery Channing and Ralph Waldo Emerson, whom he most admired and respected. Channing he judged "nearer to the kingdom of heaven than any body he had yet seen," while Emerson "love[d] that which is spoken by the word." [43] But neither man was willing to join him outside the "city of the dead." Even in friends with whom he was closest (such as Elizabeth Peabody and her circle), he detected various degrees of willfulness and disobedience, overt sins and distorted souls, spiritual disorders and neglect of divine imperatives. Unable to absorb further shocks to his delicately balanced temperament, and unwilling to abandon or drastically revise those convictions which alienated him from his contemporaries, he had little choice remaining.

> The bitterness of death is on me now,
> Before me stands its dark unclosing door;
> Yet to Thy will submissive still I bow,
> And follow Him who for me went before.[44]

In addition to his inability to leave his room, he was "still less inclined" to do so. He was totally occupied by thoughts of the collection of poetry which Emerson had promised to help him with. This was an opportunity to reach minds and hearts which he could not dismiss lightly. Knowing that neither his published poems nor the ones informally circulating in manuscript had so far succeeded as instruments of conversion, he decided to provide Emerson with additional new poems from which the final selection would be made. Isolation was necessary for the demanding task before him. Therefore when Emerson's invitation reached him, he replied only that he could not come to Concord at once but would come soon. His work-in-progress could not be interrupted. He was not yet ready to meet Emerson and settle either the matter of the book or "what is best in life."

# The New Book of Revelations

## SPRING 1839

THE PRIVATE resolve to make his book an irresistible spiritual force compelled Jones Very to adopt solitary habits in the spring of 1839. Temporary withdrawal from the world permitted him to confront troubled thoughts and feelings in ways which were impossible while the spiritual needs of others continued to absorb his attention.

Within the narrow space of his modest room there came to him the unfailing love and acceptance elsewhere withheld. Alone in intimate and familiar surroundings to which he was emotionally attached, and where fantasies could be unconsciously manipulated in satisfying patterns without the intrusion of the questioning disbelief of others, he directly encountered the Father with whom he had so long yearned to be reunited. Consistently the result was poetry:

> I sit within my room, and joy to find
> That Thou who always lov'st, art with me here,
> That I am never left by Thee behind,
> But by thyself Thou keep'st me ever near;
> The fire burns brighter when with Thee I look,

And seems a kinder servant sent to me;
With gladder heart I read thy holy book,
Because thou art the eyes by which I see;
This aged chair, that table, watch and door
Round in ready service ever wait;
Nor can I ask of Thee a menial more
To fill the measure of my large estate,
For Thou thyself, with all a father's care,
Where'er I turn art ever with me there.[1]

Sonnets written in the early months of 1839 provide the only indications of what transpired in the closed room at 154 Federal Street, just as they are the principal means of reconstructing the kind of book he was trying to assemble for Emerson's editorial approval. These poems are all dramatic, comprising speeches delivered by the chief characters in the theater of Very's mind, himself and the persons of the Trinity. The sonnets are spoken pieces, addressed by the various characters participating in the drama to the others, or to the undifferentiated humanity inhabiting the "city of the dead." Considered together with the other poems he had written since September 1838, and if arranged without regard for the exact order of composition, these sonnets comprise the only form of epic Very thought still possible in the modern world. This epic, according to the essay he had devoted to such matters, focuses upon the consciousness of the poet as it directly engages the deity and works out the terms of salvation, thereby providing an archetypal experience which other men might share to their own spiritual advantage.

Within this closed psycho-theological system, perhaps mingled with Very's scarcely differentiated recollections of Captain Very, the voice of "the Father" reconfirmed what he already knew. God speaks to him:

I come—the rushing wind that shook the place
Where those once sat who spake with tongues of fire—

O'er thee to shed the freely-given grace,
And bid the[e] speak while I thy verse inspire.

Then the world will "hear and know" that he has been dispatched by God, and has been granted the power that "wakes the dead" and performs miracles.[2] At times it is Jesus who speaks to him, in tones of love and reassurance, urging him to make known to men "My word; it speaks, will they but hear its voice."[3] Occasionally Jesus must remind him to be diligent in his "submission," promising eternal rewards in return for the poet's service:

> The words I give thee, they are not thine own:
> Give them as freely as to thee they're given,
> And thou shalt reap the grain thy hands have sown
> When thou hast reached in peace the opening heaven.
> Come—I will give thee kindred, friends, and wife
> Such as no earthly lot can have in store;
> Thou shalt receive them for eternal life.

And glorious invitations are extended him:

> My mansion is prepared; come, enter in,
> Put on the wedding dress, and you shall be
> A welcome tenant freed from every sin,
> Henceforth to walk from bondage ever free.
> In the last day I come: it cometh soon!
> Be wise—thy morning hour shall reach its noon.[4]

Similarly, in the manner of Jesus with the Disciples (John 14), the Holy Spirit directly instructs him in his "mission":

> I speak in you the word that gave you birth;
> Fear not: I call you to attend my voice.
> Walk humbly on—thy path lies through the earth,
> But thou shalt in the latter day rejoice
> If thou to all hast spoken ever true
> What thou hast heard from me who send you forth.

All Very need do is

> Speak boldly then, for 'tis not you they hear
> But Him who in you speaks the living word.[5]

Instructions to "Declare my word" frequently are repeated, to convince the poet of the necessity of his role in the drama of salvation.[6]

In spite of encouragements, the responsibilities of a God-inspired poet at times are overpowering, leaving Very exhausted; but his strength is restored by the divine gift of untroubled rest:

> I thank thee, Father, that the night is near
> When I this conscious being may resign;
> Whose only task thy words of love to hear,
> And in thy acts to find each act of mine;
> A task too great to give a child like me,
> The myriad-handed labors of the day
> Too many for my closing eyes to see,
> Thy words too frequent for my tongue to say;
> Yet when thou see'st me burthened by thy love,
> Each other gift more lovely then appears,
> For dark-robed night comes hovering from above,
> And all thine other gifts to me endears;
> And while within her darkened couch I sleep,
> Thine eyes untired above will constant vigils keep.[7]

In addition to acting as the general amanuensis of God, Very's specific appointment requires him to function as monitor of the Second Coming. Once again God the Father speaks, assigning Very a role in the cosmic scene being readied for mankind:

> I place thee as a watchman on a tower
> That thou mayst warn the city of the dead;
> The day has come, and come the appointed hour,
> When through their streets my herald's feet shall tread;
> Prepare ye all my supper to attend![8]

The poet is shocked once he realizes how ineffectual are his efforts to alert men to the approaching day of crisis and to their urgent need to avoid eternally disastrous consequences:

'Tis near the morning watch, the dim lamp burns
But scarcely shows how dark the slumbering street;
No sound of life the silent mart returns;
No friends from house to house their neighbors greet;
It is the sleep of death; a deeper sleep
Than e'er before on mortal eyelids fell;
No stars above the gloom their places keep;
No faithful watchmen of the morning tell;
Yet still they slumber on, though rising day
Hath through their windows poured the awakening light;
Or, turning in their sluggard trances, say—
"There yet are many hours to fill the night;"
They rise not yet; while on the bridegroom goes
'Till he the day's bright gates forever on them close! [9]

But God's patient explanations console him. Not all men will respond to his warnings that a new day is about to dawn:

The light will never open sightless eyes,
It comes to those who willingly would see. [10]

Very's soliloquies and prayers nevertheless disclose his continuing sense of inadequacy for the tasks assigned. As overseer and divine spokesman for the "city of the dead," he is enveloped by enervating elements. Although outside him rather than within, they yet prevent him from fully experiencing God's love:

I have not lived—the flesh has hedged me in,
I have not known the joy to be with thee;
But I must strive to loose the bonds of sin
That press me round, and be forever free.
Give me the victory o'er the tyrant death,
Whose sceptre rests now cold upon my heart;
Breathe on me, and reviving at thy breath,
The chill that o'er me steals will quick depart,
And I revive, like the ice-frosted flower

[ 315 ]

That winter seizes in his rude embrace,
When spring, with kindly sun and loving shower,
Creeps on from southern climes with welcome face,
And chides the spoilers of her children fair,
And once again restores them to her care.[11]

Another prayer relates more directly to his special role as poet:

Oh! swell my bosom deeper with thy love,
That I some river's widening mouth may be;
And ever on, for many a mile above,
May flow the floods that enter from the sea;
And may they not retreat as tides of earth,
Save but to show from Thee that they have flown;
Soon may my spirit find that better birth,
Where the retiring wave is never known;
But Thou dost flow through every channel wide,
With all a Father's love in every soul;
A stream that knows no ebb, a swelling tide
That rolls forever on and finds no goal,
Till in the hearts of all shall opened be
The ocean depths of thine eternity.[12]

As a poet exercising discretion consistent with his Father's will, Very reflects in characteristic fashion upon the circumstances of those who are spiritually dead:

There is a winter in the godless heart
More cold than that which creeps upon the year;
That will not with the opening spring depart,
But presses on though summer's heats are near.
Its blasts are words that chill the living soul,
Though heard in pleasing phrase and learned sound;
Their chilling breath nor triple folds control,
They pierce within though flesh and blood surround.
How dead the heart whence drives the arrowy shower!
The full-blown rose hangs drooping at its breath,
The bursting buds of promise feel its power,

And fixed stand incased in icy death;
And e'en the soul which Christ's warm tears fill,
Its sleety accents falling thick can chill.[13]

Finally, by means of His poet-surrogate, Jesus addresses the multitude:

My Kingdom is within you: seek it there—
Ye shall not seek in vain who work within;

and sternly directs them to "Repent!"[14] The words Very thus projects at times apply to himself as much as to others:

Serve me within; be inwardly a Jew,
And thou shalt reign with me a priest in heaven.[15]

At other times Very speaks on his own initiative, drawing upon his own experience. He addresses the unrepentant in his capacity as "watchman" over the "city of the dead":

The fairest day that ever yet has shone,
Will be when thou the day within shalt see;
The fairest rose that ever yet has blown,
When thou the flower thou lookest on shalt be.
But thou art far away among Time's toys;
Thyself the day thou lookest for in them,
Thyself the flower that now thine eye enjoys,
But wilted now thou hang'st upon thy stem.
The bird thou hearest on the budding tree,
Thou hast made sing with thy forgotten voice;
But when it swells again to melody,
The song is thine in which thou wilt rejoice;
And thou new risen 'midst these wonders live,
That now to them dost all thy substance give.[16]

And he directs the inhabitants of the "city of the dead" to recognize the change he has undergone as a result of his relationship to God:

Wouldst thou behold my features? cleanse thy heart,
Wash out the stains thy will impresses there,

And as the clay-stamped images depart,
Thou shalt behold my face: how wondrous fair,
How changed from that thine outward eye must see!
It wears no form its searching glance can know;
From flesh and blood it now has wrought it free,
And in the Spirit learns from Christ to grow.[17]

Mention repeatedly is made of a special reward—most meaningful perhaps for Very himself—which awaits those who seek salvation:

The marriage feast is ready: hasten in,
For those who tarry shall their lateness mourn.
Come, and your robes I'll wash from every sin,
And in my arms shall every son be borne.[18]

When God the Father addresses the sinful through His appointed spokesman, He warns them of the Second Coming:

Repent! why do ye still uncertain stand,
The kingdom of my son is nigh at hand![19]

Jesus, taking advantage of Very's station on the tower above the city, makes a final appeal just moments before He completes his Descent:

Come forth, come forth, my people, from the place
Where ye have lived so many days secure;
I will destroy within the wicked race,
Their walls of brass and stone shall not endure;
They fall! escape! flee fast! the foe is near!
Be wise, and of my love-sent message hear!
Stop not to take your clothes! escape for life!
For swift descends the day with sorrows rife!
Escape! the word is near you, in your heart;
Obey within, and make My pathway strait;
Hasten! from all your sinful ways depart,
And enter through the strait and narrow gate;
Be warned and flee, the morning watch is spent,
And but a moment for your flight is lent.[20]

The long-awaited moment arrives, and the announcement of the
Advent is made to the "imprisoned souls":

> Awake, ye dead! The summons has gone forth,
> That bids you leave the dark enclosing grave; . . .

The announcement is repeated:

> Awake, ye faithful! throw your grave clothes by,
> He whom ye seek is risen, bids you rise;
> The cross again on earth is lifted high;
> Turn to its healing sight your closing eyes;
> And you shall rise and gird your armor on,
> And fight till you a crown in Christ have won.[21]

From his position high above the city, Very witnesses the Son's
return to earth and recounts what is taking place. No longer is
the "vision" denied him:

> The day, the day, 'tis changed to darkest night!
> There is no beauty in its morning beams,
> But men run to and fro within its light
> As haunted by the thought of horrid dreams;
> They do not speak of what they spoke before,
> Nor greet each other now with wonted smile;
> Their hearts are pricked within them to the core,
> Nor can the sight of aught their pain beguile;
> Within their homes they hush the notes of joy,
> For like a snare their sorrow has come on;
> The slightest burdens now their souls annoy,
> And in an instant all their mirth is gone;
> For He who long has tarried is at hand,
> And comes himself his vineyard to demand.[22]

> The heavens are shaken! not the solid earth,
> But the high heavens, the spirit's own abode;
> Through the dark souls whence sin springs armed to birth,
> The miracle of miracles is showed!
> There mountains shake, there breaks a startling voice

Unknown amid its sinful depths before;
The guilty dare not, when it speaks, rejoice;
But fain within its presence would adore;
Fly! fly! it is the spirit's voice you hear,
It is an angel sent to thee from heaven,
To tell thee that the marriage feast is near,
And but a moment's warning can be given;
Oh haste! the robe, the robe of white put on,
E'er that for thee that moment shall be gone.[23]

The dead! the dead! they throw their grave clothes by,
And burst the prisons where they long have lain;
I hear them send their shouts of triumph high,
For he, the king of terrors, now is slain;
I see them; see! the dumb have found a voice;
The lame are leaping where they crawled before;
The blind with eyes of wonder see, rejoice;
The deaf stand listening to the glad uproar;
Look! each the other as a brother sees;
Hark! each the other welcomes to his home;
There are no tones of chilling breath to freeze,
No tears are dropt, no sufferers here can moan;
The joy of love o'er every feature plays,
And every new-born child rejoices in its rays.[24]

The word goes forth! I see its conquering way,
O'er seas and mountains sweeps it mighty on;
The tribes of men are bowing 'neath its sway,
The pomp of kings, the pride of wisdom's gone;
Behold, the poor have raised the victor's shout;
The meek are crowned, their triumph too is nigh;
The barren now no more a son can doubt;
The mourner wipes her cheek and glittering eye;
Hark! from the lofty palace comes a groan,
That they cannot their wealth ill-gotten hide;
The midnight darkness from the thief is flown,
The garment's rent of falsely clothed pride;

The veil is drawn; the judgment seat appears;
I see joy mingling with a world in tears.[25]

With the parting of the opaque screen which had inhibited
recognition of moral values in natural facts, and with the exposition of an untroubled future without time or injustice, the present
gains new meaning. Meditative and lyrical sonnets on familiar
natural subjects once again are appropriate. Significant, however,
is the absence of the sadness or regret which invariably had
colored their earlier counterparts in Very's canon. The world-
crisis and the personal crisis unmistakably have passed. For the
vision-struck poet, the world-as-garden has replaced the "city of
the dead":

The bubbling brook doth leap when I come by,
Because my feet find measure with its call;
The birds know when the friend they love is nigh,
For I am known to them both great and small;
The flower that on the lovely hill-side grows
Expects me there when Spring its bloom has given;
And many a tree and bush my wanderings knows,
And e'en the clouds and silent stars of heaven;
For he who with his Maker walks aright,
Shall be their lord as Adam was before;
His ear shall catch each sound with new delight,
Each object wear the dress that then it wore;
And he, as when erect in soul he stood,
Hear from his Father's lips that all is good.[26]

The past also has gained new significance. As the poet strolls
through his earthly paradise, recollections of the "inward"
Armageddon he witnessed enrich his sonnets of "memory,"
enabling them to conclude without bitterness:

I saw a war yet none the trumpet blew,
Nor in their hands the steel-wrought weapons bare;
And in that conflict armed there fought but few,

And none that in the world's loud tumults share;
They fought against their wills, the stubborn foe
That mail-clad warriors left unfought within;
And wordy champions left unslain below,
The ravening wolf though drest in fleecy skin;
They fought for peace, not that the world can give,
Whose tongue proclaims the war its hands have ceased
And bids us as each other's neighbor live,
When John within our breasts has not deceased;
They fought for him whose kingdom must increase,
Good will to men, on earth forever peace.[27]

An apocalyptic pastoral, celebrating Very's own triumphant Self, brings this remarkable sequence of epic-dramatic sonnets to a brilliant close:

I saw the spot where our first parents dwelt;
And yet it wore to me no face of change,
For while amid its fields and groves I felt
As if I had not sinned, nor thought it strange;
My eye seemed but a part of every sight,
My ear heard music in each sound that rose,
Each sense forever found a new delight,
Such as the spirit's vision only knows;
Each act some new and ever-varying joy
Did by my father's love for me prepare;
To dress the spot my ever fresh employ,
And in the glorious whole with Him to share;
No more without the flaming gate to stray,
No more for sin's dark stain the debt of death to pay.[28]

With this startling sonnet, the frenzied images of Advent were brought under firm control without jeopardizing ecstatic feelings, and the rich visions of the "Spirit Land" finally were realized. Not only had Very witnessed his own personal resurrection, but that of his poetry as well.

This then was the thematic basis for the book Very was

completing during the spring of 1839. To consist of more than a hundred poems organized in terms of the promise of the Second Coming, it would depict the prelude and consequences of this manifestation of deity on earth. The sonnets Very had written since September 1838 range through the complete spiritual cycle of man as Very understood it: from desperate self-accusation to the inner struggle between the wayward individual will and the good God-sent will; from recognition and condemnation of the "city of the dead" to redemptive suffering at Calvary; from exhortations for the spiritual awakening of the dead to the Second Coming and judgment of the wicked; finally reaching the passage of the purified Self through the perfect world of the garden. Unifying all and recurring as a leitmotiv is the love of God and enlightened man for goodness, and their corresponding denunciations of that willfulness which constitutes spiritual death.

The experiences Very depicts are symbolic in that the entire drama takes place within the consciousness of the man seeking salvation. All men, not only the poet, may be moved to this saving "vision" by the Holy Spirit; through "obedience" and "submission" all men may become the agents of God's will; all men, by virtue of divine powers working through them, may effect the regeneration of the world by first introducing the reign of peace within themselves and then within others. The book thus was conceived as a universal allegory of Self and of its varying conditions on the way to spiritual reawakening.

The most remarkable aspect of the sonnet sequence (although not always most successful in poetic terms), is the large number of deific poems—those in which components of the triune God speak either to the Self or to the disobedient multitude. Too often only verisifications of familiar Gospel incidents, phrases, and catchwords, they nevertheless manage at rare times to evoke in dramatic fashion the essence of Revelation. Prophetic sonnets, springing from Very's recollections of the New Testament as much as from deep-rooted personal tensions within him, they restate the resurrection themes which he felt were not being sufficiently stressed by Unitarianism. In this sense the work is an indictment of current theology and preaching, that dominated by the Harvard conservatives. The sonnet sequence proposes models and examples of enthusiasm, of the sort Very thought Emerson had called for in his Divinity School Address. The book Very was compiling therefore tried to set standards for a modern Christianity better suited to the spiritual needs of the present age than the ethical platitudes resounding from Unitarian pulpits. It would be, Very thought, a reforming book—for the Church as much as for individuals.

Very and Emerson and their interested friends had for several months understood that the volume would consist of his three "literary" essays in addition to a collection of his poems. Late in the spring of 1839, while still preserving the voluntary retirement which isolated him from friends, Very prepared an introduction to the book. It was designed to relate the essays to the poetry and to point up the significance of the work as a whole.

Although stimulated by Elizabeth Peabody's suggestion that he compose a "psychological autobiography" as a preface to the book,[29] what he wrote was not the kind of genetic foreword she had envisioned. Solitude and the absence of any moderating influence from family or friends further concentrated those intensities of thought and feeling which might be expected to inform his writing. The introduction was his most idiosyncratic statement of principles. Dogmatic in tone, saturated with the impersonal egotism so characteristic of him, full of scriptural echoes and paraphrase, it was a rhetorical piece in the imperative mood. Prescriptive and monitory rather than retrospective and analytical, it was not a personal account of his own spiritual life. Moreover, rhapsodic and vertiginous language often threatened to slip away into the volatile regions of sacred mystery, leaving only dazzle and paradox for the uninitiated to ponder. Obscurities, however, were caused not by incoherent rant but by the metaphors of self which made explicit his vision of human actualities and possibilities.

Underlying the introduction, if not systematically expounded in it, were Very's pneumatological conceptions, stated in the form of a Christian paradox: those who are dead are not really dead; those who are not dead are really dead. According to Very, human souls existed in three distinct conditions: either they were dead, alive, or quickening. The dead soul was an unborn or stillborn soul. By this he meant the kind possessed by most men, whose physical existence was rooted in unnatural values and actions. The unborn spirit is then willful and selfish. By contrast, the living soul (originally but no longer an unborn soul), had been given life by the intervention of a quickening agent. The living soul is will-less, since its unnatural human will is being denied in an attempt to execute the will of the Heavenly Father. The third category is that of the quickening spirit. It is distinguished by the soul's rebirth after having been born. The reborn soul lives once again a willful life, but now God's will—not the unnatural human will—motivates it.

Corresponding to the three conditions of soul are three conditions of physical existence: unnatural life, natural life, and death. Men unnaturally alive possess unborn (dead) souls, and their distinctive interests consequently are physical enjoyments. This living-death was inherited from parents who were themselves driven by physical appetites and exclusively material values. But by denying the inherited life of unnatural satisfactions, by denying physical pleasures, the body can become naturally alive; and by so doing, the soul is born. Continuation of self-denial enables the living soul finally to be *reborn*. Once all unnatural desires have ceased, rebirth is effected and the soul becomes indistinguishable from the Holy Spirit. This qualitative transformation is the highest development of the human personality and the greatest of miracles. In this third stage men possess the power of influencing the unborn, of bringing about the birth of living souls in them. This ultimate level of existence, then, is the life of good will, as distinguished from the unnatural life of the evil will, and from the natural life devoted to inward struggles between man's good and evil volitions. In this final stage of existence man's body was said by Very to be neither natural nor unnatural but dead. This was not physiological death, but the death of all gross human desires, physical pleasures, and material enjoyments, and the complete extinction of the evil will. The reborn spirit miraculously exercises God's generative power, and thereby may give life to stillborn souls.

The introduction which promulgated Very's ideas consisted of three formal letters addressed "To the Unborn." The first was "An Epistle on Birth"; the second, "An Epistle on Prayer"; and the third, "An Epistle on Miracles." [30] More insistent than persuasive, they discoursed in apostolic fashion upon the way of redemption. Instead of explaining the emotional and intellectual development of his own life, Very spoke of the condition and prospects of his readers' lives. The basis for these remarks was his conviction that the state of grace he had achieved was archetypal, and that others would gain their spiritual salvation by emulating him. Referring to himself as "I, who am what you shall be," he spoke to them confidently, directing them to abandon spiritual death and in an integral way to share the glory already illuminating his soul. The Epistles, therefore, were urgent invitations to enter into holy communion with the author.

The one on "Birth" addressed readers as creatures who in reality are "dead or still born." Very's avowed purpose was to gain for their souls a state of being identical with the quickening status of life he had achieved for himself. He had passed, he claimed, "into and through and out of" the natural world, his own "relations" with the "regular order of nature" having ceased entirely. Since his passage through the world had "perfected" him, he now comprehends the world in a manner impossible for those who have not yet done with it. Empowered by God, his comprehension entitles him to speak authoritatively. He now "predicates" of the world's "confusion, order," and thus he reveals the course which will lead others to the safety of God's kingdom. "Of *the world* in which I live, you know not; and it is, therefore, that you may know . . . that I write to you." [31]

Heretofore unknown to men, and in spite of the obstinacy of their wills, God is continually "begetting" them other natures. The first Epistle concludes with Very's call for recognition of this crucial spiritual fact. Only through human consciousness of the natural process underway, and by overtly consenting to it, may the divine work be completed and the unnatural world of the soul's stillbirth be left behind. Speaking parabolically, Very directed his readers to recall that although they themselves were "the seed of tares sown by the evil men of former generations," under the influence of God's "sun and rain" they were "daily decaying" so that new personalities might emerge from the evil and death of former selves. [32]

The controlling metaphor of self in the Epistles is organic and cyclical. It is that of the plant, whose death is the occasion for the production of seed. Through decay, brought about by the sun's warmth and the rain's damp, the sown seed gains life. Bursting its rotted husk, it stretches upward from the fertile blackness of earth, and becomes a living growth which in time of ripeness will sow its own seed. As sower of its own vital seed, the matured plant (acting "outwardly from within," said Very), is itself the reborn quickening spirit, whose God-commissioned words are the natural forces making possible the transformation from death to life by the wasting away of what is inert and corrupt.

Be you always in that condition of dying by which your words will make evident that yours is the *true* body of Jesus Christ. The decay in which you are then rooted shall keep your leaves green and fresh; so that the influence of life shall ever be thrown around you, and be for the healing of nations. . . . True life is alone the product of decay; . . . He who *is really* dying never laments the perishing of the outward man, as from its decay is ever putting forth that better body, even the incorruptible one of Jesus.[33]

The "Epistle on Prayer" discussed the second or "natural" stage of man's God-instituted transformation. Commencing with the realization of the dead soul's potential for life, this stage of existence continues until the "second birth" is brought about. By "prayer," Very meant the "action of the soul" which begins at the moment of man's natural birth.

As the denial or death of what you now are will give you birth; so will prayer, or the continuance in that denial, give you the death again of that which is so born; by which death you attain unto immortality. . . . This is your prayer if you may be said to pray. If you rise or are lifted up you shall raise and draw all who are dead to you and life.[34]

Prayer, then, is the chief activity of the natural life, and is devoted to the accomplishment of the quickening status through self-denial. Prayer includes all natural actions, the essential one of course being the inner struggle against the remnants of the selfish will. Prayer ends only with the onset of the unchallenged divine will, and with the germinal activity of the quickening spirit which accompanies it.

After referring briefly to the matter of the first two "Letters to the Unborn," the third Epistle (that on "Miracles") races to a sudden climax, reminiscent of those startling pronouncements which had outraged many in Harvard classrooms and Salem parlors, and had led most listeners to accuse Very of blasphemy and madness. But then as now, such offenses as Very committed were more apparent than real, and were linguistic rather than psychological. Where most suspect, the language of the "Epistle on Miracles" seemingly was detached from the order of realities to which language by tacit agreement refers, but actually it was parabolic. Very at such times was speaking emphatically, and as was customary under such circumstances, he was speaking obliquely. Earlier he suggested he would do precisely this. In the "Epistle on Prayer" he told his readers:

Use what language you will, you can never say anything but what you are. Whoever lives better than you knows what you are *really* saying whatever the sound of your lips. The spirit will always work whether it be good or whether it be evil.[35]

But this assertion, unmistakably anticipating the shocks to come, was inadequate preparation for the startling words in the "Epistle on Miracles." Something more decisive than the parable of the seed was to be silently appropriated from the Gospel accounts of the life of Jesus. Without hesitation it was adapted to Very's own conception of himself and of his relationship to God and to other men. Stunning and brilliant, it showed Very at the peak of self-confidence, for in dramatic fashion he was about to play God to an astonished humanity—or at least to that portion of it whom Very believed would soon read his essays and poems in the edition Emerson had promised to prepare.

I am your Resurrection and life, believe in the *Me* that speaks and you though unborn, shall be born; and he that is born and believes shall be born yet again, and shall know the *Only Begotten* of the Father. . . . He who speaks is external to you; he speaks to you from without; but it is *outward from within;* and *so* exerts an *external* influence over you. . . . I was *once* as you *now* are; but I am changed and *as such* exert this power of raising you from the dead; . . . The body which I *now* have, and which is forming in you or upon that *you;* declares of itself that it is your begetter. . . . *I* am the Resurrection; but who this I is which speaks; you the dead, or unraised cannot know; but when that change in you which gives me power to declare this of myself has taken place, then shall you also declare it of yourselves and know that I speak in truth, for you will know me.

I hide nothing from you; . . . I am loath to enter *your* dwellings but entreat me *much* and I will come in. . . . To know me in truth you yourself by a like increase in yourself must see me as I *am* from the external image there. As in a glass, face answers to face, so will my heart then answer to yours. Now *you* see *me* . . . externally with an unchanged spirit; then face to face. Now you *make* me what I am to you; then you shall see me as I *am;* for you yourself will be made like unto me. Then shall you know that it was *I* who called you forth from the grave; it was *I* who raised you from the bed of sickness; and *you* will arise and minister unto *me*. . . .[36]

In effect, Very was declaring that all the natural-born sons of man would (like himself) become Sons of God, and thus they would (also like himself) become indistinguishable from Jesus, joining the Bridegroom as an equal at the Wedding Feast. These were the miracles to which the last Epistle referred, miracles which in scope and quality went beyond all others, miracles for which God had designated Jones Very to testify by his words and by the accomplished facts of his life.

Once again—as before in Harvard and Salem, and in visits to near-strangers like Samuel Gray Ward and to important ministers like William Ellery Channing—Very was intent upon blurring the line which separated human from divine. This time it was an effort to condition readers for the truths which awaited them in his collected essays and poems, and to prepare them thoroughly for the impact he so earnestly wanted his work to have.

# XVIII

## Concord Revisited

### SUMMER 1839

AT THE END of November 1838 Jones Very had notified Emerson that he would gladly accept his offer of help for the "junking and disposal" of what was "placed" in his hands by the Holy Spirit—"whenever it is so ordered." [1] The "order" was received by Very six months later, after he had completed his work but while he was still intent upon maintaining his isolation.

So that final preparations for the publication of the book might proceed without him, Very decided (early in June 1839) to send Emerson a packet containing all his manuscripts. Since he was not "ordered" to communicate with him directly, he informed Emerson through his brother and Elizabeth Peabody that he still was not able or inclined to visit Concord, and would not do so for "some months." However, he wanted Emerson to know he would be glad to see him if Emerson considered it necessary, and if Emerson was willing to come to him. He also relayed his thoughts about arrangements for the book. At his direction Washington Very wrote to Emerson:

In regard to the publication of his poetry and essays, he says that he will send all which he has to you and that you may select from the *unpublished* pieces such as you think proper. He thinks it would be best to leave a subscription paper at the Cambridge bookstore, and he would prefer to have you send whatever money may accrue from it to me. It would give him great pleasure to see you if you should come to Salem before he is able to go out; and he is sorry that he cannot now make you a visit. . . . He would like to have the work dedicated to Professor E. T. Channing of Cambridge as a mark of gratitude and wishes that a subscription paper may be left at Cambridge as soon as possible, as there is a class with which he is well acquainted who will soon leave college.[2]

If Very's withdrawal in the spring of 1839 marked another spiritual crisis for him—as the observations of Alcott in February, and of Washington Very to Elizabeth Peabody subsequently, seem to suggest—it did not dim his appreciation of such practical matters as dedication, bookselling, and royalties. He remembered the Harvard teacher who had taken an interest in his early writings and given him encouragement; he remembered the students to whom he had so patiently ministered, and who might now wish to own a book by their former Greek tutor; and he remembered the financial need of his long-widowed mother and his unmarried sisters and brother.

The liveliness of his instincts was further demonstrated two weeks later. Alcott's gloomy predictions and his own claims to a twelve-month state of grace to the contrary, something happened later in June to Very the poet (if not to the perfected man) which caused him to change his mind about delaying the trip to Concord.

Prompting the termination of Very's retreat from the world was his sudden realization that the integrity of his muse was being threatened, and that the Voice of God was being distorted by the willful tamperings of a man not yet wholly regenerated. How Very learned this, whether through some devoted informant like Sophia Peabody or by his own devout intuitions, is not clear. Long afterward, however, Elizabeth Peabody recalled the occasion when Very and Emerson "together selected the sonnets for the volume." She said,

it was very soon after they were written *impromptue*—now and then a metaphor would not be fully carried out, but a single verbal correction was necessary.—I remember Mr Emerson said Mr Very was very averse to correction—declaring that it was the utterance of the Holy Ghost.[3]

Very's aversion to Emerson's unsolicited help in sonnet writing is elsewhere documented. Several years later a similar situation arose when Emerson edited one of Very's poems for publication in the July 1842 *Dial*. Since Very had not authorized any changes, he was upset and did not hesitate to show his displeasure upon reading the printed text. He wrote to Emerson:

I found my poem the "Evening Choir" altered considerably from what I had written—I do not know but in one or two cases for the better. Perhaps they were all improvements but I preferred my own lines. I do not know but I ought to submit to such changes as done by the rightful authority of an Editor but I felt a little sad at the aspect of the piece.[4]

Consequently, after posting his manuscripts to Emerson early in June 1839, he may have recalled Emerson's attempt to improve the sonnet "In Him we live, and move, and have our being," seven months before. In any event, contrary to his original intention to allow Emerson complete control over the contents of the volume, he decided to go to Concord in order to preserve what he had written, even at the expense of prematurely ending his solitary retreat.

On June fourteenth he set out from Salem. On the way he stopped with Alcott, always a good adversary with whom to sharpen wits prior to engaging the more magisterial Emerson. Alcott was probably the "well known person much talked of at that time for his transcendentalism" whom Very considered a "spiritual dandy." [5] This man, to whom hyperbole came easily, wrote in his journal:

Very dined with me today. He was on his way to Concord, to spend a few days with Emerson. He seemed much better both in body and soul, than when I saw him last. His interest in man and nature is reviving in him, and he may yet regain his human position, and walk about among men as one of them, and not, as heretofore, a spectre. I had a good deal of conversation with him; and feel encouraged about him.[6]

Such optimism was as premature as his former prediction of Very's impending death. If anything, Very's recent term of solitude had intensified his confidence in his unique relation to God. Although he had left his chamber he was obviously not yet prepared to "return to the ways of men."

Orestes Brownson stopped at Alcott's house while Very was still there. "What wide polarity between these two men!" Alcott later recalled. "They sat opposite each other at the table; but were sundered by spaces immeasurable." He thought their conversation "comic": however much they tried to speak to one another, "Very was unintelligible to the proud Philistine." [7] But he was quite intelligible to Alcott, who was more adept than Brownson in using "oriental" and related dialects. "J Very is to live," he concluded joyfully after Very had departed, "and aid in that new organization of the Soul presignified by all the Functions and Affects of the Times." [8] Several hours later, when Very arrived for his three-day stay in Concord, he was also intelligible to Emerson. But Emerson was neither a "spiritual dandy" nor a "proud Philistine." By the time Very was ready to return to Salem, Emerson had reached a much less sanguine conclusion than Alcott.

"The same spirit which brings me to your door," said Very on first greeting Emerson, "prepares my welcome." [9] At once Emerson sensed that his most recent fears had been without basis.

Apparently the "constant nervous twitching" of his face, which Samuel Gray Ward once had noticed, no longer "checked his words." The index of his condition probably was a "peculiarly sweet, and compassionate" expression which focused in his eyes as he spoke.[10] Very was not "dying or becoming hopelessly mad," as Alcott had led Emerson to believe three months before.[11] But initial relief at finding his "brave saint" reasonably well-tempered was equivocal. The curious greeting had another effect, one Very could not have anticipated. It struck an unusually sensitive nerve in Emerson. It seemed to repeat, "in a form not agreeable," an idea which had "agitated" Emerson many years before.[12] Although for a time concealed from Very, his annoyance with such pieties did not quickly pass, and it did not foreshadow a happy outcome to the visit.

Sensitivities of another sort caused him to miscalculate Very's mood, and made him disregard something Elizabeth Peabody had told him. She said she found that Very's "apprehension of a real sympathy with his views" invariably would dissipate his "isolated feeling," which in turn would forestall the "violence of expression" he otherwise might resort to.[13] Such advice, however, failed to take into account Emerson's own present humor. Once they began discussing the forthcoming book and disagreements arose, the character of the visit changed in a way neither man expected. To Emerson's discredit, he baited his guest relentlessly, showing him little sympathy, generosity, or patience.

The unpleasant fact was that Emerson could not always resist the temptation to "blaspheme" this friend "now and then," nor was he the only one so inclined. All who were acquainted with Very knew how easily he was roused to extravagant statement, and that he placed "inordinate vaules on all his own thoughts." The confidence with which he characteristically spoke (due to his "excessively *conceited*" nature, said Susan Burley), sometimes exposed him to the uncharitable laughter of even close friends.[14] Having a distinctive style and point of view, his speech was easily mimicked. His "tall, angular figure" and his "solemn, fervent" manner, the high forehead (even more prominent than it had been during college days), the thin, smooth face from whose expression it "seemed as if he had left off thinking since he had become so happy as he expressed himself to be," his large black hat, his meticulous black suit and frockcoat, and his black walking stick were all easily caricatured—as Caroline Sturgis demonstrated to the amusement of Margaret Fuller and Emerson.[15] Indeed, at his expense much "sweet fun" could readily be had, although fortunately it often was "checked" by the "benevolent regret" of the wits themselves.[16] On June fourteenth, however, to their mutual disadvantage, Emerson boldly exploited the peculiar weakness of his guest.

As soon as Very explained the purpose of his visit, to his dismay he found his original suspicions emphatically confirmed. Emerson's conception of the book, including the origins and significance of its contents, differed widely from his own. When he explained that he wanted the book to begin with the three "Letters to the Unborn," Emerson refused to include them anywhere in the compilation, probably arguing that the three essays ("Epic Poetry," "Shakespeare," and "Hamlet") were sufficient introduction, and that the manner and substance of the "Letters" were likely to confuse and discourage readers. When Very said he wanted his poems arranged thematically, so that the spiritual cycle would be unfolded in systematic fashion, Emerson objected, insisting that this was not necessary or desirable, and that they must be arranged essentially in order of composition and without regard to any rigid scheme. When Very said he wanted only unpublished poems in the volume (reiterating more strongly what his brother's recent letter had already made clear), Emerson expressed his frank opinion: all of these, with perhaps three or four exceptions, were "unworthy [of] publication," [17] and of the more than 150 poems already published in periodicals, scarcely one-third deserved reprinting. When Very, in exasperation, insisted that none of the poems acceptable to Emerson should be altered in any way (each, he claimed, must be left "exactly as it was done the first time" because "such was the will of God"), Emerson made his most crushing retort. He asked him bluntly: "Cannot the spirit parse and spell?" In a patronizing tone he added, "We cannot permit the Holy Ghost to be careless (and in one instance) to talk bad grammar." [18] He was quick to answer every one of Very's "speeches," and later (for the entertainment of mutual friends) he recounted in detail how cleverly he had "dealt" with him.

The result of this one-sided editorial conference was that Emerson made clear he would proceed with arrangements for the book only if he were allowed to "select and combine with sovereign will." He overrode all Very's objections with the assurance that if his own judgments were allowed to prevail, the result would be a "little gem of a volume," one likely to find a sizeable audience, and which would respect the intentions of the Spirit while spelling, grammar, punctuation, and organization conformed to standard usage. Jones Very capitulated. [19]

As Emerson conceived it, the book would de-emphasize the prophetic, apocalyptic, and overtly evangelic aspects of Very's work. While not absent entirely, the more idiosyncratic poems (particularly those written in 1839, immediately before and during his period of withdrawal), would not be conspicuous. The emphasis of the collection would fall on poems of more gentle mood and feeling, on those derived from Very's experiencing of the world of nature more than that of man, on poems less likely to offend the sensibilities of more orthodox readers, and on poems which did not manifestly derive from those exorbitant claims which had led to Very's one-month confinement at McLean's hospital and to consequent notoriety. Traces of world-destruction fantasies and paranoiac exaltations in the deific mode would nevertheless remain, but these would largely be neutralized since the focus of the book would be shifted to less controversial ground.

The most extreme characteristics of Very's life and ideas—especially his self-Jesus equation, marriage-feast imagery, Armageddon visions, and personal reconciliation with the Father—would therefore be implicit rather than stated directly. Emerson was planning to blunt the edge of Veryism.

In effect, the book Emerson intended to assemble in Very's name was designed to restore his earlier reputation as a devout, independent soul, a writer of poems of substantial beauty and originality, simple and lyrical poems, poems in a quiet but expectant mood. It would be a prudent collection, based on relatively conservative principles and tastes, chosen from among poems which were soundest in terms of reasonably liberal theological doctrine as well as soundest in terms of conventional poetic values. It would be a volume which certainly would not jeopardize the interests and reputation of those individuals with whom Very's name had already been linked, at the same time as it might possibly dispel whatever doubts existed about Very's sanity. The Veryist heresies, if not quite expunged, would at least be played down. From an editorial standpoint, the book to a significant extent would reflect Emerson's own more balanced preferences with regard to the relationship between natural facts and spiritual truths, and would underplay the mediating role of language, personality, imagination, and vision. While the substance of the book nevertheless remained Very's rather than Emerson's, the image of the author it projected belonged to a Very normalized and sobered by Emersonian discretion.

No matter how sound his editorial judgments or how well-intentioned his plan for using the book to promote the worldly fortunes of a reluctant Jones Very and Transcendentalist friends, Emerson's success in overpowering his sensitive guest scarcely stabilized their relationship. But instead of responding to Emerson's wit and sarcasm by declaring a "day of hate" and being moved by the Spirit to accuse Emerson of spiritual willfulness and disobedience (as most certainly he would have done under similar circumstances before adopting his recent solitary habits), Very became strangely resigned. Once he realized that all his demands and protestations were being ignored by Emerson, he expressed his several disappointments in more disciplined if no less dramatic fashion. He redirected his energies and emotions in order to salvage some measure of victory following the stunning defeat by an uncompromising editor.

Since he believed that Lidian Emerson had "received more of his mission" than her husband during the October 1838 visit,[20] it is not surprising that he sought out her company on this particular occasion. Moreover, several previous encounters had established their friendship on a rather familiar basis. As early as September 1838, in the ecstatic letter to Emerson which accompanied his Shakespeare essay (the letter which according to Emerson "betrayed the state of his mind"), Very had openly spoken of the "love" he already felt for Lidian—feelings which of course he identified with those "wherewith the Father has loved me."[21] The way then was prepared. Very looked to her for the enthusiastic acceptance and unqualified acknowledgments denied him elsewhere in the Emerson household. And apparently Very gauged her earlier reactions accurately. She warmly welcomed his sudden attentions in June 1839. Whatever her motives, whether personal sympathy of the sort Elizabeth Peabody mustered upon occasion, or sincere interest in pious ideas for their own sake, she provided the kind of direct response still important for Very.

The thirty-three-year-old Lydia Jackson whom Waldo Emerson married in 1835 was a sensitive woman, deeply religious without being "strait laced orthodox."[22] Nominally Unitarian, hers was a more emotional, less rationalistic faith than was currently fashionable. Despite her maturity, she still possessed the dreamy, romantic qualities of her girlhood, expressed now through intensely religious habits of mind, making her susceptible at times to "half-mystical" visionary experiences of a sort which led Lydia Maria Child and others to call her, however inaccurately, a "Swedenborgian lady." Highly developed piety joined with a ready appreciation of strong character, and led her to find in Aunt Mary Moody Emerson (that prickly old Calvinist who functioned as eccentric matriarch to the Emerson clan), a "congenial soul" with whom she could have "high and sweet communion." After becoming Lidian Emerson and mistress of Concord's "Coolidge Castle," she even succeeded in establishing a routine of morning and evening prayers, a domestic ritual eventually neglected only because her husband insisted upon greater intellectual and spiritual freedom.

In some ways, as Thoreau discovered during the two years he lived with the family, Lidian was a "motherly woman." Not at all hesitant about supervising a bustling household, Lidian from the outset of her marriage tried to be hospitable to "the transcendentals" and other friends of her husband, and she welcomed them as houseguests, often for several weeks at a time. But friendship was a much less abstract and imperonal matter for her than it was for Emerson or for them. She responded primarily to persons, not to conceptions. Hers was essentially a sociable nature. But however much she enjoyed entertaining visitors, her "strong ties" to more conventional religious attitudes prevented her from becoming involved with them on an intellectual level. It was not so much that she was indifferent to ideas; rather, she was not particularly interested in their ideas. She therefore was considered something of an anachronism in the heady world of Concord she had married into. Indeed, exasperation mixed uneasily with amusement in 1838 when Emerson described her to Carlyle as "an incarnation of Christianity." He called her "Asia," presumably referring to her affectionate nature and deep feelings, and to her intensely Christian commitment and inflexible conservatism. Primarily because of his impatience with what he considered her narrow outlook and lack of sympathy for intellectual adventures of the kind advocates of "the Newness" excelled at, by 1840 a "certain estrangement" developed between them.[23] Similar tensions already had been introduced into Emerson's relationship with Jones Very, with whom Lidian temperamentally had much in common.

Another point of contact between Jones Very and Lidian Emerson was her tendency to hypochondria. In this respect she resembled Sophia Peabody, in whom Very had already shown a lively interest, as Lidian learned from an exchange of letters with Elizabeth Peabody. At the age of nineteen Lidian had suffered a severe attack of scarlet fever. She was convinced that the after-effects of this illness lingered. Even after her marriage she frequently was given to vague illnesses and periods of depression which often led her to speculate on her state of mind and body.[24] In December 1838 Elizabeth Peabody, aware of Lidian's recurring malaise, inquired whether she accepted Very's psychological explanation of the nature of Sophia's chronic infirmity. According to Elizabeth, he contended that "perfect yielding of wilfulness" would release her from "the *sensation of pain* itself," and he delivered various "dicta" for her benefit, to the effect that there was no such thing as "physical evil." [25] "All despondency *is* founded on delusion," Lidian wrote to Elizabeth in January 1839. "With me, and I think with most, it originates in bodily disease—or fatigue at least—It is in the nerves,—the soul disowns it." [26]

Whether or not Lidian accepted Very's explanation of Sophia's condition and his suggested remedy, she certainly was interested in hearing from Very himself about such matters, and also about Sophia's "Angelic sin" of Imagination and its consequences.[27] Moreover, she probably was also curious about the portion of his "discourse" which Elizabeth considered "most harmful" and "a step beyond Swedenborg." According to her account, Very did away with "that meaning of the senses that answers to the Understanding; saying that Moses did so when he discovered that men should not 'kill.' " [28] This was precisely the sort of assertion likely to arouse Lidian's interest and engage her religious feelings in a way other of Emerson's friends could not.

Whatever the form or basis of Lidian's interest in him, he appreciated her kind attempts at drawing him out on his own terms during private conversations. He wrote several poems during his visit, and read them to her. She was delighted by them, even though she realized they were not the kind Emerson wanted to accentuate in the collection he was assembling. She asked Very for copies of the two she liked best, "The Tenant" and "The Morn." [29]

The first consisted of proposals for a spiritual elopement. It was an invitation to follow him to where the wedding feast was being celebrated—at which he was already in attendance:

Trees shall rise around thy dwelling,
When thy house from heaven appears.
          .  .  .  .  .
Thou canst ne'er have leave to enter
That new dwelling's open door;
Where thy hopes and wishes centre,
Where thy friend has gone before;

Till the hut where now thou livest
Low is leveled with the ground;
          .  .  .  .  .
Houseless left, thou shalt not perish
          .  .  .  .  .
Quick, then, leave some poorer dweller
That wherein thou livest now; . . . [30]

The second was both a condemnation of willfulness (perhaps Emerson's own), in seeking mastery over God's gratuitous offerings, and a denunciation of efforts to employ them for selfish purposes:

When comes the sun to visit thee at morn,
Art thou prepared to give him welcome then?
Or is the day, that with his light is born,

With thee a day that has already been?
Hast thou filled up its yet unnumbered hours
With thy heart's thoughts, and made them now thine own?
Then for thee cannot bloom its budding flowers;
The day to thee hast past and onward flown.
The noon may follow with its quickening heat,
The grain grow yellow in its ripening rays,
And slow-paced evening mark the noon's retreat;
Yet thou as dead to them live all thy days,
For thou hast made of God's free gifts a gain,
And wouldst the sovereign day a slave in bonds retain.[31]

Emerson was disturbed by the unexpected turn the visit had
taken on the first day. After preliminary arrangements for the
book were concluded, he saw relatively little of his guest. Very
was deliberately avoiding him. He said he wished to be left alone.
He seemed sullen, reluctant to speak to Emerson, and to others in
his presence; but when he did speak he adopted his most severe
manner, restating familiar views relentlessly, in their least attractive aspect. When pressed by Emerson for an explanation, Very
replied with cryptic evasiveness: "I work hard without moving
hand or foot." [32] Yet Lidian Emerson reported she was finding
Very quite agreeable. Alone with her he was at his most charming, considerate and not self-conscious, radiating a gentle piety
which contrasted with his zealousness elsewhere, much as Elizabeth Peabody predicted he would were he not badgered or
mocked.

Once Emerson recognized this inconsistent behavior, it struck
him as strange. The journal entry he made on the second day of
the visit reflected his perplexity. It was difficult for him to reconcile the solemn reserve Very showed him with the favorable
impression he was making upon his wife. There also was a trace
of bitterness to his comments, as if he regretted their friendship
and even more regretted his inability to see Very either objec-
tively or with Lidian's sympathetic understanding. Very's self-

composure and unusual reticence were ever more irritating than his once furious "mono*Sania.*" [33]

Certainly the progress of character and of art teaches to treat all persons with an infinite freedom. What are persons but certain good or evil thoughts masquerading before me in curious frocks of flesh and blood? I were a fool to mind the color or figure of the frock, and slight the deep, aboriginal thoughts which so arrays itself. In this sense you cannot overestimate persons. And now in my house, as I see them pass, or hear their steps on the stair, it seems to me the steps of Ages and Nations.

And truly these walls do not lack variety in the few individuals they hold. Here is Simeon the Stylite, or John of Patmos in the shape of Jones Very, religion for religion's sake, religion divorced, detached from man, from the world, from science and art; grim, unmarried, insulated, accusing, yet true in itself, and speaking things in every word. The lie is in the detachment; and when he is in the room with other persons, speech stops as if there were a corpse in the apartment. Then here is mine Asia, not without a deep tinge herself of the same old land, and exaggerated and detached pietism, and so she serves as bridge between Very and the Americans.[34]

The tone of the entry, with its gloomy implications, differs strikingly from that of a passage written less than two weeks before Very's arrival, and before Emerson had examined the bulky collection of manuscripts. Then he thought Very was a spokesman, along with Alcott, for the present "Revolutionary age"—whose distinguishing mark was that "man is coming back to Consciousness." On June third Emerson still counted him among those who were announcing "the new ideas," among those who did not belong to "the traditional age in philosophy and religion." By relying on his own genius and through awareness of his own self-sustaining powers, Very could "abhor books" (the repositories of the "old learning") without disadvantage, while "the sticklers to tradition" could not.[35] This hopeful estimate of Very's prospects and his inclusion among "the transcendentals," was significantly changed by Emerson's study of the entire corpus of Very's work and by the unexpected turn the visit had taken. In writing to Elizabeth Peabody on June seventeenth, however, he was more cautious than he was in his journal entry the day before.

I cannot persuade Mr Very to remain with me another day. He says, he is not permitted [by the Spirit], and no assurances that his retirement shall be secured, are of any avail: He has been serene, intelligent and true in all the conversation I have had with him, which is not much. He gives me pleasure, and much relief after all I had heard concerning him. His case is unique. And I have no guess as to its issue, which I trust will be best and happiest. I shall go to town this week and settle what I can of the printing of his book, from which however I dare not now assure him any pecuniary advantage. Yet perhaps there will be such. I will write to him or to his brother when I have better information.[36]

The next morning, without further explanation, Emerson simply recorded in his journal: "Yesterday departed Jones Very from my house."[37] Hours later, after evaluating all he had read, heard, and witnessed, he was certain Very's departure marked a turning point in their relationship. Emerson was still determined to preserve his own independence, even if it meant alienating a friend—a friend whose intellectual and emotional demands were contrary to his nature.

There is no history, only biography. The private soul ascends to transcendent virtue. Like Very, he works hard without moving hand or foot; like Agathon, he loves the goddess and not the woman; like Alcott, he refuses to pay a debt without injustice; but this liberty is not transferable to any disciple, no, nor to the man himself, when he falls out of his trance and comes down from the tripod.

I will surrender to the Divine,—to nothing less: not to Jove, not to ephod or cross.[38]

Before setting out for Salem, Very apparently had broken his Johannine "trance" and had descended from his Simeonic "tripod," uttering mortal words instead of those belonging to the Holy Spirit he claimed to represent—or so it seemed to Emerson in retrospect. Given the particular cluster of temperaments gathered at "Coolidge Castle" for three days in the middle of June 1839, Lidian Emerson most likely was the one who stimulated Very's show of manliness at the expense of his divinity. If so, her influence upon him went counter to that of the other Lydia in his life—his mother, the widow Very. Her furious atheism and materialism originally caused him to repress his worldly, masculine self, and to incarnate the Son as the only means of bringing about her belated reconciliation with the Father. But the former Lydia Jackson, with her feminine ways and sensitivities, devout thoughts and encouragements, innocently roused in Jones Very human feelings he long ago learned to despise. Thirty-seven-year-old Mrs. Emerson unwittingly made the twenty-six-year-old poet conscious once again of the natural self he thought he had exorcised for his mother's sake. The visit to Concord, therefore, with a suddenness he had not foreseen, thrust him from the world of spirit into the world of men.

His return on June seventeenth to the austere frame house on Federal Street meant both resumption of lonely isolation and translation into poetry of the effects of his three-day sojourn in Concord. Four poems, none of them sonnets, indicate that Emerson's was not the only outlook radically altered by Very's most recent encounter with "Beauty." Diffused feelings of guilt, reminiscent of the anguish which preceded the completion of his "sacrifice" at Harvard in 1835, took the form of a personal summons from the Father. Familiar words, not long since addressed through "watchman" Very to the unfortunate inhabitants of the dismal City, now were dramatically evoked by the recurrence of his own spiritual sleep-in-death. This was his way

of accusing himself of having fallen from a state of grace. God
speaks:

> Why art thou not awake, my son?
> The morning breaks I formed for thee;
> And I thus early by thee stand,
> Thy new-awakening life to see.
>
> . . . . .
>
> I come to wake thee; haste, arise,
> Or thou no share with me can find;
> Thy sandals seize, gird on thy clothes,
> Or I must leave thee here behind.[39]

But, like countless other wretched residents of the City of the
Dead, the sleeping son cannot hear this call. Believing himself
deprived of access to the "Spirit Land" because he no longer is
free from the sin of willfulness and thus no longer a "quickening
spirit," he is (or seems) unaware of God's presence as he sits in
his room before his writing desk. Even solitary walks through the
lovely garden stretching down to the banks of the North River
fail to moderate his self-accusations and sense of estrangement. In
seeming ignorance of what has already been proffered by a
merciful God, he prays for the restoration of his former privileged state:

> Wilt Thou not visit me?
> The plant beside me feels thy gentle dew;
> And every blade of grass I see,
> From thy deep earth its moisture drew.
>
> . . . . .
>
> Come, for I need thy love,
> More than the flower the dew, or the grass the rain;
> Come, gently as thy holy dove;
> And let me in thy sight rejoice to live again.

I will not hide from them,
When thy storms come, though fierce may be their wrath;
But bow with leafy stem,
And strengthened follow on thy chosen path.

Yes, Thou wilt visit me;
Nor plant nor tree thy parent eye delight so well,
As when from sin set free
My spirit loves with thine in peace to dwell.[40]

The third of these post-Concord poems placed Very's special friendship with Lidian Emerson in perspective. She of course was not the only woman to engage his affections in an extraordinary manner. As an undergraduate at Harvard he discovered he could control "unbridled passions" for women only by a "monkish austerity and selfdenial" requiring temporary renunciation of all contacts with women. Subsequently his ambivalent attitude toward his mother, which combined love with hatred in equal measure, culminated in the total acceptance by her of his saving mission. His attraction to Elizabeth and Sophia Peabody, while far less startling in effect, involved similar objectives and tensions for Very. Simultaneously drawn to and repelled by the sisters as women, he seems to have tried to remove the physical threat they posed to his spiritual well-being by transporting them to the innocent world of his religious fantasies. Since whatever friendships could be sustained on such an ephemeral basis actually derived from mixtures of worldly and spiritual motives, they accordingly resulted in various combinations of frustration and disappointment for him, although he was not always willing to admit this to himself.

"The Bride," written in July 1839, was prompted by Very's recent approaches to Lidian Emerson. But his moral imagination concentrated and refracted in it all of his experiences with women. Taking the form of a Christian parable, the poem drew upon his repressed desires as well as his immediate need to regain his status as a perfected man worthy of the heavenly wedding feast.

> I sought of Thee my promised wife,
>     She of the golden hair;
> But though I toiled with manly strife,
>     Thou gave me one less fair.
>
> Again I toiled, and many a day,
>     My hands to labor flew;
> But Thou withheld again my pay,
>     And gave me one less true.
>
> And still once more my limbs they plied
>     Their strength to serve Thee Lord;
> But Thou wouldst not, though long I tried
>     With her my pains reward.
>
> But still for her I loved in youth,
>     My nerves again are strung;
> And I will serve Thee still in truth,
>     As when my limbs were young.
>
> And though the snows fall on my head,
>     And lightless grows my eye;
> She of my youth I still may wed,
>     And dwell with her on high.[41]

By understanding the disappointments of his life as part of God's continual testing of his fidelity, Very could hold himself responsible for his failures while still preserving both his innocent love-fantasies and spiritual optimism. Self-condemnation was the tactic by which he was insuring his prospects for the future.

The last in this series of poems depicts the unhappy poet as a man deprived by God of his material legacy, the "poor and clay-built" house left him by his "earthly parent." Loss of physical being proves a spiritual advantage, however, since it enables him to find the friendship he prized above all others. Rooted in love, it is friendship without sin, friendship without guilt, friendship without misunderstanding, friendship without limit.

> But soon the light and open air
> Received me as a wandering child,
> And I soon thought their house more fair,
> And all my grief their love beguiled.
>
> Mine was the grove, the pleasant field
> Where dwelt the flowers I daily trod;
> And there beside them too I kneeled
> And called their friend my friend and God.[42]

In June Very had lost his earthly paradise, jeopardized his relationship with the divine, and forfeited his eternal reward. By August however, when the last of these poems was written, he had managed to re-enter the Edenic Garden, reconfirm the mutual love between God and himself, and once again feel he merited glory. In two months his spiritual progress between 1835 and 1838 was retraced.

Since the purpose of the four poems, like that of the forthcoming book, was to encourage others to undertake the same course, he forwarded the poems to Emerson. The letter enclosing the last poem reveals that he was trying to use them also as a means of regaining Emerson's confidence. He still hoped to make a "disciple" of him.

I send you these by letter that they may come earlier to hand—I hardly dared to write *them* and that will excuse me from a letter. They are the true letter as I am true. There is more joy and freedom as I advance yet still I long to be clothed upon with my house from heaven. In you too may mo[re] of the old pass away and the new and abiding be more and more felt.[43]

Emerson had already concluded preliminary arrangements with Little and Brown for publication of Very's work. In July he wrote to Margaret Fuller:

I am editing Very's little book. Three Essays; and verses. Out of two hundred poems, I have selected sixty six that really possess rare merit. The book is to cost 75 cents, and I beg you to announce its coming value to all buyers. If it sells, our prophet will get $150 which, little though it be, he wants.[44]

Nevertheless Emerson was sufficiently impressed by the new poems to change the contents of the volume. He decided to include three of them in the collection, rejecting only "The Bride."

Emerson could not help but admire Very's tenacity. Upon receiving his short letter he wrote in his journal:

This old complaint of the Unitarians, that the Calvinists deny them fellowship and access to the communion table, is a plain confession that their religion is nought, that they have no vision. Whoso has, never begs allowance; he commands and awes men. Fox and Penn, Swedenborg and Very, never complain of not being admitted [to fellowship and communion], but complain that none come and ask admittance [of them].[45]

However impatient he may have been in the presence of Very the man nine weeks before, when seen from a distance—either through his writings or filtered through Emerson's own enlarging and generalizing imagination—Very possessed an elemental power and significance which made him seem a semi-mythical figure. Like the Quakers and Swedenborg, Very's forceful manner, his intuitive judgments, his single-minded intensity, and his radical self-confidence did not yield before opposition. Like their religious enthusiasms, his was deemed remarkable not for its specifications but for its significations. Emerson could admire Very not for what he was, but for what he represented. For this reason he valued Veryism without being compelled to join in "fellowship" with Very or feeling the need to gain access to his "communion table." He was prepared, he said, to "surrender" to nothing less than the Divine itself. The incarnations, the rituals, the priesthood, the vestments, the systemic organization of the believing individual, all the symbols and symptoms of Divinity were mere outward show. They were incidental rather than integral, with functions limited by particular circumstances. They served only as substitutes in the absence of the undifferentiated essence to which they related. Nevertheless, they could not be entirely ignored.

In September 1839, just one year after the Tutor in Greek and sometime divinity student had thrown Harvard into momentary confusion by announcing he was the Son of God, *Essays and Poems by Jones Very* was published. Emerson's efforts in obtaining a publisher, selecting and arranging manuscripts, reading proof, and in other ways coping with the problems of seeing a book through the presses, were concealed from the general public. His name did not appear on the title page, nor did the author anywhere acknowledge indebtedness to an editor. The simple dedication followed Very's original instructions passed on to Emerson by his brother: "To Edward Tyrrel Channing, Boylston Professor in Harvard University, This Volume is Inscribed, As a Token of Gratitude, By the Author."

# Denouement

SEPTEMBER 1839–DECEMBER 1840

A s w a s to be expected from the specialized inflections of the book and the reputation of its author, the circulation of *Essays and Poems* was "limited."[1] Nowhere except in the small group of Very's friends and acquaintances did the publication cause any detectable stir. And even here, because the three essays and most of the poems had already circulated in manuscript, and because of growing disenchantment with Very's intellectual and emotional inflexibility, reaction to the book was slight. Certainly its editor did not promote it vigorously. While on a lecture trip to New York City in the spring of 1840 Emerson did promise a copy of the book to someone, most likely his kinsman Orville Dewey, or his literary friend William Cullen Bryant; and he also did agree to send copies to Carlyle and Wordsworth. But it was only at Very's insistence that he considered doing so. These were gifts bestowed with reluctance, if indeed they ever were sent.[2] Rather than publicize the book he was instrumental in having printed, rather than praise essays he once called among the finest of their kind, rather than recommend poems he once considered worthy of being read "to all who have ears to hear," Emerson (especially when among close friends) preferred to repeat Very's most recent "speeches," and to relate how he had "dealt" with them.[3]

Others reacted differently. Lidian Emerson viewed the book from the perspective of her congenial relationship with Very, and so it was with "affectionate regards" that she presented a copy to Aunt Mary Moody Emerson.[4] James Freeman Clarke, who had been deeply moved by Very's confident yet self-denying assertions to Channing in December 1838, received a copy from his thoughtful sister,[5] and during the next two years printed thirteen new poems by Very in the *Western Messenger*. Hawthorne probably received his copy in a gesture of "brotherly" friendship by the author, and although he was guarded in his estimate of the book, he acknowledged it possessed at least a quaint and musty beauty.[6] James Russell Lowell mused and commented at length in the margins of his copy, arguing frequently with the essays but judging "some of the sonnets . . . better poetry than has yet been published in America."[7] Even Professor Longfellow kept *Essays and Poems* in the Craigie House Library.[8]

Richard Henry Dana, Sr., who had known Very as a bright Harvard student singled out by Professor Channing for special encouragement, sent the book to William Cullen Bryant. He did so because he thought the sonnets would interest him. "I am sure," Dana wrote, "that they will please you wonderfully." He had himself been favorably impressed by them:

The thought is deeply spiritual; and while there is a certain character of *peculiarity* which we so often find in like things from our old writers, there is freedom from quaintness. You will be much struck with the collocation, simplicity and expressiveness of the language. Indeed, I know not where you would turn away from yourself, and find any thing in this country to compare with these Sonnets.

Dana had only a single objection: "I am sorry, . . . that Very did not follow the true [Italian] sonnet rhyme." As for the essays, he reserved judgment. He said he had "looked a little" at the one on Epic Poetry, but as a matter of principle he refused to read the other two. "I may wish to write more about S— myself," he explained, "and I keep as clear of other men's thoughts as I can in such cases. That on Hamlet I am told, is well done." [9] Bryant in turn agreed with Dana's general estimate of the book. He "prized" the slender volume "very highly," and spoke to Parke Godwin about the "outstanding grace and originality" of the poems.[10]

The Peabody family, heretofore a center of good will toward Very, had meanwhile become strangely reticent. After hearing about Very from Emerson, Elizabeth Peabody admitted to herself, and afterward to sister Sophia, that she had been "very stupid." As a result of her high estimate of Very as a man and poet, she had been deluded into believing herself spiritually *"awake* for about two months!" But Emerson, whom she found "very luminous, and wiser than ever," at last made her see the truth. He alluded to the almost scandalous personal interest Very was taking in Lidian and her spiritual welfare, and showed how absurd if not dangerous Very actually was, "amidst all his sublimities." Elizabeth consequently was now certain that Emerson—not Very—was the one who was "beautiful, and good, and great." [11] It is not known how Sophia, the most ardent Veryist in the Peabody household, received her sister's recantation. However, after the family moved from Salem to Boston in 1840, all contact with him was lost. Elizabeth was under the "impression" that it was "painful" to Very "to recur to a season—in which he certainly was in a degree *beside himself."* She did not write to him because she was "afraid" she might "wound him" by alluding to that "season." Neither sister ever saw or heard from him again.[12]

Of those of the Transcendental persuasion, only Bronson Alcott responded to *Essays and Poems* with genuine enthusiasm. He considered it "one of the neatest issues of the American press," a book as important as Orestes Brownson's *New Views of Christianity, Society, and the Church,* George Ripley's *Specimens of Foreign Standard Literature,* Emerson's "Address at Cambridge," and of course his own prized manuscript, "Psyche." (As late as 1880 he thought the "subtlety and simplicity of execution" of the sonnets and Shakespeare essays "surpass any that have since appeared.") In addition to sending a copy to one of his English correspondents a few days after the book's appearance, Alcott managed to extract a promise from Margaret Fuller to review it for Heraud's *New Monthly Magazine,* a radical British journal he currently was interested in.[13] She never wrote this article,[14] but not because she failed to recognize any merit to the book. The piece she finally did write appeared in the January 1840 issue of Orestes Brownson's *Boston Quarterly Review.* It was the first critical notice of Very's book to appear in print.

The occasion was her first "Chat in Boston Bookstores," a proposed series of articles on the contemporary literary scene. She used the pseudonym "Dahlia," which more than a decade later Hawthorne used as the personal emblem for Zenobia in *The Blithedale Romance.* Margaret Fuller wrote that Very's poems possessed "an elasticity of spirit, a genuine flow of thought, an unsought nobleness and purity." In no other poems by an American, she said, could be detected such straightforward virtues. Even if "unfinished in style, and homely of mien," his sonnets still represented a fresh and striking departure from the "self-seeking, factitious sentiment and weak movement of our over-taught and over-ambitious literature, if indeed, we can say we have one."[15]

Margaret Fuller did not try to base her appreciation of Very's poems on moral or theological grounds. She viewed them as poetic facts, not as biographical statements or religious documents. The poems functioned in their own terms, and not as reflections of the personality and circumstances of their author. She approached the essays in much the same way. Moreover, although she had once soundly criticized them in a letter to Emerson,[16] and even though in her review she took exception to some of what Very said, she still publicly welcomed the prose more than the poetry. If the "merits" of the poems were "unobtrusive," the same could not be said about the essays.

Without indicating the specific themes which were the substance of Very's work, she commended the essays "Shakespeare" and "Hamlet" in view of the dearth of good Shakespeare criticism. The only discussions she considered worth recalling were

a dozen or more fineries by Schlegel, two or three just views by Goethe, and some invaluable hints by Coleridge. . . . Amid such destitution, Mr. Very's observations seem well worth considering. His view, whether you agree with it or not, boasts a height and breadth not unworthy of his subject; and in details, he is delicate and penetrating.

Her opinion of the two essays was best expressed when she described them as being "full of genuine thought, but not, I think, of just criticism." She found fault with Very's decision to strive "too resolutely for unity" at the expense of what she called "condition." She accused him of having strained many points in an effort to discover "the center of the Shakespearean circle." [17]

Nevertheless, in spite of the abstract and remote tone she adopted, it would seem that if the self-conscious literary posture she assumed for the "Chat" were set aside, her estimate of Very's critical judgment would have been more purposive. Her article took the form of a dialogue between the Reverend Mr. Nightshade and Professor Partridge, the latter more often the spokesman for her own views. The dialectical structure of her remarks only served to confuse the matter of appraising Very's work. Earlier she simply told Emerson that she found "excellent things" in his study of Shakespeare, especially its "tone" which she considered "very noble." [18] She made no mention of the first essay in the volume, "Epic Poetry."

Unlike Emerson, Margaret Fuller approached Very as a writer, not as a personality. Her contacts with him had been more limited, and her emotions were in no way intimately engaged by him. His importance for her—"he seems worthy to be well known," she had told Emerson [19]—was justified by his capacity for writing poetry and criticism. She did not allow her opinions of him as a man or evangelist to interfere with her literary judgments. Unlike Emerson, her stance was impersonal. She was not primarily interested in his "inspired and prophetical side." [20]

However varied its significance to others, publication of Very's book early in September 1839 was viewed by the author himself as an extraordinary event. Its appearance coincided with the first anniversary of his spiritual purification and the onset of that "double-consciousness" which had abruptly ended his brilliant academic career at Harvard. *Essays and Poems* therefore signaled the termination of his withdrawal from "the ways of men." His sense of his spiritual separation from the evils inherent in unnatural, "unborn" men had led him to various strategies for redeeming those whom he wanted to have join him in the exclusive world of his moral imagination. During the final six months of his supernatural grace, while his energies were directed toward poetry as the chief instrument of salvation, he completed his own spiritual uniqueness by physically isolating himself from the society of friends and neighbors. This divinely-ordered course of solitude had been interrupted only once, divided precisely in half by the urgent visit to Emerson in June 1839. But with the publication of his book three months later, and the exposure to the world of his spiritual self which it afforded, the less cadenced and symmetrical rhythms of his former outward life were restored, and he literally returned to the familiar scenes of human willfulness and sin. His separatist days were over. He celebrated his resumption of a social existence the same way he had his discharge from McLean Hospital almost a year before. He undertook the short journey to Concord and Cambridge, returning to Salem several days later by way of Boston. The purpose of the trip was to see Emerson and his wife, to consult with College and Divinity School officials, and to visit his publisher.

He lingered with Emerson in September 1839 only long enough to have him write a letter introducing him to Messrs. Little and Brown, and directing them to give him some copies of his book. The account with the publishers stood in Emerson's name as editor rather than in Very's as author, and Emerson explained to him that whatever royalties accrued would be sent to Concord rather than directly to Salem.[21] After concluding this business, Very spent an hour or two with Lidian Emerson. He spoke longer with her than with her husband since the ill-feeling generated between the two men during the June editorial meeting still persisted. Upon returning to Salem several days later he therefore wrote to her instead of to Emerson, and thanked her for the kindness she once again had shown him. He spoke of Emerson only incidentally.

My return a few days since from Concord through Watertown, Cambridge and Boston was as pleasant as one but little accustomed to travelling and its fatigues has a right to expect. Your cake was well supplied by a piece of white bread and a cup of milk and water from a poor yet worthy woman on your turnpike at whose house I rested a little while on my way. Alas, it went to my heart to take it; for I feel I could not as yet give her the true bread in return. I was wearied much by a few days stay at Cambridge, but am now as if with you again and well; waiting for that daily direction which is a path unseen through the world and its visible evils;—in which that we all may walk forever and ever I pray always. . . .

I had occasion to stop at Mess Little's and Brown's as I came through Boston; and Mr Emerson's order was readily received. The four copies of "Essays and Poems" which I then took fell off to three before I reached home; my neighbor whose horse and wagon helped me on from Chel[s]ea bridge receiving one for his little children.[22]

At Cambridge he visited with Divinity School officials, making clear his intention to resume preparations for the ministry. He was given no encouragement, or at least he was not allowed to enroll as a divinity student. And of course he was again refused reappointment to the College faculty. He remained at Cambridge for several days nevertheless, visiting friends and former students. During his stay he confirmed the wisdom of the professors who had denied him regular access to Harvard classrooms. He called on his brother Washington, now beginning his Sophomore year, and found him studying Livy. "I asked him," Very subsequently recalled,

if the Romans were masters of the world? My brother said they had been: I told him they were still. Then I went into the room of a senior who lived opposite, and found him writing a theme. I asked him what was his subject? And he said, Cicero's Vanity. I asked him if the Romans were masters of the world? He replied that they had been: I told him they were still. This was in the garret of Mr. Ware's house. Then I went down into Mr. Ware's study, and found him reading Bishop Butler, and asked him if the Romans were the masters of the world? He said they had been: I told him they were still.[23]

Although his twelve-month state of grace terminated in September 1839, as he had predicted it would, its effects remained. But the sort of behavior he formerly attributed to submission to the inner "Voice," and which had demanded he suspend all deliberative thinking of his own, now actually became a pose. It could now be maintained only in dramatic fashion—that is, by self-conscious application of his own human will to recollections of his previous spiritual condition. Memories provided him with a standard of being, a model which he now was trying to project on his own initiative, with full knowledge he was doing so without special authorization or guidance. He was, he now knew, acting by his own decision and at his own discretion. In effect, Jones Very felt it necessary in September 1839 to deliberately cast

[ 360 ]

himself in the role of the man who during the preceding year had contributed so much to the excitements of Cambridge, Salem, Concord, and Boston. Although the part he now was playing was thoroughly known to him since he was both actor and the original upon whom it was based, it was a part nevertheless.

At first the absence of distinctively divine imperatives made little if any outward difference in his manner, or so the letter to Lidian Emerson and the pattern of incidents in the home of the Professor of Pulpit Eloquence suggest. By December 1839, however, a change was becoming evident to some of his friends. A qualitative decline had set in. It was becoming increasingly difficult for him to play the vatic role successfully. Without the belief he was acting by special dispensation, without the spontaneous impulses ascribable to some divine source within himself, it was a strain for him to continue imitating his former glory-filled life.

The first to suspect the disintegration of Very's perfected being was Bronson Alcott, in whose home on Boston's Beach Street he passed a winter night. During the evening Very read him several sonnets, which Alcott thought "very fine." But it seemed as if his visitor were "even more preternatural than ever." And yet, surprisingly, during their conversations Very said nothing "worth repeating." [24] Alcott did not try to account for the apparent discrepancy. He may have opportunely remembered that Very had once accused him of committing the "Angelic sin" of "spiritual curioisty."

Another friend, less reverent than Alcott, was more perceptive. A day or two later Margaret Fuller discovered what Alcott stopped short of comprehending. Her habit of making subtle distinctions with the help of literary allusions enabled her to see through Very's ecstatic claims. She admitted she was bored with the clichés and inflated rhetoric by which Very was striving to maintain the appearance of a spiritually superior man. He was trying too hard to live up to his reputation as a saintly visionary, and thereby his pretensions were exposed to her inquiring intelligence. She wrote in her journal:

> I saw Mr Very this morning, and was disappointed. His state is imperfect. He *thought* himself a Son, he should therefore abide in the desert and let the ravens bring him food. But he sometimes uses his human will and understanding, and so falsifies his thought. It is the same state which Balzac has aimed at depicting in Louis Lambert. That conception is higher than Very's state, . . . I hate the ever-recurring "sublime," "immense," "exquis[ite]" etc.[25]

One of Very's more labored efforts to reassert himself as a Son of God took dramatic form in December, and was forwarded to Alcott with the request he read it to friends participating in his Sunday evening series of "Conversations." Very explained its meaning by using the verbal style already familiar to those acquainted with his vision of an earthly resurrection. "That which they hear and see daily," he told Alcott, "let them and you hold fast and encrease until the senses of the new man are born and exercised in you all. The grace and peace which are of life eternal be and remain with such as hear and understand."[26] He called this short work "The Morning: A Dialogue." It was an attempt to reassure others as well as himself that although he had left his house he had not departed from the apocalyptic course originally chartered by the "Voice" within him. In effect he was saying that the piece was itself an exercise of the "senses of the new man." However that may be, it does seem a feeble prose variation on themes associated with sonnets written early in 1839. Appropriately, the time and setting of the "Dialogue" are not specified.

ONE MAN: What brightening is that in the east; is it day? and yet it seems brighter by far;—Men surprised are running to and fro as if the sun had risen before his accustomed hour.

## Denouement

SECOND: 'Tis not the light of day; it shines into my heart as that lightens my dwelling;—I feel I am in it, yet I can neither escape from it nor see it.

FIRST: I see it, but as yet I cannot walk in it as the natural day; my sight fails me at every other step.

SECOND: Can one see and walk in this light as in that of the sun? I am wholly blind then; for I cannot move, nor discern a single object by it.

FIRST: Where is he who lodged with you last night?

SECOND: Alas! he is more blind than I am; I left him in bed; he did not even hear the noise in the street. Lead me in neighbor, I would not be seen by the people crowding by. God gr[ant] I may see as well as you before night.

FIRST: Here, step there; that is safe;—This is your fence; there, touch there;—Now we are at your door. I will call again in the evening to see how you do.

SECOND: Thank you, thank you.

ANOTHER: Who was that you [were] leading home as I came up?

FIRST: One who lives in the next house to mine; who came out, but could not find his way back again.

THE OTHER: This is a sad morning for many;—you seem to walk feebly yourself.

FIRST: Yes I do so;—but I am glad even thus, when I see some wholly blind. But you walk as if you had recovered your sight.

THE OTHER: Yes, this is the day that I have prayed for; and my eye[s] are blessed even in its dawn; yet I must hasten on; an[d] take care lest I stumble when the night comes on, as I sa[w] your neighbor do just now.

THE FIRST: Is that your companion? I did not see him before.

THE OTHER: 'Tis no one, the light only casts my shadow on the wall. Goodby; I hope to see you well when we meet again.

[ 363 ]

FIRST, to himself: I will try to find my way home again, it is yet too dark for me to venture far.[27]

In succeeding months Very made additional efforts, all with similar unsatisfactory results, to resume his outward life where it had left off in the winter of 1838–1839. In May 1840 he joined Frederic Henry Hedge, Bronson Alcott, Thoreau, Margaret Fuller, and several others for an informal meeting of the Transcendental Club at Emerson's house, the first he had attended since December 1838. The group discussed "the inspiration of the Prophet and Bard, the nature of Poetry, and the causes of the sterility of Poetic Inspiration in our age and country." Although these topics seemed perfectly suited to Very's intellectual and emotional preferences, Alcott once again thought Very said nothing "worth repeating." [28] This was the last meeting of the Transcendental Club that Very ever attended, and the last time he saw Bronson Alcott.

Also in May he called on Richard Henry Dana, Sr., and made another unfavorable impression. Very "uttered some deep truths," Dana admitted, "but in strange phraseology, and connected with much that could only be as a dream to himself." Mistakenly he assumed Very was "clearly insane." But when Very read him "a little thing which he had just written," Dana drew the more significant conclusion that "it was sane enough, but not striking." [29] Very never called upon him again.

On several occasions Very attended sessions of Margaret Fuller's "Conversations." His presence here was more irritating and disruptive than triumphant. Only by "exert[ing] herself very much" could the moderator keep the discussion away from "a comparison of the religious privileges of the Greeks and our own." She shrewdly wished to avoid "endless theological discussions." [30] This was her final encounter with Very.

In November 1840 he attended sessions of the "Chardon Street Convention of Friends of Universal Reform," where he was one of many persons of a "mystical or sectarian or philosophic renown," including Dr. Channing, Alcott, Theodore Parker, Edward Taylor (Melville's "Father Mapple"), William Lloyd Garrison, and Maria W. Chapman.[31] Here, where frenetic utterances were openly encouraged, Very failed to distinguish himself. When another assembly at Boston's Chardon Street Chapel was announced for November 1841, a "Bible Convention," he was not even certain that he wanted to attend.[32]

Of all Very's prominent friends, it is ironic that the only one who continued to think about him and have anything more than perfunctory contacts with him after the publication of *Essays and Poems* was the one he alienated first, Ralph Waldo Emerson. Of course his feelings toward Very had changed drastically since that day in April 1838 when they met for the first time at the insistence of Elizabeth Peabody. Nevertheless, in spite of the tensions that recently had developed between them, Emerson could not completely dismiss him from his thoughts.

The first indication that he did not consider their estrangement beyond remedy came most unexpectedly. In a letter to Lidian in March 1840, six months after the abrupt, business-like confrontation in Concord, Emerson referred to Very parenthetically, recalling something he once had told him during an untroubled moment: "as Very said of his Angels,—'they make one wish to be good.' "[33] Less than two weeks later Very himself showed up in Concord. Emerson welcomed him as if nothing had occured to disrupt their former relationship.

Both men were invigorated as much by the bright spring day which greeted them as by the contagious good humor each brought to their encounter. Nature seemed to be sanctioning their reconciliation. Even the gentle breeze scattered whatever remained of the old bitterness. "We walked this afternoon to Edmund Hosmer's and Walden Pond," Emerson recorded in his journal, and Jones Very again was a "treasure of a companion." It was as if their relationship had been renewed with the year.

The South wind blew and filled with bland and warm light and dry sunny woods. The last year's leaves flew like birds through the air. As I sat on the bank of the Drop, or God's Pond, and saw the amplitude of the little water, what space, what verge, the little scudding fleets of ripples found to scatter and spread from side to side and take so much time to cross the pond, and saw how the water seemed made for the wind, and the wind for the water, dear playfellows for each other,—I said to my companion, I declare this world is so beautiful that I can hardly believe it exists. At Walden Pond the waves were larger, and the whole lake in pretty uproar. Jones Very said, "See how each wave rises from the midst with an original force, at the same time that it partakes the general movement!" [34]

By way of illustrating the sort of individualism the Pond's surface was reflecting, Very related what he had said and done in Henry Ware's house during his September visit to Cambridge. Emerson was delighted by the story of the innocent's return to the insensitive world of the ever-powerful "Romans." Later, in addition to transcribing it for his journal, Emerson was moved to add his own reactions and general impressions. These included a self-critical reappraisal of their entire relationship. He placed his former antipathy in perspective, and attributed most of the blame to his own narrow, cold, distrustful nature. The result was a passage which by June became a part of his essay on "Friendship":

We parry and fend the approach of our fellow-man by compliments, by gossip, by amusements, by affairs. We cover up our thought from him under a hundred folds. I knew a man who under a certain religious frenzy cast off this drapery, and omitting all compliment and commonplace, spoke to the conscience of every person he encountered, and that with great insight and beauty. At first he was resisted, and all men agreed he was mad. But persisting—as indeed he could not help doing—for some time in this course, he attained to the advantage of bringing every man of his acquaintance into true relations with him. No man would think of speaking falsely with him, or of putting him off with any chat of markets or reading-rooms.

But every man was constrained by so much sincerity to the like plain-dealing, and what love of nature, what poetry, what symbol of truth he had, he did certainly show him. But to most of us society shows not its face and eye, but its side and its back. To stand in true relations with men in a false age is worth a fit of insanity, is it not? [35]

This remarkable passage—in which Emerson alluded to his initial high estimate of Very's abilities, the subsequent rumors of madness and intrigue, the thoughtless fun at Very's expense, and even the intimate soul-searching which involved Lidian Emerson's pieties—shows that Jones Very was more than another curiosity in Emerson's collection of distinctive human types. The impersonal "we" employed by the essayist concealed something more than belated regret at having failed to respect a "friend's" innocent integrity. It was an admission of his own hypocrisy and restlessness of spirit, and a condemnation of his earlier reluctance to abandon an uncharitably moralistic attitude toward Very. His radical manifestation of a religious individualism at least should have been tolerated, even if it were directed toward Lidian Emerson.

The more sympathetic attitude Emerson cultivated in 1840 did not mean that he had become a disciple of Veryism. On the contrary, he was still capable of taking vigorous exception to what seemed from his own point of view to be Very's parochial outlook. But in spite of his dissent, he could not avoid admiring Very's intensity and stamina. Even when, like Alcott and Margaret Fuller before him, he realized that it was no longer possible for Very to carry the mantle of his former brilliance, he still thought of Very in terms of the new "friendship." In October random thoughts on this subject found their way into his journal:

To what purpose should you tell me of your faith, of your happiness, if you do not make me feel that you are at rest and blessed. Jones Very's words were loaded with his fact. What he said, held; was not personal to him; was no more disputable than the shining of yonder sun or the blowing of this south wind. But I do not know that you are looking at universal facts.[36]

It was no coincidence that "sun" and "south wind," images which had been conspicuous in his account of their reconciliation in April, reappeared. Out of ambivalent feelings, a mixture of admiration with revulsion, and of "friendly" love with intellectual reservation, Emerson was trying to extract a consistent attitude which would focus Very's significance for him.

That Emerson still retained equivocal thoughts about him more than thirty years after all communication between them had ended, suggests that he never was able to lay Very's ghost to lasting rest. Not even the knowledge that Very no longer believed himself the beneficiary of impulses from God could make Emerson forget that once his "words were loaded with his fact."

In spite of their renewal of contact in 1840, it was the Very of 1838 and 1839 that Emerson preferred to remember. It may have been about him he was thinking when he wrote in September or October: "But ah we impute the virtues to our friends and afterwards worship the face and feature to which we ascribe these divine tenants."[37] Even in the essay on "Friendship" Emerson spoke of him in the past tense, as if the man no longer existed. In terms of the essential Very—the Very who wrote startling poems and brilliant essays, the Very who disrupted Harvard's stolid classrooms and Salem's genteel drawing rooms, the Very who carried his self-reliance into Concord and Boston without regard for practical consequences, the Very who refused to exercise reasonable restraints which might betray his genius, the Very intent upon winning salvation for the souls of all his friends, the Very whom he called "our brave saint"—Emerson was right. This man no longer existed. He passed out of the world the moment the mortal Jones Very ended his year-long retirement in September 1839. By walking out of his house into the blinding light of Federal Street, the supernatural illumination within him was exchanged for the diurnal sun outside. All that remained to him were memories of his vision of an earthly eternity. As in "The Morning: A Dialogue," the shadows which continued to follow him (some not of his own making), were not adequate substitutes for the inward experience of grace, nor for the confidence it had brought.

Of the more than thirty poems Very wrote after the publication of his book and before the end of 1840, only four made poetically satisfactory use of the remembered past. Three of these were written in October or early November 1839, while his recollections were still sharp and he was still capable of generating an approximation of the excitements of relevation. In "The Hand and Foot" paradox served to narrow the distance between experience and memory:

The hand and foot that stir not, they shall find
Sooner than all the rightful place to go;
Now in their motion free as roving wind,
Though first no snail so limited and slow;
I mark them full of labor all the day,
Each active motion made in perfect rest;
They cannot from their path mistaken stray,
Though 'tis not theirs, yet in it they are blest;
The bird has not their hidden track found out,
The cunning fox though full of art he be;
It is the way unseen, the certain route,
Where ever bound, yet thou art ever free;
The path of Him, whose perfect law of love
Bids spheres and atoms in just order move.[38]

The informing idea, and thus the conception of this sonnet, goes back at least to the spring of 1839. After Very's abrupt departure from Concord in June, Emerson had wondered about the "private soul" ascending to "transcendent virtue," and he explained that it resembled Jones Very in so far as it "works hard without moving hand or foot." [39] The sonnet therefore derives from the period before Very permanently ended his solitary withdrawal, and before publication of *Essays and Poems*.

The same is true for "Yourself." This sonnet is rooted in that sense of his own uniqueness and spiritual superiority which produced the "Epistles to the Unborn." Like them, the sonnet celebrates the vital, quickening "self," with its power of raising readers up from the living-dead.

> 'Tis to yourself I speak; you cannot know
> Him whom I call in speaking such a one,
> For you beneath the earth lie buried low,
> Which he alone as living walks upon:
> You may at times have heard him speak to you,
> And often wished perchance that you were he;
> And I must ever wish that it were true,
> For then you could hold fellowship with me:
> But now you hear us talk as strangers, met
> Above the room wherein you lie abed;
> A word perhaps loud spoken you may get,
> Or hear our feet when heavily they tread;
> But he who speaks, or him who's spoken to,
> Must both remain as strangers still to you. [40]

Only the muted wish to achieve communion with those from whom he was estranged sets this sonnet apart from those written earlier in 1839. The dim figures hovering above the poem seem unsatisfactory substitutes for the manly intercourse Very had deprived himself of. The soul partners or spiritual brothers have little to say worth repeating, although the conception itself is appropriately evocative.

"Thy Neighbor" resorts to the familiar imagery of the living plant, the earthly and spiritual dwellings, the marriage feast, and the death of the unnatural self. Only this particular conjunction of components, all salvaged from earlier work, is new—nothing more. At best it is an act of conservation:

I am thy other self; what thou wilt be
When thou art I, the one thou seest now;
In finding thy true self thou wilt find me,
The springing blade where now thou dost but plough;
I am thy neighbor, a new house I've built
Which thou as yet hast never entered in;
I come to call thee; come in when thou wilt,
The feast is always waiting to begin;
Thou shouldst love me as thou dost love thyself;
For I am but another self beside;
To show thee him thou lov'st in better health,
What thou wouldst be when thou to him have died;
Then visit me, I make thee many a call;
Nor live I near to thee alone but all.[41]

That this synthesis of elements no longer urgent or personally meaningful to Very was still possible and valid, offered some measure of hope for his future as a poet. But the promise was never fulfilled.

A year later he had not yet found present experiences to provide the substance and tone for new poems. Instead he continued to rewrite old ones, and the result was as expected. He insisted upon clinging to a past which he was finding impossible to convert into effective poetry. All that remained to him was the habit of writing poems, and the best he could do under these circumstances was such a sonnet as "Death":

Men live and die in secret; none can see
When going out or lighting up the flame,
Save the all-seeing eye;—frail mortals, we
Call death and life what are but so in name;
Death is that shunning Him who bids thee die,
Which thou but disobedience learnst to call;
Words cannot hide thee from the searching eye,
That sees thy corse beneath their sable pall;
And life the lifting up that thou dost feel,
When thy feet follow where he bids thee go;

A life beyond disease, or severing steel,
That nought but him who gives it, fear below;
This be thy life, and death shall flee away,
For thou hast learned forever to obey.[42]

While not much inferior in a technical sense to his better poems, "Death" is a disjointed verbal structure, one which no longer made connection with Very's vital experience of life. The kind of integrated meaning which once related to real tensions or degrees of serenity within himself, and which had enabled him to overcome the limited range of his language, is completely lacking in "Death." Unfortunately, in the remaining forty years of his life Jones Very could never bring himself to abandon an effete sort of poetry. As a poet, the rest was anticlimax. The lesson of obedience may have been well learned, but in poetry at least there was nothing to which it might apply. The "Voice" which he once claimed spoke to readers willing to hear, was permanently silenced after 1840. Not even the renewed interest Emerson was showing could move him to justify that gesture. His was a fatal conservatism.

Until 1840 the distinctive qualities of his life and work were sufficient to give them inherent interest and value. But after 1840, whatever significance Jones Very possessed depended almost entirely upon those relatively infrequent occasions when a mental construct corresponding to him managed to invade the consciousness of Ralph Waldo Emerson, and succeeded in holding his attention long enough for him to leave some record of it in his letters, journals, and published essays. That record properly belongs to the life of Emerson rather than to that of Jones Very. All that Very provided was the material for thought. The rest was Emerson's.[43]

Although he lived until 1880, Very's effective life was over by the end of 1840.[44] By then all his significant achievements were behind him, and gone was the energy which for a brief time had sustained him, as a successful teacher of Greek at Harvard; as a man of rare charm and sensitivity; as a writer of a number of skillful and forceful sonnets and a handful of lovely lyrics; as a critic of epic and dramatic poetry; as an examiner of Shakespeare's "mind"; as a somewhat troublesome contributor to a "transcendental" way of life; as a friend or acquaintance of Elizabeth and Sophia Peabody, of Emerson and his wife, of Bronson Alcott, Thoreau, Hawthorne, Margaret Fuller, Professor Channing and Dr. Channing, the elder Dana, James Freeman Clarke, and the Transcendentalist company in general; as a saintly foil to the wordly-wise; and as a controversial figure and unsettling force in that emphatic little world whose chief cities were Boston, Concord, Cambridge, and Salem.

During his last forty years he was cut off by choice and circumstance from the ideas, people, and activities which gave special meaning to his earlier life. These long years before death he spent in Salem, reading pious tracts and sentimental stories; writing more than a hundred tedious sermons, and delivering them as "supply minister" to various churches in the vicinity; walking about the countryside, observing flowers, trees, birds, and sky, or just daydreaming; smiling kindly and offering bland words to the neighborhood children; examining ancient tombstones in out-of-the-way cemeteries and studying old documents for traces of his ancestors; visiting local newspaper offices where he looked at out-of-town papers and current magazines; composing solemn hymns for churches celebrating special public occasions; rhyming verses about the latest mechanical inventions and scientific discoveries, or about man's need to lead a better life; listening to sober lectures at the Essex Institute, and examining its museum collections; working in his garden or lounging in the tiny summerhouse he built there; reading his dog-eared, slip-marked Bible in his upstairs bedroom, or staring out at the industrial clutter which was growing up on the far bank of the North River; answering trivial "literary" questions for neighbors in his role of town pundit; muttering about the large Catholic

Church erected on the lot adjoining his house; following a bachelor's routine with the help of two spinster sisters after the death of his long-widowed mother; and reminiscing silently and without purpose about the first twenty-seven years of his life.

That prolonged anticlimax followed a life once so promising and so charged with excitement is attributable to his own personal failure. He was a victim of his own genius, trapped by the peculiar individuality he willfully created for himself, a martyr to the yearning of his spirit for special grace, and a casualty of his capacities for self-hatred and self-love. When he should have been at the peak of his powers and in full command of his talents and perceptions, cheerful resignation concealed his disappointment and disillusionment over the impossibility of further triumphs (and defeats), and thus he lacked that combination of tension and ambition which drives a man in the direction of greatness. The sources of energy which had once given a distinctive style to his life had failed, leaving him exhausted and but little troubled. Everything about Jones Very which had prevented mediocrity, and which now is worth recalling, was restricted to his first twenty-seven years.

# NOTES AND BIBLIOGRAPHY

# ABBREVIATIONS USED IN THE NOTES

The following system of abbreviations has been used for the most frequent references:

| | |
|---|---|
| Bartlett | William I. Bartlett, *Jones Very: Emerson's "Brave Saint"* (1942). |
| C.B. I | "Journal for 1833," in "Three Commonplace Books by Jones Very." |
| C.B. II | "Scrap Book, 1834," in "Three Commonplace Books by Jones Very." |
| C.B. III | Commonplace Book "III," in "Three Commonplace Books by Jones Very." |
| *E & P* | *Essays and Poems by Jones Very* (1839). |
| *EIHC* | *Essex Institute Historical Collections.* |
| EPP | Elizabeth Palmer Peabody. |
| *ESQ* | *Emerson Society Quarterly.* |
| *J* | *The Journals of Ralph Waldo Emerson* (1909–1914). |
| JV | Jones Very. |
| *L* | *The Letters of Ralph Waldo Emerson* (1939). |
| "Letters" | "Letters of Jones Very to Ralph Waldo Emerson, 1838–1846." |
| "Memoir" | William P. Andrews, Introductory "Memoir," in *Poems by Jones Very* (1883). |
| "Notebook" | "Notebook of William P. Andrews on Jones Very." |
| *Obs.* | Salem *Observer.* |
| *P* | *Poems by Jones Very* (1883). |
| *P & E* | *Poems and Essays by Jones Very* (1886). |
| RWE | Ralph Waldo Emerson. |
| *W* | *The Complete Works of Ralph Waldo Emerson* (1903–1904). |
| WPA | William P. Andrews. |

Short titles are keyed to expanded entries in the Selected Bibliography. The location of manuscripts is given in the Selected Bibliography. Full citations are made in the Notes for items omitted from the Selected Bibliography.

# Notes

### Introduction

1. Ambitious attempts to present coherent accounts of Jones Very's life, accomplishments, and significance have been made by William P. Andrews, Bessie W. Proudfoot, Percy P. Burns, Carlos Baker, Yvor Winters, William I. Bartlett, and Warner B. Berthoff. These, and other scholarly studies and critical estimates, are discussed in my unpublished Master's Thesis on Jones Very, pp. 2–9, 48–59. (See Selected Bibliography for details.)

### Chapter 1

### *The Matrix of Maturity: 1813–1833*

1. The brief genealogy and family history in this chapter is based on JV's own detailed study, "The Very Family," *EIHC,* I (1859), 116, and II (1860), 33–38. It is supplemented by a MS written by him in 1872, printed in "The Father of Rev. Jones Very," May 17, 1880 Salem *Register.*

2. No evidence of formal marriage is on file in Essex County record repositories, and a search of local newspaper holdings in the Essex Institute has failed to disclose any published announcement. Neither

WPA in "Memoir," nor J. F. Clarke in "Biographical Notice of Jones Very," cite any date or comment on the absence of documentary evidence. (Both writers had access to Very family papers.) Bartlett, p. 6, follows JV's own account in *EIHC*, II (1860), 37, giving the fictitious date of February 13, 1813, and notes that JV was born six and a half months later. The brief biographical sketch of Captain Very in "History of the Essex Lodge of Freemasons," *EIHC*, III (1861), 211, gives the date as March 1, 1813, making JV's birth even more "premature."

3. "Memoir," p. 3. None of their poems have been preserved.

4. EPP December 3, 1838 letter to RWE, p. 1; EPP October 20, 1838 letter to RWE, p. 2; EPP November 12, 1880 letter to WPA, p. 12.

5. "Memoir," pp. 4–5; Bartlett, p. 18; C. T. Brooks December 11, 1880 letter to Essex Institute, in *Life and Services*, p. 29.

6. May 17, 1880 Salem *Register;* R. G. Albion, "From Sails to Spindles: Essex County in Transition," *EIHC*, XCV (1959), 116; Osgood and Batchelder, *Historical Sketch*, pp. 132–33.

7. See the portrait of Captain Very in the Essex Institute; reprinted by Bartlett, facing p. 6.

8. According to Leavitt, *EIHC*, III (1861), 211, Captain Very joined the Salem Lodge in January 1815.

9. EPP November 12, 1880 letter to WPA, p. 12.

10. *EIHC,* II (1860), 37.

11. "Memoir," p. 5.

12. "The sun was shining on the deck," in Bartlett, p. 10.

13. RWE September 25, 1841 letter to Rufus W. Griswold.

14. In 1871 JV recalled the 1823–1824 voyage in "The Barque Aurelia of Boston," Bartlett, pp. 174–75. See also May 17, 1880 Salem *Register.*

15. May 17, 1880 Salem *Register.*

16. "Memoir," p. 3.

17. Captain Very's October 8, 1824 will, reprinted from Essex County *Probate Book* (*Wills*) by Bartlett, pp. 13–14.

18. The text of the December 21, 1824 will apparently has not survived. See Interrogatory 6 and Answer, in "The Trial of Lydia Very," reprinted from Essex County *Probate Book* by Bartlett, pp.

178–81. The "Complaint" identifies Pickering as administrator of the estate. The Essex County *Deed Book* (*Grantees*), cited by Bartlett in another connection, p. 20, indicates that Cheever was appointed guardian. Lydia Very's lack of legal status necessitated that appointment, and accounts for the references to him in the Trial proceedings.

19. "The Trial of Lydia Very" (Interrogatory 17 and Answer), in Bartlett, p. 180.

20. May 17, 1880 Salem *Register.*

21. "The Trial of Lydia Very" (Interrogatory 20 and Answer), in Bartlett, p. 180.

22. Bartlett, pp. 20, 176. Lydia Louisa Ann bequeathed the Very house to the Essex Institute. The house was demolished in 1964 to permit construction of the St. James Parish School.

23. L. L. A. Very, *An Old-Fashioned Garden,* p. 38.

24. EPP November 12, 1880 letter to WPA, p. 12; "Memoir," p. 5.

25. Except as otherwise indicated, this account of Lydia Very has been developed from Bartlett's report of interviews conducted with elderly Salem residents in 1937, pp. 16–17, 121.

26. "Memoir," pp. 4–6; "The Voice of Nature in Youth and Age," "The Scholar Dreaming," and "The Child's Dream of Reaching the Horizon," *P & E,* pp. 404–5, 494–95, 496–97.

27. "Memoir," p. 6; Osgood and Batchelder, pp. 102–3.

28. C. T. Brooks, "Augustus Story," *EIHC,* XX (1883), 115–37; *DAB, s.v.* "Oliver."

29. "Memoir," p. 6.

30. C.B. I, p. 56.

31. See especially C.B. I, pp. 9–13 *passim,* and C.B. II, pp. 36–37. The Harvard College "Library Charging Lists" disclose that he also read Mackintosh in May 1835 and May 1838.

32. See JV's "Individuality."

33. See Mackintosh's account of Butler's moral philosophy, in *Dissertation on the Progress of Ethical Philosophy,* ed. William Whewell (Edinburgh, 1862), pp. 143–57.

34. See C.B. II, pp. 36–37, 52, 106–12, 128; C.B. III, pp. 14–15.

35. Mackintosh, *Dissertation,* pp. 338–41.

36. C.B. I, pp. 35–38, 49–54, 55–58.

37. *The Origin and Progress of Language,* 2nd ed. (Edinburgh,

1774), I, 46–52, 219–26, and II, 456–61. A number of JV's later notebook entries stemmed from an interest in exotic cultures and related esoterica which Monboddo stimulated. See C.B. II, p. 121; C.B. III, pp. 1–3.

38. See JV's "Individuality," p. 8.

39. C.B. I, p. 53.

40. C.B. I, p. 54. The full quotation may be found in Channing, *Works*, I, 272.

41. C.B. I, pp. 49–54 *passim*.

42. William Paley, *Natural Theology* (Boston, 1829), pp. 295–97.

43. Paley's premises and conclusions are embodied in JV's "Hast thou ever heard the voice of nature," Bartlett, pp. 183–84.

44. JV read Pope carefully. See C.B. I, pp. 23–26; C.B. II, p. 30.

45. Bartlett, pp. 181–82.

46. See "Lines—Written on Reading Stuart's Account of the Treatment of Slaves in Charlestown," reprinted Bartlett, pp. 182–83.

47. "Memoir," p. 6. Andrews was mistaken when he said that the unnamed uncle came forward in 1834. He was under the impression that JV entered Harvard early in 1834.

## Chapter 11

### *Excursions in Cambridge and Salem: 1833–1834*

1. Incomplete college records have confused biographers about the date JV joined the class at Harvard with which he graduated in 1836. However, such documents as the surviving Term Scales, "Library Charging Lists, 1833–1834," and the records of the Institute of 1770, make clear that he enrolled in September 1833. Cf. "Memoir," p. 6, and Bartlett, p. 23.

2. WPA "Remarks," *Life and Services*, p. 5.

3. "Samuel Gray Ward's Account."

4. J. T. G. Nichols letter to Editor, in "[Class of] 1836: [Death of] Jones Very, at Salem, May 8," in June 1880 *Harvard Register*.

5. John Healy Heywood, quoted in J. Ward, "Jones Very: The Finest Sonnet Writer in America," May 16, 1880 Boston *Sunday Herald;* "Samuel Gray Ward's Account."

6. "Memoir," p. 7; Nichols letter, in June 1880 *Harvard Register*.

7. "Library Charging Lists, 1833–1834," p. 178 (2nd ser.).

8. "Institute of 1770—Records: 1832–1837," vol. A (September 11, September 25, 1833 minutes); "Institute of 1770—Accounts: 1825–1836," vol. A, p. 21.

9. WPA "Remarks," *Life and Services,* p. 5.

10. Rusk, *Life,* pp. 67–68.

11. C. Beck April 29, 1834 letter to Committee of Overseers, *Overseers Reports,* IV (1834–1836), 79.

12. C. C. Felton April 28, 1834 letter to Committee of Overseers, *Overseers Reports,* IV (1834–1836), 81.

13. J. Ward, May 16, 1880 Boston *Sunday Herald.* As an honor student in October 1835, JV participated in "Mathematical Exercises" at the Harvard Exhibition.

14. *E & P,* the only book by JV published during his lifetime, was dedicated to Edward Tyrrel Channing "as a token of gratitude."

15. Rusk, *Life,* p. 78.

16. E. T. Channing April 29, 1834 letter to Committee of Overseers, *Overseers Reports,* IV (1834–1836), 74.

17. Townsend Scudder, "Henry David Thoreau," in *Literary History of the United States,* ed. Robert E. Spiller, *et al.* (New York, 1949), I, 390; Alexander Kern, "The Rise of Transcendentalism, 1815–1860," in *Transitions in American Literary History,* ed. Harry Hayden Clark (Durham, 1953), p. 293.

18. Nichols letter, in June 1880 *Harvard Register.*

19. C.B. I, p. 57.

20. Foote, "Rev. Jones Very," May 11, 1880 Salem *Gazette.*

21. C. T. Brooks December 11, 1880 letter to Essex Institute, in *Life and Services,* p. 29.

22. See R. H. Dana, Sr. May 21, 1840 letter to W. C. Bryant; Charvat, *Origins of American Critical Thought,* pp. 178–79.

23. C.B. I, pp. 55–103 *passim;* "Library Charging Lists, 1833–1834," September 10, 1833 to February 25, 1834 entries, p. 178 (2nd ser.).

24. Nichols letter, in June 1880 *Harvard Register.*

25. J. Ward, May 16, 1880 Boston *Sunday Herald;* Rusk, *Life,* p. 71.

26. J. Ward, May 16, 1880 Boston *Sunday Herald.* See Term Scales reprinted in facsimile by Cameron, in *ESQ,* No. 19 (II Quarter 1960),

pp. 52–57. Robert Bartlett, JV, and West ranked in that order at the head of their class in the Sophomore year, as well as at the time of their graduation in 1836. From 1838 to 1840 West was the superintendent of the North Church Sunday School. (*The First Century of the North Church and Society* [Salem, 1873], p. 166.)

27. Nichols letter, in June 1880 *Harvard Register*.

28. See "Lines on Mount Auburn, December 1833," in Bartlett, pp. 148–49.

29. "Institute of 1770—Accounts: 1825–1836," vol. A.

30. J. Ward, May 16, 1880 Boston *Sunday Herald;* Nichols letter, in June 1880 *Harvard Register*.

31. See secretary's minutes for October 23, 1833, January 8 and 22, 1834, March 5 and 19, 1834, in vol. A, "Institute of 1770—Records: 1832–1837."

32. C.B. I, p. 87 (April 18–25, 1834).

33. Reprinted by Bartlett, pp. 183–84.

34. "Hast thou ever heard the voice of nature," dated April 7, 1834, in April 26, 1834 *Obs.;* reprinted Bartlett, pp. 183–84.

35. C.B. I, pp. 87–88 (April 25, May 2, 1834); "Library Charging Lists, 1833–1834," p. 178 (2nd ser.).

36. Dated August 13, 1833, in August 24, 1833 *Obs.;* reprinted Bartlett, pp. 182–83. On p. 53 of C.B. I, JV noted that he had finished reading Stuart's *Three Years in North America* (Edinburgh, 1833), on August 13, 1833.

37. Bartlett, pp. 150–51.

38. Bartlett, p. 150.

39. Osgood and Batchelder, *Historical Sketch,* pp. 231, 248.

40. C.B. I, p. 111. References are to Thomas Hobbes' *Human Nature,* the Earl of Shaftesbury's *Moralists,* Samuel Parr's *Discourse on Education,* and probably William Godwin's *Political Justice.*

41. C.B. I, p. 88.

42. "Rev. Jones Very: College Life of Jones Very," May 21, 1880 Salem *Gazette.*

43. Bartlett, pp. 26–27; Samuel Eliot Morison, *Three Centuries of Harvard: 1636–1936* (Cambridge, 1936), pp. 252–53.

44. *College Papers,* 2nd ser., VI, 113; *Faculty Records,* XI (1829–1840), 150.

45. Untitled poem ("What [is] more delightful than to wander forth"), dated June 8, 1834, in Bartlett, pp. 153–54.

46. Dated June 21, 1834, in June 28, 1834 *Obs.;* reprinted Bartlett, pp. 184–85. Lafayette died at Paris on May 20, 1834. JV's burst of energy in this poem may have been prompted in part by having seen Lafayette during his second visit to Salem, on August 31, 1824. This was the day Captain Very and his son returned from their last sea voyage. (See Bartlett, pp. 12, 27.) If true that the Verys participated in this celebration, then Lydia Very may have seen and spoken to her intellectual "idol," Fanny Wright, who accompanied Lafayette on his triumphal tour of the United States.

47. "Pleasure," dated July 22, 1834, in August 2, 1834 *Obs.;* reprinted Bartlett, pp. 188–89.

48. VI, 227–57; in C.B. II, pp. 1–2.

49. C.B. II, p. 2.

50. C.B. II, p. 4.

51. V, 367–78; in C.B. II, p. 5.

52. C.B. II, p. 3.

53. See Charvat, *Origins of American Critical Thought,* pp. 186–87; Brooks, *Flowering of New England,* pp. 93–114 *passim.*

54. V, 379–82; in C.B. II, p. 5.

55. C.B. II, p. 16.

56. C.B. II, p. 6.

57. II, xxxviii; in C.B. II, pp. 16–17.

58. III, xlii; in C.B. II, p. 13.

59. C.B. II, pp. 13, 21.

60. Dated July 6, 1834, in July 12, 1834 *Obs.;* reprinted Bartlett, pp. 186–87.

61. "Kind Words," dated July 16, 1834, in July 19, 1834 *Obs.;* reprinted Bartlett, p. 187.

## Chapter III

### *The Expanding Field: 1834–1835*

1. *Faculty Records,* XI (1829–1840), 179, 184.

2. Brooks, *Flowering of New England,* pp. 90–91.

3. "Notes on Ticknor's Course, 1834."

4. Lecture 2, p. 6.

5. Lectures 7 and 8, pp. 21–26.

6. Lecture 9, p. 28.

7. Lecture 10, p. 29.

8. Lecture 11, p. 30.

9. Lectures 13 and 14, pp. 37–38.

10. Lecture 18, p. 48.

11. See Charvat, *Origins of American Critical Thought,* pp. 62–63.

12. C.B. II, p. 6; "Library Charging Lists, 1834–1835," October 8 and 12, 1834 entries, p. 92 (2nd ser.).

13. Lines 247–67; C.B. II, p. 8.

14. "Lines: Suggested by Seeing a Butterfly Sculptured On a Tomb," Bartlett, pp. 186–87.

15. C.B. II, p. 8.

16. See C.B. II, pp. 10, 35, 39, 58, 65, 68.

17. James Marsh, ed. (Burlington, 1831), III, 455; C.B. II, p. 10.

18. Boston 1842 edition, pp. 10–14; C.B. II, pp. 9–10.

19. XXXVI, 565–66; C.B. II, p. 20.

20. C.B. II, p. 20.

21. C.B. II, p. 33.

22. C.B. II, pp. 11–12.

23. C.B. II, pp. 12–13.

24. *Childe Harold's Pilgrimage,* II, xxxvii; III, xcvi, xcvii, lxvii; III, lxxv, xiii, xiv; III, xiv (5–9); C.B. II, pp. 16–17, 22–23, 32, 41.

25. C.B. II, p. 14.

26. III, xcvii; C.B. II, p. 22.

27. C.B. II, p. 32.

28. See C.B. II, pp. 22–23.

29. "Shakespeare," *E & P,* p. 65.

30. III, xiv (5–9); C.B. II, p. 41.

31. "The New Year," in January 3, 1835 *Obs.;* reprinted *P & E,* pp. 167–68.

32. "Health of Body Dependent on the Soul," *P & E,* p. 328; with variants, p. 521.

33. "Sleigh Ride," dated January 5, 1835, in January 10, 1835 *Obs.;* reprinted Bartlett, p. 189. (Italics added.)

34. "The Snow-Drop," dated Salem April 8, 1835, in April 11, 1835 *Obs.;* reprinted *P & E,* pp. 173–74.

35. Secretary's July 3 and September 5, 1834 minutes, in vol. A, "Institute of 1770—Records: 1832–1837."

36. C. C. Felton September 9, 1834 letter to T. W. Harris, inserted between pp. 178–79 (2nd ser.) of "Library Charging Lists, 1833–1834." See September 11, 1834 entries, pp. 92, 178 (2nd ser.).

37. Secretary's September 15, 1834 minutes, in vol. A. "Institute of 1770—Records: 1832–1837." The kind of verse he could write for such an occasion may be surmised from a parody of Robert Burns he composed for the "Class-Supper of the Sophomore Class of 1834." See Cameron, *ESQ*, No. 5 (IV Quarter 1956), pp. 12–13.

38. Chapt. I, art. 4 of "Constitution," in vol. B, "Institute of 1770—Constitution." JV is not mentioned in the minutes after September 15, 1834.

39. JV *c*. 1856 letter to D. H. Conrad.

40. The editor's preface to JV's "Hymn: Sung at the Dedication of the New Stone Church of the North Society, in Salem, June 22, 1836," in June 25, 1836 *Obs.*, identifies JV as a member of the North Society (Unitarian).

41. JV *c*. 1856 letter to Conrad; Samuel Longfellow, "Memoir," in Samuel Johnson's *Lectures, Essays, and Sermons* (Boston and New York, 1883), p. 7.

42. Rusk, *Life*, p. 135.

43. "Theodore Parker's Experience as a Minister," *Transcendentalists* (ed. Miller), pp. 488–89.

44. Hale, in *Autobiography of J. F. Clarke*, p. 89.

45. "Samuel Gray Ward's Account."

46. See "Landmark's Preface" to JV's "My Mother's Voice," in June 4, 1836 *Obs.*

47. C.B. I, p. 87 (April 28, 1834).

48. "A Greek Version: Extracts from Webster's 'Oration.' "

49. "Practical Application," p. 4.

## Chapter IV

### *The Composition of Greatness: 1835*

1. "Library Charging Lists, 1834–1835," pp. 58, 92, 95 (2nd ser.); "Library Charging Lists, 1835–1836," pp. 76 (2nd ser.), 224 (1st ser.); C.B. II, pp. 58–121.

2. See C.B. II, pp. 31, 39–52 *passim*.

3. C.B. II, p. 39.

4. C.B. II, p. 67.

5. C.B. II, p. 33.

6. C.B. II, pp. 50–52.

7. C.B. I, p. 54.

8. C.B. I, pp. 79–80.

9. *Paradise Lost*, I, 24; *Hamlet*, IV, iv, 53–54; C.B. II, p. 38.

10. C.B. I, p. 53.

11. Francis Lieber, *Letters to a Gentleman in Germany* (Philadelphia, 1834), pp. 335–37; C.B. II, pp. 26–27.

12. C.B. II, p. 25.

13. C.B. II, p. 23.

14. C.B. II, p. 28.

15. C.B. II, p. 28.

16. C.B. II, p. 35.

17. C.B. II, p. 39.

18. C.B. II, p. 38.

19. C.B. II, p. 29.

20. C.B. II, p. 35.

21. Channing, *Works*, I, 118–20.

22. C.B. II, pp. 50–52.

23. "The Humming-Bird," dated August 1, 1835, in August 8, 1835 *Obs.;* reprinted with variant spelling and punctuation, in *Harvardiana*, II (1836), 326; *E & P*, pp. 107–8; *P*, pp. 136–37; *P & E*, p. 154.

24. In August 1, 1835 *Obs.;* reprinted with variant spelling and punctuation, in *E & P*, p. 109; *P*, pp. 142–43; *P & E*, p. 155. Title from Horace's *Odes*, II, xiv, 1: "Alas, O Posthumus, Posthumus, the fleeting years are slipping by."

25. "Nature," dated August 15, 1835, in August 22, 1835 *Obs.;* reprinted *P & E*, pp. 420–21; reprinted with minor variants, in *P*, pp. 123–24; *P & E*, pp. 178–79. See C.B. III, p. 128, for early MS version with cancellations.

26. "Religion," dated August 24, 1835, in August 29, 1835 *Obs.;* reprinted *P & E*, p. 166.

27. See "Samuel Gray Ward's Account."

28. See Term Scales for 3rd term of JV's Junior year, and for the first two terms of his Senior year; facsimiles in Cameron, "Jones Very's Academic Standing at Harvard," *ESQ*, No. 19 (II Quarter 1960), pp. 54–56. JV ranked third in his class for these periods, while at other times (including his final standing at graduation), he ranked second. His high position in spite of relatively poor current grades for these three terms was due mainly to "points" accumulated during earlier, less troubled periods.

29. JV December 29, 1838 letter to Bellows, p. 1.

30. Wheeler September 15, 1838 journal entry, in Eidson, *C.S. Wheeler*, p. 47.

31. JV December 29, 1838 letter to Bellows, p. 1.

32. "Samuel Gray Ward's Account."

33. JV December 29, 1838 letter to Bellows, p. 1.

34. JV December 29, 1838 letter to Bellows, p. 1.

35. JV *c.* 1856 letter to Conrad; J. F. Clarke December 10, 1880 and C. T. Brooks December 11, 1880 letters to Essex Institute, in *Life and Services*, pp. 26, 29.

## Chapter v

### *In Private: 1835–1836*

1. R. C. Waterston December 13, 1880 letter to Essex Institute, in *Life and Services*, p. 27.

2. J. Quincy November 4, 1835 letter to S. T. Armstrong, in *Overseers Reports*, IV (1834–1836), 251; his February 18, 1836 report, in *College Papers* (2nd ser.), VII, 257.

3. See September 1835 to June 1836 entries in "Library Charging Lists, 1835–1836," p. 76 (2nd ser.).

4. See August 1835 entries in "Library Charging Lists, 1834–1835," p. 95 (2nd ser.); September 1835 to May 1836 entries in "Library Charging Lists, 1835–1836," p. 76 (2nd ser.); C.B. II, pp. 54–82 *passim*.

5. See September 1835 entries in "Library Charging Lists, 1834–1835," p. 95 (2nd ser.); October 1835 to June 1836 entries in "Library Charging Lists, 1835–1836," p. 76 (2nd ser.); C.B. II, pp. 58–95 *passim*.

6. C.B. II, p. 75.

7. C.B. II, p. 65.

8. *Biographia Literaria* (Boston, 1834), II, 248; *Aids to Reflection,* ed. James Marsh (Burlington, 1829), p. 366; passage attributed by JV to *The Friend* (Burlington, 1831); C.B. II, pp. 58, 65, 68.

9. New York, 1833, II, 195; C.B. II, p. 62.

10. *Wilhelm Meister's Apprenticeship* (trans., Boston, 1828) I, 22; C.B. II, p. 77.

11. *Wilhelm Meister,* I, 25; C.B. II, p. 77.

12. *Wilhelm Meister,* I, 29; C.B. II, p. 78. Italics added by JV, who also scored the margin opposite the last sentence.

13. *Faust* (trans. A. Hayward), Act I; C.B. II, pp. 91–92.

14. JV attribution to Schiller's "Uber das Erhoben"; C.B. II, pp. 90–91.

15. [Mrs. William Minot], "Cousin's Philosophy," *North American Review,* XXXV (1832), 28; C.B. II, p. 93.

16. C.B. II, p. 89.

17. C.B. II, p. 94.

18. C.B. II, p. 69.

19. C.B. II, p. 93.

20. "A Withered Leaf—Seen on a Poet's Table," dated November 24, 1835, in December 5, 1835 *Obs.;* reprinted with variants, in *E & P,* p. 110; *P,* pp. 137–38; *P & E,* p. 156. (Last stanza, quoted in part, appears only in *Obs.* version.)

21. "The Stars," dated December 22, 1835, in December 26, 1835 *Obs.;* reprinted *Harvardiana, II* (1836), 199; *P & E,* pp. 205–6.

22. "The Snow-Bird," dated December 25, 1835, in January 2, 1836 *Obs.;* reprinted with variant spelling and punctuation, in *Harvardiana,* II (1836), 200; *P & E,* pp. 168–69.

23. "The Painted Columbine," *Harvardiana,* II (1836), 231–32; reprinted April 23, 1836 *Obs.;* as "To the Painted Columbine" with variants, in *E & P,* pp. 112–13; *P,* pp. 128–29; *P & E,* pp. 157–58.

24. "My Mother's Voice," *Harvardiana,* II (1836), 248; reprinted June 4, 1836 *Obs.;* with variant punctuation, in *P,* pp. 145–46; *P & E,* p. 182. According to the paragraph introducing the *Obs.* text, signed "Landmark," the poem originally had been written in a "Lady's Album."

Chapter VI

*Public Exhibitions: 1836*

1. See prefatory note to Essex Institute MS of JV's "Epic Poetry"; also 1836 Bowdoin Prize Announcement, preceding No. 4 in *Bowdoin Prize Dissertations,* VI (1835–1839).

2. "Song," No. 5 on the program.

3. *College Papers* (2nd ser.), VII, 236; VIII, 27; *Overseers Reports,* V (1837–1840), 19; *Faculty Records,* XI (1829–1840), 281.

4. Four passages were transferred from "Practical Application" without change, and similar or identical words and phrases were retained throughout.

5. The Essex Institute MS of "Epic Poetry" bears JV's note: "written in April—delivered July, 1836." The MS JV actually delivered in July, entitled "What Reasons Are There For Not Expecting Another Great Epic Poem?" is bound as No. 4 in *Bowdoin Prize Dissertations,* VI (1835–1839). Notes at the bottom of pp. 2, 3, 11, 42 of the Essex Institute MS were included in the Bowdoin version.

6. "Samuel Gray Ward's Account."

7. Bowdoin MS, p. 17; Essex Institute MS, p. 47, n. 7. (This addendum, excluded from the surviving "final" versions, may have been used in the texts delivered later as lectures at the Salem and Concord Lyceums.)

8. The third text is "Influence of Christianity and of the Progress of Civilization on Epic Poetry." Most of the addenda at the end of the Essex Institute MS, pp. 46–48, do not appear in the Bowdoin MS but were included in this version.

9. John Pierce's "Journal," extracts included in the account of the January 1890 meeting of the Massachusetts Historical Society. See *Proceedings,* 2nd ser., V (1889–1890), 218.

10. The corresponding dissidence of Emerson, Bronson Alcott, Margaret Fuller, and of a number of other New England radicals of the time, may have derived also from feelings of personal inadequacy. However, their feelings seem to have been effectively purged by their "protests," while JV's public accusations made him more intensely

aware of his moral deficiencies. His "protestantism" was therefore essentially an act of self-condemnation, not of regeneration.

11. "An English Oration: Individuality," pp. 1–3.

## Chapter VII

*Gladly Would He Learn and Gladly Teach: 1836–1837*

1. WPA "Remarks," *Life and Services,* p. 6; "Memoir," p. 7; Rusk, *Life,* p. 110; Hale, in *Autobiography of J. F. Clarke,* p. 88.

2. Blau, in *American Philosophic Addresses,* p. 587.

3. "Form of Admission to the Church in Harvard University Nov$^r$ 1 1814," printed by Cameron, *ESQ,* No. 14 (I Quarter 1959), p. 18.

4. Schneider, *American Philosophy,* pp. 60–1, 227; Blau, in *American Philosophic Addresses,* pp. 538–39.

5. Hale, in *Autobiography of J. F. Clarke,* p. 89–90; Schneider, *American Philosophy,* p. 227; Miller, in *Transcendentalists,* pp. 6, 157–58; Pochmann, *German Culture in America,* p. 537, n. 160.

6. See *Transcendentalists* (ed. Miller), pp. 49–105.

7. Hale, in *Autobiography of J. F. Clarke,* p. 90; Miller, in *Transcendentalists,* pp. 159, 210.

8. Smith, *Changing Conceptions,* pp. 69, 76–77.

9. Hale, in *Autobiography of J. F. Clarke,* p. 89.

10. C. C. Felton May 3, 1837 letter to the Committee of the Board of Overseers, in *Overseers Reports,* V (1837–1840), 35; Cameron, "Jones Very and Thoreau—The 'Greek Myth,'" *ESQ,* No. 7 (II Quarter 1957), p. 39.

11. See "Records of the Theological School: 1819–1892."

12. R. C. Waterston August 18, 1880 letter to WPA, p. 3, in "Notebook"; his December 13, 1880 letter to Essex Institute, in *Life and Services,* p. 27.

13. Moore, "Diary," V (September 6, 1836).

14. "Library Charging Lists, 1835–1836," p. 224 (1st ser.); "Library Charging Lists, 1836–1837," p. 133 (1st ser.).

15. "Library Charging Lists, 1835–1836," p. 224 (1st ser.); "Library Charging Lists, 1836–1837," p. 133 (1st ser.); C.B. II, pp. 104–26 *passim.*

16. Rusk, *Life*, pp. 238–39.

17. Charvat, "A Chronological List of Emerson's American Lecture Engagements," *Bulletin of the New York Public Library*, LXIV (1960), 500–1.

18. Mr. Parkman D. Howe of Needham, Mass. generously made JV's copy of *Nature* available for examination, and granted permission to report on the marginalia.

19. *Nature* (Boston, 1836), pp. 65, 73, 85, 88.

20. Almost certainly these "desires" were the source of JV's deep-seated anxieties and troubled conscience about his relationship with his mother and about his recollections of his father. His declared intention to have nothing further to do with women, his continuing self-hatred, and his rejection of all thought, seem to have stemmed from his determination to overcome these "two evil desires."

21. *Transcendentalists* (ed. Miller), pp. 174–78.

22. See Cameron, "Jones Very and Emerson's Friends in College Church Records," *ESQ*, No. 14 (I Quarter 1959), p. 18.

23. JV October [16] 1837 and May 1, 1838 letters to Harvard Overseers, in *Overseers Reports*, V (1837–1840), 83, 141.

24. J. Ward, May 16, 1880 Boston *Sunday Herald;* R. C. Waterston December 13, 1880 letter to Essex Institute, in *Life and Services*, p. 27; R. C. Waterston August 18, 1880 letter to WPA, p. 2, in "Notebook."

25. *J*, IX, 504 (April 20, 1863); W. O. White December 13, 1880 letter to Essex Institute, in *Life and Services*, p. 32; Cabot, *Memoir*, I, 349.

26. C. B. II, p. 97.

27. *Life and Services*, p. 32; "Memoir," p. 7; G. Bradford, Jr. review of *P & E*.

28. Waterston August 18, 1880 letter to WPA, p. 2, and EPP November 12, 1880 letter to WPA, p. 6, in "Notebook."

29. C.B. II, p. 105.

30. C.B. II, p. 125.

31. C.B. II, p. 126.

32. Waterston August 18, 1880 letter to WPA, pp. 2–3, and EPP November 12, 1880 letter to WPA, p. 7, in "Notebook"; Cabot, *Memoir*, I, 349.

33. Cabot, *Memoir*, I, 349; S. Johnson September 28, 1838 letter, p. 1; *Life and Services*, pp. 27, 32; "A Pupil's Testimony," May 21, 1880 Salem *Gazette*.

34. "A Pupil's Testimony," May 21, 1880 Salem *Gazette;* "Memoir," p. 7.

35. C. C. Felton October 16, 1838 letter to Harvard Overseers, in *Overseers Reports*, V (1837–1840), 184.

36. "MS Journal," XI, 439 (*c.* December 10, 1838).

37. Letter of May 1, 1838 to Harvard Overseers, in *Overseers Reports*, V (1837–1840), 141.

38. *Life and Services*, p. 32.

## Chapter VIII

### *A Poet Steps Forth: 1837*

1. C.B. II, p. 126.

2. C.B. II, p. 107.

3. C.B. II p. 112.

4. C.B. II, pp. 124–25.

5. JV December 29, 1838 letter to Bellows, p. 1.

6. C.B. II, p. 126.

7. JV December 29, 1838 letter to Bellows, p. 1.

8. "The Autumn Leaf," in October 1, 1836 *Obs.;* reprinted Bartlett, p. 192.

9. "The Winter Bird," in December 31, 1836 *Obs.;* reprinted with variants, in *P*, pp. 135–36; *P & E*, p. 190.

10. C.B. II, p. 121.

11. "To the Canary Bird," in April 15, 1837 *Obs.;* reprinted *E & P*, p. 117; *P*, p. 95–96; *P & E*, p. 69.

12. "An English Oration: Individuality," p. 8.

13. "What Reasons," pp. 16, 42.

14. JV December 29, 1838 letter to Bellows, p. 1; "Samuel Gray Ward's Account."

15. "The Tree," in April 22, 1837 *Obs.;* reprinted *E & P*, p. 119; *P*, pp. 89–90; *P & E*, p. 70.

16. "White Hills Journal," p. 1; in C.B. II, following p. 111.

17. C.B. II, p. 125.
18. "White Hills Journal," p. 4.
19. "Shakespeare," *E & P*, pp. 39–40.
20. "Library Charging Lists, 1837–1838," p. 59 (1st ser.).
21. "The Voice of God," in December 2, 1837 *Obs.;* reprinted *P & E*, pp. 175–76.
22. "The Wind-Flower," in December 23, 1837 *Obs.;* reprinted in January 6, 1838 issue; reprinted with variant spelling and punctuation, in *E & P*, p. 123; *P*, pp. 91–92; *P & E*, p. 72.
23. "Beauty," in December 30, 1837 *Obs.;* reprinted in January 6, 1838 issue (correcting typographical error in line 3: "weary" *v.* "every"); reprinted with variant punctuation, in *E & P*, p. 122; *P*, pp. 154–55; *P & E*, p. 71. (*E & P* text.)

Chapter IX

*Befriended: 1837–1838*

1. See M. C. D. Silsbee, *A Half Century in Salem* (Boston and New York, 1887), p. 97; Caroline Howard King, *When I Lived in Salem: 1822–1866* (Brattleboro, 1937), pp. 167–68; Brooks, *Flowering of New England*, p. 234.
2. December 23, 1837 *Obs.*
3. Except as otherwise noted, this account of EPP's first encounter with JV is based on her November 12, 1880 letter to WPA, pp. 1–5.
4. EPP November 12, 1880 letter to WPA, pp. 3–4.
5. RWE January 20, 1838 letter to S. Peabody, in Lathrop, *Memories,* p. 183.
6. EPP November 12, 1880 letter to WPA, p. 7.
7. S. F. Clarke, MS 3, p. 7; her December 31, 1837–January 1, 1838 letter to J. F. Clarke.
8. S. Peabody *c.* January 1839 letter to EPP, in Lathrop, *Memories,* p. 24.
9. M. Peabody February 5, 1839 letter to S. Peabody, p. 3.
10. S. Peabody May 4–6 1838 letter to EPP, p. 4.
11. S. Peabody June 29, 1839 letter to EPP, in Lathrop, *Memories,* p. 30.
12. EPP February 26, 1838 letter to R. C. Waterston.

13. EPP November 12, 1880 letter to WPA, p. 6.

14. *J*, V, 411 (1840).

15. "Concord Lyceum Record Book, 1828-1859," p. 151, in the Concord Free Public Library.

16. EPP November 12, 1880 letter to WPA, p. 5.

17. EPP November 12, 1880 letter to WPA, pp. 7-8.

18. C.B. III, pp. 1-3, 7.

19. EPP November 12, 1880 letter to WPA, p. 5.

20. RWE wrote his undated inscription in a penciled scrawl which is now badly faded.

21. RWE April 5, 1838 letter to EPP (copy in hand of WPA), in "Notebook."

22. Rusk, *Life*, p. 255.

23. *J*, IV, 432 (April 26, 1838).

24. *J*, IV, 423 (April 19, 1838).

25. "Typescript Journal C," p. 212 (May 20, 1838).

26. C.B. III, p. 12.

27. JV December 29, 1838 letter to Bellows, p. 1.

28. Eidson, *C. S. Wheeler*, pp. 30-1, 106.

29. S. F. Clarke July 23, 1838 letter to J. F. Clarke.

30. R. H. Dana, Sr. May 21, 1840 letter to W. C. Bryant, p. 2.

31. S. F. Clarke July 23, 1838 letter to J. F. Clarke.

32. JV December 29, 1838 letter to Bellows, pp. 1-2.

33. C.B. III, pp. 3-4, 8.

34. XXIV (1838), 33-34.

35. "Thy Beauty Fades," in April 21, 1838 *Obs.*; reprinted *E & P*, p. 121; *P*, p. 154; *P & E*, p. 71.

36. "The Columbine," in June 9, 1838 *Obs.*; reprinted *E & P*, p. 125; *P*, p. 93; *P & E*, p. 73. (*Obs.* punctuation adjusted to later versions.)

37. C.B. III, p. 2.

38. "Nature," in *E & P*, p. 118; reprinted *P*, p. 83; *P & E*, p. 69.

39. C.B. III, p. 18.

40. "The Song," in *E & P*, p. 133; reprinted *P*, pp. 83-84; *P & E*, p. 77.

41. "To the Pure All Things Are Pure," in *E & P*, p. 166; reprinted *P*, p. 84; as "Man in Harmony with Nature," in *P & E*, p. 93.

42. "The Stranger's Gift," in August 18, 1838 *Obs.;* reprinted with variants in punctuation and line 10, *E & P,* p. 120; *P,* p. 96; *P & E,* p. 70.

43. JV September [15], 1838 letter to RWE, in "Letters."

44. *L,* II, 154.

## Chapter x

### *The Rhetoric of Grace: September 1838*

1. See Rusk, *Life,* pp. 267–68.

2. Miller, in *Transcendentalists,* p. 198.

3. *W,* I, 119–51.

4. *Correspondence of Carlyle and Emerson* (ed. Norton), I, 183.

5. "The New School in Literature and Religion," in *Transcendentalists* (ed. Miller), pp. 193–96.

6. S. Johnson September 6, 1838 letter, pp. 2, 4; his September 28, 1838 letter, p. 1.

7. S. Johnson September [14], 1838 letter, pp. 2–3.

8. JV December 29, 1838 letter to Bellows, p. 2.

9. S. Johnson September [14], 1838 letter, p. 3.

10. S. Johnson *c.* September 21, 1838 letter, p. 1.

11. *Records of the College Faculty,* XI (1829–1840), 287.

12. JV December 29, 1838 letter to Bellows, p. 2.

13. JV December 29, 1838 letter to Bellows, p. 2.

14. Moore, "Diary," V (September 13, 1838).

15. J. Ward, May 16, 1880 Boston *Sunday Herald.*

16. Moore, "Diary," V (September 13, 1838).

17. S. Johnson September [14] letter, p. 3.

18. S. Johnson *c.* September 21, 1838 letter, pp. 1–2.

19. G. Bradford, Jr., "Jones Very," *Unitarian Review,* XXVII (1887), 111 n.

20. Moore, "Diary," V (September 14, 1838).

21. Eidson, *C. S. Wheeler,* p. 17.

22. Wheeler September 15, 1838 journal entry; quoted by Eidson, p. 17.

23. Moore, "Diary," V (September 17, 1838).

24. Henry Ware, Jr., *The Personality of the Deity,* pp. 7–23.

25. EPP November 12, 1880 letter to WPA, p. 16.
26. JV September [15], 1838 letter to RWE, in "Letters."
27. *L,* II, 165 (to Margaret Fuller, September 28–29, 1838).

## Chapter XI

### *The Genius and the Saint: September 1838*

1. Franklin B. Sanborn, *Recollections of Seventy Years* (Boston, 1909), II, 438; quoted by Bartlett, p. 80.
2. *J,* V, 105 (October 28, 1838).
3. EPP November 12, 1880 letter to WPA, p. 22. Cf. *J,* X, 108 (July 23, 1865).
4. Page references cited in the discussion of "Shakespeare" are from *E & P,* the only version published during JV's lifetime. No MS has survived.
5. *J,* IV, 432 (April 26, 1838).
6. The following passages from the New Testament, quoted or paraphrased by JV in "Shakespeare," have been identified: I Cor. 9:22 (p. 55); John 3:7–8 (p. 55); Acts 17:28 (p. 57); Mark 10:14 (pp. 57–58); Jude 13 (p. 71); Luke 22:42 (p. 72).

## Chapter XII

### *Crisis-Comedy in Salem: September 1838*

1. JV December 29, 1838 letter to Bellows, p. 2.
2. EPP September 24, 1838 letter to RWE, and her November 12, 1880 letter to WPA, relate the events of September 16, 1838 in detail.
3. This incident probably involved Margaret Fuller, who at this time was living in Groton, but none of her papers refer to any unusual occurrence involving JV.
4. C. W. Upham November 5, 1836 letter to Andrews Norton; quoted by William R. Hutchinson, *The Transcendentalist Ministers* (New Haven, 1959), p. 63.
5. EPP probably meant that Lydia Very had already learned of Upham's threats, having heard them from her son upon his return home.

6. EPP [September 17, 1838] letter to E[lizabeth Manning Hathorne].

7. S. Johnson *c.* September 21, 1838 letter, pp. 1–3.

8. G. B. Loring September 19, 1838 letter to J. R. Lowell.

9. R. H. Dana, Sr. May 21, 1840 letter to W. C. Bryant.

10. Quoted by Eidson, *C. S. Wheeler,* p. 47. (Wheeler was misinformed about the actual circumstances of Upham's two encounters with JV on September 16, 1838.)

11. EPP October 20, 1838 letter to RWE, p. 1.

12. RWE September 20, 1838 letter to W. H. Furness; quoted by Bartlett, p. 52.

13. EPP September 24, 1838 letter to RWE.

14. *L,* II, 164–65 (to Margaret Fuller, September 28–29, 1838).

15. *E & P,* p. 68.

Chapter xiii

*From Bedlam to Concord: September–October 1838*

1. JV December 29, 1838 letter to Bellows, p. 2.

2. *J,* VI, 290 (October 26, 1842).

3. EPP October 20, 1838 letter to RWE.

4. EPP October 20, 1838 letter to RWE gives a detailed account of this meeting.

5. EPP October 20, 1838 letter to RWE, pp. 2–3.

6. G. Bradford, Jr., "Jones Very," *Unitarian Review,* XXVII (1887), 111 n.

7. *E & P,* p. 68.

8. *E & P,* p. 83. Page references incorporated in the discussion of "Hamlet" are from *E & P,* the only version published during JV's lifetime. No MS has survived.

9. Rev. 20:11. In 1836 JV noted this passage in the margin of his copy of *Nature,* p. 64.

10. EPP October 20, 1838 letter to RWE, p. 1.

11. S. Johnson, *c.* November 3, 1838, letter, p. 1.

12. *J,* V, 98 (October 26, 1838).

13. *J,* V, 98–99; *L,* II, 171 (to EPP, October 30, 1838).

14. *J*, V, 105 (October 28, 1838).
15. *J*, V, 141 (November 17, 1838).
16. *J*, V, 105.
17. RWE "Typescript Journal C," p. 212 (May 20, 1838).
18. See JV December 29, 1838 letter to Bellows, pp. 1–3.
19. New Testament quotations from Matt. 3:3, 3:10–11, John 3:30.
20. JV December 29, 1838 letter to Bellows, pp. 2–3.
21. EPP September 24, 1838 letter to RWE, p. 2.
22. *J*, VI, 198 (April 13, 1842).
23. EPP December 3, 1838 letter to RWE, p. 1; Alcott, "MS Journal," XII, 100 (January 15, 1839).
24. *J*, V, 114–15 (November 3, 1838).
25. *J*, V, 104–5 (October 28, 1838).
26. *J*, V, 104.
27. *J*, V, 105.
28. *J*, V, 105; VI, 132 (November 22, 1841).
29. *L*, II, 171 (to EPP, October 30, 1838).
30. *J*, V, 106 (October 29, 1838).
31. When Heliodorus, the prime minister of Seleucis IV, tried to seize the treasure at the Temple in Jerusalem, a horse suddenly appeared carrying a "dreadful rider" who wore magnificent golden armor. The horse rushed forward, reared, and struck Heliodorus with its forefeet, driving him back. Then two angels appeared and flogged him until he "fell suddenly to the ground and was enveloped in deep darkness." (II Macc. 3.)
32. *J*, V, 110–11 (October 30, 1838). JV's "victim" probably was Barzillai Frost, the local minister. See Rusk, *Life*, p. 255.
33. *L*, II, 171 (to EPP, October 30, 1838).
34. *L*, II, 170–71 (to EPP, October 30, 1838).
35. *J*, V, 104 (October 18, 1838).
36. *J*, V, 105 (October 28, 1838). Cf. "Hamlet," p. 84.
37. *J*, V, 104.
38. *J*, V, 105.
39. *J*, V, 106 (October 29, 1838).
40. EPP September 24, 1838 letter to RWE, p. 3.
41. *L*, II, 171 (to EPP, October 30, 1838).
42. *L*, II, 173 (to Margaret Fuller, November 9, 1838).

43. *J*, V, 143 (November 25, 1838).

44. Moore, "Diary," V (September 17, 1838); S. Johnson *c.* September 21, 1838 letter, pp. 2–3.

45. S. Johnson *c.* November 3, 1838 letter, pp. 1–2.

46. *Overseers Reports*, V (1837–1840), 219.

Chapter xiv

*Friendly Evaluations: Winter 1838–1839*

1. JV December 29, 1838 to Bellows, p. 2.

2. "The New Birth," in October 27, 1838 *Obs.;* reprinted *E & P,* p. 126; *P*, p. 49; *P & E*, p. 73. (*Obs.* punctuation adjusted to *E & P.*)

3. *L*, II, 170 (to EPP, October 30, 1838); RWE November 18, 1838 letter to JV, p. 1.

4. *L*, II, 173 (to Margaret Fuller, November 9, 1838); *J*, V, 133 (November 12, 1838).

5. *L*, II, 175 (to Susan Burley, November [18], 1838).

6. RWE November 18, 1838 letter to JV, p. 1.

7. See *L*, II, 173.

8. RWE November 18, 1838 letter to JV, p. 2.

9. In November 10, 1838 *Obs.* "In Him we live" reprinted *E & P,* p. 128; *P*, pp. 39–40; *P & E*, p. 74. "Enoch" reprinted *E & P*, p. 129; *P*, pp. 70–1; *P & E*, p. 75. (*Obs.* punctuation adjusted to *E & P.*)

10. RWE November 18, 1838 letter to JV, p. 3.

11. *E & P*, p. 129.

12. RWE November 18, 1838 letter to JV, p. 3.

13. EPP December 3, 1838 letter to RWE, p. 4.

14. JV December 24, 1838 letter to unidentified former pupil; quoted by G. Bradford, Jr., "Jones Very," *Unitarian Review*, XXVII (1887), 111.

15. S. Peabody *c.* January 1839 letter to EPP, in Lathrop, *Memories,* p. 24; *J*, VI, 51 (September 12, 1841).

16. *E & P*, pp. 97–98.

17. *J*, VI, 132 (November 22, 1841).

18. *E & P*, p. 40.

19. JV November 30, 1838 letter to RWE, p. 1, in "Letters."

20. JV November 30, 1838 letter to RWE, pp. 1–2.

21. EPP October 20, 1838 letter to RWE, p. 2.

22. JV November 30, 1838 letter to RWE, p. 3.

23. JV November 30, 1838 letter to RWE, p. 3.

24. EPP December 3, 1838 letter to RWE, pp. 1–3, describes this visit in detail.

25. EPP November 12, 1880 letter to WPA, pp. 20–21.

26. EPP November 12, 1880 letter to WPA, p. 20.

27. J. F. Clarke, "Biographical Notice," p. xxv.

28. EPP November 12, 1880 letter to WPA, p. 18.

29. J. F. Clarke, "Biographical Notice," p. xxv.

30. EPP November 12, 1880 letter to WPA, pp. 19–20; EPP *c.* December 10, 1838 letter to Lidian Emerson.

31. EPP November 12, 1880 letter to WPA, pp. 18–19.

32. S. F. Clarke July 23, 1838 letter to J. F. Clarke; EPP December 3, 1838 letter to RWE, p. 3.

33. J. F. Clarke, Introduction to "Religious Sonnets By Jones Very," *Western Messenger,* VI (1839), 309–11.

34. Alcott, "MS Journal," XI, 429–30 (*c.* December 6, 1838).

35. Alcott, "MS Journal," XI, 446 (*c.* December 10, 1838).


Chapter xv

*The Prices of Deification: Winter 1838–1839*

1. EPP November 12, 1880 letter to WPA, pp. 16–17.

2. EPP November 12, 1880 letter to WPA, p. 17.

3. JV December 29, 1838 letter to Bellows, p. 3.

4. EPP November 12, 1880 letter to WPA, p. 17; JV December 29, 1838 letter to Bellows, pp. 1–2.

5. See "Samuel Gray Ward's Account."

6. EPP November 12, 1880 letter to WPA, p. 17; EPP *c.* December 10, 1838 letter to Lidian Emerson, p. 1; EPP December 3, 1838 letter to RWE, p. 1.

7. EPP *c.* December 10, 1838 letter to Lidian Emerson, pp. 1–2; JV December 8, 1838 letter to Alcott; S. Peabody *c.* January 1839 letter to EPP, in Lathrop, *Memories,* pp. 23–24; EPP December 3, 1838 letter to RWE, p. 1.

8. EPP November 12, 1880 letter to WPA, p. 20.

9. EPP *c.* December 10, 1838 letter to Lidian Emerson, p. 2.

10. XI, 440 (*c.* December 10, 1838); reprinted in *Journals* (ed. Shepard), p. 108.

11. "The Weary and Heavy Laden," subsequently printed in January 19, 1839 *Obs.;* reprinted *P & E,* p. 101; as "The Soul's Rest," with variant lines 9–14, in *P,* p. 79; *P & E,* p. 244.

12. Alcott was conducting a series of weekly "conversations" on the "transcendental topics."

13. JV December 8, 1838 letter to Alcott.

14. EPP November 12, 1880 letter to WPA, p. 21.

15. EPP November 12, 1880 letter to WPA, p. 21.

16. "Samuel Gray Ward's Account" gives a detailed report of this visit.

17. Cf. "Hamlet," *E & P,* pp. 93–94: "It is at the root of the tree of self within the heart that Christ has laid the axe; and . . . here fall the blows that sound loudest and farthest through the kingdom of Satan."

18. M. Peabody February 5, 1839 letter to S. Peabody, p. 3.

19. EPP December 3, 1838 letter to RWE, p. 3.

20. EPP November 12, 1880 letter to WPA, p. 22.

21. EPP 1882 MS, in Norman Holmes Pearson, "Elizabeth Peabody on Hawthorne," *EIHC,* XCIV (1958), 261–62.

22. EPP November 12, 1880 letter to WPA, p. 22.

23. EPP December 3, 1838 letter to RWE, pp. 3–4. Hawthorne's judgment has recently received independent confirmation from a psychiatrist who was informally asked to examine the more important documents pertaining to JV's mental condition, including some poems. He said that if JV had been referred to him as a patient, not only would he not have recommended confinement, but he would have hesitated to commence any course of therapy. He said that he would be reluctant to interfere with psychological processes which had so valuable a yield as an occasional good sonnet. So long as JV was able to lead a personally satisfying life which at the same time was socially beneficial, it was his opinion that JV did not need psychiatric attention.

24. S. Peabody *c.* January 1839 letter to EPP, in Lathrop, *Memories,* p. 26.

25. M. Peabody February 5, 1839 letter to S. Peabody, p. 3.

26. Hawthorne July 10, 1840 letter to S. Peabody, in Julian Hawthorne, *Nathaniel Hawthorne and His Wife* (Boston and New York, 1884), I, 221.

27. "A Virtuoso's Collection," in *Boston Miscellany,* I (1842), 198. Hawthorne's equivocal statement was inscribed by the Essex Institute on a bronze plaque which, until 1964, identified the Very house at 154 Federal Street. The tablet is now in the custody of the Institute.

28. "The Hall of Fantasy," *The Pioneer,* I (1843), 53.

29. S. Peabody *c.* January 1839 letter to EPP, in Lathrop, *Memories,* pp. 23–25.

30. S. Peabody June 29, 1839 letter to EPP, in Lathrop, *Memories,* p. 30. Reference is to first paragraph of Introduction to *Nature.*

31. EPP December 3, 1838 letter to RWE, p. 1.

32. S. Peabody *c.* January 1839 letter to EPP, in Lathrop, *Memories,* pp. 23–24.

33. EPP December 3, 1838 letter to RWE, p. 3.

34. S. Peabody *c.* January 1839 letter to EPP, in Lathrop, *Memories,* p. 24.

Chapter xvi

*Calls to Glory: Winter 1838–1839*

1. EPP December 3, 1838 letter to RWE, p. 1.

2. Alcott, "MS Journal," XI, 449–50 (*c.* December 13–14, 1838).

3. JV December 29, 1838 letter to Bellows, p. 4.

4. JV December 24, 1838 letter; quoted by G. Bradford, Jr., "Jones Very," *Unitarian Review,* XXVII (1887), 111.

5. *Western Messenger,* VI (1839), 308.

6. See Kenneth W. Cameron, *The Transcendentalists and Minerva* (Hartford, 1958), I, 272–73.

7. "Love," in November 17, 1838 *Obs.;* reprinted *E & P,* p. 134; *P,* p. 153; *P & E,* p. 77. (*Obs.* punctuation adjusted to *E & P.*)

8. "The Son," in November 17, 1838 *Obs.;* reprinted *E & P,* p. 127; *P,* p. 39; *P & E,* p. 74. (*Obs.* punctuation adjusted to *P.*)

9. Alcott, "MS Journal," XII, 550 (March 28, 1839).

10. Alcott, "MS Journal," XI, 465–66 (*c.* December 20, 1838).

11. "The Spirit Land," in December 15, 1838 *Obs.;* reprinted *E & P*, p. 140; *P*, p. 52; *P & E*, p. 80. (*Obs.* text pasted in Alcott, "MS Journal," XI, 465.)

12. "Worship," in December 15, 1838 *Obs.;* reprinted *E & P*, p. 141; *P*, p. 71; *P & E*, p. 81.

13. Alcott, "MS Journal," XII, 93 (*c.* January 15, 1839).

14. See JV December 8, 1838 letter to Alcott, p. 5.

15. *L*, II, 179 (to Margaret Fuller, January 18, 1839); *L*, II, 184 (to Margaret Fuller, February 8, 1839); Margaret Fuller March 4, 1839 letter to C. S. Tappan.

16. Alcott, "MS Journal," XI, 498 (*c.* December 26–29, 1838). By "forty, and more" is probably meant the number of poems already printed in Salem newspapers.

17. Alcott, "MS Journal," XII, 86–88 (January 14, 1839).

18. Alcott, "MS Journal," XII, 102 (January 16, 1839).

19. Alcott, "MS Journal," XII, 103–4 (January 16, 1839); printed (in part) in *Journals* (ed. Shepard).

20. Alcott, "MS Journal," XII, 207–10 (January 29, 1839); printed (in part) in *Journals* (ed. Shepard).

21. "Time," in December 22, 1838 *Obs.;* reprinted *E & P*, p. 172; *P*, p. 40; *P & E*, p. 96.

22. "The Spirit," in December 29, 1838 *Obs.;* reprinted *E & P*, p. 144; *P*, pp. 87–88; *P & E*, p. 82. (Entitled "The Breath," in "Manuscript Poems.")

23. "The Dead," in January 5, 1839 *Obs.;* reprinted *E & P*, p. 146; *P*, p. 67; *P & E*, p. 83. (*Obs.* punctuation adjusted to *E & P*.)

24. "The Grave Yard," in February 2, 1839 *Obs.;* reprinted *E & P*, p. 153; *P*, pp. 67–68; *P & E*, p. 87.

25. "The Eagles," in "Manuscript Poems"; printed Bartlett, p. 144. Cf. Matt. 24:28.

26. "The Prison," in *Western Messenger*, VI (1839), 373; reprinted *P*, p. 68.

27. "He Was Acquainted With Grief," in *Western Messenger*, VI (1839), 312; reprinted *E & P*, p. 167; *P*, p. 69; *P & E*, p. 94.

28. EPP December 3, 1838 letter to RWE, p. 1.

29. "The Jew," in March 2, 1839 *Obs.;* reprinted *E & P*, p. 155; *P*, p. 72; *P & E*, p. 88.

30. "Behold He is at Hand That Doth Betray Me," in *Western Messenger*, VI (1839), 312; reprinted Bartlett, pp. 197–98.

31. "Thy Brother's Blood," in February 2, 1839 *Obs.;* reprinted *E & P*, p. 154; *P*, p. 72; *P & E*, p. 87. (*Obs.* text adjusted to *E & P*.)

32. JV December 29, 1838 letter to Bellows, p. 1.

33. "The Trees of Life," in December 29, 1838 *Obs.;* reprinted *E & P*, p. 143; *P*, p. 99; *P & E*, p. 82.

34. Alcott, "MS Journal," XII, 382 (February 27, 1839).

35. *L*, II, 191 (to Margaret Fuller, March 8, 1839).

36. *L*, II, 190 (Margaret Fuller to RWE, March 4, 1839).

37. *L*, II, 191.

38. RWE March 19, 1839 letter to JV, in "Notebook."

39. RWE April 16, 1839 letter to EPP, in "Notebook."

40. RWE April 16, 1839 letter to EPP.

41. EPP December 3, 1838 letter to RWE, p. 1.

42. EPP *c.* June 3, 1839 letter to RWE, pp. 1–2.

43. EPP November 12, 1880 letter to WPA, p. 20; JV November 30, 1838 letter to RWE, p. 1, in "Letters."

44. "The Cup," in February 23, 1839 *Obs.;* reprinted *P & E*, p. 122.

Chapter xvii

*The New Book of Revelations: Spring 1839*

1. "The Presence," in January 5, 1839 *Obs.;* reprinted *E & P*, p. 145; *P*, p. 51; *P & E*, p. 83. (*E & P* text.)

2. "The Promise," no. 31, in Bartlett, pp. 163–64. (Punctuation added.)

3. "The Preacher," in Bartlett, p. 156. (Punctuation added.)

4. "The Promise," no. 48, in Bartlett, p. 170. (Punctuation added.)

5. "The Charge," in Bartlett, p. 155. (Punctuation added.)

6. "The Apostle," in Bartlett, p. 173.

7. "Night," in November 24, 1838 *Obs.;* reprinted *E & P*, p. 136; *P*, p. 55; *P & E*, p. 78. (*Obs.* punctuation adjusted to *E & P*.)

8. "The Watchman," in *Western Messenger*, VI (1839), 372; reprinted Bartlett, p. 202.

9. "The Morning Watch," in December 1, 1838 *Obs.;* reprinted *E & P*, p. 130; *P*, p. 66; *P & E*, p. 75.

10. "Morning," in March 23, 1839 *Obs.;* reprinted *E & P*, p. 160; *P*, p. 56; *P & E*, p. 90.

11. "Spring," in Bartlett, pp. 166–67. (Punctuation added.)

12. "The River," in *Western Messenger*, VI (1839), 366; reprinted *P*, p. 45.

13. "Winter," in Bartlett, p. 144.

14. "The Kingdom of God Is Within You," in Bartlett, p. 154. (Punctuation added.)

15. "Obedience," in Bartlett, p. 164. (Punctuation added.)

16. "The Lost," in *P*, p. 62; reprinted *P & E*, p. 132.

17. "The Seed," in Bartlett, p. 172. (Punctuation added.)

18. "Come Unto Me," in Bartlett, p. 160. (Punctuation added.)

19. "Terror," in May 4, 1839 *Obs.;* reprinted *P & E*, p. 110. Cf. John 15:1–5, Rev. 18:5.

20. "The Flight," in January 19, 1839 *Obs.;* reprinted *P & E*, p. 106.

21. "Christmas," in February 16, 1839 *Obs.;* reprinted *P*, p. 77; *P & E*, p. 102. The title literally refers to the "sending of Christ."

22. "Then Shall All the Tribes of the Earth Mourn," in *P & E*, p. 149.

23. "Yet Once More," in Bartlett, p. 143.

24. "The Resurrection," in January 19, 1839 *Obs.;* reprinted *P & E*, p. 107.

25. "The White Horse," in March 9, 1839 *Obs.;* reprinted *P & E*, p. 108. Cf. Rev. 19:11–16.

26. "Nature," in March 23, 1839 *Obs.;* reprinted *E & P*, p. 161; *P*, p. 85; *P & E*, p. 91.

27. "The War," in January 12, 1839 *Obs.;* reprinted *E & P*, p. 152; *P*, pp. 151–52; *P & E*, p. 86.

28. "The Garden," in *E & P*, p. 132; reprinted *P*, pp. 50–51; *P & E*, p. 76.

29. EPP December 3, 1838 letter to RWE, p. 2.

30. In "Letters."
31. "Birth," pp. 1–2.
32. "Birth," pp. 3–4.
33. "Prayer," pp. 2–3; "Miracles," p. 6.
34. "Prayer," pp. 1–2.
35. "Prayer," p. 2. Cf. Alcott, "MS Journal," XIII, 451 (December 3, 1839); *J*, VI, 132 (November 22, 1841); "Typescript Journal ZO," p. 78 (*c*. December 3, 1856.)
36. "Miracles," pp. 1–5.

### Chapter XVIII

### *Concord Revisited: Summer 1839*

1. JV November 30, 1838 letter to RWE, p. 3, in "Letters."
2. Washington Very June 3, 1839 letter to RWE, in "Letters." (Italics added.)
3. EPP November 12, 1880 letter to WPA, pp. 23–24.
4. JV November 23, 1842 letter to RWE, p. 2, in "Letters."
5. EPP November 12, 1880 letter to WPA, pp. 17–18.
6. Alcott, "MS Journal," XII, 880 (June 14, 1839).
7. Alcott, "MS Journal," XII, 880.
8. Alcott, "MS Journal," XII, 944 (June 26, 1839).
9. *J*, V, 289 (October 18, 1839).
10. See "Samuel Gray Ward's Account."
11. *L*, II, 191 (to Margaret Fuller, March 8, 1839).
12. *J*, V, 289.
13. EPP December 3, 1838 letter to RWE, pp. 1–2.
14. EPP October 20, 1838 letter to RWE, p. 1; EPP December 3, 1838 letter to RWE, p. 2.
15. Cabot, *Memoir*, I, 348; "Samuel Gray Ward's Account"; C. F. W. Archer, "Clippings from the Salem *Evening News*, 1922–1924," p. 14 (May 31, 1922), in Essex Institute; *L*, II, 190 (Margaret Fuller to RWE, March 4, 1839).
16. EPP October 20, 1838 letter to RWE, p. 1.
17. R. H. Dana, Sr. May 21, 1840 letter to W. C. Bryant, pp. 1–2.
18. *J*, VIII, 211 (May 1851); *L*, II, 331 (to Elizabeth Hoar, September 12, 1840); EPP November 12, 1880 letter to WPA, p. 24.

19. EPP June 23, 1839 letter to S. Peabody, in Lathrop, *Memories,* pp. 29–30.

20. EPP December 3, 1838 letter to RWE, p. 3.

21. *L,* II, 165 (to Margaret Fuller, September 28–29, 1838); JV September [15], 1838 letter to RWE, in "Letters."

22. Unless otherwise noted, the following account of Lidian Emerson is derived from Rusk, *Life,* pp. 215, 219–21, 224–26, 290.

23. Stephen E. Whicher, ed., *Selections from Ralph Waldo Emerson* (Boston, 1957), p. 480 (p. 142 note).

24. Rusk, *Life,* p. 261.

25. EPP December 3, 1838 letter to RWE, pp. 1, 3.

26. Quoted in Rusk, *Life,* p. 261.

27. EPP *c.* December 10, 1838 letter to Lidian Emerson, pp. 1–2; S. Peabody *c.* January 1839 letter to EPP, in Lathrop, *Memories,* pp. 23–24.

28. EPP December 3, 1838 letter to RWE, p. 3.

29. JV *c.* September 30, 1839 letter to Mrs. Ralph Waldo Emerson, in "Letters."

30. "The Tenant," printed in *P,* p. 115.

31. "The Morn," printed in November 26, 1839 Salem *Gazette* as "The Slaveholder"; reprinted as "The Day Not For Gain," with variants, in *P,* p. 65; *P & E,* p. 257. Cf. RWE "Days."

32. "Typescript Journal OP Gulistan," p. 52 (1848).

33. *L,* II, 173 (to Margaret Fuller, November 9, 1838).

34. *J,* V, 220–21 (June 16, 1839). St. Simeon Stylites (390–459) was the first and most famous of the pillar hermits. He lived for thirty years without descending from his sixty-foot perch, during which time his preaching converted the Syrian heathen who came to stare at him. John of Patmos (the Apostle John), according to tradition, composed the Apocalypse during his banishment to that Aegean island.

35. *J,* V, 214 (June 3, 1839).

36. RWE June 17, 1839 letter to EPP, in "Notebook."

37. *J,* V, 221 (June 18, 1839).

38. *J,* V, 223 (June 18, 1839). In Plato's "Symposium," Agathon praised Love as a deity, instead of praising the beloved.

39. "The Call," in July 13, 1839 *Obs.;* reprinted with variant

punctuation, in *E & P*, p. 173; *P*, p. 113 (last stanza omitted); *P & E*, p. 160.

40. "The Prayer," in July 20, 1839 *Obs.;* reprinted with variants, in September 10, 1839 Salem *Gazette; E & P*, p. 175; *P*, p. 311; *P & E*, p. 161.

41. "The Bride," in July 27, 1839 *Obs.;* reprinted Bartlett, p. 194.

42. "The Cottage," enclosed in JV August 13, 1839 letter to RWE, in "Letters"; printed *E & P*, p. 174; reprinted *P*, p. 114; *P & E*, p. 160.

43. JV August 13, 1839 letter to RWE, in "Letters." In addition to "The Cottage," the letter transmitted "The Immortal" and "The Serving Man."

44. *L*, II, 209 (to Margaret Fuller, July 9, 1839). The published book contained sixty-five poems, not sixty-six.

45. *J*, V, 243 (August 19, 1839).

Chapter xix

*Denouement: September 1839–December 1840*

1. Fuller, "Literary Notices," *Boston Quarterly Review,* III (1840), 132. As late as 1865 the original printing was not yet exhausted, although copies were difficult to locate. (See JV January 14, 1865 letter to R. H. Dana, Sr., p. 1.)

2. *L*, II, 261 (to Lidian Emerson, March 8, 1840); Rusk, *Life,* p. 285; *J*, V, 377 (March 28, 1840); RWE May 30, 1841 letter to Carlyle, in *Correspondence of Carlyle and Emerson* (ed. Norton), I, 359–60.

3. EPP June 23, 1839 letter to S. Peabody, in Lathrop, *Memories,* p. 30. See also *L*, II, 405 (to Margaret Fuller, June 15, 1841).

4. Copy now located in NE upstairs bedroom of the Emerson House in Concord. (The official catalog of books indicates that it belongs in the SW downstairs parlor library.)

5. S. F. Clarke September 18, 1839 letter to J. F. Clarke.

6. "A Virtuoso's Collection," *Boston Miscellany,* I (1842), 198.

7. Lowell's copy now kept in Houghton Library. See Bartlett, pp. 100–2, for detailed description of marginalia.

8. Now kept in Houghton Library.

9. R. H. Dana, Sr. May 21, 1840 letter to W. C. Bryant, pp. 1–2.

10. Parke Godwin December 8, 1880 letter to WPA, in "Notebook."

11. EPP June 23, 1839 letter to S. Peabody, in Lathrop, *Memories,* p. 30.

12. EPP November 12, 1880 letter to WPA, pp. 24–25.

13. Alcott, "MS Journal," XIII, 226 (September 7, 1839), 310–11 (October 16, 1839), 409 (November 18, 1839); *Journals* (ed. Shepard), p. 517 (May 16, 1880).

14. See Thomas Wentworth Higginson, *Margaret Fuller Ossoli* (Boston, 1884), p. 146.

15. III (1840), 132.

16. *L,* II, 190 (Margaret Fuller to RWE, March 4, 1839).

17. III (1840), 132–33.

18. *L,* II, 190.

19. *L,* II, 190.

20. *L,* II, 191 (to Margaret Fuller, March 8, 1839).

21. See JV letters to RWE, in "Letters": March 26, 1841, p. 2; April 11, 1841, p. 1; November 21, 1841, p. 3; November 23, 1842, p. 1.

22. JV *c.* September 30, 1839 letter to Mrs. Ralph Waldo Emerson, in "Letters."

23. *J,* V, 382 (April 9, 1840).

24. Alcott, "MS Journal," XIII, 461 (December 6, 1839).

25. "Extracts from Journals," I, 607–9 (*c.* December 7, 1839). (Italics added.)

26. JV *c.* December 4, 1839 letter to Alcott, p. 3.

27. "The Morning," pp. 1–3.

28. See Alcott "Diary," p. 39, incomplete transcription from "MS Journal" (May 1840), made for Franklin B. Sanborn, in Houghton Library; F. B. Sanborn, *Henry D. Thoreau* (Boston, 1893), p. 190.

29. R. H. Dana, Sr. May 21, 1840 letter to W. C. Bryant, p. 2.

30. S. F. Clarke November 17, 1839 letter to J. F. Clarke; Caroline Dall, *Margaret Fuller and Her Friends* (Boston, 1895), p. 94.

31. *W,* X, 375; S. F. Clarke November 22, 1840 letter to J. F. Clarke.

32. JV March 26, 1841 letter to RWE, p. 2, in "Letters."

33. *L,* II, 265 (to Lidian Emerson, March 28, 1840). Cf. *E & P,* p. 81.

34. *J,* V, 381–82 (April 9, 1840).

35. *W,* II, 203. Cf. *J,* V, 383 (April 9, 1840).

36. "Typescript Journal F(2)," p. 48 (*c.* October 24, 1840); *J*, V, 482.

37. "Typescript Journal F(2)," p. 17.

38. "The Hand and Foot," in November 19, 1839 Salem *Gazette;* reprinted *P*, p. 42; *P & E*, p. 128.

39. *J*, V, 223 (June 18, 1839); "Typescript Journal OP Gullistan," p. 52 (1848).

40. "Yourself," in November 23, 1839 *Obs.;* reprinted without archaisms, in *P*, p. 61; *P & E*, p. 116. (*P* text.)

41. "Thy Neighbor," in November 23, 1839 *Obs.;* reprinted *P & E*, p. 117; as "Thy Better Self" with variants, in *P & E*, p. 254.

42. "Death," in *Western Messenger*, VIII (1841), 462; reprinted Bartlett, p. 203.

43. There is no satisfactory study of the impact of JV on RWE after 1840. Some of the relevant documents were referred to by Bartlett, pp. 112–13, 118–19, 126. Carlos Baker's study of the JV-RWE relationship, in *New England Quarterly*, VII (1934), 90–99, was based on incomplete evidence.

44. Bartlett's brief sketch of JV's life after 1840 was based on incomplete evidence.

# A Selected Bibliography

W HAT F O L L O W S is not an exhaustive bibliographical statement. Although there is a relative abundance of manuscript material relating to Very's last forty years, it is not listed here. Only the more important material used in the preparation of the text is included. Brief annotations are provided for some of the entries.

Alcott, Amos Bronson. *The Journals of Amos Bronson Alcott*. Edited by Odell Shepard. Boston, Little, Brown and Co., 1938. Includes about one-twentieth of Alcott's "Manuscript Journals."
———— "Manuscript Journals." Vol. XI: "Journal for 1838." Vol. XII: "Diary for 1839" [January–June]. Vol. XIII: "Diary for 1839" [July–December]. Houghton Library "Alcott Papers" Collection.
Andrews, William P. "Memoir," in *Poems by Jones Very*. Boston, Houghton Mifflin Co., 1883.
Baker, Carlos. "Emerson and Jones Very," *New England Quarterly*, VII (March 1934), 90–99.
Bartlett, William Irving. *Jones Very: Emerson's "Brave Saint."* Durham, Duke University Press, 1942. Chapter VIII and Appendices include unpublished and uncollected poems.
Berthoff, Warner B. "Jones Very: New England Mystic," *Boston Public Library Quarterly*, II (January 1950), 63–75.

# A Selected Bibliography

Blau, Joseph L., ed. *American Philosophic Addresses: 1700–1900.* New York, Columbia University Press, 1946.

Bradford, Jr., G[eorge]. "Jones Very," *Unitarian Review,* XXVII (February 1887), 11–18.

Brooks, Van Wyck. *The Flowering of New England.* New York, E. P. Dutton & Co., 1952.

Burns, Percy Pratt. "Jones Very," *Howard College Bulletin,* LXXX (June 1922), 42–66.

Cabot, James Elliot. *A Memoir of Ralph Waldo Emerson.* 2 vols. Cambridge, Mass., Riverside Press, 1887.

Cameron, Kenneth Walter. "Jones Very and Emerson's Friends in College Church Records," *Emerson Society Quarterly,* No. 14 (1 Quarter 1959), p. 18. Reprints "Form of Admission to the Church in Harvard University Nov$^r$ 1 1814," signed by Very on May 17, 1837.

Cameron, K[enneth] W[alter]. "Jones Very and Thoreau—The 'Greek Myth,'" *Emerson Society Quarterly,* No. 7 (II Quarter 1957), pp. 39–40.

Cameron, Kenneth Walter. "Jones Very's Academic Standing at Harvard," *Emerson Society Quarterly,* No. 19 (II Quarter 1960), pp. 52–57. Facsimile reprint of Term Scales preserved in Harvard University Archives.

Channing, William Ellery. *Works of William Ellery Channing.* Vol. I. Boston, J. Munroe, 1855.

Charvat, William. *Origins of American Critical Thought: 1810–1835.* Perpetua Book Ed. New York, A. S. Barnes & Co., 1961.

Clarke, James Freeman. "Biographical Notice of Jones Very," in *Poems and Essays by Jones Very.* Boston and New York, Houghton Mifflin Co., 1886.

—— Introduction to "Religious Sonnets by Jones Very, Salem, Mass.," *The Western Messenger,* VI (March 1839), 309–11.

Clarke, Sarah Freeman. Manuscript 3: "Impressions and Recollections of Miss [Elizabeth Palmer] Peabody . . . Written for the Memorial Meeting, 1894." Boston Public Library Manuscript Collection.

—— Letter of December 31, 1837–January 1, 1838 to James Freeman Clarke. Houghton Library "James Freeman Clarke Manuscript Collection."

## A Selected Bibliography

——— "The Letters of a Sister." Galley-sheets in Houghton Library "James Freeman Clarke Manuscript Collection." Letters of July 23, 1838, January 27, 1839, September 18, 1839, November 17, 1839, and November 22, 1840 contain material about Very.

"[Class of] 1836: [Death of] Jones Very, at Salem, May 8 [1880]." June 1880 *Harvard Register*.

*College Papers*. 2nd ser. Vols. VI–VIII. Harvard University Archives.

Dana, Sr., R[ichard] H[enry]. Letter of May 21, 1840 to W[illiam] C[ullen] Bryant. Massachusetts Historical Society "Dana Papers" Collection.

Eidson, John Olin. *Charles Stearns Wheeler: Friend of Emerson*. Athens, Ga., University of Georgia Press, 1951.

Emerson, Ralph Waldo. *The Complete Works of Ralph Waldo Emerson*. Centenary Edition. Biographical Introduction and Notes by Edward Waldo Emerson. Vol. I: *Nature, Addresses and Lectures*. Vol. II: *Essays: First Series*. Vol. VIII: *Letters and Social Aims*. Vol. X: *Lectures and Biographical Sketches*. Boston and New York, Houghton Mifflin Co., 1903–1904.

——— *The Correspondence of Thomas Carlyle and Ralph Waldo Emerson, 1834–1872*. Edited by Charles Eliot Norton. Vol. I. Boston, J. R. Osgood, 1883.

——— *Journals of Ralph Waldo Emerson*. Edited by Edward Waldo Emerson and Waldo Emerson Forbes. Vol. IV: 1836–1838. Vol. V: 1838–1841. Vol. VI: 1841–1844. Vol. VII: 1845–1848. Vol. VIII: 1849–1855. Vol. IX: 1856–1863. Vol. X: 1864–1876. Boston and New York, Houghton Mifflin Co., 1909–1914.

——— Letter of November 18, 1838 to Jones Very. Essex Institute Autograph Collection. Printed in facsimile by William I. Bartlett in his *Jones Very: Emerson's "Brave Saint,"* between pp. 58–59.

——— Letter of September 25, 1841 to Rufus W. Griswold. In Passages from *The Correspondence of Rufus Wilmot Griswold*. Edited by William McCrillis Griswold. Cambridge, Mass., privately printed by the editor, 1898. P. 98. Provided Griswold with biographical data for his sketch of Very in *The Poets and Poetry of America* (Philadelphia, 1842).

——— *The Letters of Ralph Waldo Emerson*. Edited by Ralph L. Rusk. Vol. II: 1836–1841. Vol. III: 1842–1847. New York, Columbia University Press, 1939.

# A Selected Bibliography

Emerson, Ralph Waldo. *Nature*. Boston, James Munroe, 1836. Copy owned by Jones Very, with his signature and date, marginal notes, comments, and scored passages, and with an unsigned Emerson inscription. Presently in the personal library of Mr. Parkman D. Howe, of Needham, Mass.

—— "Typescript Journals of Ralph Waldo Emerson." Journals: C, GL, OP Gullistan, TU, ZO, F(2). Special Collections of Columbia University Library.

*Faculty Records.* Vol. XI (1829–1840). Harvard University Archives.

"The Father of Rev. Jones Very." May 17, 1880 Salem *Register.*

Felton, C[ornelius] C. Letter of September 9, 1834 to Dr. [Thaddeus William] Harris. Loosely inserted between pp. 178–79 (2nd ser.) of "Library Charging Lists, 1833–1834." Harvard University Archives.

[Foote, Henry W.] "Rev. Jones Very," May 11, 1880 Salem *Gazette.*

Fuller, Margaret. "Extracts from Journals, 1833–1839." In "Manuscript Works of S. M. F. Ossoli." Vol. I. Houghton Library.

—— Letter of March 4, 1839 to Caroline [Sturgis] Tappan. In "Tappan Papers: Ossoli-Tappan." Houghton Library.

[Fuller, Margaret]. "Literary Notices—Chat in Boston Bookstores—No. I," *Boston Quarterly Review,* III (January 1840), 127–34.

Gittleman, Edwin. "Jones Very's Quest for Poetry." Unpublished Master's Thesis, Columbia University, 1957.

Hale, Edward Everett, ed. *Autobiography, Diary and Correspondence of James Feeeman Clarke.* Boston and New York, Houghton Mifflin Co., 1891.

Hawthorne, Nathaniel. "The Hall of Fantasy," *The Pioneer,* I (February 1843), 53.

—— "A Virtuoso's Collection," *The Boston Miscellany of Literature and Fashion,* I (May 1842), 198. Reprinted in *Mosses from an Old Manse.*

"Institute of 1770—Accounts: 1825–1836." Vol. A. Harvard University Archives.

"Institute of 1770—Constitution, etc. with a Library Catalogue: 1835–1848." Vol. B. Harvard University Archives.

"Institute of 1770—Records: 1832–1837." Vol. A. Harvard University Archives.

Johnson, Jr., Samuel. Five letters to Dr. Samuel Johnson, of Salem: September 6, 1838, September [14], 1838, *c.* September 21, 1838, September 28, 1838, and *c.* November 3, 1838. Essex Institute Samuel Johnson, Jr. Manuscript Collection. Letters about Very by a sensitive Harvard student.

Lathrop, Rose Hawthorne. *Memories of Hawthorne.* Boston and New York, Houghton Mifflin Co., 1897.

Leavitt, William. "History of the Essex Lodge of Freemasons," *Essex Institute Historical Collections,* III (August 1861), 211.

"Library Charging Lists." Vols. 1833–1834, 1834–1835, 1835–1836, 1836–1837, and 1837–1838. Harvard University Archives.

"The Life and Services to Literature of Jones Very: A Memorial Meeting, Dec. 14, 1880." Salem, printed for the Essex Institute, 1881. Reprinted from *The Bulletin of the Essex Institute,* XIII (January–June 1881). This meeting occasioned remarks and letters by friends of Very.

Loring, George B. Letter of September 19, 1838 to James Russell Lowell. In "James Russell Lowell Manuscript Collection." Houghton Library.

Miller, Perry, ed. *The Transcendentalists: An Anthology.* Cambridge, Harvard University Press, 1950. Includes abridged versions of "Epic Poetry," "Shakespeare," and "Hamlet," and a generous selection of Very's poems.

Moore, George. "Diary." Vol. V: August 1836–December 1840. American Antiquarian Society Library, Worcester, Mass.

"Notebook of William P. Andrews on Jones Very." Wellesley College Library. In addition to newspaper and magazine clippings, this contains originals and copies of letters about Very by Emerson, R. H. Dana, Sr., Parke Godwin, Robert C. Waterston, and Elizabeth Palmer Peabody. Five of the Emerson letters are uncollected or have hitherto been known only in part.

Osgood, Charles S., and H. M. Batchelder. *Historical Sketch of Salem: 1626–1879.* Salem, Essex Institute, 1879.

*Overseers Reports.* Vol. IV: 1834–1836. Vol. V: 1837–1840. Harvard University Archives.

Peabody, Elizabeth Palmer. Four letters to Ralph Waldo Emerson: September 24, 1838, October 20, 1838, December 3, 1838, and *c.* June 3, 1839. Essex Institute Autograph Collection.

Peabody, Elizabeth Palmer. Letter of February 26, 1838 to Robert C. Waterston. Essex Institute Autograph Collection.

—— Letter of July 31, 1838 to Sophia Peabody. Berg Collection, New York Public Library.

—— Letter of [September 17, 1838] to E[lizabeth Manning Hathorne]. Berg Collection, New York Public Library.

—— Letter of *c.* December 10, 1838 to Lidian Emerson. Essex Institute Autograph Collection.

—— Letter of November 12, 1880 to William P. Andrews. In "Notebook of William P. Andrews on Jones Very." Wellesley College Library. This 27-page letter is the most detailed account of Very's life by one who knew him intimately. Andrews made ineffectual use of it in his "Memoir."

—— Untitled manuscript of 1882. Printed by Norman Holmes Pearson, in "Elizabeth Peabody on Hawthorne," *Essex Institute Historical Collections,* XCIV (July 1958), 256–76.

Peabody, Mary. Letter of February 5, 1839 to Sophia Peabody. Berg Collection, New York Public Library.

Peabody, Sophia. Letter of May 4–6, 1838 to Elizabeth Palmer Peabody. [Copy in the latter's hand.] Berg Collection, New York Public Library.

Pochmann, Henry A. *German Culture in America: Philosophical and Literary Influences, 1600–1900.* Madison, University of Wisconsin Press, 1957.

Proudfoot, Bessie Whitmore. "Jones Very: A Biographical Study." Unpublished Ph.D. dissertation, University of Chicago, 1918. Typescript in New York Public Library.

"A Pupil's Testimony to Mr. Very as a Teacher." May 21, 1880 Salem *Gazette.* Bologna, Italy April 1880 letter to Jones Very from an unidentified correspondent.

*Records of the College Faculty.* Vol. XI: 1829–1840. Harvard University Archives.

"Records of the Theological School: 1819–1892." Andover–Harvard Theological Library, Cambridge, Mass.

*The Records of the Theological School, 1827–1893.* Andover–Harvard Theological Library, Cambridge, Mass.

"Rev. Jones Very: College Life of Jones Very." May 21, 1880 Salem *Gazette.*

Rusk, Ralph L. *The Life of Ralph Waldo Emerson.* New York, Charles Scribner's Sons, 1949.

"Samuel Gray Ward's Account of a Visit from Jones Very in 1839." In L[yman] H. Butterfield, "Come with Me to the Feast; or Transcendentalism in Action," *Massachusetts Historical Society Miscellany,* No. 6 (December 1960), pp. 3–4.

Schneider, Herbert W. *A History of American Philosophy.* New York, Columbia University Press, 1946.

Smith, H. Shelton. *Changing Conceptions of Original Sin: A Study in American Theology Since 1750.* New York, Charles Scribner's Sons, 1955.

Very, Jones. "The Barometric Method of describing the height of hills." Manuscript No. 11 of the October 20, 1835 "Mathematical Exercises." In *Exhibition and Commencement Performances (1834–1835).* Harvard University Archives. Prepared and performed with Robert Bartlett and William Minot.

——— "Captain Jones Very." Dated January 1872. In "The Father of Rev. Jones Very." May 17, 1880 Salem *Register.*

——— "An English Oration: The Heroic Character." Manuscript No. 12 of the May 3, 1836 program. In *Exhibition and Commencement Performances (1835–1836).* Harvard University Archives.

——— "An English Oration: Individuality." Manuscript No. 12 of the August 31, 1836 program. In *Exhibition and Commencement Performances (1835–1836).* Harvard University Archives.

——— "Epic Poetry." Essex Institute Manuscript Collection.

——— *Essays and Poems by Jones Very.* [Edited by Ralph Waldo Emerson.] Boston, Charles C. Little and James Brown, 1839.

——— "A Greek Version: Extracts from Webster's 'Oration at Plymouth.'" Manuscript No. 12 of the April 28, 1835 program. In *Exhibition and Commencement Performances (1834–1835).* Harvard University Archives. Reprinted with an English translation by Kenneth Walter Cameron, in "Jones Very's Harvard Greek Exhibition and Daniel Webster," *Emerson Society Quarterly,* No. 38 (I Quarter 1965), pp. 133–35.

——— "Influence of Christianity on Epic Poetry." *Christian Exam-*

*iner,* XXIV (May 1838), 201–21. Reprinted as "Epic Poetry," in the 1839 and 1886 collections.

────── Letter of October [16], 1837 to Harvard Overseers. In *Overseers Reports,* V (1837–1840), 83. Harvard University Archives.

────── Letter of May 1, 1838 to Harvard Overseers. In *Overseers Reports,* V (1837–1840), 141. Harvard University Archives.

────── Letter of December 8, 1838 to Bronson Alcott. In Alcott's *c.* December 10, 1838 "Journal" entry, XI, 441–45. Houghton Library "Alcott Papers" Collection. Copy in Alcott's hand.

────── Letter of December 29, 1838 to Henry W. Bellows. Massachusetts Historical Society "Bellows Papers" Collection. Very traces in detail the psychological changes he underwent between 1834 and 1838.

────── Letter *c.* January 1839 to James Freeman Clarke. *The Western Messenger,* VI (March 1839), 308.

────── Letter *c.* December 4, 1839 to Bronson Alcott. Inserted in Alcott's December 5–6, 1839 "Journal" entry, XIII, 457. Houghton Library "Alcott Papers" Collection.

────── Letter *c.* 1856 to David Holmes Conrad. In Conrad's *Memoir of Rev. James Chisholm A.M.* New York, Protestant Episcopal Society for the Promotion of Evangelical Knowledge, 1856. Pp. 12–13.

────── Letter of January 14, 1865 to Richard Henry Dana, Sr. Massachusetts Historical Society "Dana Papers" Collection.

────── "Letters of Jones Very to Ralph Waldo Emerson, 1838–1846." Wellesley College Library. Includes Very's three formal "Letters to the Unborn," written *c.* May 1839: "An Epistle on Birth," "An Epistle on Prayer," and "An Epistle on Miracles."

────── "Manuscript Poems." Houghton Library. Textual basis for 1886 edition of *Poems and Essays by Jones Very.* Formerly in Andover–Harvard Theological Library.

────── "The Morning: A Dialogue." Appended to Very's *c.* December 4, 1839 letter to Bronson Alcott. Inserted in Alcott's December 5–6, 1839 "Journal" entry, XIII, 457. Houghton Library "Alcott Papers" Collection.

────── "Notes on Ticknor's Course, 1834." Harvard University Archives. Classroom notes and comments made while attending George Ticknor's course in Spanish literature.

## A Selected Bibliography

Very, Jones. *Poems and Essays by Jones Very: Complete and Revised Edition*. With a Biographical Sketch by James Freeman Clarke and a Preface by C[yrus] A. Bartol. Boston and New York, Houghton Mifflin Co., 1886.

——— *Poems by Jones Very with an Introductory Memoir by William P. Andrews*. Boston, Houghton Mifflin Co., 1883.

——— Poems. "Manuscripts in the Andover Theological Seminary, Cambridge, Massachusetts." Eleven poems printed by William I. Bartlett in Chapter VIII of *Jones Very: Emerson's "Brave Saint*," pp. 141–48.

——— Poems. "Manuscripts in the Harris Collection of American Poetry, at Brown University, Providence, Rhode Island." Sixty poems printed by William I. Bartlett in Chapter VIII of *Jones Very: Emerson's "Brave Saint*," pp. 148–75.

——— Poems. Printed in *Harvardiana*. Vol. II. February 1836: 119 and 200. March 1836: 231–32. April–May 1836: 248. June 1836: 326.

——— Poems. Printed in Salem *Gazette*, 1839–1840. References to specific titles and issues are included in notes accompanying my discussion of individual poems.

——— Poems. Printed in Salem *Observer*, 1833–1843. References to specific titles and issues are included in notes accompanying my discussion of individual poems.

——— Poems. Printed in *The Western Messenger*. Vol. VI. March 1839: 311–14. April 1839: 366–73. Vol. VIII. May 1840: 43. January 1841: 424. February 1841: 449, 462, 467, 472. April 1841: 549–52.

——— "The Practical Application in This Life, by Men as Social and Intellectual Beings, of the Certainty of a Future State." Manuscript No. 2 in *Bowdoin Prize Dissertations*, VI (1835–1839). Harvard University Archives. Awarded first prize in the Junior Class competition of July 1835.

——— "A Song composed by Mr J. Very, to be sung at the Class-Supper of the Sophomore Class of 1834." Printed by Kenneth Walter Cameron, in *Emerson Society Quarterly*, No. 5 (IV Quarter 1956), pp. 12–13.

——— "Song." No. 5 on the program of Valedictory Exercises of the Senior Class of 1836. Broadside in Houghton Library. Reprinted in facsimile by Kenneth Walter Cameron, in *Emerson Society Quarterly*, No. 29 (IV Quarter 1962), p. 50.

—— "Spiritual Navigation." Manuscript dated October 12, 1843. Yale University Library. Includes an untitled prose prayer.

—— "Three Commonplace Books by Jones Very." Harvard University Archives. Contains "Journal for 1833," "Scrap Book, 1834," and Commonplace Book "III." Bound with the "Scrap Book" is the "Journal of a Journey to the White Hills, 1837." Bound with Commonplace Book "III" is the "Journal: From Eastport, Me. to Salem, 1846."

—— "The Very Family." *Essex Institute Historical Collections,* I (July 1859), 116; II (Part 2, February 1860), 33–38.

—— "What Reasons Are There For Not Expecting Another Great Epic Poem?" Bound as No. 4 in *Bowdoin Prize Dissertations,* VI (1835–1839). Harvard University Archives. Awarded first prize in the Senior Class competition of July 1836. Reprinted by Kenneth Walter Cameron in *Emerson Society Quarterly,* No. 12 (III Quarter 1958), pp. 25–32.

Very, L[ydia] L[ouisa] A[nn]. *An Old-Fashioned Garden—and Walks and Musings Therein.* Salem, Salem Press, 1899.

—— Undated letter to The Editor. Printed in "Jones Very Again," June 6, 1880 Boston *Sunday Herald.*

[Ward, Julius]. "Jones Very: The Finest Sonnet Writer in America," May 16, 1880 Boston *Sunday Herald.*

Ware, Jr., Henry. *The Personality of the Deity: A Sermon, preached in the Chapel of Harvard University, September 23, 1838.* Boston, James Munroe, 1838.

Winters, Yvor. "Jones Very: A New England Mystic," *The American Review,* VII (May 1936), 159–78. Reprinted as "Jones Very and R. W. Emerson: Aspects of New England Mysticism," in *Maule's Curse: Seven Studies in the History of American Obscurantism* (New York, New Directions, 1938). Subsequently reprinted in *In Defense of Reason* (New York, The Swallow Press and W. Murrow, n.d.).

# Index

# Index

"Barometric Method of describing the height of hills, The" (JV), 85

Bartlett, Robert, 97, 382n. 26

Bartol, Cyrus A., 131, 167, 268, 271, 279

*Bassvilliana* (Monti), 104

Beattie, James, 56

"Beauty" (JV), 79, 152–55

Beauty: JV's sacrifice of, *see* Sacrifice: of Beauty

Beck, Charles, 23, 28

"Behold He Is at Hand That Doth Betray Me" (JV), 303

Beke, Charles T., 86

Bell, Dr., 227, 232, 234

Bellows, Henry W., 289

Bentley, Richard, 28

Bentley, William, 116

Bible, JV's paraphrase and quotation from, 188, 189, 195, 213, 216–17, 223, 242, 244, 294, 313–14, 323, 396n. 6, 398n. 19, 405n. 25

*Biographia Literaria* (Coleridge), 53, 86

Birth: JV's concept of, *see* "Epistle on Birth"

*Blackwood's Edinburgh Magazine,* 54

Blake, Harrison G. O., 131

*Blithedale Romance, The* (Hawthorne), 356

Bolles, Lucius, 219

Bonaparte, Napoleon, 25

Book of Revelation (John), 123, 125, 126, 129

*Book of the Church* (Southey), 86, 120

*Boston Miscellany,* 285

*Boston Quarterly Review,* 356

Bowen, Francis, 130

Brazer, John, 219, 227, 235, 288

"Bride, The" (JV), 348–49, 351

Brownson, Orestes A., 86, 118, 334, 356

Bryant, Jacob, 25

Bryant, William Cullen, 76, 228, 353, 354

Bulwer-Lytton, Edward, 56, 88, 90, 120

Burke, Edmund, 120

Burley, Susan, 156–58, 161, 257, 266, 282, 285, 335

Burnett, James, *see* Monboddo, James Burnett, Lord

Burns, Robert, 56, 385n. 37

Butler, Joseph, 14–15, 16, 18, 19, 20, 31, 35, 39, 46, 47, 66, 70, 79, 154

Butler, Samuel, 56, 86

Byron, George G. N. B., 6th Baron, 44–48, 49, 50, 52, 55, 58, 65, 66, 72, 74, 79, 99–100, 106, 122, 132, 154, 211; quoted, 45, 46–47, 57, 58

"Call, The" (JV), 347

Campbell, George, 25

*Canterbury Tales* (Chaucer), 86

Carlyle, Thomas, 42, 72, 86, 106, 120, 148, 168, 183, 340, 353

Cedar Pond, 3, 11

Cervantes, Miguel de, 51

*"Change of heart":* JV's experience of, 82–83, 92, 98, 99, 100, 122, 145, 168

Channing, Edward Tyrrel, 24, 25, 38, 39, 50, 65, 66, 70, 86, 104, 131, 148, 169, 193, 196; *Essays and Poems* dedicated to, 332, 352

Channing, William Ellery, 16–17, 18, 31, 39, 46, 47, 74, 79, 82, 97, 154, 160, 279, 309, 365; JV's visit, 264, 268–69; "sacrifice" needed, 277; quoted, 16, 77

Channing, William Henry, 131

Chapman, Maria W., 365

"Characteristics" (Carlyle), 86

# Index

# Index